GRAMMAR
AND BEYOND

John D. Bunting
Luciana Diniz
with Randi Reppen

4

CAMBRIDGE
UNIVERSITY PRESS

CAMBRIDGE UNIVERSITY PRESS
Cambridge, New York, Melbourne, Madrid, Cape Town,
Singapore, São Paulo, Delhi, Mexico City

Cambridge University Press
32 Avenue of the Americas, New York, NY 10013-2473, USA

www.cambridge.org
Information on this title: www.cambridge.org/9780521143011

First published 2013

Printed in Hong Kong, China, by Golden Cup Printing Company Limited

A catalog record for this publication is available from the British Library.

ISBN 978-0-521-14301-1 Student's Book 4
ISBN 978-0-521-14323-3 Student's Book 4A
ISBN 978-0-521-14328-8 Student's Book 4B
ISBN 978-1-107-60409-4 Workbook 4
ISBN 978-1-107-60410-0 Workbook 4A
ISBN 978-1-107-60411-7 Workbook 4B
ISBN 978-1-107-67297-0 Teacher Support Resource Book with CD-ROM 4
ISBN 978-0-521-14343-1 Class Audio CD 4
ISBN 978-1-139-06188-9 Writing Skills Interactive 4

Art direction, book design, layout services, and photo research: Integra
Audio production: John Marshall Media

Contents

Introduction to *Grammar and Beyond*   vii

About the Authors   xi

Acknowledgments   xii

Tour of a Unit   xiv

PART 1 Cause and Effect | Social Responsibility

UNIT 1 Cause and Effect 1 The Environment and You   2

Sentence Structure: Simple and Compound Sentences   4

Complex Sentences   8

Common Patterns with Nouns That Show Cause   11

The Writing Process: Thesis Statements   15

UNIT 2 Cause and Effect 2 Consumer Behavior   18

Subordinators and Prepositions That Show
Cause, Reason, or Purpose   20

Transition Words and Phrases That Show Effect   23

Common Patterns with Nouns That Show Effect   26

The Writing Process: Hooks   30

UNIT 3 Cause and Effect 3 Social Responsibility   34

Present and Future Real Conditionals   36

Present and Future Unreal Conditionals   40

Common Phrases with *Unless* and *If*   43

The Writing Process: Paragraph Order   46

UNIT 4 Cause and Effect 4 Alternative Energy Sources   50

-ing Participle Phrases That Show Effect   52

-ing Participle Phrases That Show Cause   54

Verbs That Show Cause and Effect   57

The Writing Process: Paraphrasing   60

PART 2 Comparison and Contrast | Human Behavior

UNIT 5 Comparison and Contrast 1 Family Size and Personality   64

Identifying Relative Clauses   66

Comparatives with *As . . . As*   70

Common Patterns That Show Contrast   73

The Writing Process: Topic Sentences   76

UNIT **6 Comparison and Contrast 2 Men, Women, and Equality**   **80**
Complex Noun Phrases   82
Parallel Structure   85
Common Quantifiers   88
The Writing Process: Supporting Details   92

UNIT **7 Comparison and Contrast 3**
Family Values in Different Cultures   **96**
Comparative and Superlative Adjectives and Adverbs   98
Articles   104
Common Expressions That Show Similarity   107
The Writing Process: Summarizing   110

UNIT **8 Comparison and Contrast 4 Intercultural Communication**   **114**
Adverb Clauses of Contrast and Concession   116
Transition Words and Phrases That Show Contrast and Concession   120
The Writing Process: Conclusions   124

PART 3 Narrative | Society and Culture

UNIT **9 Narrative 1 The American Dream**   **128**
Past Perfect and Past Perfect Progressive   130
Past Modals and Modal-like Expressions   133
Common Time Clauses   137
The Writing Process: Sentence Variety   142

UNIT **10 Narrative 2 Immigration**   **146**
Demonstratives   148
Common Time Signals   151
The Writing Process: Audience and Purpose   154

PART 4 Classification and Definition | Business

UNIT **11 Classification and Definition 1 Job Interviews**   **158**
The Passive   160
Common Words and Phrases Used in Classification Writing   164
The Writing Process: Classifying   169

UNIT **12 Classification and Definition 2 Your Ideal Job**   **172**
The Language of Definition   174
Appositives   178
The Writing Process: Cohesive Devices   183

PART 5 Problem–Solution | Nutrition and Health

UNIT 13 Problem–Solution 1 Food and Technology   188

Present Perfect and Present Perfect Progressive   190

Common Noun Phrase Structures   194

The Writing Process: Emphasizing the Significance of a Problem   199

UNIT 14 Problem–Solution 2 Children and Health   202

Reporting Verbs   204

Adverb Clauses and Phrases with *As*   208

Common Vocabulary for Describing Information in Graphics   211

The Writing Process: Narrowing Down a Topic   214

UNIT 15 Problem–Solution 3 Health and Technology   218

Adverb Clauses of Purpose and Infinitives of Purpose   220

Reducing Adverb Clauses to Phrases   224

Common Vocabulary to Describe Problems and Solutions   227

The Writing Process: Evaluating Proposed Solutions   231

UNIT 16 Problem–Solution 4 Leading a Healthy Life   234

It Constructions   236

Common Transition Words to Indicate Steps of a Solution   241

The Writing Process: Describing the Steps of a Solution   245

PART 6 Summary–Response and Persuasion | Social Issues and Technology

UNIT 17 Summary–Response Privacy in the Digital Age   248

Past Unreal Conditionals   251

Common Phrases Used in Summary–Response Writing   254

The Writing Process: Summary–Response Writing   258

UNIT 18 Persuasion 1 Violence in the Media   262

Nonidentifying Relative Clauses in Persuasive Writing   264

Phrases That Limit Overgeneralization   268

The Writing Process: The Introductory Paragraph to a Persuasive Essay   271

UNIT 19 Persuasion 2 Living in an Age of Information Overload   274

Noun Clauses with *Wh-* Words and *If/Whether*   276

Phrases for Argumentation   279

The Writing Process: Presenting and Refuting Opposing Views   283

UNIT 20 Persuasion 3 Social Networking   286

Expressing Future Actions   288

Common Words and Phrases in Persuasive Writing   292

The Writing Process: Writing Strong Arguments   295

References R1

Sources S1

Appendices

1 Parts of an Essay A1
2 Writer's Checklist A2
3 About Plagiarism A3
4 Academic Word List (AWL) Words and Definitions A6
Glossary of Grammar and Writing Terms G1
Index I1
Art Credits I8

Introduction to *Grammar and Beyond*

Grammar and Beyond is a research-based and content-rich grammar series for beginning- to advanced-level students of North American English. The series focuses on the grammar structures most commonly used in North American English, with an emphasis on the application of these grammar structures to academic writing. The series practices all four skills in a variety of authentic and communicative contexts. It is designed for use both in the classroom and as a self-study learning tool.

Grammar and Beyond Is Research-Based

The grammar presented in this series is informed by years of research on the grammar of written and spoken North American English as it is used in college lectures, textbooks, academic essays, high school classrooms, and conversations between instructors and students. This research, and the analysis of over one billion words of authentic written and spoken language data known as the *Cambridge International Corpus*, has enabled the authors to:

• Present grammar rules that accurately represent how North American English is actually spoken and written

• Identify and teach differences between the grammar of written and spoken English

• Focus more attention on the structures that are commonly used, and less attention on those that are rarely used, in written and spoken North American English

• Help students avoid the most common mistakes that English language learners make

• Choose reading and writing topics that will naturally elicit examples of the target grammar structure

• Introduce important vocabulary from the Academic Word List

Grammar and Beyond Teaches Academic Writing Skills

Grammar and Beyond helps students make the transition from understanding grammar structures to applying them in their academic writing.

In the Student's Books

At Levels 1 through 3 of the series, every Student's Book unit ends with a section devoted to the hands-on application of grammar to writing. This section, called Grammar for Writing, explores how and where the target grammar structures function in writing and offers controlled practice, exposure to writing models, and a guided but open-ended writing task.

At Level 4, the most advanced level, the syllabus is organized around the academic essay types that college students write (e.g., narrative, cause and effect) and is aimed at teaching students the grammar, vocabulary, and writing skills that they need in order to be successful at writing those kinds of essays.

Online

Grammar and Beyond also offers *Writing Skills Interactive*, an interactive online course in academic writing skills and vocabulary that correlates with the Student's Books. Each unit of the writing skills course focuses on a specific writing skill, such as avoiding sentence fragments or developing strong topic sentences.

Special Features of *Grammar and Beyond*

Realistic Grammar Presentations

Grammar is presented in clear and simple charts. The grammar points presented in these charts have been tested against real-world data from the *Cambridge International Corpus* to ensure that they are authentic representations of actual use of North American English.

At Level 4 vocabulary charts present words and phrases that naturally occur in each writing genre.

Data from the Real World

Many of the grammar presentations and application sections in the Student's Book include a feature called Data from the Real World, in which concrete and useful points discovered through analysis of corpus data are presented. These points are practiced in the exercises that follow.

Avoid Common Mistakes

Each Student's Book unit features an Avoid Common Mistakes section that develops students' awareness of the most common mistakes made by English language learners and gives them an opportunity to practice detecting and correcting these errors in running text. This section helps students avoid these mistakes in their own work. The mistakes highlighted in this section are drawn from a body of authentic data on learner English known as the *Cambridge Learner Corpus*, a database of over 35 million words from student essays written by nonnative speakers of English and information from experienced classroom teachers.

Academic Vocabulary

Every unit in *Grammar and Beyond* includes words from the Academic Word List (AWL), a research-based list of words and word families that appear with high frequency in English-language academic texts. These words are introduced in the opening text of the unit, recycled in the charts and exercises, and used to support the theme throughout the unit. The same vocabulary items are reviewed and practiced in *Writing Skills Interactive*, the online writing skills course. By the time students finish each level, they will have been exposed several times to a carefully selected set of level-appropriate AWL words, as well as content words from a variety of academic disciplines.

Series Levels

The following table provides a general idea of the difficulty of the material at each level of *Grammar and Beyond*. These are not meant to be interpreted as precise correlations.

	Description	TOEFL IBT	CEFR Levels
Level 1	beginning	20 – 34	A1 – A2
Level 2	low intermediate to intermediate	35 – 54	A2 – B1
Level 3	high intermediate	55 – 74	B1 – B2
Level 4	advanced	75 – 95	B2 – C1

Components for Students

Student's Book

The Student's Books for Levels 1 through 3 teach all of the grammar points appropriate at each level in short, manageable cycles of presentation and practice organized around a high-interest unit theme. The Level 4 Student's Book focuses on the structure of the academic essay in addition to the grammar rules, conventions, and structures that students need to master in order to be successful college writers. Please see the Tour of a Unit on pages xiv–xvii for a more detailed view of the contents and structure of the Student's Book units.

Workbook

The Workbook provides additional practice of the grammar presented in each unit of the Student's Book. The exercises offer both discrete and consolidated practice of grammar points and can be used for homework or in class. Each unit also offers practice correcting the errors highlighted in the Avoid Common Mistakes section in the Student's Book to help students master these troublesome errors. Self-Assessment sections at the end of each unit allow students to test their mastery of what they have learned.

Writing Skills Interactive

This online course provides graduated instruction and practice in writing skills, while reinforcing vocabulary presented in the Student's Books. Each unit includes a vocabulary review activity, followed by a short text that builds on the theme presented in the Student's Book and provides an additional context for the vocabulary. The text is followed by an animated interactive presentation of the target writing skill of the unit, after which students have the opportunity to practice the target skill in three different activities. Each unit closes with a quiz, which allows students to assess their progress.

Teacher Resources

Teacher Support Resource Book with CD-ROM

This comprehensive book provides a range of support materials for instructors, including:

- Suggestions for applying the target grammar to all four major skill areas, helping instructors facilitate dynamic and comprehensive grammar classes

- An answer key and audio script for the Student's Book

- A CD-ROM containing:

  - Ready-made, easily scored Unit Tests

  - PowerPoint presentations to streamline lesson preparation and encourage lively heads-up interaction

Class Audio CD

The class audio CD for each level provides the Student's Book listening material for in-class use.

Teacher Support Website

www.cambridge.org/grammarandbeyond

The website for *Grammar and Beyond* contains even more resources for instructors, including:

- Unit-by-unit teaching tips, helping instructors plan their lessons

- Downloadable communicative activities to add more in-class speaking practice

- A monthly newsletter on grammar teaching, providing ongoing professional development

We hope you enjoy using this series, and we welcome your feedback! Please send any comments to the authors and editorial staff at Cambridge University Press, at grammarandbeyond@cambridge.org.

About the Authors

John D. Bunting is a Senior Lecturer in the Intensive English Program in the Department of Applied Linguistics & ESL at Georgia State University. Prior to this, John taught EFL in Venezuela. He wrote *College Vocabulary 4* (Cengage, 2006) and worked on a revision of *Vocabulary in Use High Intermediate* (Cambridge, 2010). His research interests are corpus linguistics, vocabulary, academic writing, technology in language learning, and teacher education.

Luciana Diniz is the ESOL Department Chair at Portland Community College and an instructor. She has an MA and a PhD in Applied Linguistics from Georgia State University, and she has been teaching EFL/ESL for nearly 15 years. Luciana's research interests focus on the use of corpus linguistics in vocabulary and grammar teaching/learning. She has presented a number of papers at national and international conferences.

Randi Reppen is Professor of Applied Linguistics and TESL at Northern Arizona University (NAU) in Flagstaff, Arizona. She has over 20 years' experience teaching ESL students and training ESL teachers, including 11 years as the Director of NAU's Program in Intensive English. Randi's research interests focus on the use of corpora for language teaching and materials development. In addition to numerous academic articles and books, she is the author of *Using Corpora in the Language Classroom* and a co-author of *Basic Vocabulary in Use*, 2nd edition, both published by Cambridge University Press.

Advisory Panel

The ESL advisory panel has helped to guide the development of this series and provided invaluable information about the needs of ESL students and teachers in high schools, colleges, universities, and private language schools throughout North America.

Neta Simpkins Cahill, Skagit Valley College, Mount Vernon, WA

Shelly Hedstrom, Palm Beach State College, Lake Worth, FL

Richard Morasci, Foothill College, Los Altos Hills, CA

Stacey Russo, East Hampton High School, East Hampton, NY

Alice Savage, North Harris College, Houston, TX

Authors' Acknowledgments

In addition to our gratitude toward the many people who have collaborated in the preparation of this book, Luciana would like to thank her husband and best friend – Sergio – for his love and support. John wishes to acknowledge the insights and guidance provided by his friend and colleague, Sharon Cavusgil. He is also indebted to his wonderful wife Mayira and to Chris and James – their love and support sustain him.

Acknowledgments

The publisher and authors would like to thank these reviewers and consultants for their insights and participation:

Marty Attiyeh, The College of DuPage, Glen Ellyn, IL

Shannon Bailey, Austin Community College, Austin, TX

Jamila Barton, North Seattle Community College, Seattle, WA

Kim Bayer, Hunter College IELI, New York, NY

Linda Berendsen, Oakton Community College, Skokie, IL

Anita Biber, Tarrant County College Northwest, Fort Worth, TX

Jane Breaux, Community College of Aurora, Aurora, CO

Anna Budzinski, San Antonio College, San Antonio, TX

Britta Burton, Mission College, Santa Clara, CA

Jean Carroll, Fresno City College, Fresno, CA

Chris Cashman, Oak Park High School and Elmwood Park High School, Chicago, IL

Annette M. Charron, Bakersfield College, Bakersfield, CA

Patrick Colabucci, ALI at San Diego State University, San Diego, CA

Lin Cui, Harper College, Palatine, IL

Jennifer Duclos, Boston University CELOP, Boston, MA

Joy Durighello, San Francisco City College, San Francisco, CA

Kathleen Flynn, Glendale Community College, Glendale, CA

Raquel Fundora, Miami Dade College, Miami, FL

Patricia Gillie, New Trier Township High School District, Winnetka, IL

Laurie Gluck, LaGuardia Community College, Long Island City, NY

Kathleen Golata, Galileo Academy of Science & Technology, San Francisco, CA

Ellen Goldman, Mission College, Santa Clara, CA

Ekaterina Goussakova, Seminole Community College, Sanford, FL

Marianne Grayston, Prince George's Community College, Largo, MD

Mary Greiss Shipley, Georgia Gwinnett College, Lawrenceville, GA

Sudeepa Gulati, Long Beach City College, Long Beach, CA

Nicole Hammond Carrasquel, University of Central Florida, Orlando, FL

Vicki Hendricks, Broward College, Fort Lauderdale, FL

Kelly Hernandez, Miami Dade College, Miami, FL

Ann Johnston, Tidewater Community College, Virginia Beach, VA

Julia Karet, Chaffey College, Claremont, CA

Jeanne Lachowski, English Language Institute, University of Utah, Salt Lake City, UT

Noga Laor, Rennert, New York, NY

Min Lu, Central Florida Community College, Ocala, FL

Michael Luchuk, Kaplan International Centers, New York, NY

Craig Machado, Norwalk Community College, Norwalk, CT

Denise Maduli-Williams, City College of San Francisco, San Francisco, CA

Diane Mahin, University of Miami, Coral Gables, FL

Melanie Majeski, Naugatuck Valley Community College, Waterbury, CT

Jeanne Malcolm, University of North Carolina at Charlotte, Charlotte, NC

Lourdes Marx, Palm Beach State College, Boca Raton, FL

Susan G. McFalls, Maryville College, Maryville, TN

Nancy McKay, Cuyahoga Community College, Cleveland, OH

Dominika McPartland, Long Island Business Institute, Flushing, NY

Amy Metcalf, UNR/Intensive English Language Center, University of Nevada, Reno, NV

Robert Miller, EF International Language School San Francisco – Mills, San Francisco, CA

Marcie Pachino, Jordan High School, Durham, NC

Myshie Pagel, El Paso Community College, El Paso, TX

Bernadette Pedagno, University of San Francisco, San Francisco, CA

Tam Q Pham, Dallas Theological Seminary, Fort Smith, AR

Mary Beth Pickett, Global-LT, Rochester, MI

Maria Reamore, Baltimore City Public Schools, Baltimore, MD

Alison M. Rice, Hunter College IELI, New York, NY

Sydney Rice, Imperial Valley College, Imperial, CA

Kathleen Romstedt, Ohio State University, Columbus, OH

Alexandra Rowe, University of South Carolina, Columbia, SC

Irma Sanders, Baldwin Park Adult and Community Education, Baldwin Park, CA

Caren Shoup, Lone Star College – CyFair, Cypress, TX

Karen Sid, Mission College, Foothill College, De Anza College, Santa Clara, CA

Michelle Thomas, Miami Dade College, Miami, FL

Sharon Van Houte, Lorain County Community College, Elyria, OH

Margi Wald, UC Berkeley, Berkeley, CA

Walli Weitz, Riverside County Office of Ed., Indio, CA

Bart Weyand, University of Southern Maine, Portland, ME

Donna Weyrich, Columbus State Community College, Columbus, OH

Marilyn Whitehorse, Santa Barbara City College, Ojai, CA

Jessica Wilson, Rutgers University – Newark, Newark, NJ

Sue Wilson, San Jose City College, San Jose, CA

Margaret Wilster, Mid-Florida Tech, Orlando, FL

Anne York-Herjeczki, Santa Monica College, Santa Monica, CA

Hoda Zaki, Camden County College, Camden, NJ

We would also like to thank these teachers and programs for allowing us to visit:

Richard Appelbaum, Broward College, Fort Lauderdale, FL

Carmela Arnoldt, Glendale Community College, Glendale, AZ

JaNae Barrow, Desert Vista High School, Phoenix, AZ

Ted Christensen, Mesa Community College, Mesa, AZ

Richard Ciriello, Lower East Side Preparatory High School, New York, NY

Virginia Edwards, Chandler-Gilbert Community College, Chandler, AZ

Nusia Frankel, Miami Dade College, Miami, FL

Raquel Fundora, Miami Dade College, Miami, FL

Vicki Hendricks, Broward College, Fort Lauderdale, FL

Kelly Hernandez, Miami Dade College, Miami, FL

Stephen Johnson, Miami Dade College, Miami, FL

Barbara Jordan, Mesa Community College, Mesa, AZ

Nancy Kersten, GateWay Community College, Phoenix, AZ

Lewis Levine, Hostos Community College, Bronx, NY

John Liffiton, Scottsdale Community College, Scottsdale, AZ

Cheryl Lira-Layne, Gilbert Public School District, Gilbert, AZ

Mary Livingston, Arizona State University, Tempe, AZ

Elizabeth Macdonald, Thunderbird School of Global Management, Glendale, AZ

Terri Martinez, Mesa Community College, Mesa, AZ

Lourdes Marx, Palm Beach State College, Boca Raton, FL

Paul Kei Matsuda, Arizona State University, Tempe, AZ

David Miller, Glendale Community College, Glendale, AZ

Martha Polin, Lower East Side Preparatory High School, New York, NY

Patricia Pullenza, Mesa Community College, Mesa, AZ

Victoria Rasinskaya, Lower East Side Preparatory High School, New York, NY

Vanda Salls, Tempe Union High School District, Tempe, AZ

Kim Sanabria, Hostos Community College, Bronx, NY

Cynthia Schuemann, Miami Dade College, Miami, FL

Michelle Thomas, Miami Dade College, Miami, FL

Dongmei Zeng, Borough of Manhattan Community College, New York, NY

Tour of a Unit

> Each unit presents grammar and vocabulary structures that **naturally occur** in a specific writing genre.

UNIT 5

Comparison and Contrast 1: Identifying Relative Clauses; Comparatives with *As . . . As*; Common Patterns That Show Contrast

Family Size and Personality

1 Grammar in the Real World

You will read an essay that discusses how a child's birth order in the family – being the oldest child, middle child, youngest child, or an only child – may affect his or her personality as an adult. The essay is an example of a type of comparison and contrast writing in which the ideas are organized using the block method.

A *Before You Read* How many siblings (brothers and sisters) do you have? Do you think that some of their personality traits come from the order of their birth? Read the essay. How strong are the effects of birth order, according to the information in the essay?

Birth Order and Adult Sibling Relationships

What do Jimmy Carter, Bill Clinton, and George W. Bush all have in common? In addition to being elected president of the United States, these men all share the same birth order. Each one is the oldest child in his family. In fact, many very successful people in government and business have been "firstborn" children. While there is always some
5 variation, some experts agree that birth order can have an influence on a person's personality in childhood and in adulthood.

Firstborn children often share several traits. First, in contrast to their siblings, they are more likely to be responsible, ambitious, and authoritarian. This is probably because they are born into an environment of high expectations, and they usually receive a great deal of
10 attention. They are used to being leaders, taking responsibility for others, and sometimes taking on an almost parental role.

Middle children, on the other hand, exhibit different characteristics from firstborns. They are often not as determined as firstborns. They tend to be more passive and solitary. Having to share family attention with older and younger siblings, middle children have a
15 tendency to be more realistic, creative, and insightful.

Youngest children are often more protected than their older siblings. As a result, they are more likely to be dependent and controlling. They are often as creative as middle children, but usually more easygoing and social.

A child with no siblings, or an "only child," also exhibits some unique characteristics.
20 While some parents worry that an only child will have difficulties socializing and making friends, studies show that an only child is just as intelligent, accomplished, and sociable as a child with siblings. In fact, some research indicates that being an only child has some benefits. These children tend to have better vocabulary, perform better at school, and maintain closer relationships with their parents than children with siblings (Petersen,
25 2010, p. 2).

Even though it is assumed that birth order dictates some personality traits, individuals can free themselves from the roles they played when they were young, but it can be difficult. According to Vikki Stark, family therapist and author of *My Sister, My Self*, change requires letting go of familiar ways of being and patiently asserting new behaviors that
30 express one's true self (Kochan, 2006, para. 10).

B *Comprehension Check* Answer the questions.

1. How are former presidents Bill Clinton and George W. Bush connected to the main idea of the text?
2. According to the writer, why are firstborn children usually more ambitious than their siblings?
3. Which of the different birth order types – firstborn, middle born, youngest, and only child – do you think has the fewest advantages in life? Explain.

C *Notice*

1 Comparison and Contrast Writing Complete the outline below with information from the essay. The essay is organized using the block method. In this method, the main points that describe one part of the issue are presented together in "one block" or paragraph, and the main points that describe the second side of the issue are presented in the next paragraph, and so on.

Block Method: Birth Order and Adult Sibling Relationships

Introductory paragraph. Thesis statement: Some experts agree that birth order can have an influence on a person's personality in childhood and adulthood.

Body Paragraph 1. Topic: *Firstborn children*
(1)
Personality traits: responsible, ambitious, authoritarian

Body Paragraph 2. Topic: _____
(2)
Personality traits: passive, solitary, _____ , creative, _____
(3) (4)

Body Paragraph 3. Topic: _____
(5)
Personality traits: dependent, _____ , creative, easygoing, _____
(6) (7)

Body Paragraph 4. Topic: _____
(8)
Personality traits: intelligent, _____ , sociable
(9)

> ***Grammar in the Real World*** presents the grammar and vocabulary structures in an **essay on a contemporary topic**.

> ***Notice*** activities first draw students' attention to the **structure of the genre**.

Additional *Notice* activities help **students analyze** the grammar, vocabulary, and writing skill.

Grammar and Vocabulary charts provide clear guidance on the form, meaning, and use of the target language **for ease of instruction and reference**.

2 Grammar Follow the instructions below to help you notice and understand comparison and contrast sentences from the essay that use *as . . . as*.

1. Read the *as . . . as* sentence in the third paragraph. Are middle children likely to be equally determined, more determined, or less determined than firstborn children? Explain.
2. Read the *as . . . as* sentence in the fourth paragraph. Are youngest children likely to be equally creative, more creative, or less creative than middle children? Explain.
3. Read the *as . . . as* sentence in the fifth paragraph. Are only children likely to be equally intelligent, more intelligent, or less intelligent than children with siblings? Explain.

3 The Writing Process Underline the sentence that gives the main idea of each body paragraph. This sentence is called the *topic sentence*.

2 Identifying Relative Clauses

▶ Grammar Presentation

A relative clause modifies a noun and follows the noun it modifies. Identifying relative clauses provide necessary information about the noun. They are used in all kinds of academic writing, but they are especially useful in comparison and contrast writing to describe characteristics of elements that are being compared.

*Children **who / that have no siblings** are often very close to their parents.*
*People gradually behave in ways **which / that are more consistent with their preferred self-image.***

2.1 Identifying Relative Clauses

a. An identifying relative clause modifies a noun. It begins with a pronoun: *that, which, who, whom,* or *whose.* (It is often called a *restrictive relative clause.*)

An identifying relative clause answers the question, "Which one?" It gives necessary information about the noun or noun phrase in the main clause. Without that information, the sentence would be incomplete.

IDENTIFYING RELATIVE CLAUSE
*People **who do not have children** may not be aware of differences in birth order.*

IDENTIFYING RELATIVE CLAUSE
*Creativity is a trait **that all middle children share.***

b. *Who, that,* and *whom* refer to people. Use *whom* for object relative clauses. In informal speaking and writing, the use of *who* for *whom* is common.

PEOPLE
*Researchers **who / that study families** have different views.*
*My siblings are the people in my life **whom** I will always trust.*

4 Common Patterns That Show Contrast 🌐

▶ Vocabulary Presentation

Useful words and phrases that show contrast in academic writing include *difference(s), differ, in contrast,* and *unlike.* These words are important in comparison and contrast writing.

*One **major difference** in some cultures is the role of adult children.*
***In contrast to** the past, more U.S. children now live with their parents into their early adulthood.*

4.1 Difference(s), Differ, In Contrast, Unlike

a. A common pattern with the noun *difference* is:

NOUN PHRASE
The difference between _____
NOUN PHRASE
and _____ is . . .

*One **significant difference between** youngest children **and** their older siblings **is** that youngest children receive a lot of attention.*

b. A common pattern with the verb *differ* is:

NOUN PHRASE   NOUN PHRASE
_____ differ(s) from _____ in that . . .

*The results of current research **differ from** earlier results **in that** they show a definite relationship between birth order and personality.*

c. Common expressions and patterns used with the phrase *in contrast* are:

NOUN PHRASE   INDEPENDENT CLAUSE
In contrast to _____ , _____ .

INDEPENDENT CLAUSE
In contrast, _____ .

***In contrast to** traditional American families, the Chinese have had several generations of one-child families.*
*Many children without siblings receive a lot of attention. **In contrast**, children with siblings often share their parents' attention.*

d. A common pattern with the adjective *unlike* is:

NOUN PHRASE   INDEPENDENT CLAUSE
Unlike _____ , _____ .

***Unlike** firstborn children, youngest children are generally very creative.*

Data from the Real World, a feature unique to this series, takes students **beyond traditional information** and teaches them how the unit's **grammar and vocabulary** are used in authentic situations, including the differences between spoken and written use.

Students learn to **Avoid Common Mistakes** based on research in student writing.

2.2 Using Identifying Relative Clauses *(continued)*

b. Relative clauses are similar to subordinate clauses in that they are fragments if they appear alone.

| FRAGMENT: | *A recent study reports that firstborns are generally smarter than siblings.* **Who are born later.** |
| CORRECT: | *A recent study reports that firstborns are generally smarter than siblings* **who are born later.** |

Data from the Real World

In academic writing, the relative pronoun **who** is more commonly used than **that** to refer to people.

| Who | |
| That | |

In speaking, the relative pronoun **that** is more commonly used than **who** to refer to people.

| Who | |
| That | |

▶ **Grammar Application**

Exercise 2.1 Identifying Relative Clauses

A Read the paragraph about birth order. Complete each sentence with *that, who,* *whom,* or *whose.* Sometimes more than one answer is possible.

Birth order researchers have discovered some interesting information __*that*__ can help us understand
(1)
our colleagues better. Do you have a difficult boss
_____ authoritarian personality makes
(2)
your life difficult? If so, your boss might be a firstborn child.
Children _____ are born first are often
(3)
more authoritarian than their younger siblings. Do you
have a co-worker _____ is passive, but particularly creative and insightful?
(4)
This person may be a middle child. People _____ have both older and
(5)
younger siblings are often passive because their older siblings were responsible for their
well-being when they were young. The creativity _____ they exhibit might
(6)
be the effect of their having spent a lot of time on their own due to having to share parental
attention with their older and younger siblings. People _____ you work with
(7)

---

5 Avoid Common Mistakes ⚠

1. Do not use *who* **with inanimate nouns.**
    that
    A study who showed the benefits of being an only child was published last year.

2. Do not omit the relative pronoun in subject relative clauses.
    who
    Children ˌhave older siblings tend to be somewhat dependent.

3. Remember that the subject and the verb must agree in relative clauses.
    have
    Children who has siblings often become secure and confident adults.

4. Use *the same as,* **not** *the same than.*
    as
    Middle children often have the same level of creativity than youngest children.

Editing Task

Find and correct eight more mistakes in this body paragraph from an essay comparing trends in families in the past and today.

Families Past and Present

          that
    A major way that families have changed is the number of families ˌhave only one child.
The number of families had only one child was low in the United States in the 1950s and
1960s. However, one-child families began increasing in the 1970s and are very common
today. This is especially true in households who have only one parent. One reason families
5 are smaller is the cost of living. It is not the same than it was 40 years ago. For example, it
costs about 10 times more to send a child to college than it did 40 years ago. As a result, many
parents choose to have only one child because they do not have enough money for more
children. In addition, attitudes about only children are also
not the same than attitudes about them in the past. In the
10 1950s and 1960s, people avoided having only one child. At
that time, many people thought that children did not have
siblings had many disadvantages. For example, people
thought that they did not learn good social skills. However,
recent studies who focus on only children show a different
15 picture. These studies show that only children tend to have
the same social skills than children who has siblings.

Theme-related exercises allow students to **apply the grammar and vocabulary** in a variety of natural contexts.

Next, students apply what they learn in **realistic editing tasks.**

The Writing Process section begins with presentation and practice of a **writing skill** and culminates in a *Writing Task*.

Before starting the *Writing Task*, students **organize and discuss their ideas**.

6 The Writing Process

In this section, you will write an outline and one body paragraph for a comparison and contrast essay using the block method. Before you start writing, you will learn how to write effective topic sentences.

About Topic Sentences

Topic sentences introduce the main idea of a body paragraph. In academic essays, they often appear at the beginning of body paragraphs. Although not all body paragraphs have topic sentences, it will help you to organize your writing if you always include one.

The following guidelines will help you write effective topic sentences:

1. An effective topic sentence should contain a claim or an opinion that needs to be supported with evidence. It should not be a fact that is widely accepted as true. Notice the difference in the following sentences:
   - Some families are small. (a fact)
   - Small families are better than large families. (a claim that needs to be supported with evidence)
2. The content of the topic sentences should relate back to the thesis statement of the essay.
   - Siblings have different personality traits because of birth order. (thesis statement)
   - Firstborn children are generally leaders. (topic sentence)
3. The topic sentence is usually a general statement. It rarely contains detailed information. The details will come in the rest of the paragraph in sentences that convince the reader that the claim in the topic sentence is valid or true.
   - Middle children can be more solitary. (general statement)
   - Middle children do not always get a lot of attention. (detail to support the topic sentence)
4. Include words and phrases that connect one body paragraph to another.
   - *Unlike* middle children, those born last are often more easygoing.
   - *In addition to* being more easygoing, the youngest are also . . .
   - *Another* common trait of the youngest child is . . .

Organize Your Ideas

A For this assignment, you will use the block method of comparison and contrast for organizing your ideas.

Look at the block method outline for the essay on birth order below. Use the blank outline that follows to create an outline for your topic.

Title of Essay: Birth Order
Paragraph 1. Introductory paragraph. Thesis Statement: Experts agree that birth order tends to dictate some basic personality traits in children and adults.
Paragraph 2. Topic Sentence: Firstborn children often share several common traits. • Traits: responsible, ambitious, authoritarian
Paragraph 3. Topic Sentence: Middle children exhibit unique characteristics. • Traits: passive, solitary, realistic, creative, insightful
Paragraph 4. Topic Sentence: Youngest children have typical characteristics as well. • Traits: dependent, controlling, creative, easygoing, social

Title of Essay: _____
Paragraph 1. Introductory paragraph. Thesis Statement: _____ _____ _____
Paragraph 2. Topic Sentence: _____ _____
• Details: _____ _____
Paragraph 3. Topic Sentence: _____ _____
• Details: _____ _____
Paragraph 4. Topic Sentence: _____ _____
• Details: _____ _____

B *Pair Work* Share your outline with a partner and discuss your ideas.

Writing Task

Write one of the body paragraphs from your outline. Follow the steps below.

1. Make sure that you have a clear topic sentence that follows the guidelines in About Topic Sentences on page 76.
2. Include the following in your paragraph:
   - identifying relative clauses;
   - *as . . . as;*
   - common patterns that show contrast;
   - at least three of these academic words from the essay in this unit: *adulthood, assumed, author, benefit, creative, environment, exhibit, expert, indicate, individual, insightful, intelligent, maintain, passive, research, role, unique.*
3. After you write your paragraph, review it and make sure that you avoided the mistakes in the Avoid Common Mistakes chart on page 75.

> **Academic Writing Tip**
>
> **Improving Your Internet Searches**
> When you do an Internet search, use quotation marks around important ideas. For example, "large families" will eliminate results with only "large" or "family" alone.

Peer Review

A Exchange your outline and paragraph with a partner. Answer the following questions as you read your partner's outline and work, and share your responses.

1. Is the outline organized using the block method?
2. Does the topic sentence relate to the thesis statement?
3. Are any identifying relative clauses, *as . . . as,* or common patterns that show contrast used in the paragraph?
4. Is anything confusing? Write a question mark (?) next to it.
5. Provide one compliment (something you found interesting or unusual).

B Use your partner's comments to help you revise your paragraph. Use the Writer's Checklist on page A2 to review your paragraph for organization, grammar, and vocabulary.

In the *Writing Task*, students **apply** the Unit's grammar, vocabulary, and writing skill.

Peer Review offers a structured way for students to give **constructive feedback** on each other's writing.

Cause and Effect 1: Sentence Structure; Common Patterns with Nouns That Show Cause

The Environment and You

1 Grammar in the Real World 🌍

You will read an essay about ecological footprints, a measurement of the impact each person has on the world's natural resources. The essay is an example of one kind of cause and effect writing in which one cause leads to several effects.

A *Before You Read* What are three common things that people do in their everyday lives that have an impact on the environment? Read the essay. According to the writer, what might be one effect of mining for natural resources such as coal and oil?

Ecological Footprints

Environmentalists have been concerned about the impact that individuals have on our planet, and many people wonder what they can do to help protect the environment. A good place to start is by reducing one's ecological footprint. An ecological footprint is an estimate of how much land, water, and other natural resources are being used by a person or a group. Because
5 resources are easily accessible in developed countries like the United States, people in these countries tend to have large ecological footprints. For example, they may take long showers, leave their computers on for the whole day, and buy new things they do not need because the items are on sale. The consequences of large ecological footprints can be disastrous.[1]

One of the worst effects of large ecological footprints is the loss of natural resources, such
10 as oil, water, and wood. These resources are being consumed so fast that the Earth does not have time to renew them. According to Adam Grubb (2011, para. 1), co-founder of Energy Bulletin, 85 million barrels of oil are produced daily in the world. People use oil to run their cars, heat their homes, and create products such as clothes, paint, and plastic. In "Forest Facts," the United Nations Environment Programme (2011) reveals that "36 million acres of natural forest
15 are lost each year" (para. 2). As more people consume products like oil and wood, these natural resources will become even scarcer.[2]

Large ecological footprints also lead to higher greenhouse gas emissions. The mining of oil, natural gas, and coal, as well as the use of these resources in electrical power plants and automobiles, releases dangerous gases into the air, where they trap[3] heat. As a result, the
20 Earth gets warmer.

Another result of large ecological footprints is the increased pollution of rivers and streams. A great deal of waste is thrown into rivers and streams daily. Because of pollution, the water in many bodies of water is becoming or has already become unsuitable for human consumption.

[1]**disastrous:** causing a lot of damage | [2]**scarce:** difficult to find | [3]**trap:** prevent from leaving

It is our responsibility to find ways to decrease our
25 impact on our planet. Even small changes can make a
difference and help to protect the environment. If we
do not start reducing our ecological footprints right
away, it may be too late for future generations
to contain[4] the damage.

[4]**contain:** limit

B *Comprehension Check* Answer the questions.

1. In your own words, what is an ecological footprint? Provide examples of activities that could cause a large and a small ecological footprint.
2. According to the essay, what are three major consequences of large ecological footprints?
3. "We do not inherit the Earth from our ancestors; we borrow it from our children" is a Native American proverb. How is this proverb related to the essay?

C *Notice*

1 Cause and Effect Writing In the essay, underline the three effects, or results, of large ecological footprints. There is one in each body paragraph (the paragraphs that follow the introduction and explain each of the writer's main ideas). Draw a chart like the one below on a separate sheet of paper and write the effects.

2 Grammar Follow the instructions below to help you notice sentence structures that state causes and describe effects.

1. In the first paragraph find the sentence about easily accessible resources and large ecological footprints on lines 4–6. Write *C* above the clause that gives a reason or cause and *E* above the clause that states the effect. Circle the word that introduces the cause.
2. In the third paragraph find the sentence that states the effect of releasing dangerous gases in the air. Circle the phrase that introduces the effect.
3. In the fourth paragraph underline the first sentence. Does the sentence describe a cause or an effect? What phrase does the writer use to introduce it?

3 The Writing Process Reread the introductory paragraph of the essay and underline the sentence that tells the reader the main idea. This sentence is called the *thesis statement*.

2 Sentence Structure: Simple and Compound Sentences

▶ Grammar Presentation

In cause and effect writing and in academic writing in general, it is effective to use a variety of sentence types. Writers use simple sentences to express facts or opinions strongly. They use compound sentences to link related ideas such as causes and effects.

Simple sentence:
Lack of natural resources is one of the results of large ecological footprints.

Compound sentence:
Large ecological footprints cause many problems, and it is our social responsibility to solve them.

2.1 Simple Sentences

a. A simple sentence has only one clause, called a *main clause* or an *independent clause*. Like all sentences, a simple sentence must have a subject and a verb.	SUBJECT VERB *A great deal of waste is thrown into rivers and streams daily.*
Many different elements may come after the verb, including: object prepositional phrase adjective adverb	SUBJECT VERB OBJECT *Pollution has devastated **many rivers**.* SUBJECT VERB PREP. PHRASE *Ozone and other greenhouse gases are often **in the news**.* SUBJECT VERB ADJECTIVE *The Earth is becoming **warmer**.* SUBJECT VERB ADVERB *Natural resources that provide energy will run out **eventually**.*
b. The subject of a sentence must be a noun phrase. There are many different kinds of noun phrases, including: adjective + noun pronoun noun *and* noun noun + prepositional phrase noun + relative clause gerund	* **Small changes** can make a difference.* ***This** has devastated many rivers.* ***Ozone and other greenhouse gases** are often in the news.* ***The health of our oceans** remains critical.* ***Natural resources that provide energy** will run out eventually.* ***Reducing our ecological footprints** is crucial.*

2.1 Simple Sentences *(continued)*

c. The verb of a sentence can consist of a single main verb or a main verb with an auxiliary verb such as *be*, *do*, and *have*, or a modal such as *can* and *will*.	MAIN VERB *The health of our oceans **remains** critical.* AUXILIARY VERB *This **has** devastated many rivers.* MODAL *People **may** take long showers.*
A verb phrase can consist of more than one verb.	*The average temperature **rises and falls**.*

2.2 Using Simple Sentences

a. Use short simple sentences to emphasize an important point within the larger discourse.	*The consequences of these footprints can be disastrous.*
b. If the subject or a verb is missing, the sentence is incomplete. It is called a *fragment*. Avoid fragments by making sure all sentences have a subject and a verb.	FRAGMENT (MISSING SUBJECT): *In the future, will probably be much warmer on Earth.* CORRECTION: *In the future, **the temperature** will probably be much warmer on Earth.* FRAGMENT (MISSING VERB): *The worst effect of large ecological footprints the loss of natural resources.* CORRECTION: *The worst effect of large ecological footprints **is** the loss of natural resources.*
c. Academic writers connect independent clauses with transition words to make the relationship between two ideas very clear. Some examples of transition words are: *as a result, consequently, furthermore, however* You can use a period or a semicolon before a transition word to connect the independent clauses. Use a comma after a transition word.	*These gases trap heat in the air. **As a result**, the Earth gets warmer.* *These gases trap heat in the air; **as a result**, the Earth gets warmer.*
d. You can connect two independent clauses with a semicolon. This is a good choice if the ideas in the two clauses are closely related.	INDEPENDENT CLAUSE 1 INDEPENDENT CLAUSE 2 *People should buy less; they should replace items only when absolutely necessary.*

2.3 Compound Sentences

a. Use compound sentences to connect two ideas. A compound sentence includes at least two independent clauses that are connected by a coordinating conjunction (*and, but, or, so, yet*). Use a comma before the coordinating conjunction.

INDEPENDENT CLAUSE 1
Some people are concerned about the environment,
INDEPENDENT CLAUSE 2
so they recycle as much as they can.

b. Avoid run-on sentences and comma splices. A run-on sentence is two independent clauses without a coordinating conjunction.

Use a comma and coordinating conjunction when connecting two independent clauses.

A comma splice is two independent clauses combined with a comma.

Use a period between the two independent clauses.

RUN-ON: *These gases trap heat in the air the Earth gets warmer.*

CORRECTION: *These gases trap heat in the air, **so** the Earth gets warmer.*

COMMA SPLICE: *Humans are the cause of many environmental problems, it is our responsibility to resolve them.*

CORRECTION: *Humans are the cause of many environmental problems. It is our responsibility to resolve them.*

c. The use of *and* and *but* to introduce a sentence is common in some types of writing, such as in newspapers and magazines. However, it is not usually appropriate in academic writing.

*Natural resources are being consumed so fast that the Earth does not have time to renew them. **And** as a result, these resources are becoming scarce.*

*There are efforts to clean up the oceans. **But** the health of our oceans remains critical.*

▶ Grammar Application

Exercise 2.1 Subjects and Verbs

Read about energy resources in Iceland. Underline the subject, and circle the verb in each independent clause.

1. Iceland has huge frozen glaciers, but it also has more than 100 volcanoes.
2. In 1998, Iceland decided to become independent from fossil fuels.
3. It began to increase its use of renewable energy sources.
4. Electricity in Iceland's homes is generated by geothermal springs, or it comes from the energy of the rivers and glaciers.
5. The water in geothermal springs is already hot, so Icelanders use it instead of fossil fuels to heat their homes.
6. Basic services such as transportation in Iceland are switching to electric vehicles, and all ships in the large fishing industry may eventually operate on hydrogen fuel.
7. Iceland satisfies its country's need for energy without relying heavily on fossil fuels.

Exercise 2.2 Fragments, Run-on Sentences, and Comma Splices

A Read the following sentences about the environment. Check (✓) each complete sentence. Write *F* for each fragment, *R-O* for each run-on, and *CS* for each comma splice.

1. (a) ___✓___ Over time, people have destroyed the natural habitats of many plants and animals in order to build more homes and grow more food. (b) ___F___ For this reason, many of our forests now gone. (c) ___R-O___ Plants and animals are losing their homes they may become extinct.

2. (a) _____ Water pollution a serious problem. (b) _____ For many years, people got rid of waste by dumping it into the water. (c) _____ As a result, the quality of the water in many of our oceans, rivers, and lakes unacceptable. (d) _____ In fact, nearly a billion people in the world do not have safe drinking water, and over two million people die each year from diseases related to water.

3. (a) _____ Environmentalists are constantly trying to come up with ideas to protect the environment nobody knows what the environment will be like in the future.

   (b) _____ However, researchers believe that much has already improved.

   (c) _____ Individuals are becoming more aware of the environment around them.

4. (a) _____ Trying to protect nature in various ways. (b) _____ Some people are helping to clean up the environment by driving electric cars, others are working to preserve endangered plants and animals. (c) _____ These efforts will allow future generations to have clean air and water and to enjoy the world's natural beauty.

5. (a) _____ The forests of the Earth are being cut down. (b) _____ The destruction of the forests is the result of human and natural disasters. (c) _____ Has negative consequences on the environment.

B Rewrite the fragments, run-ons, and comma splices in A. Use coordinating conjunctions, transition words, and punctuation to correct run-ons and comma splices. Check your answers with a partner.

1. *For this reason, many of our forests are now gone. Plants and animals are losing their homes. As a result, they may become extinct.*

2. _____

   _____

3. _____

   _____

4. _____

   _____

5. _____

   _____

3 | Complex Sentences

▶ Grammar Presentation

Another way to link cause and effect ideas is with complex sentences. Complex sentences have one independent clause and at least one dependent clause.

Because resources are readily accessible in developed countries like the United States, people in these countries tend to have large ecological footprints.

3.1 Complex Sentences

A complex sentence has an independent clause and a dependent clause introduced by a subordinator. Subordinators show the relationship between the two ideas.

Some examples of subordinators are:
although, after, as if, because, before, if, since, whereas, whether, while

When the dependent clause comes first, use a comma to separate it from the independent clause.

INDEPENDENT CLAUSE
Future generations will suffer

DEPENDENT CLAUSE
if pollution is not reduced.

DEPENDENT CLAUSE
***Although** people try to save energy,*

INDEPENDENT CLAUSE
global demand for energy increases every year.

3.2 Using Complex Sentences

a. In academic writing, use complex sentences with the subordinators *because, if, since,* and *when* to express cause and effect relationships.

CAUSE   EFFECT
***If** pollution is reduced, global health will improve.*

b. A dependent clause that is not connected to an independent clause is a fragment.

Avoid dependent clause fragments in the following ways:

Connect the dependent clause to an independent clause. (Remember to use a comma after a dependent clause if it comes before an independent clause.)

OR

Change the subordinator to a transition word that can introduce an independent clause.

FRAGMENT: ***Because** energy use is high in the developed world. People there use a lot of resources.*

DEPENDENT CLAUSE
CORRECTION: ***Because** energy use is high in the*

INDEPENDENT CLAUSE
developed world, people there use a lot of resources.

CORRECTION: *Energy use is high in the developed world. **As a result**, people there use a lot of resources.*

▶ Grammar Application

Exercise 3.1 Complex Sentences

A For each pair of sentences about bald eagles, write *C* next to the sentence that shows the cause and *E* next to the sentence that shows the effect. Next, combine the sentences using *because*, *if*, *since*, or *when*. Sometimes more than one answer is possible.

1. _*E*_ The United States government declared bald eagles an endangered species.

   _*C*_ Bald eagles were almost extinct in the 1960s.
   Because bald eagles were almost extinct
   in the 1960s, the United States government
   declared them an endangered species.

2. _____ The bald eagle showed the qualities of impressive strength and courage.

   _____ The bald eagle was chosen in 1782 to be the symbol for the United States.

   _____

   _____

3. _____ The government enacted laws that included banning the use of the pesticide DDT.

   _____ The bald eagle population began to recover.

   _____

   _____

4. _____ In 2007, the bald eagle was taken off the Endangered Species Act's "threatened" list.

   _____ The bald eagles' numbers had greatly increased since the 1960s.

   _____

   _____

5. _____ The bald eagle population may decrease once more.

   _____ The habitats of the bald eagles are not protected in the future.

   _____

   _____

6. _____ Some biologists are urging wind energy companies to develop safer turbines.

   _____ The birds are sometimes killed by the blades of wind turbines.

   _____

   _____

7. _____ People can help protect the bald eagle.

   _____ People volunteer to clean up the habitats where eagles nest.

   _____

   _____

B *Pair Work* With a partner, think of two endangered animals. Discuss why the animals are endangered (habitat loss, pesticides, overfishing, etc.) and what is being done to protect the animals. Next, do the role play below. Use *because*, *if*, *since*, and *when* where possible.

A You are a reporter. Interview Partner B about one of the animals you talked about. Ask why the animal is endangered and what the impact of environmental policies has been.

B You are an environmentalist. Answer Partner A's questions.

Partner A Tell me about an endangered animal that people should know about.
Partner B Sea turtles are an endangered animal.
Partner A Why are they endangered?
Partner B One reason is the fishing industry. Many turtles die when they bite the hooks and get caught in the fishing lines.
Partner A How are they today?
Partner B Since there are now programs that protect the turtles, their numbers have improved in recent years.

Switch roles and do the role play again using information about the second animal.

Exercise 3.2 ◀ッ More Complex Sentences

Read the questions below. Then listen to the radio interview about bikeshare programs in large cities. As you listen, take notes. Finally, answer the questions. Use *because*, *if*, *since*, and *when*.

1. Why are bikeshares becoming so popular in large cities?
   Bikeshares are becoming popular because
   they are a great way to reduce pollution.

2. Why do people use a bikeshare?
   _____
   _____
   _____

3. What do people have to do if they want to use the bikes?
   _____
   _____
   _____

4. What happens when riders get a flat tire?
   _____
   _____
   _____

5. If a city wants a bikeshare program to be successful, what two things are required?

_____

_____

6. What can bikeshare riders do in some cities when they want to find a bike or an empty space at a station?

_____

_____

7. Why do some people feel uncomfortable riding the bikes?

_____

_____

4 Common Patterns with Nouns That Show Cause

▶ Vocabulary Presentation

Cause and effect relationships can be shown in many different ways. One important way is through the use of the nouns *cause*, *reason*, and *factor*.

One important cause of overpopulation is lack of education.

Low cost **is the primary reason why** many communities use coal for energy.

Emissions from cars **are a major factor in** the increase in air pollution.

4.1 Nouns That Show Cause: *Cause, Reason, Factor*

a. The following expressions and patterns are commonly used with the noun *cause* and a form of the verb *be*: NOUN PHRASE NOUN PHRASE _____ is a/one cause of _____ . NOUN PHRASE NOUN PHRASE Another cause of _____ is _____ .	A higher birth rate **is one** major **cause of** overpopulation. **Another** leading **cause of** overpopulation **is** the decline in death rates.
b. Expressions with *cause* generally describe a negative effect. *Cause* does not usually occur with words that are related to success or positive results.	Some researchers believe that the primary cause of **global warming** is large ecological footprints.

4.1 Nouns That Show Cause: *Cause, Reason, Factor* (continued)

c. These expressions and patterns are commonly used with the noun *reason* and a form of the verb *be*:

CLAUSE   CLAUSE
One reason (why) _____ *is* _____ .

CLAUSE   NOUN PHRASE
One reason (why) _____ *is* _____ .

NOUN PHRASE   CLAUSE
The reason for _____ *is* _____ .

NOUN PHRASE   NOUN PHRASE
The reason for _____ *is* _____ .

SENTENCE
_____ . *For this reason / these reasons,*

CLAUSE
_____ .

One reason (why) *the population **is** growing so fast **is** that death rates have fallen dramatically.*

One reason (why) *the population is growing so fast **is** the decline in the death rate.*

The *real* **reason for** *our concern about overpopulation **is** that our resources are limited.*

The *primary* **reason for** *our concern about overpopulation **is** limited resources.*

People are living longer, healthier lives. **For this reason,** *the population has been increasing.*

d. These expressions and patterns are commonly used with the noun *factor* and a form of the verb *be*:

NOUN PHRASE   NOUN PHRASE
_____ *is a / one factor in* _____ .

NOUN PHRASE   NOUN PHRASE
Another factor in _____ *is* _____ .

*Mortality **is one** key **factor in** the current growth in population.*

Another *critical* **factor in** *water pollution **is** the increase in fertilizer use by farmers.*

Data from the Real World 🌐

Adjectives that most frequently occur with *cause* are:

leading, probable, common, root, underlying, exact, major, likely, main, important, primary
*Scholars are not sure whether poverty is an **underlying cause** of overpopulation.*

Adjectives that most frequently occur with *reason* are:

good, major, real, main, primary, biggest
*One **good reason** to recycle is to save money.*

Adjectives that most frequently occur with *factor* are:

important, another, major, key, significant, critical
*Decreasing the number of cars on the road is a **critical factor** in the effort to reduce air pollution.*

▶ Vocabulary Application

Exercise 4.1 Nouns That Show Cause

A Complete the online article about ways to get around. Use *cause*, *reason*, or *factor* and appropriate adjectives from the Data from the Real World box above.

=== Changing with the Times ===

Some experts say that one <u>*leading cause*</u> of air pollution is the carbon emissions from
(1)

cars. To reduce these emissions, many people have changed how they get around. James

Kendall of Cincinnati, Ohio, sold his gas-guzzling car and purchased a hybrid vehicle. Kendall

says, "One _____ _____ I bought a hybrid is that it's better
(2)

for the environment. However, another _____ _____ in my
(3)

decision was money. I spend a lot less on gas now."

Linda Wong of Los Angeles, California, takes public transportation as often as she

can. "Carbon emissions from cars is the _____ _____
(4)

of smog and air pollution in L.A.," she explains. "I don't want to add to that. That's

the _____ _____ why I don't like to drive. Another
(5)

_____ _____ in my decision is that driving in L.A. is
(6)

very stressful."

Pedro Sandoval of Missoula, Montana, started using a carpool to get to and from

work two years ago because of his concern for the environment, but he says that the

_____ _____ that he has stuck with it has to do with other
(7)

incentives. "I've met a lot of really nice people and saved a lot of money." He'll take public

transportation, but, as he says, buses are a _____ _____ of
(8)

pollution, too.

B *Pair Work* With a partner, choose three environmentally related issues. Below are some
ideas. Explain possible causes and effects for each one using expressions with *factor*, *reason*,
and *cause*.

| noise pollution | nuclear safety | overpopulation | water pollution |

The use of medicines is a factor in water pollution. The medicines we use end up in our
water. For this reason, some communities have started to collect unused medicines so that
they don't end up in our water.

Exercise 4.2 More Nouns That Show Cause

A Answer the questions about ways that people and cities are lessening their impact on the environment. Use expressions and patterns with *cause*, *reason*, or *factor*, and adjectives from *Data from the Real World*.

1. What is one reason why some people prefer not to eat meat?

   One primary reason why some people prefer not to eat meat is that they don't want animals to be killed for food.

2. What do you think is one reason for the rising interest in locally grown food?

   _____

3. What are two causes of pollution in cities?

   _____

4. What is one important factor in a city's decision to start a bikeshare program?

   _____

5. Some cities have decided to ban the use of plastic bags in grocery stores. What do you think is the reason for this ban?

   _____

B *Pair Work* With a partner, take turns asking and answering the questions in A. Do you agree or disagree with each other's answers? Tell why.

I disagree that people don't eat meat because they don't want animals to be killed.
I think that some people don't eat meat because they can't afford it.

5 | Avoid Common Mistakes ⚠

1. Avoid fragments. Make sure sentences have a subject and a verb.

   The result of a large ecological footprint ^is^ often pollution.

2. Use *because*, not *cuz or coz*, in written academic English.

   Animals are becoming extinct ~~cuz~~ *because* humans have moved into their habitats.

3. Do not confuse *cause* with *because*.

   Because
   ~~Cause~~ water pollution is widespread, there is a shortage of clean drinking water in many parts of the world.

4. Avoid beginning sentences with *and* in written academic English.

   Shoppers should bring their own bags to stores because paper bags lead to ~~deforestation. And~~ *deforestation, and*

   plastic bags are dangerous for birds and marine life.

Editing Task

Find and correct eight more mistakes in this paragraph from an essay about ocean pollution.

One significant cause of ocean pollution is the accidental spilling of crude oil by large ocean-going ships. The consequences of oil spills can be disastrous to both plant and animal marine life. For example, oil that spills on the surface of the water blocks oxygen from getting to marine plant life. Cause oxygen is necessary for survival, marine plants die. And the
5   fish that eat them can die as well. In addition, oil spills can coat the feathers of marine birds. Oil-coated birds can become weighted down, so cannot fly. Furthermore, oil often removes the natural coating on marine bird feathers. As a result, the birds can die from overexposure cuz the coating protects them from the elements. Oil spills also affect the human food chain. This occurs coz shellfish such as mussels and clams filter water through their bodies. If the
10   water is polluted with oil, the flesh of the shellfish becomes polluted as well. And this makes them harmful for human consumption. Cause oil spills affect human, animal, and plant life, many people agree that these spills one of the most serious environmental problems in the world today.

6 | The Writing Process

In this section, you will write an introductory paragraph for a cause and effect essay that describes one cause leading to several effects. Before you start writing, you will learn how to write effective thesis statements.

About Thesis Statements

The introductory paragraph of an essay has three parts: the hook, which introduces the topic; additional background information on the topic; and a thesis statement. A thesis statement states the main idea of the essay and gives a preview of what the writer is going to say about the topic. It usually comes at the end of the paragraph.

There are two types of thesis statements:

1. **General thesis statements** A general thesis statement tells the reader the topic of the essay, but not the exact points that will be made. The specific points will appear later in the topic sentences of the body paragraphs.

   NON-SPECIFIC IDEAS

   *There are **three main reasons** for not driving a car to help build a better future.*

   NON-SPECIFIC IDEAS

   *Drastic lifestyle changes will have both **positive and negative effects**.*

2. **Specific thesis statements** A specific thesis statement tells the reader the exact arguments or points that will be developed in the essay. Usually, the points are listed in the same order in which they appear in the body paragraphs.

SPECIFIC ARGUMENTS

*Becoming a strict vegetarian can lead to **a healthier body**, **a smaller ecological footprint**, **and a more spiritual life**.*

SPECIFIC POINTS

*Some ways to lead a healthy life include **waking up early**, **exercising**, **and meditating**.*

Exercise

A Read the thesis statements below. Label each one as general (*G*) or specific (*S*).

_____ 1. A dramatic increase in population will cause several major environmental changes.

_____ 2. Environmental policies can reduce air pollution, traffic congestion, and water use.

_____ 3. "Green" office buildings will lead to cleaner air, lower costs, and healthier workers.

_____ 4. Neighborhood groups can improve the environment in several important ways.

B Imagine that each thesis statement in A was in the introduction to an essay. Match each statement below to a thesis statement in A. Write the number (1, 2, 3, 4) on the line.

_____ a. People can start community gardens that provide fresh local produce.

_____ b. Installing solar panels in buildings could reduce heat and electricity costs.

_____ c. Water resources may become scarce.

_____ d. Raising the tax on gasoline will discourage people from driving.

Pre-writing Tasks

Choose a Topic

A Choose one of the essay topics listed below. You will write an introductory paragraph for a cause and effect essay on this topic. This essay will describe one cause (your topic) leading to several effects.

- The impact of overpopulation on the environment
- Lifestyle changes that can decrease one's ecological footprint
- A topic of your own approved by your teacher

B *Pair Work* Write a list of effects that you might include in an essay on this topic. Choose three major effects. Then share your ideas with a partner.

Organize Your Ideas

A Draw a chart like the one below on a separate sheet of paper, and complete it to organize your ideas.

B *Pair Work* Explain your chart to your partner, and discuss how you will organize your introductory paragraph.

Writing Task

Write an introductory paragraph. Follow the steps below.

1. Use the information from your chart in Organize Your Ideas to write your introductory paragraph. Your thesis statement should state the cause and three effects.

2. Include the following in your paragraph:
   • a variety of sentence types: simple, compound, and complex;
   • at least one of the phrases that you learned with *cause, reason*, and *factor*;
   • at least three of these academic words from the essay in this unit: *accessible, consequences, consume, consumption, create, environment, environmentalist, estimate, generation, impact, individual, item, release, resource*.

3. After you write your introductory paragraph, review it and make sure you avoided the mistakes in the Avoid Common Mistakes chart on page 14.

> **Academic Writing Tip**
>
> **Avoid Fragments with *Because***
> Remember to connect *because* to an independent clause.
> *People buy locally produced food because it is in their long-term interest.*

Peer Review

A Exchange your paragraph with a partner. Answer the following questions as you read your partner's paragraph, and then share your responses.

1. What is the topic?

2. What is the thesis statement? Is the thesis statement general or specific? Underline it.

3. What are the cause and effects that will be addressed in the essay?

4. Are all the sentences complete? Are there any fragments, run-ons, or comma splices?

5. Does the paragraph contain a variety of sentence types and transition words?

6. Is anything confusing? Write a question mark (?) next to it.

7. Provide one compliment (something you found interesting or unusual).

B Use your partner's comments to help you revise your paragraph. Use the Writer's Checklist on page A2 to review your paragraph for organization, grammar, and vocabulary.

2

Cause and Effect 2: Subordinators and Prepositions That Show Cause; Transition Words and Common Patterns with Nouns That Show Effect

Consumer Behavior

1 Grammar in the Real World

You will read an essay about the factors that influence consumers' buying behavior. The essay is an example of one type of cause and effect writing in which several causes lead to one effect.

A *Before You Read* What is the biggest purchase you made in the past six months? What influenced you in making your decision? Read the essay. What does the writer state are the key factors that affect consumer buying behavior?

Understanding Consumer Behavior

Consumer behavior is the process consumers go through in making purchasing decisions. This process includes the steps they take from the moment they become aware of a particular need through the final decision to purchase or not purchase a product. According to Perner (2008), this process includes the time spent planning where to shop and comparison shopping.
5 Along the way, consumers are influenced by many factors, including psychological and physical ones. Many experts agree on four factors that have a significant effect on consumer behavior.

One set of factors that influence consumer behavior is physical factors – how a person physically feels when shopping. For example, being hungry when grocery shopping affects how people shop. The result is that people often buy more food than they would if they were not
10 hungry. In contrast, feeling tired leads people to buy less.

Cultural and social factors also have an effect on consumer behavior. Some people make choices because of what their friends do. One example is the importance attached to owning a particular item, such as an expensive pair of jeans, in a person's social network. Another social factor is whether the culture encourages or discourages a behavior, such as bargaining for a
15 lower price.

A third factor that impacts consumer behavior is a person's self-image. People often try to match their purchases, from paper towels to cars, to their idea of self. For example, some people care very much about the environment and health of the planet. Therefore, they might choose to drive a hybrid car[1] due to its low impact on the environment. Other people might
20 see themselves as economical shoppers. As a result, they might buy only simple, inexpensive clothing in order to maintain that aspect of their self-image.

Finally, a person's own experience is a factor. Memories about a certain product or place can have a direct effect on later decisions. For instance, people will tend to go back to a restaurant because they had a good eating experience there. On the other hand, if a person becomes ill
25 eating seafood, it might have a negative effect on his or her future desire for that kind of food.

Every day, people make choices about what to buy. However, they are often unaware of the process behind their decision making. As a result, they can become vulnerable to[2] advertising and other marketing techniques that target the factors that convince people to buy more. Consumers may want to make changes in their purchasing patterns, but they might not know
30 how to make these changes. One important step is for them to become more aware of why they make choices. Becoming educated about their behavior as consumers is an important way for people to make better buying decisions.

[1]**hybrid car:** a car that can run on both gasoline and an electric motor | [2]**vulnerable to:** able to be easily hurt or influenced

B *Comprehension Check* Answer the questions.

1. According to the text, what is the definition of consumer behavior? Use your own words.
2. Name one factor from the essay that might influence someone to buy more and one factor from the essay that might influence someone to buy less.
3. Why does the writer believe it is important to understand consumer behavior?

C *Notice*

1 Cause and Effect Writing Draw the chart below on a separate sheet of paper. Write the four factors, or causes, mentioned in the essay that have an effect on consumer behavior.

Factors / Causes	Effect
1.	
2.	Consumer behavior
3.	
4.	

2 Grammar Follow the instructions below to help you notice the words the writer uses to state causes and describe effects.

1. Find the word *effect* in the first paragraph and circle it. Underline the verb, adjective, and preposition that combine with the word *effect*. Notice how the author uses the word *effect* twice in the fifth paragraph with different adjectives. Underline the phrases with *effect* and circle the adjectives.

2. Find the sentence in the second paragraph that describes a possible effect of being hungry when one shops. Circle the words that introduce the result in the sentence that follows it.

3. Find the sentence in the fourth paragraph that explains why people might buy a hybrid car. Circle the two words that introduce the reason why.

3 The Writing Process How does the writer begin the introductory paragraph? What type of opening sentence does the writer use to attract the reader's attention? Check (✔) the answer.

1. _____ Definition   2. _____ Interesting fact   3. _____ Provocative question

2 | Subordinators and Prepositions That Show Cause, Reason, or Purpose

▶ Grammar Presentation

Some subordinators and prepositions show cause, reason, or purpose in academic writing. They answer the question *why*. Both subordinators and prepositions may be a word or a phrase.

*Some people buy products they do not need only **because** they are on sale.*
*We often choose what products to buy **as a result of** past experience.*

2.1 Using Subordinators That Show Cause, Reason, or Purpose

a. Subordinators connect dependent clauses to independent clauses. These dependent clauses are adverb clauses.	INDEPENDENT CLAUSE DEPENDENT CLAUSE *Some consumers purchase certain products **because** they want to maintain their self-image.*
b. As taught in Unit 1, use the subordinators *because* and *since* to indicate the cause or reason.	EFFECT CAUSE / REASON *Some consumers buy products **because** they want to be like their friends.*
c. Use the following subordinators to indicate purpose: *so / so that*	PURPOSE *Some consumers buy "green" products **so (that)** they can appear environmentally aware.*

2.2 Using Prepositions That Show Cause or Reason

Use the following prepositions to indicate cause or reason. Unlike subordinators, they are followed by noun phrases: *because of, as a result of, due to*	EFFECT CAUSE / REASON *Some people choose products* **because of** *their past experiences.* EFFECT CAUSE / REASON *Shoppers will buy more food* **as a result of** *being hungry when they shop.* EFFECT CAUSE / REASON *Some consumers choose a hybrid car* **due to** *its low impact on the environment.*

▶ # Grammar Application

Exercise 2.1 Subordinators That Show Cause, Reason, or Purpose

A In each pair of clauses about consumer behavior, write *C* above the clause that states a cause and *E* above the clause that states an effect. Next, combine the clauses using the words in parentheses. Sometimes more than one answer is possible.

          C   E

1. our decisions affect our financial future / it is important for us to make responsible buying decisions (*because*) *It is important for us to make responsible buying decisions because they affect our financial future.*

2. it is not easy to ignore advertising / consumers need to learn how to shop wisely (*since*)

3. make a list before you leave home / you do not buy something you do not need (*so that*)

4. people can get into debt easily / it is easy to buy things using a credit card (*because*)

5. children see the snack foods and ask their parents for them / stores put snack foods on low shelves (*so that*)

6. people will impulsively buy products that they don't need / stores put fun items like candy and toys by the checkout counters (*so*)

B *Group Work* Complete the sentences with your own ideas on a separate sheet of paper. Then share your sentences with your group and explain them. Ask your classmates if they agree or disagree with your ideas and tell why.

1. Sometimes people buy things they don't need because . . .
2. Sometimes people spend more money than they make because . . .
3. Manufacturers of cereals often include cartoon characters in their commercials so . . .

4. Fast-food restaurants often air commercials during late-night TV so that . . .
5. Stores sometimes advertise a few items at very low prices because . . .
6. Some people prefer to buy products online since . . .

A *My sentence is* People buy things they don't need because they want to feel better. *For example, when I have a bad day, sometimes I go out and buy something – even something small like a book – to make myself feel better.*

B *I agree with you because I do that, too, but I think more often people buy things they don't need because they are bored.*

Exercise 2.2 Subordinators and Prepositions That Show Cause, Reason, or Purpose

Complete the sentences about consumer buying habits. The subordinators and prepositions are missing one word each. Write the missing word.

Consumers buy things for a lot of different reasons. Most frequently, people buy products <u>*because*</u> of their individual tastes. For example, they might buy the same snacks or cereals
(1)

every time they go shopping _____ to their family's likes and dislikes. They
(2)

don't even think about whether or not they want those items. People also make purchases

as a _____ of need. They buy an air conditioner _____ of
(3)   (4)

severe hot weather, or they purchase fire alarms in their house _____ that
(5)

their family stays safe. Finally, sometimes people make impulse purchases. They buy things

they haven't planned to buy and may not necessarily need or even want. Sometimes they

make these purchases _____ a result of effective advertising or in the case of
(6)

food, because _____ hunger while they are shopping. They also make impulse
(7)

purchases due _____ their own personalities. Some people are more prone to
(8)

impulse buying than others are.

Exercise 2.3 More Subordinators and Prepositions That Show Cause, Reason, or Purpose

A You will listen to an interview about a person's buying habits. First read the questions. Then listen and take notes on the answers. Finally, write answers to the questions using sentences with the words in parentheses.

1. Why does Roger sometimes go shopping when he doesn't need anything?

(because) <u>*He goes shopping when he doesn't need anything*</u>
<u>*because he's happy when he is shopping.*</u>

2. How does he control his spending?

    (so that) _____

    _____

3. Does he use a credit card or debit card for his purchases? Why or why not?

    (because of) _____

    _____

4. Why does he do a lot of research when he has to buy an expensive product?

    (as a result of) _____

    _____

5. Does he eat out a lot?

    (due to) _____

    _____

B *Pair Work* Rewrite questions 2–5 in A to interview your partner. On a separate sheet of paper, write sentences with his or her answers. Try to use the same prepositions and subordinating conjunctions. Share your sentences with another pair. How similar are your habits and experiences?

3 | Transition Words and Phrases That Show Effect

▶ Grammar Presentation

> Another important way to link cause and effect in academic writing is with transition words and phrases. Transition words often signal a cause, a reason, or an effect.
>
> *Sometimes people buy products that show that they are part of a social network.* **Therefore,** *they might choose an expensive pair of jeans because the jeans are popular with their friends.*

3.1 Using Transition Words and Phrases That Show Effect

a. Transition words and phrases connect two independent clauses. Separate the clauses with a semicolon or use two separate sentences. Use a comma after the transition word or phrase.	*Environmental values might affect some purchases;* ***consequently,*** *many merchants offer green products.* *Environmental values might affect some purchases.* ***Consequently,*** *many merchants offer green products.*

3.1 Using Transition Words and Phrases That Show Effect *(continued)*

b. The following transition words and phrases are used to show effect or result:

as a consequence, as a result, consequently, therefore, thus

Note: Thus is rarely used in informal speech or informal writing.

Many consumers are concerned about the environment. **As a result**, they buy products that are environmentally safe.

Some consumers feel the need to be part of a certain group; **therefore**, they buy products that are expensive and fashionable.

▶ Grammar Application

Exercise 3.1 Transition Words and Phrases

A Unscramble the sentences about the effects of advertisements on consumers, using the prompts in parentheses. Remember to use a comma after the transition words and phrases.

1. People see and hear over 2,500 advertisements per day.

   As a result, people need to be aware of the effects of advertising.
   (of advertising / be / people / need to / aware of / the effects / as a result)

2. Candy and sugary cereals are advertised during children's television shows.

   _____
   (for them / a desire / children / develop / as a consequence)

3. Public television does not show advertisements for sugary foods.

   _____
   (exposed to / not / children / are / them / as a result)

4. The effects of smoking are serious and possibly deadly.

   _____
   (it / not / on TV / them / legal / to advertise / is / therefore)

5. Happy people are often shown eating snack foods.

   _____
   (think / them / viewers / too / snack foods / happy / will make / eating / consequently)

B *Pair Work* With a partner, choose two different products. How is each product advertised? What effects do you think the advertisements have on consumers? On a separate sheet of paper, write five sentences about each product using the cause and effect words in A. Then share your ideas with another pair of students.

The first product we discussed was an exercise shoe. Every ad shows young, thin women who are very pretty wearing the shoes. They have handsome boyfriends, and they seem very happy. Consequently, when I see the advertisements, I always think I should buy the shoes.

Exercise 3.2 More Transition Words and Phrases

A Match the causes and effects of advertising techniques and their influence on consumers' buying decisions.

Causes	Effects
1. Advertisements equate high prices with effectiveness. 2. Some advertisements target children. 3. Prices for large quantities of food are discounted. 4. Advertisements often show beautiful people. 5. Sometimes ads do not focus on the ill effects of the products.	___1___ a. Consumers end up buying expensive brands. _____ b. Consumers buy more than they need. _____ c. Consumers sometimes buy products that might not be good for them. _____ d. Children start to become consumers early. _____ e. Consumers believe the products will make them beautiful, too.

B Combine each pair of causes and effects in A. Write sentences using *as a consequence, as a result, consequently,* and *therefore.* Use each transition word or phrase once.

1. *Advertisements equate high prices with effectiveness. As a result, consumers end up buying more expensive brands.*

2. _____

    _____

3. _____

    _____

4. _____

    _____

5. _____

    _____

C *Group Work* Discuss recent purchases that your group has made. What factors influenced you in your buying decision? Write five sentences based on the answers from your group using transition words and phrases such as *as a consequence, as a result, for this reason,* and *therefore.* Share the information with another group of students.

A friend of Amy's daughter had her ears pierced recently. For this reason, Amy's daughter wanted to get her ears pierced, too.

Julia Rozzio watched a very funny commercial about laptop computers. As a result, when it was time to buy a new computer, she decided to buy a laptop.

4 Common Patterns with Nouns That Show Effect 🌐

▶ Vocabulary Presentation

There are several common expressions with the nouns *effect* and *result* that are used to show effect in cause and effect writing.

Advertising **can have a big effect on** children and teens.
The increase in sales **is a direct result of** our ad campaign.

4.1 Expressions with *Effect* and *Result*

a. Some common expressions and patterns with the noun *effect* are:

NOUN PHRASE   NOUN PHRASE
The / One effect of _____ *on* _____ *is*

NOUN PHRASE
_____ .

NOUN PHRASE   NOUN PHRASE
_____ *have an effect on* _____ .

One effect of advertising **on** the public **is** overconsumption.

Advertising **can have a** significant **effect on** children and teens.

b. Some common expressions and patterns with the noun *result* are:

NOUN PHRASE   NOUN PHRASE
_____ *is a result of* _____ .

CLAUSE   NOUN PHRASE
When / If _____ , *the result is* _____ .

NOUN PHRASE
_____ *have a result.*

Overconsumption **is a** predictable **result of** consumers' unawareness of sophisticated advertising techniques.

When / If consumers are unaware of their behavior, **the** primary **result may be** overconsumption.

Consumer awareness of advertising techniques often **has a** positive **result**.

Data from the Real World 🌐

Adjectives that most frequently occur with *effect* are:

no, little, significant, some
    Research suggests that advertising has **little effect** on a family's food budget.

Adjectives that most frequently occur with *result* are:

direct, positive, predictable, primary
    Women's desire to be thin is a **direct result** of advertising.

▶ Vocabulary Application

Exercise 4.1 Common Patterns with Nouns That Show Effect

A Complete the following paragraph about the consumer behavior of working parents using the phrases in the box. Add appropriate punctuation as needed.

a direct result can be	one effect of	effect on
a positive effect on	effect of	~~have a significant effect on~~

These days in many families both parents work full-time. This fact can

have a significant effect on their consumer behavior. In general, too, the behavioral
(1)

change will have _____ the economy. Parents with full-time
(2)

jobs may not have time to cook dinner when they get home from work. As a result, they

may spend more money in restaurants than families with non-working parents do.

Dual-income families may eat out a lot or bring prepared food home. Some parents who work

full-time may want to spend a lot of time with their children when they are not working.

_____ that they do special activities with their children that
(3)

cost money. For example, they might take their children to amusement parks or go to the

movies with them on the weekends. Some parents may also have to wear business attire for

their jobs, which has an _____ their clothing expenses. Another
(4)

_____ a dual-income lifestyle may be higher commuting expenses.
(5)

The working parents may have two cars or pay twice the amount in public transportation

costs. In sum, _____ a dual-income lifestyle is that it will
(6)

benefit the economy.

B *Pair Work* Write answers to the questions about the consumer behavior of parents below. Then share your answers with a partner. Use the common patterns with nouns to show effect with an appropriate adjective in each sentence.

1. How does having two working parents in a family affect the family's consumer behavior?

    One positive effect of working parents on children is that the children need to become more responsible.

2. How does the fact that working parents may not have time to cook dinner affect their lives?

    _____

3. What effect can having a dual income have on entertainment expenses?

    _____

4. How might working parents' jobs affect a family's clothing expenses?

    _____

5. How does a dual-income lifestyle affect a family's commuting expenses?

    _____

Exercise 4.2 More Common Patterns with Nouns That Show Effect

A Answer the questions about consumer behavior. Use the expressions with *effect* and *result* and adjectives from Data from the Real World where appropriate in your answers.

1. Some stores, especially clothing stores, play loud music. If a store plays loud music, does the store have a positive or negative effect on you? Why? Would you walk into the store or not?

    Music always has a positive effect on me. If I like the music, then I'll go into the store.

2. Do brand names have a significant effect on your decision to buy clothes? Why or why not?

    _____

3. Why do some people prefer to buy expensive brands? What is it a direct result of? Explain your opinion.

    _____

4. What do you think the primary result of advertising is on young children?

    _____

5. What kind of effect do consumer reviews on websites have on you as a consumer?

    _____

6. Why are some people thrifty? What could it be the result of?

    _____

B *Group Work* Share your answers in a group. Decide on answers to each question that you all agree on. Share them with the class.

5 | Avoid Common Mistakes ⚠️

1. **Do not confuse *affect* and *effect*. *Affect* is almost always a verb; *effect* is almost always a noun.**

   Product placement in movies usually has a strong ~~affect~~ ^{effect} on sales.

2. **Remember to use the correct preposition in expressions with *cause*, *result*, and *effect*.**

   Cartoon characters in ads have a significant effect ~~in~~ ^{on} children.

   As a result ~~on~~ ^{of} advertising on Saturday mornings, the company reached their target market – children.

3. **Do not confuse *because* with *because of*. Follow *because* with a subject and verb; follow *because of* with a noun.**

   Advertisers are coming up with new ways to market products because ~~of~~ young consumers are paying less attention to ads.

   Advertisers are coming up with new ways to market products because _{of} young people's disinterest in ads.

Editing Task

Find and correct six more mistakes in this body paragraph from an essay about effective advertising campaigns.

Over the years, overexposure to advertising has gradually resulted ~~on~~ ⁱⁿ consumer
inattention. In fact, studies have shown that most advertisements have little affect in the
average consumer. One way in which manufacturers and retailers are responding to this
problem is by using a technique known as product placement. Rather than spending money
5 to produce advertisements that consumers will ignore, companies simply place their products
in television programs or films. For example, they have characters drink a particular brand
of soda, drive a particular type of car, or carry a certain handbag. One example of successful
product placement is the use of Apple products in various television programs and films over
the years. Product placement must have resulted on higher sales because of in 2010 Apple's
10 products were present in 30 percent of the year's top 33 films, including *Toy Story 3*, *Iron
Man 2*, and *The Social Network*. Between 2008 and 2010, the number of American homes
with Apple computers increased 9 percent. Product placement has a second beneficial affect,
as well. By placing products in their shows and movies, television and film companies are able

to lower their production costs because of they use products free of cost or they are paid
15 to use a company's products. For example, the reality TV show *My Fair Wedding* features
several jewelry and makeup brands in each episode. Without product placement, the show's
producers might have to purchase the jewelry and makeup. Because the inclusion of the
products in the show, the show's producers are able to use the jewelry and makeup for free.

6 | The Writing Process

In this section, you will write an introductory paragraph for a cause and effect essay. Before you start writing, you will learn how to write engaging hooks.

About Hooks

Writers create interest and motivate readers to keep reading by including a "hook" in the introductory paragraph of an essay. The hook is usually the first or second sentence of the paragraph.

The following are four types of hooks:

1. **An unusual or surprising fact**

   Essay Topic: Overconsumption in the United States

   Hook: *Americans use 71 million tons of paper annually, or more than 900 million trees (U.S. EPA, 2011).*

2. **A definition of a key term or concept**

   Essay Topic: Consumer behavior

   Hook: *Consumer behavior is the process consumers go through in making purchasing decisions. This process includes the steps one takes from the moment he or she becomes aware of a particular need through the final decision to purchase or not purchase a product (Perner, 2008).*

3. **A thought-provoking question**

   Essay Topic: What the government can do to prevent negative effects of advertisements on children

   Hook: *Should the government prohibit all advertisements on children's TV programs?*

4. **A quotation**

   Essay Topic: The effects of overconsumption

   Hook: *"Too many people spend money they haven't earned, to buy things they don't want, to impress people they don't like" (Will Rogers, American humorist).*

Exercise

A Match the examples of hooks below to the types of hooks in the box.

definition of a key term	thought-provoking question
quotation	unusual or surprising fact

1. Should the government have the power to stop parents from smoking in their own homes?
   thought-provoking question

2. "There are two ways to get enough: one is to continue to accumulate more and more. The other is to desire less" (G. K. Chesterton, 1874–1936). _____

3. Every ton of recycled office paper saves 380 gallons of oil. _____

4. Many people define advertising as the marketing and promotion of a product. _____

5. Glass produced from recycled glass instead of raw materials reduces related air pollution by 20 percent, and water pollution by 50 percent. _____

B *Group Work* In a small group, read the following thesis statements, and discuss possible hooks that could begin an essay containing each one. Share your ideas with another group.

1. Three main factors in childhood determine how people approach eating throughout their lives.
2. In order to stick to a budget, consumers need to address both internal and external forces before and during shopping.
3. Traffic jams can be the result of accidents, bad weather, and a lack of public transportation.

Pre-writing Tasks

Choose a Topic

A Choose one of the essay topics listed below. You will write an introductory paragraph for a cause and effect essay on this topic. This essay will describe many causes leading to one effect.

- Factors that influence your buying behavior
- Social and cultural influences on behavior
- A topic of your own approved by your teacher

B *Pair Work* Share your topic with a partner. Describe the multiple causes and the one effect you are going to write about. Give each other suggestions about ideas or facts to include.

Organize Your Ideas

A Use the chart below to organize your ideas.

Factors / Causes	Effect
1.	
2.	
3.	
4.	
5.	

B *Group Work* In a small group, share your completed chart and discuss these questions: Are all the causes clear? Are any important causes missing? Then modify your chart following the discussion.

Writing Task

Write an introductory paragraph. Follow the steps below.

1. Use the information in your chart in Organize Your Ideas to write a thesis statement. The thesis statement should include several causes and one effect that you are going to describe.

2. Write a hook that will work well for your topic. Use the description and examples in About Hooks to help you.

3. Include the following in your paragraph:
   - subordinating conjunctions and transition words and phrases to link the ideas in your paragraph;
   - common patterns with the nouns *effect* and *result* to show effect;
   - at least three of these academic words from the essay in this unit: *affect, aspect, attached, aware, consumer, convince, culture, economical, environment, expert, factor, final, finally, image, impact, item, maintain, negative, network, physical, physically, process, psychological, purchase, significant, target, technique, unaware.*

4. After you write your introductory paragraph, review it and make sure you avoided the mistakes in the Avoid Common Mistakes chart on page 29.

Peer Review

A Exchange your paragraph with a partner. Answer the following questions as you read your partner's paragraph, and then share your responses.

1. What is the thesis statement? Underline it.

2. Is the hook interesting and effective? Why? Which of the four kinds of hooks was used?

3. What are the several causes and one effect that will be addressed in the essay?

4. What subordinating conjunctions and transition words did your partner use in the paragraph?

5. Is anything confusing? Write a question mark (?) next to it.

6. Provide one compliment (something you found interesting or unusual).

B Use your partner's comments to help you revise your paragraph. Use the Writer's Checklist on page A2 to review your paragraph for organization, grammar, and vocabulary.

Cause and Effect 3:
Real and Unreal Conditionals;
Common Phrases with *If* and *Unless*

Social Responsibility

1 | Grammar in the Real World

You will read an essay that describes what might happen if corporations were to make socially responsible decisions. The essay is another example of cause and effect writing in which one cause leads to several effects.

A *Before You Read* What do you think it means for a company to act in a socially responsible manner? What can companies do to help local communities? Read the essay. According to the writer, what are the benefits of companies being socially responsible?

Corporate Social Responsibility:
The Wave of the Future

Most managers would be in agreement that the main goal of a modern company is to make a profit. If a company does not make money, it will go out of business. In addition, while pursuing profit, companies should be ethical in their business practices. However, more and more people believe that the ethical pursuit of profit is no longer enough for
5 modern companies. They argue that companies should also incorporate a strong sense of "corporate social responsibility" (Burstein, 2012). This means managing a business while attempting to have a positive impact on the community. There are many reasons why companies may choose to embrace social responsibility.

According to proponents of corporate social responsibility, if companies make socially
10 responsible decisions, they can improve life in the community. For example, companies can make an impact on a local community when they sponsor local cultural events or science fairs for high school students. To make a broader impact, companies can give money to charitable organizations that are connected to the core beliefs of the company. An example of this is Green Mountain Coffee, which donates money to a nonprofit organization that
15 improves life for children in the company's coffee-growing areas (Waite, 2007, para. 4). Companies can also try to improve public policy. For instance, they may stop doing business with companies that use child labor, even if that means higher manufacturing costs and lower profits.

Corporate social responsibility can also benefit the environment. For example,
20 companies can implement green policies, such as restricting printing to important
documents, buying locally grown products, or conducting an electronics recycling fair.
When companies conduct their business with an awareness of the environment, they set
an example for the community. If these policies are part of the culture of the company,
employees are likely to follow them outside the workplace.

25   Finally, if a company makes social responsibility part of its corporate mission, it can
potentially have a better public image. A socially responsible company will be seen as
an ally[1] of the community. This positive public image may set the company apart from
its competitors. It will also attract investors, which will improve the company's finances.
Companies like Patagonia, Inc. are already very aware of this benefit. They hire executives
30 to focus on corporate social responsibility throughout the business (Patagonia, 2011, p. 3).

Many companies already see the value of corporate social responsibility for the
community as well as for their own organization. However, corporate social responsibility
could play a role in every company. Supporters say that it is not just that a company makes
money, but how it makes money. They argue that if more companies embraced corporate
35 social responsibility, there would be more instances of positive social change in the world.

[1]**ally**: a person, country, or organization that provides help and support

B *Comprehension Check* Answer the questions.

1. According to the writer, how can corporate social responsibility benefit the community?
2. Why does the writer argue that it is important that companies implement green policies?
3. Explain this sentence in the last paragraph: "Supporters say that it is not just that a company makes money, but *how* it makes money."

C *Notice*

1 Cause and Effect Writing Each body paragraph of the essay (the paragraphs that follow the introduction and explain each of the writer's main points) describes an effect that would happen to companies as a result of making more socially responsible decisions. Complete the chart below with each effect.

Effects of Corporate Social Responsibility
1. Body Paragraph 1: *Companies can improve life in the community.*
2. Body Paragraph 2: _____
3. Body Paragraph 3: _____

2 Grammar Follow the instructions below to help you notice sentence structures that state causes and describe effects.

1. Find a sentence in the first paragraph that contains an *if* clause. This sentence contains ideas that express cause and effect. Does the *if* clause or the main clause state the effect (result)? How certain is the writer of this effect? What word in the main clause gives the certainty?

2. Underline the sentence in the fifth paragraph that contains an *if* clause. Compare the meaning of this sentence with the sentence in 1. Which effect seems more likely to happen? Why?

3. Look at lines 22–24. Compare the sentence containing the *when* clause with the one containing the *if* clause that immediately follows it. Which sentence contains an effect that is more likely to happen? Which words tell you?

3 The Writing Process Look at the effects which you listed in the chart in 1 Cause and Effect Writing. How did the writer order them? Check the way that you think best describes the order in which the effects are listed:

_____ In chronological order

_____ From most familiar (to the reader) to least familiar

_____ In a sequence of events, where one event leads to the next

_____ In order of importance (from least important point to most important point)

Discuss your answer with your classmates. Why do you think the writer put the topics in that order?

2 | Present and Future Real Conditionals

▶ Grammar Presentation

> Present and future real conditionals describe possible situations or conditions in the present and future and their likely results. They are often used to express cause and effect relationships in academic writing.
>
> *Companies **improve** life in the community **if** they **are** socially responsible.*
> ***If** companies **follow** green policies, they **will set** a good example for their employees.*

2.1 Present Real Conditionals

The present real conditional is formed as follows: *If* clause (present), + main clause (present)	IF CLAUSE (PRESENT) ***If** companies **donate** to charity programs,* MAIN CLAUSE (PRESENT) *they **set** good examples for other companies.*
The *if* clause can come first or last in the sentence. When the *if* clause comes first, use a comma to separate the clauses. If it comes last, do not use a comma.	*Companies **set** a good example for other companies **if** they **donate** to charity programs.*
Note: You can use *then* to start the main clause. The meaning does not change.	*If companies donate to charity programs, **then** they set a good example for other companies.*

2.2 Using Present Real Conditionals

a. You can use present real conditionals to describe general truths, habits, routines, and scientific facts.	*If companies **recycle**, employees generally **recycle**, too.*
b. In real conditional sentences, the *if* clause describes what action or event is necessary (the condition) for the action or event in the main clause to happen (the result).	IF CLAUSE: CONDITION *If companies **contribute** to charity,* MAIN CLAUSE: RESULT *many programs **benefit**.*
c. You can use *when* or *whenever* to replace *if* when something is a general fact or a routine.	*Companies help the community **if / when / whenever** they are socially responsible.*

2.3 Future Real Conditionals

a. The future real conditional is formed as follows: *If* clause (present) + main clause (*be going to / modal* + base form of verb) The *if* clause can come first or last. Use a comma only when the *if* clause comes first.	IF CLAUSE (PRESENT) *If we **get** a tax refund this year,* MAIN CLAUSE (*BE GOING TO* + BASE FORM) *(then) we **are going to buy** a hybrid car.* MAIN CLAUSE (MODAL + BASE FORM) *We **will / might buy** a hybrid car* IF CLAUSE (PRESENT) *if we **get** a tax refund this year.*
b. The *if* clause states a possible future situation or condition, and the main clause states the likely result.	CONDITION RESULT ***If I get a raise**, we will be able to buy a new car.*

2.4 Using Future Real Conditionals

a. You can use future real conditionals to offer predictions. They describe possible future situations and their likely result.	*If a company **does not make** a profit, it **will go** bankrupt.*
b. You can use different modals in the main clause. The modal indicates how likely the result is. *will* = It is certain.	*If a company has a good public image, it **will** attract investors.*
can / could = It is possible.	*If a company addresses social responsibility, it **can** result in a better public image.*
should = It is a strong possibility.	*If the company installs solar panels at its factories, this **should** cut energy costs in half within two years.*
may / might = It is not certain.	*Employees **might** consider ways to make their companies greener if they receive rewards for their ideas.*

▶ Grammar Application

Exercise 2.1 Present Real Conditionals

A Each pair of sentences below describes a way (condition) for companies to be socially responsible and the effect that the condition can have. Write *C* next to each condition and *E* next to each effect.

1. ___C___ Car companies produce hybrid cars.

   ___E___ The companies help decrease the amount of pollution in the atmosphere.

2. _____ Workers are happier and more productive.

   _____ Companies offer generous salaries.

3. _____ The government gives tax breaks to companies that donate to organizations.

   _____ Company donations to schools increase.

4. _____ Employees feel good about themselves, and the community benefits.

   _____ Companies encourage their employees to volunteer.

5. _____ The countries that allow child labor feel more pressure to change their laws.

   _____ Companies refuse to do business in countries that allow child labor.

6. _____ The companies help the environment and save money.

   _____ Companies use environmentally friendly (green) technology.

B Combine the pairs of sentences in A. Write sentences using an *if* clause in the way indicated in parentheses. Remember to use commas where necessary.

1. (*if* clause first) _If car companies produce hybrid cars, they help decrease the_ _amount of pollution in the atmosphere._

2. (main clause first) _____

   _____

3. (*if* clause first) _____

   _____

4. (main clause first) _____

   _____

5. (*if* clause first) _____

   _____

6. (main clause first) _____

   _____

C *Pair Work* Take turns reading the sentences in B aloud with a partner. Replace *if* in the sentences with *when* or *whenever*. Talk with a partner. Does the meaning of each sentence change? Why or why not?

Exercise 2.2 Future Real Conditionals

A Johnny's Chicken Restaurant has poor sales. Below are some suggested actions and results to improve sales. Match the actions and results.

Suggested Actions

___*f*___ 1. Offer inexpensive lunch specials.

_____ 2. Donate the profit of a sandwich to a nonprofit organization.

_____ 3. Have some vegetarian choices.

_____ 4. Create a website.

_____ 5. Install energy-efficient ovens.

_____ 6. Use bikes – not cars – to deliver food.

_____ 7. Buy local produce.

Results

a. Save money on gas.

b. Attract customers who don't eat meat.

c. Lower its electricity bills.

d. Show people that it supports local farmers.

e. Improve its public image.

f̶. See an increase in its lunch business.

g. Get more online orders.

B Combine the actions and results in A and write suggestions for improving the restaurant. Use future real conditionals and modals that best express the meanings of the words in parentheses.

1. (strong possibility) *If the company offers inexpensive lunch specials, it should see an increase in its lunch business.*

2. (possible) _____

3. (strong possibility) _____

4. (not certain) _____

5. (possible) _____

6. (certain) _____

7. (certain) _____

C *Pair Work* Work with a partner. Think of a company you know that is not doing well. On a separate sheet of paper, list three reasons why the company is having problems. Next to each reason, write a suggestion to the manager to fix the problem. Use a future real conditional and the appropriate modal to show how confident you are that your suggestion would work. Next, trade papers with another pair. Read their reasons and suggestions. Do you agree that the suggestions would work? Explain your opinions.

For the problem of rude waiters, your suggestion is If you train your waiters to be kind and helpful, your business will improve. *We agree that training is helpful, but we think* could *is more accurate because we don't think training is enough to change people's behavior. We believe that employees will change if they also feel respected by management.*

3 | Present and Future Unreal Conditionals

▶ Grammar Presentation

Present and future unreal conditional sentences describe situations that are not true. They describe imaginary situations, and then give the results of those situations as if they were true. In cause and effect writing, unreal conditional sentences are used to propose changes and predict the results of those changes.

If employees became involved in the community, they would feel good about themselves.
If the restaurant donated money to a community organization, its public image would improve.

3.1 Present and Future Unreal Conditionals

a. The unreal conditional is formed as follows: *If* clause (past) + main clause (modal + base form of the verb). The modal *would* is the most commonly used. The *if* clause can come first or last. Use a comma only when the clause comes first.	IF CLAUSE (PAST) *If we **were** socially responsible,* MAIN CLAUSE (MODAL + BASE FORM) *we **would** attract more customers.* *Charitable programs **would** help more people if more companies **contributed** to their programs.*
b. Use *were*, not *was*, for singular subjects, including *I*, in formal writing. *Was* is more common in speaking and informal writing.	FORMAL: *If I **were** socially responsible, I would recycle.* MORE COMMON: *If I **was** socially responsible, I would recycle.*
c. The modals *would*, *might*, and *could* are used in the main clause: *Would* expresses a more certain or desired effect or result. It is often used in unreal conditionals. *Might* and *could* express less certain results. *Could not* expresses impossibility.	*Communities **would** benefit if more companies donated time and money to local charities.* *If your company advertised more, you **might** get more business.* *If the organization did not receive donations, it **could not** exist.*

3.2 Using Present and Future Unreal Conditionals

a. In unreal conditional sentences, use the *if* clause to describe a situation that is not real or true. However, the situation may be possible in the present or future. The main clause describes the result of the situation.	IF CLAUSE: CONDITION *If the company **used** more resources on social issues,* MAIN CLAUSE: RESULT *it **would** attract more investors.* (It does **not** currently use many resources on social issues, but it might in the future.)

3.2 Using Present and Future Unreal Conditionals *(continued)*

b. Present unreal conditionals are often used in cause and effect writing to propose changes and predict the results of those changes.	*Less energy **would** be consumed in the world **if** more companies **used** green technology.* (Not enough companies use green technology in the present. The situation is not real or true at the present time.)

▶ Grammar Application

Exercise 3.1 Present and Future Unreal Conditionals

A Read the article with tips on how individuals can be more socially responsible. Underline four more sentences containing present unreal conditional clauses.

It always feels good to help other people and know that you are making a positive difference in someone's life. Here are a few tips to get you started. First, decide who you want to help. If you want to help your community, visit a local school and ask if they need help. The school would probably appreciate your help. If there were more volunteers in classrooms,

5 teachers could spend more time with students who need special help. If there's a park or other public place near you that is full of trash, get a group of friends together and volunteer to clean it up. Your actions would have a huge impact. If these places were cleaned up, more people would visit them. As a result of all these visitors, local shops would get more business and hire more staff.

10 If you want to help people outside of your community or country, find an organization that sends money, supplies, and clothes to troubled areas. Your contributions are crucial. If these organizations didn't get donations and help, they couldn't be as effective as they are.

You could also spend your time or money helping an organization that works for a special cause like cancer or heart disease. If you spent time volunteering for one of these

15 organizations, you might learn more about the organizations and find ways to help them receive more donations. These donations could be used to fund research and lead to breakthroughs or cures. If you made a donation today, you would know that your money is going toward an important cause.

B *Pair Work* Explain your choices to a partner. Do you agree or disagree?

Exercise 3.2 More Present and Future Unreal Conditionals

A 🔊 You will listen to a radio interview about ways to improve your community. First, read the questions. Then listen and take notes on the answers. Finally, write answers to the questions using unreal conditional sentences and the modals *would*, *might*, or *could*, depending on the certainty of the speaker's comments.

1. Why is it important for more people to safely recycle their old electronics?

   If more people safely recycled their old electronics, it would reduce toxins

   in the environment.

2. Why is it important for more people to donate their old clothes to community organizations?

   _____

   _____

3. Why should more people volunteer at a school?

   _____

   _____

4. Why should teenagers volunteer?

   _____

   _____

5. Why should more people donate money to community organizations?

   _____

   _____

B *Group Work* With your group, decide how the community can encourage people to become involved in solving issues that affect the quality of living. How could the community get more young and old people involved? What would motivate residents to get involved? Explain why you think people – both young and old – are not involved. Then think of five suggestions explaining how you might motivate them and how you would reward them. Present your ideas to another group or the class.

We think that teenagers are very busy with school, so they don't have time. But they also want to socialize and feel accepted. Teenagers would become more involved if the volunteering was combined with a social event. The city could . . .

4 Common Phrases with *Unless* and *If*

▶ Vocabulary Presentation

Unless, if . . . not, only if, and *even if* can also introduce conditions.

Unless *cities require solar panels for new construction, builders may continue to use older forms of energy delivery.*

People will recycle **only if** *it is required by law.*

Even if *companies do a lot for the community, they still need to make a profit.*

4.1 Negative Conditions: *Unless, If . . . not*

Unless can be used to describe a possible negative condition in the present or future. It suggests that failing to meet the condition will lead to an undesirable or unpleasant result.	NEGATIVE CONDITION **Unless** *the organization gets more donations,* UNDESIRABLE RESULT *it will have to cut some programs.* **Unless** *someone speaks up, the city will not fix the problems.* (= **If no one** *speaks up, the city will not fix the problems.)*
If with a negative subject (*no one*) or *if . . . not* has the same meaning as *unless*.	**Unless** *more employees volunteer for the event, it will be canceled.* (= *If more employees* **don't** *volunteer for the event, it will be canceled.)*

4.2 Exclusive Condition: *Only if*

Only if is used to show that the result / effect will happen when a specific condition becomes true. No other condition will have this result.	*Consumers will change their habits* **only if** *prices increase dramatically.*
When a sentence begins with *only if*, do not use a comma. The modal in the independent clause comes before the subject.	ONLY IF + CONDITION MODAL + SUBJECT **Only if** *prices increase dramatically* **will consumers** *change their habits.*

4.3 Emphatic Condition: *Even if*

Even if emphasizes that the condition does not matter. The condition may occur or be fulfilled, but the result will be the same.	EVEN IF + CONDITION **Even if** *many people start driving electric cars,* UNCHANGED RESULT *the country's energy needs will not decrease.* (Despite the fulfillment of the condition, the expected change will not occur.)
In contrast, there is an expectation that the change will occur with *if* clauses.	IF + CONDITION EXPECTED RESULT *If many people start driving electric cars, the country's energy needs will be lower.* (We would expect this change.)

► Vocabulary Application

Exercise 4.1 *Unless, Only If, Even If*

A Complete the sentences about the rules for refunds and exchanges for employees of a retail company that values social responsibility. Use *unless*, *only if*, and *even if*.

1. _Even if_ the product is broken, offer to exchange the item for another one.

2. The customer can exchange the product _____ he or she has bought the item within the last 60 days. If it is more than 60 days, get a manager's approval before you make the exchange.

3. Offer an exchange first _____ the customer appears upset and asks for the money right away. In that case, give them the money.

4. _____ the customer has a receipt, can you offer an exchange. Do not offer one otherwise.

5. Do not offer the customer a store credit _____ the product is in good condition because we need to be able to resell it.

6. Give a cash refund _____ the customer refuses an exchange and a store credit. In general, try to avoid giving full cash refunds.

7. You cannot give a full cash refund _____ you have approval from a manager. His or her approval is required.

8. _____ the customer becomes upset, stay calm and patiently explain that you are doing everything you can to help him or her.

B *Pair Work* Rewrite the sentences with *unless* using *if . . . not*. You will need to change some words.

Exercise 4.2 More *Unless, Only If, Even If*

Complete the sentences about social responsibility in your city with a condition or a result. Use your own ideas and *unless*, *even if*, and *only if* where necessary.

1. Unless the city provides free recycling pick-up, _____ .

2. Even if people recycle, _____ .

3. If the city doesn't clean up the parks, _____ .

4. Only if the city adds more buses and subway trains, _____ .

5. _____ will people volunteer in the community.

6. _____ , there will continue to be crime downtown.

7. _____ , children won't have a safe place to play.

8. _____ , people will continue to throw litter on the streets.

5 | Avoid Common Mistakes ⚠️

1. **Remember that the subject and verb in an *if* clause must agree.**

   buys
   The restaurant will have more customers if it ~~buy~~ local produce.

2. **Remember that the base form of the verb follows a modal.**

   make
   If a company improves its image, it can ~~makes~~ a higher profit.

3. **Remember to use the correct form of the modal in real and unreal conditional sentences.**

   will
   Real: If companies use recycled paper, they ~~would~~ save money.

   would
   Unreal: Telecommuting ~~will~~ work if employees had laptops.

4. **Do not confuse *otherwise* with *unless*.**

   unless
   Our dependence on oil will not decrease ~~otherwise~~ we start making more electric cars.

Editing Task

Find and correct seven more mistakes in a body paragraph from an essay about how companies can make changes to create a better world.

Making a Better World

create
   If a company allows telecommuting, it can ~~creates~~ a better working lifestyle for its

employees and a better world. If a business have a telecommuting program, it not only

improves the environment, it also improves the quality of life for its employees. Take, for

example, an employee who usually drives to the office. If he or she can works from home

5 a few days a week, there is one less car on the road. This reduces the levels of carbon

dioxide in the air. If there is less carbon dioxide, there would be less pollution in the future.

Telecommuting also improves the communities that employees live in. Often employees

are too busy to get involved in their communities. If employees spent fewer hours at the

office, they will spend more time in their communities. Employees can gets involved in local

10 programs if they can structure their own working days. For example, many telecommuters

cannot volunteer in local schools or other neighborhood activities otherwise they have some

free time during the week. If more companies offered telecommuting, both the environment

and our communities will benefit.

6 | The Writing Process

In this section, you will write an introduction and three body paragraphs for a cause and effect essay. Before you start writing, you will learn about different ways to order your ideas in your writing so that your ideas can be communicated as effectively as possible.

About Paragraph Order

In academic writing, a good introductory paragraph previews the points that will be covered in the body paragraphs of the essay. Writers must then consider the best order to present these points.

The following are some ways to order the main points in an essay.

1. **By time (chronological)** Points can be presented from earliest to latest or latest to earliest.

   Essay topic: History of recycling

   Order of points: Earliest to latest
   1. Littering problems in 1960s
   2. Garbage problems in the 1980s
   3. Recycling efforts in the 21st century

2. **By importance of ideas** Writers can start or end with what they consider to be the most important point.

   Essay topic: Environmental issues

   Order of points: End with the most important effect
   1. Issues of convenience (more expensive gasoline = important)
   2. Issues that could possibly harm lives (increased diseases = more important)
   3. Issues that could create widespread disaster (mass starvation, floods = most important)

3. **By familiarity** Writers can start with a point that is familiar to readers. This will help readers follow points more easily. This strategy requires determining who the readers are, and basing the ordering on, for example, the readers' location, the readers' area of expertise or interest, or their general knowledge.

   Essay topic: Green initiatives around the world (written by a Southern Californian)

   Order of points: Based on more familiar topic being first
   1. Green initiatives in the Southern California local community
   2. Green initiatives in other parts of the country
   3. Green initiatives in other parts of the world

4. **By sequence of events** Sometimes a cause leads to an effect, which then becomes a cause for something else. In this instance, writers often list causes or reasons in the order in which they occur, making a storyline that moves along as each effect or result happens.

   Essay topic: How cars have become more fuel efficient

Order of points: Sequential

1. Public pressure on the government to pass stricter new laws on fuel efficiency
   ↓
2. The effect of these new laws on the manufacture of cars
   ↓
3. The automakers' decisions to market the newly required fuel-efficient cars
   ↓
4. The public's embrace of hybrid cars in the 2000s

Exercise

For each thesis statement below, select one of the ordering patterns that the writer might use in writing the body paragraphs. Write the name of the ordering pattern on the line after the thesis statement.

familiarity   importance   sequence   time

1. Young people want to make changes to improve the future for three main reasons: to fix problems of the past, to live a healthier life now, and to provide a better environment for the next generation. _____

2. There are many ways a young person can make changes to create a better world: by changing personal habits, becoming involved locally, and learning more about the world. _____

3. Before joining an environmental organization, a young person should first research the organization online, meet and interview organization members, and then attend some meetings as a guest. _____

4. There are three main reasons why a young person might want to pursue a career in environmental protection. _____

Pre-writing Tasks

Choose a Topic

A Choose one of the essay topics listed below. You will write an introductory paragraph and three body paragraphs for a cause and effect essay on this topic.

- Changes that individuals can make in their lives to create a better world and the possible impact of these changes on the world
- Changes that groups of people (for example, neighborhood groups) can make to create a better world and the possible impact of these changes on the world
- A topic of your own approved by your teacher

B Brainstorm a list of ideas for your chosen topic. Then discuss your ideas with your classmates.

Organize Your Ideas

Use the ideas below to organize your ideas.

1. Select the idea you feel you can best develop.
2. Decide which ordering pattern you will use to organize the ideas. Then explain to a partner the ordering pattern you chose (by time, importance, familiarity, sequence) and why.
3. In the chart below, write a thesis statement, a hook, and three main points. The thesis statement should reflect the ordering pattern you decided to use. The main points in the body paragraphs should appear in the same order as they appear in your thesis statement.

Introductory Paragraph
Hook:
Thesis Statement:
Body Paragraph 1 Main Point:
Body Paragraph 2 Main Point:
Body Paragraph 3 Main Point:

Writing Task

Write your introductory and body paragraphs for your cause and effect essay. Follow the steps below.

1. Write your introductory paragraph, using the thesis statement and "hook" from your chart.
2. Write the body paragraphs, using your main points from your chart. Make sure the body paragraphs follow the order of the list of points in your thesis statement.

> **Academic Writing Tip**
>
> **Avoid Using the Pronoun *You***
> Sentences with *you* tend to be informal. Instead use words such as *individuals, people,* or *one* in academic writing.
>
> *Individuals   their*
> ~~You~~ can help ~~your~~ community by volunteering.

3. Include the following in your essay:
   - real or unreal conditional statements in your body paragraphs;
   - phrases like *unless, if . . . not, only if,* and *even if;*
   - at least three of these academic words from the unit: *area, aware, benefit, community, conduct, core, corporate, cultural, culture, document, environment, ethical, finance, focus, goal, image, impact, implement, incorporate, instance, investor, labor, policy, positive, pursuit, restrict, role.*
4. After you write, review your work and make sure you avoided the mistakes in the Avoid Common Mistakes chart on page 45.

Peer Review

A Exchange your work with a partner. Answer the following questions as you read your partner's work, and then share your responses.

1. What is the thesis statement? Underline it.

2. What is the main point that the writer is making in each body paragraph? Identify the main points in each body paragraph and underline them.

3. Which order did your partner use to present his or her points: time, importance, familiarity, or sequence? Was this order a good choice for the essay topic? Why or why not?

4. Identify the real and unreal conditionals used in the essay, and any uses of *unless*, *if . . . not*, *only if*, and *even if*. Were they used properly?

5. Is anything confusing? Write a question mark (?) next to it.

6. Provide one compliment (something you found interesting or unusual).

B Use your partner's comments to help you revise your work. Use the Writer's Checklist on page A2 to review your paragraphs for organization, grammar, and vocabulary.

Cause and Effect 4:
-ing Participle Phrases and Verbs
That Show Cause and Effect

Alternative Energy Sources

1 | Grammar in the Real World 🌐

You will read an essay that contains several cause and effect ideas about solar energy. In order to persuade the reader that solar energy is a good energy alternative, the writer uses ideas from experts.

A *Before You Read* What are the advantages and disadvantages of traditional sources of energy, such as oil, natural gas, and coal? Read the essay. What does the writer believe are the advantages of solar energy?

Making the Dream a Reality:
Never Running out of Energy

The demand for energy is always increasing. In fact, ACCENT, a European research company, claims that despite greater efficiency in many technical processes, each person's energy use has risen dramatically in the last few decades and will continue to rise ("Energy Today and Tomorrow," 2008, para. 2). Currently, electricity is produced mainly with nonrenewable fossil fuels, such as
5 coal, oil, and natural gas. Although this use of fossil fuels can meet the world's current energy needs, it can potentially lead to negative consequences. These may include global warming, scarcity of[1] resources, and high prices. Environmental analyst Lester Brown (2009, p. 56) warns us that the reserves of oil in the world are gradually shrinking. Fortunately, there are other alternatives for energy sources. Many experts note that solar energy is one excellent substitute
10 because it is feasible[2] to use and is a clean source of energy.

Solar energy is feasible for several reasons. There are already solar thermal[3] power stations located in many places in the world, including in the United States, Spain, Australia, and Germany. In these power stations, solar energy is converted into thermal energy, providing hot water and heat for homes and offices. In an interview, Noah Kaye, a representative for the Solar Energy
15 Industries Association, points out that the price of solar power decreases almost 20 percent whenever solar usage doubles (cited in Sweet, 2007, para. 11). This lower cost for solar energy will make it easier to use in more places in the future.

In addition to its feasibility, solar energy is very clean, unlike fossil fuels. It does not create pollution like coal, gas, and oil. It is true that many other materials can also produce energy, such
20 as recycled automobile tires and aluminum cans. However, these materials are nonrenewable

[1]**scarcity of:** lack of | [2]**feasible:** possible to succeed | [3]**thermal:** related to or caused by heat

and create pollution. Solar energy consumes far fewer nonrenewable materials, making less of an impact on the environment. For example, solar energy uses long-lasting solar panels to convert energy from sunlight, thereby reducing our dependence on coal, oil, and gas.

25 Being such a clean energy, solar energy is a sensible alternative to fossil fuels. It reduces our dependence on imported fuels and improves the quality of the air we breathe. The world needs energy sources like solar energy that can save resources, thus preserving the environment.

B *Comprehension Check* Answer these questions.

1. Why does the writer believe that it is important to switch from traditional energy sources to alternative energy sources, such as solar power?
2. What is the difference between renewable and nonrenewable resources? Give examples.
3. Does the writer believe that solar energy is a feasible alternative to traditional energy sources? Explain.

C *Notice*

1 Cause and Effect Writing Draw a chart like the one below, and complete it with causes and effects from the essay.

Cause		Effect
Electricity is produced mainly with nonrenewable fossil fuels.	→	Using nonrenewable fossil fuels can potentially lead to global warming, scarcity of resources, and high prices.
Solar energy is converted into thermal energy.	→	
Solar power output doubles.	→	
	→	It reduces our use of coal, oil, and natural gas.

2 Grammar Follow the instructions to help you notice and understand *-ing* participle phrases that show effects and causes.

1. The last sentences in the third and fourth paragraphs talk about an effect. Circle the word in each sentence that signals that the writer is going to state an effect of using solar energy.

2. Notice the -*ing* form of the verbs that follow the words that you found in item 1. Underline the verb and all the words that complete each phrase. Notice how you can use *As a result* to restate each phrase as a sentence.

3. Reread the -*ing* phrase in the first sentence in the last paragraph. Does the phrase state a cause or an effect? How is its position different from the -*ing* phrases in item 1?

3 The Writing Process Notice how the writer includes the ideas of experts to support his or her own ideas. In each case, the writer gives the source, a reporting verb, and the expert's ideas. Complete the chart below with the missing information.

The Source	The Reporting Verb	The Expert's Ideas
ACCENT, a European research company		. . . each person's energy use has risen dramatically.
	warns	. . . reserves of oil in the world are gradually shrinking.
Noah Kaye		

2 | -*ing* Participle Phrases That Show Effect

▶ Grammar Presentation

-*ing* participle phrases begin with the -*ing* form of a verb. They can show effects in academic writing.

*Solar energy is converted into thermal energy, **providing hot water and heat for homes**. Nuclear plants are expensive to build, **limiting their desirability**.*

2.1 -*ing* Participle Phrases That Show Effect

a. -*ing* participle phrases that show effect usually come after the independent clause.	INDEPENDENT CLAUSE *Solar energy is very clean,* -*ING* PARTICIPLE PHRASE ***causing less pollution**.*
b. A comma separates the -*ing* participle phrase from the independent clause.	*The government is investing large sums of money in alternative energy projects, **creating thousands of new jobs**.*

2.2 Using -*ing* Participle Phrases That Show Effect

a. Use an -*ing* participle phrase to show the effect or result of the situation or action in the independent clause.	CAUSE *Some countries give tax credits for wind energy,* EFFECT / RESULT ***lowering costs for consumers**.*

2.2 Using *-ing* Participle Phrases That Show Effect *(continued)*

b. You can use *thus* or *thereby* to start *-ing* participle phrases. These words strengthen the cause and effect relationship of the ideas.	*The manufacturing of solar energy systems can create jobs, **thus** stimulating the economy.* *Most solar panels have no moving parts, **thereby** lowering maintenance costs.*

▶ Grammar Application

Exercise 2.1 *-ing* Participle Phrases That Show Effect

A 🔊 Listen to the lecture about wind power. Match each cause with its effect.

Causes

<u> *d* </u> 1. Wind power costs about the same as coal and oil.

_____ 2. The technology of wind power is improving.

_____ 3. Wind power will not involve many costs in the near future.

_____ 4. Wind power produces zero carbon dioxide emissions.

_____ 5. Wind energy is renewable.

Effects

a. It provides low cost power to everyone.

b. It is a steady source of power.

c. It reduces air pollution.

 d. This makes it an affordable source of alternative energy.

e. It lowers the costs even further.

B Combine the causes and effects in A and write sentences with *-ing* participle phrases that show effect. Remember to put a comma before the phrases.

1. <u>*Wind power costs about the same as coal or oil, making it an affordable source of alternative energy.*</u>

2. _____

3. _____

4. _____

5. _____

Exercise 2.2 -ing Participle Phrases That Show Effect

A In each pair of sentences about alternative energy, label the sentences *C* for cause and
E for effect.

1. _*C*_ Solar energy technology continues to improve.

    _*E*_ Solar energy provides more efficient and cost-effective choices.

2. _____ Solar energy reduces noise pollution.

    _____ Solar cells are silent when collecting energy.

3. _____ Solar energy helps keep our air clean.

    _____ Solar energy does not release any harmful gases into the atmosphere.

4. _____ Homeowners can sell excess electricity they create through solar energy.

    _____ Homeowners can produce extra income with no extra effort.

5. _____ Governments often give tax credits for solar power generation.

    _____ Tax credits lower the cost of installing a solar energy system.

6. _____ Solar energy provides a long-term source of energy.

    _____ Solar energy exists in the sunlight we enjoy every day.

7. _____ Wind power is another clean source of energy.

    _____ Wind power offers another renewable option for our future energy needs.

B *Pair Work* On a separate sheet of paper, combine each pair of sentences in A. Introduce
the effect using *thus* or *thereby* and an *-ing* participle phrase. Compare your sentences with
a partner.

1. *Solar energy technology continues to improve, thereby providing more efficient and*
   cost-effective choices.

3 | -ing Participle Phrases That Show Cause

▶ Grammar Presentation

In academic writing *-ing* participle phrases can show causes or reasons.

Producing very little waste, *solar power creates an environmentally friendly source of*
energy.

Being such a new technology, *solar energy is still in the development stage in many*
countries.

3.1 -ing Participle Phrases That Show Cause

a. *-ing* participle phrases that show cause or reason almost always come before the independent clause.	***Providing an almost unlimited clean source of electricity***, *solar energy will certainly grow in importance.*

3.1 *-ing* Participle Phrases That Show Cause (continued)

b. The omitted subject of the *-ing* participle phrase must be the same as the subject of the independent clause.	***Being widely accessible,*** <u>hot rocks</u> *deep in the earth could be an unlimited source of energy.*
c. Do not confuse *-ing* participle phrases and gerunds. Gerunds can be the subject or object of a sentence.	*-ING* PARTICIPLE PHRASE ***Investing in alternative sources of energy,*** *the country will be ready for increases in oil prices.* GERUND PHRASE ***Investing in solar energy*** *was once considered a high risk.*

3.2 Using *-ing* Participle Phrases That Show Cause

a. Use an *-ing* participle phrase to show the cause of or reason for the situation or action in the independent clause.	CAUSE / REASON ***Using wind energy,*** EFFECT *we can lower the cost of electricity for consumers.*
b. You can start *-ing* participle phrases with the prepositions *by* and *in*. Using these words to begin the phrase can strengthen the cause and effect relationship of the ideas. *By* is more frequent than *in* in these expressions.	CAUSE EFFECT ***By*** <u>using solar energy</u>, *we can reduce our ecological footprint.* ***In*** <u>cutting tax credits for alternative energy</u>, *the government has increased our dependence on fossil fuel.*

▶ Grammar Application

Exercise 3.1 *-ing* Participle Phrases That Show Cause

A Read the online article about saving energy in the home. Underline each *-ing* participle phrase that expresses a cause. Circle each *-ing* participle phrase that shows an effect.

Tips for Saving Energy

Many people want to save energy in their homes, but they're not sure how. The truth is there are several simple ways to begin saving energy and money. First, people can keep their appliances unplugged when they're not in use, (decreasing) small amounts of energy use with each unplugged appliance. In taking that simple step, some consumers have saved hundreds
5 of dollars in energy costs in a single year. Along the same lines, people should not leave the lights on when they're not in a room. By making this change, people can easily save a few dollars a month on their energy bills. Also, by purchasing and installing energy-efficient

appliances, people can reduce their energy use. These appliances may cost more money to buy. However, they save consumers money in the long run, using less electricity than

10 regular appliances. Keeping doors and windows closed, people can reduce their use of air conditioning and heating. By setting thermostats lower while they are away or sleeping, people can reduce their energy costs by up to 10 percent. All consumers should take these simple steps, making a positive difference in energy use and reducing electricity bills.

B *Pair Work* Explain your choices in A to a partner.

I circled "decreasing" because it describes the effect of unplugging appliances when they are not in use.

Exercise 3.2 *-ing* Participle Phrases That Show Cause

A Complete the sentences about ways to reduce energy consumption. Use *-ing* participle phrases and the prepositions in parentheses. Use the information from 3.1 or your own ideas. Remember to use commas after the phrases.

1. (by) *By using dimmers and timers for all the lighting,* hospitals can bring their energy costs down.

2. (in) _____ restaurants can reduce their use of electricity.

3. (by) _____ hotels would be able to reduce energy costs.

4. (by) _____ offices could reduce waste and energy bills.

5. (in) _____ airports might be able to reduce their energy costs.

6. (by) _____ schools could probably reduce their energy bills.

B *Pair Work* Discuss with a partner three things that a government can do to reduce people's energy use. Agree on three things and write sentences using *in* or *by* and *-ing* participle phrases. Share your sentences with another pair. Are any of your ideas the same?

I think that by increasing taxes on energy use, people will want to use energy more efficiently.

4 | Verbs That Show Cause and Effect

▶ Vocabulary Presentation

> The verbs *cause, lead to, produce, contribute to, result in,* and *result from* are commonly used to show cause and effect in academic writing.
>
> *Curiously, increases in efficiency may have **led to** greater demand.*
>
> *Higher gas prices have **contributed to** more consumer awareness of energy issues.*

4.1 Verbs That Show Cause and Effect

a. *Cause* as a verb can be used in active or passive (*be + caused + by*) sentences. It is usually used to discuss negative issues (disasters, crises, etc.).	*The accident **caused** a shutdown of the plant's central operations.* *The slow development of alternative energy **is caused by** cheap oil.*
b. *Lead to* and *produce* are other ways to link cause and effect. They are more neutral than *cause* and are used to discuss positive or negative issues.	*New laws **have led to** an increase in wind-generated electricity.* *Overreliance on fossil fuels **could produce** an uncertain future for all of us.*
c. *Contribute to* is used to show one of a number of causes.	*Pollution **contributes to** many health problems.* *Increased use of wind power **contributes** directly **to** a cleaner environment.*
d. *Result in* and *result from* show a connection between cause and effect. Use *result in* to refer to the effect. Use *result from* to refer to the cause.	CAUSE EFFECT *Strict standards for cars **will result in** a reduction in energy use.* EFFECT CAUSE *A reduction in energy use **will result from** strict standards for cars.*

▶ Vocabulary Application

Exercise 4.1 Common Verbs That Show Cause and Effect

Rewrite the sentences about energy sources with the verb phrases in parentheses.

1. The sharp increase in oil prices in the 1970s created a surge in state-funded energy research and development. (result in)

   The sharp increase in oil prices in the 1970s
   resulted in a surge in state-funded energy
   research and development.

2. Growing concerns about environmental issues were a factor in the government's decision in the 1970s to promote alternative energy sources. (contribute to)

_____

3. Increase in oil supplies and falling prices in the 1980s were a result of a reduction in U.S. rules requiring more fuel-efficient cars. (result from)

_____

4. An increase in fossil fuel usage and nuclear plants was a result of a lack of consistent solar and wind energy supplies. (was caused by)

_____

5. In the future, hydrogen-based energy sources could give us pollution-free cities. (lead to)

_____

6. Continued overreliance on oil could create political conflicts in the future. (cause)

_____

Exercise 4.2 More Common Verbs That Show Cause and Effect

A Read the sentences about international energy issues. Circle the correct verbs to complete the sentences.

1. The Japanese nuclear power plant accident in 2010 **resulted in** / **was caused by** widespread protests against nuclear plants.

2. Japan's position as the world's leading manufacturer of household solar technology **was a result of** / **produced** the Japanese government's financial assistance for solar roof panels in 1994.

3. High energy needs and low energy production **were caused by** / **contributed to** Japan's interest in renewable energy sources.

4. In Denmark, a high tax on electricity **produced** / **resulted from** an incentive for consumers to use less energy.

5. Denmark's interest in reducing dependence on foreign fossil fuels **resulted from** / **led to** the country's commitment to using natural sources of energy.

6. In Italy, a lack of natural resources **resulted in** / **resulted from** a need to import foreign electricity.

7. A desire to reduce use of foreign electricity **has been caused by** / **has contributed to** Italy's current focus on energy efficiency.

B *Pair Work* Discuss with a partner events that occurred in other countries as a result of energy issues. Use the verbs in A to explain the causes and effects.

In Ecuador in 2009 and 2010, there was an energy crisis. Severe droughts resulted in very low water levels at hydroelectric plants. This led to many blackouts.

5 | Avoid Common Mistakes ⚠️

1. **Remember to use *result in*, not *result of* for verbs that are followed by an effect.**

    The increased demand for oil has resulted ~~of~~ *in* higher prices for gas.

2. **Remember to use *result from*, not *result by* for verbs that are followed by a cause.**

    A decrease in carbon dioxide emissions will result ~~by~~ *from* an increase in electric cars.

3. **Remember to use *contribute to*, not *contribute for*.**

    The use of solar energy will contribute ~~for~~ *to* a healthier environment.

4. **Remember that the subject and the verb must agree when using *contribute to*.**

    This factor ~~contribute~~ *contributes* to climate change.

Editing Task

Find and correct six more mistakes in these paragraphs about alternative energy sources.

Rising awareness of the dangers of carbon emissions and the limits of our natural resources has contributed ~~for~~ *to* some creative ideas for alternative energy sources. While most scientists think of ways to use renewable resources in the environment to make energy, others are finding ways to generate electricity from the movements of the human body. In

5 2010, Michael McAlpine of Princeton University and some of his colleagues placed a material called PZT into flexible silicone rubber sheets. The PZT-filled sheets generate an electrical current when they are bent. Bending the sheets repeatedly results of a significant amount of energy. Placing these crystals in a pair of shoes or even directly into the body could result of enough electricity to charge devices like cell phones or tablets.

10 Our body heat can help create energy, too. In 2007 and 2008, Belgian nanotechnology engineers built thermoelectric devices that allow a person's body heat to contribute for powering medical devices such as EKG machines and brain monitors. In 2010, engineers in Paris discovered a different way to use body heat to conserve electricity. The engineers developed a system that uses geothermal technology to move heat from a metro, or subway,

15 station to heating pipes in a public-housing project above the station. Their system resulted from a 33 percent cut in carbon dioxide emissions in the housing project's heating system. Innovative approaches like these contributes to solving our ongoing need for alternative energy sources.

6 The Writing Process ✎

In this section, you will write a cause and effect essay. Before you write, you will learn some effective ways to paraphrase.

About Paraphrasing

Much of the supporting information in an academic essay may come from various sources. When writers include information from a source but do not directly quote it, the information needs to be paraphrased and cited. *Paraphrasing* means stating the information in a different way from the original without changing its meaning. *Citing* means stating who wrote the original material and / or what publication the original material came from. By paraphrasing and citing, writers avoid plagiarizing, that is, they avoid copying someone's exact words and using them as if they were their own.

The following will help you write effective paraphrases. In each case, the writer is paraphrasing this sentence below:

"Denmark leads the world in wind energy, generating 20 percent of its energy from wind power" (Evans, 2007, para. 2).

1. **Use synonyms.** It is helpful to look at a thesaurus for synonyms, but be careful deciding which ones to use. If you are not sure what a word means, use your dictionary. A good learner dictionary will often have additional information that can help you find appropriate synonyms. Here the writer uses *producing* instead of *generating*.

   Producing *20 percent of its energy from wind power, Denmark is the world leader in wind energy (Evans, 2007, para. 2).*

2. **Change the order of the ideas in the sentences.** Here the writer mentions Denmark's energy production before mentioning it is the world leader.

   *Producing 20 percent of its energy from wind power, Denmark **is the world leader in wind energy production** (Evans, 2007, para. 2).*

3. **Break long sentences into shorter ones. Alternatively, combine sentences, changing shorter ones into longer ones.** Here the writer has created two sentences from the original sentence.

   *Denmark is the world leader in wind energy. **Twenty percent of its energy comes from wind power** (Evans, 2007, para. 2).*

4. **Change the word form of key words, and shift grammar as needed to fit the new word forms.** Here the writer uses *leader* instead of *lead* and makes the necessary changes to the grammar.

   *Denmark is the world **leader** in wind energy. Twenty percent of its energy comes from wind power (Evans, 2007, para. 2).*

5. **Switch between active and passive voice.**

   *Denmark is the world leader in wind energy. Twenty percent of its energy **is produced** from wind power (Evans, 2007, para. 2).*

6. **Combine several of the strategies (1–5 above) to create your paraphrase.**

   One-fifth of the energy in Denmark is produced from wind power. This makes Denmark a world leader in wind energy production (Evans, 2007, para. 2).

7. **Always include a citation that recognizes the source of the material that you are paraphrasing.** This should go after the first mention of the author, or if the author is not mentioned, at the end of the material being paraphrased.

   *One-fifth of the energy in Denmark is produced from wind power. This makes Denmark a world leader in wind energy production **(Evans, 2007, para. 2)**.*

8. **Make sure that you do not change the meaning of the original material when you paraphrase.** The following paraphrase contains two inaccuracies. According to the source information, Denmark is *the* leader in the world and produces only *one-fifth* of its energy from wind.

   Denmark is one of the leading producers of wind energy in the world; almost one-half of its domestic energy is provided by wind power (Evans, 2007, para. 2).

Exercise

A Paraphrase each quotation below, using at least two of the strategies described above.

1. "Population and income growth are the two most powerful driving forces behind the demand for energy" ("BP Energy Outlook 2030," 2011, p. 9).

   _____

2. "About 42 percent of the world's energy-related CO_2 emissions come from oil" ("Our Dependence on Oil," 2010, p. 2).

   _____

3. "Even though many technical processes have become more efficient, the energy needs per person have also greatly increased" ("Energy Today and Tomorrow," 2008, para. 2).

   _____

4. "Every time solar power output doubles, the price drops by 18 percent" (cited in Sweet, 2007, para. 11).

   _____

5. "'Car culture,' both in the cities and suburbs, causes the smog that helps make many California cities unhealthful" ("The True Costs of Petroleum: The Community Map," 2003, p. 3).

   _____

B *Pair Work* Work with a partner. Read each other's paraphrases and identify which of the strategies your partner used. Did you use the same ones? Then discuss ways you each could improve your paraphrases.

Pre-writing Tasks

Choose a Topic

A Choose one of the essay topics listed below. You will write an essay that discusses several causes that lead to one effect or one cause that leads to several effects.

- Things that can be done to make energy more affordable
- The causes and effects of improving energy use in the home
- A topic of your own approved by your teacher

B *Pair Work* Share your topic with a partner. Describe the causes and effects that are important for your topic. Provide suggestions to each other about what to include.

Organize Your Ideas

A Research your chosen topic. Find at least two direct quotations from your sources that you might include in your essay. Complete the chart below with the name of the source, the quotation, and a paraphrase of the quotation.

Source	Quotation	Paraphrase
1.		
2.		

B *Pair Work* Work with a partner. Share your quotations and your paraphrases. Tell your partner why you chose the quotations. Have your partner check your paraphrases to make sure you are not plagiarizing.

Writing Task

Write your cause and effect essay. Follow the steps below.

1. Write an introductory paragraph with a hook and a thesis statement.
2. Write body paragraphs that express your main points.
3. Order your paragraphs in the most logical way according to your main points.

> **Academic Writing Tip**
>
> **Use Quotations and References**
> Taking material directly from any source without using quotations and citing it correctly is considered plagiarism. For more information on ways to avoid plagiarism, see About Plagiarism, page A3.

4. Include the following in your essay:
   - ways to show cause and effect that you learned in Units 1–4;
   - *-ing* participle phrases and verbs such as *contribute to* and *result from* to link cause and effect;
   - at least three academic words from this unit: *alternative, analyst, cite, consequence, convert, create, decade, despite, dramatically, energy, environment, environmental, expert, impact, negative, percent, potential, process, research, resource, substitute*;
   - paraphrases and quotations from your sources. Do not forget to include the name of the author, year of publication, and page number for your sources (if available).

5. After you write your essay, review it and make sure you avoided the mistakes in the Avoid Common Mistakes chart on page 59.

Peer Review

A Exchange your essay with a partner. Answer the following questions as you read your partner's paragraph, and share your responses.

1. What is the topic? Underline the thesis statement.

2. What are the cause(s) and effect(s) the writer addresses in the essay?

3. Does the essay contain several causes leading to one effect, or one cause leading to several effects?

4. Look at the lists of causes and effects. Did the writer choose a specific order, such as familiarity or importance?

5. What paraphrases and quotations are used in the essay? Are they effective? Why or why not?

6. Identify any *-ing* participle phrases. Do they show cause or effect?

7. Is anything confusing? Write a question mark (?) next to it.

8. Provide one compliment (something you found interesting or unusual).

B Use your partner's comments to help you revise your essay. Use the Writer's Checklist on page A2 to review your essay for organization, grammar, and vocabulary.

Comparison and Contrast 1: Identifying Relative Clauses; Comparatives with *As . . . As*; Common Patterns That Show Contrast

Family Size and Personality

1 Grammar in the Real World

You will read an essay that discusses how a child's birth order in the family – being the oldest child, middle child, youngest child, or an only child – may affect his or her personality as an adult. The essay is an example of a type of comparison and contrast writing in which the ideas are organized using the block method.

A *Before You Read* How many siblings (brothers and sisters) do you have? Do you think that some of their personality traits come from the order of their birth? Read the essay. How strong are the effects of birth order, according to the information in the essay?

Birth Order and Adult Sibling Relationships

What do Jimmy Carter, Bill Clinton, and George W. Bush all have in common? In addition to being elected president of the United States, these men all share the same birth order. Each one is the oldest child in his family. In fact, many very successful people in government and business have been "firstborn" children. While there is always some
5 variation, some experts agree that birth order can have an influence on a person's personality in childhood and in adulthood.

Firstborn children often share several traits. First, in contrast to their siblings, they are more likely to be responsible, ambitious, and authoritarian. This is probably because they are born into an environment of high expectations, and they usually receive a great deal of
10 attention. They are used to being leaders, taking responsibility for others, and sometimes taking on an almost parental role.

Middle children, on the other hand, exhibit different characteristics from firstborns. They are often not as determined as firstborns. They tend to be more passive and solitary. Having to share family attention with older and younger siblings, middle children have a
15 tendency to be more realistic, creative, and insightful.

Youngest children are often more protected than their older siblings. As a result, they are more likely to be dependent and controlling. They are often as creative as middle children, but usually more easygoing and social.

A child with no siblings, or an "only child," also exhibits some unique characteristics.
20 While some parents worry that an only child will have difficulties socializing and making friends, studies show that an only child is just as intelligent, accomplished, and sociable as a child with siblings. In fact, some research indicates that being an only child has some benefits. These children tend to have better vocabulary, perform better at school, and maintain closer relationships with their parents than children with siblings (Petersen,
25 2010, p. 2).

Even though it is assumed that birth order dictates some personality traits, individuals can free themselves from the roles they played when they were young, but it can be difficult. According to Vikki Stark, family therapist and author of *My Sister, My Self*, change requires letting go of familiar ways of being and patiently asserting new behaviors that
30 express one's true self (Kochan, 2006, para. 10).

B *Comprehension Check* Answer the questions.

1. How are former presidents Bill Clinton and George W. Bush connected to the main idea of the text?
2. According to the writer, why are firstborn children usually more ambitious than their siblings?
3. Which of the different birth order types – firstborn, middle born, youngest, and only child – do you think has the fewest advantages in life? Explain.

C *Notice*

1 Comparison and Contrast Writing Complete the outline below with information from the essay. The essay is organized using the block method. In this method, the main points that describe one part of the issue are presented together in "one block" or paragraph, and the main points that describe the second side of the issue are presented in the next paragraph, and so on.

Block Method: Birth Order and Adult Sibling Relationships

Introductory paragraph. Thesis statement: Some experts agree that birth order can have an influence on a person's personality in childhood and adulthood.

Body Paragraph 1. Topic: _Firstborn children_
(1)
Personality traits: responsible, ambitious, authoritarian

Body Paragraph 2. Topic: _____
(2)
Personality traits: passive, solitary, _____ , creative, _____
(3)   (4)

Body Paragraph 3. Topic: _____
(5)
Personality traits: dependent, _____ , creative, easygoing, _____
(6)   (7)

Body Paragraph 4. Topic: _____
(8)
Personality traits: intelligent, _____ , sociable
(9)

---

2 Grammar Follow the instructions below to help you notice and understand comparison and contrast sentences from the essay that use *as . . . as*.

1. Read the *as . . . as* sentence in the third paragraph. Are middle children likely to be equally determined, more determined, or less determined than firstborn children? Explain.
2. Read the *as . . . as* sentence in the fourth paragraph. Are youngest children likely to be equally creative, more creative, or less creative than middle children? Explain.
3. Read the *as . . . as* sentence in the fifth paragraph. Are only children likely to be equally intelligent, more intelligent, or less intelligent than children with siblings? Explain.

3 The Writing Process Underline the sentence that gives the main idea of each body paragraph. This sentence is called the *topic sentence*.

2 | Identifying Relative Clauses

▶ Grammar Presentation

A relative clause modifies a noun and follows the noun it modifies. Identifying relative clauses provide necessary information about the noun. They are used in all kinds of academic writing, but they are especially useful in comparison and contrast writing to describe characteristics of elements that are being compared.

*Children **who / that have no siblings** are often very close to their parents.*
*People gradually behave in ways **which / that are more consistent with their preferred self-image**.*

2.1 Identifying Relative Clauses

a. An identifying relative clause modifies a noun. It begins with a relative pronoun: *that, which, who, whom,* or *whose*. (It is often called a *restrictive relative clause*.)	IDENTIFYING RELATIVE CLAUSE *People **who do not have children** may not be aware of differences in birth order.*
An identifying relative clause answers the question, "Which one?" It gives necessary information about the noun or noun phrase in the main clause. Without that information, the sentence would be incomplete.	IDENTIFYING RELATIVE CLAUSE *Creativity is a trait **that all middle children share**.*
b. *Who, that,* and *whom* refer to people. Use *whom* for object relative clauses. In informal speaking and writing, the use of *who* for *whom* is common.	PEOPLE *Researchers **who / that study families** have different views.* *My siblings are the people in my life **whom** I will always trust.*

2.1 Identifying Relative Clauses *(continued)*

c. *Whose* shows possession. It is followed by an animate or inanimate noun in academic writing.	POSSESSION *Researchers **whose work focuses on families** disagree about the importance of birth order.* *She cited a study **whose** results supported previous research.*
Which and *that* refer to things. In academic writing, *that* is often preferred to *which* in identifying relative clauses.	THINGS *The study examines characteristics **that / which are common in firstborn children**.*
d. In a subject relative clause, the relative pronoun is the subject. In an object relative clause, the relative pronoun is the object of the verb. *Note:* The relative pronoun in object relative clauses can be omitted, but it is better not to do so in academic writing. The relative pronoun may not be omitted in subject relative clauses.	*Psychologists <u>**who**</u> **work with only children and their parents** can help the children learn to share attention.* (*Who* is the subject of the verb *work* in the relative clause.) *There are several strategies <u>**that**</u> **parents use to help their only children**.* (*That* is the object of the verb *use* in the relative clause.) *The research **(that) they just published on sibling order** was inconclusive.*
e. A preposition can also come at the beginning of the clause, but this is only used in very formal writing. *Note:* The relative pronoun may not be omitted in the formal version.	FORMAL WRITING: *An older sibling is someone **on whom** you can always rely.* MORE COMMON: *An older sibling is someone **that / who** you can always rely **on**.* *Researchers studied the ways **in which** parents interacted with their only child.*

Data from the Real World

In academic writing, 75 percent of relative clauses with *whose* modify inanimate nouns:

*The report included the results of a study funded by an organization **whose** mission is to help children reach their potential.*

2.2 Using Identifying Relative Clauses

a. Use identifying relative clauses in comparison and contrast writing to provide characteristics or information that shows the differences between the elements you are comparing.	*My friend **who lives in Boston** always remembers my birthday, but my friend **who lives in New Jersey** does not.* *Some people like to play games **that involve competition,** while others like to play games **that encourage collaboration**.*

2.2 Using Identifying Relative Clauses (continued)

b. Relative clauses are similar to subordinate clauses in that they are fragments if they appear alone.	FRAGMENT: *A recent study reports that firstborns are generally smarter than siblings.* **Who are born later.**
	CORRECT: *A recent study reports that firstborns are generally smarter than siblings* **who are born later.**

Data from the Real World

In academic writing, the relative pronoun **who** is more commonly used than **that** to refer to people.	
In speaking, the relative pronoun **that** is more commonly used than **who** to refer to people.	

► Grammar Application

Exercise 2.1 Identifying Relative Clauses

A Read the paragraph about birth order. Complete each sentence with *that, who, whom,* or *whose*. Sometimes more than one answer is possible.

Birth order researchers have discovered some interesting information ___*that*___ can help us understand
(1)
our colleagues better. Do you have a difficult boss

_____ authoritarian personality makes
(2)
your life difficult? If so, your boss might be a firstborn child.

Children _____ are born first are often
(3)
more authoritarian than their younger siblings. Do you

have a co-worker _____ is passive, but particularly creative and insightful?
(4)
This person may be a middle child. People _____ have both older and
(5)
younger siblings are often passive because their older siblings were responsible for their

well-being when they were young. The creativity _____ they exhibit might
(6)
be the effect of their having spent a lot of time on their own due to having to share parental

attention with their older and younger siblings. People _____ you work with
(7)

_____ are controlling may be youngest children. These people are also likely
(8)
to be more social than co-workers _____ are middle children. Of course, these
(9)
are only generalizations. There are countless factors _____ help form people's
(10)
personalities, but birth order research may shed some helpful light on people's behavior in the
workplace.

B Look at the relative pronouns you wrote in A. Write *S* above each relative pronoun that is
the subject of the clause, *O* above each relative pronoun that is the object of the clause, and
P above each relative pronoun that shows possession.

Exercise 2.2 More Identifying Relative Clauses

A Combine each pair of sentences that describe opinions about parental behavior using an
identifying relative clause.

1. Some parents often focus too much attention on their son or daughter. These parents have
   only one child.

   Some parents who have only one child often focus too much attention on
   their son or daughter.

2. Parents put a lot of pressure on their children to do a lot of activities. These parents want
   their children to excel.

   _____

3. Children often feel a lot of stress. Their parents have high expectations of them.

   _____

4. Sports practice and music lessons are examples of activities. Some parents expect their
   children to do these activities after school.

   _____

5. Parents raise more independent adults. These parents give proper emotional support to
   their children.

   _____

6. Some children have behavioral problems at school. Their parents both work long hours.

   _____

B *Pair Work* Tell a partner whether you agree or disagree with each opinion in A. Use
identifying relative clauses where possible.

A I don't think it's true that parents who have only one child focus too much attention on
that child. I was an only child, and I don't think that I received too much attention from
my parents.

B I disagree. In my experience, parents who have an only child often want to give that
child everything. The child doesn't realize what it's like to share, either.

3 | Comparatives with *As . . . As*

▶ Grammar Presentation

Writers show similarities and differences in comparison and contrast writing by using *as . . . as*.

*Some people think that youngest children might not be **as mature as** their siblings.*

*Sometimes younger children do not get **as much attention as** their older siblings.*

3.1 *As . . . As*

a. *As . . . as* can be used in the following patterns: (*not*) *as* + adjective / adverb + *as*	ADJECTIVE *Youngest children are not as **independent*** NOUN PHRASE *as **their older siblings**.* ADVERB *An only child socializes as **well** as children with siblings.* NOUN PHRASE
(*not*) *as* + noun phrase + *as*	*An only child has as **many close friends** as children with siblings.*
b. *As . . . as* can also be used to compare quantities with count and noncount nouns: (*not*) *as much* + noncount noun phrase + *as*	*Younger children sometimes don't get as **much attention** from parents as firstborn children.*
(*not*) *as many* + count noun phrase + *as*	*Growing up as an only child has as **many advantages** as growing up in a large family.*

3.2 Using *As . . . As*

Use *as . . . as* in the following ways: to emphasize two equal elements: _____ (*just*) *as . . . as* _____	*Only children usually turn out **just as well as** children from large families.*
to show that two things are slightly unequal: _____ *almost / nearly / about / not quite as . . . as*	*Firstborn children are **almost as open to new experiences as** their younger siblings.*
to emphasize a difference: _____ *not nearly as . . . as* _____	*Genuine concern over sibling order may **not be nearly as widespread as** it seems at first glance.*

▶ Grammar Application

Exercise 3.1 Comparatives with *As . . . As*

A Complete the sentences about personality traits and birth order using the information in the chart and *as . . . as* phrases.

	Firstborn Children	Middle Children	Youngest Children
Responsible	Very	Somewhat	Not Very
Social	Somewhat	Not Very	Very
Creative	Not Very	Very	Very
Realistic	Very	Very	Not Very
Dependent	Not Very	Not Very	Very

1. Middle children *are not as responsible as* (responsible) firstborns.

2. Firstborn children _____ (social) youngest children.

3. Middle children _____ (creative) youngest children.

4. Youngest children _____ (realistic) middle children.

5. Middle children _____ (dependent) firstborn children.

6. Firstborn children _____ (realistic) middle children.

7. Firstborn children _____ (creative) youngest children.

8. Middle children _____ (dependent) youngest children.

B Look at the information in the chart in A about firstborn children, middle children, and youngest children again. Think about your birth order and the birth order of people you know. Does the information accurately describe your personality and their personalities? Why or why not? Give at least one example for each birth order.

I'm a middle child and my brother is a firstborn child. According to the chart, I'm not as responsible as firstborn children, but actually, I'm much more responsible than my brother. Maybe it's because I was given the responsibility of taking care of everyone while my parents worked. I think I have always felt responsible for my siblings. I agree with the idea that youngest children are social. My younger brother is really outgoing and has a lot of friends . . .

Exercise 3.2 Comparatives with *As . . . As*

A 🔊) Listen to the story of two famous sisters – Venus and Serena Williams. Complete the chart.

	Venus Williams	Serena Williams
1. Birth date	June 17, 1980	
2. Height	6'1"	
3. Year turned professional		
4. Wimbledon singles victories (individual years)		
5. U.S. Open singles victories (individual years)		

B On a separate sheet of paper, use the information from A and the cues below to write sentences with the following *as . . . as* phrases: *almost as . . . as*; *just as . . . as*; *not nearly as . . . as* and *not quite as . . . as*. Sometimes more than one answer is possible.

1. Serena / is / tall / Venus.

   <u>*Serena is not quite as tall as Venus.*</u>

2. Serena / has / played / long / Venus.

3. Serena / is / old / Venus.

4. Serena / has / experience / Venus.

5. Serena / is / important to U.S. sports / Venus.

6. Serena / has / won / Wimbledon singles / Venus.

7. Venus / is / famous / Serena.

8. Serena / has had / Wimbledon singles victories / Venus has had.

9. Venus / has had / success in business / Serena. They are both successful businesswomen.

Serena and Venus Williams

C *Pair Work* Tell a partner about two people you know well. Compare them using *as . . . as* structures. Next, write five sentences about them using *as . . . as*. Use adjectives, adverbs, and noun phrases as well as phrases such as *almost*, *not nearly*, and *not quite* in your sentences where possible.

Younsil does not have as many children as Victoria.
Younsil is not quite as shy as Victoria.

4 | Common Patterns That Show Contrast 🌐

▶ Vocabulary Presentation

Useful words and phrases that show contrast in academic writing include *difference(s)*, *differ*, *in contrast*, and *unlike*. These words are important in comparison and contrast writing.

One **major difference** *in some cultures is the role of adult children.*

In contrast to *the past, more U.S. children now live with their parents into their early adulthood.*

4.1 Difference(s), Differ, In Contrast, Unlike

a. A common pattern with the noun *difference* is:

NOUN PHRASE

The difference between _____

NOUN PHRASE

and _____ *is . . .*

One **significant difference between** *youngest children* **and** *their older siblings* **is** *that youngest children receive a lot of attention.*

b. A common pattern with the verb *differ* is:

NOUN PHRASE   NOUN PHRASE

_____ *differ(s) from* _____ *in that . . .*

The results of current research **differ from** *earlier results* **in that** *they show a definite relationship between birth order and personality.*

c. Common expressions and patterns used with the phrase *in contrast* are:

NOUN PHRASE   INDEPENDENT CLAUSE

In contrast to _____ , _____ .

INDEPENDENT CLAUSE

In contrast, _____ .

In contrast to *traditional American families, the Chinese have had several generations of one-child families.*

Many children without siblings receive a lot of attention. **In contrast**, *children with siblings often share their parents' attention.*

d. A common pattern with the adjective *unlike* is:

NOUN PHRASE   INDEPENDENT CLAUSE

Unlike _____ , _____ .

Unlike *firstborn children, youngest children are generally very creative.*

▶ Vocabulary Application

Exercise 4.1 Vocabulary That Shows Contrast

A Complete the following sentences about children in the United States using the words and phrases in the box.

differ from	~~major difference between~~	unlike
in contrast	significantly different from	

1. One *major difference between* children in the United States in 1900 and now is that children in the past didn't get a lot of individual attention from their parents, while children today get a lot of individual attention.

2. Another way that today's children are _____ _____ children in the past is that in the past, children often worked to help their families, but children now often work for their own extra spending money.

3. Today's children also _____ children in 1900 in that they are required to attend school.

4. Children in the past often had large families with several siblings. _____ , many children today have one or two siblings or are only children.

5. In 1900, children were very independent. _____ them, children today depend on their parents a lot.

B *Pair Work* With a partner, draw a chart like the one below. Write five contrasting pieces of information about children in the 1900s and now in a culture that you are familiar with. Then present your information to the class, using vocabulary from A.

Children in the 1900s	Children Now

One major difference between young children in my native country today and in the 1900s is that in the 1900s, they used to work in factories. Today that's illegal.

5 | Avoid Common Mistakes ⚠️

1. Do not use *who* with inanimate nouns.

that
A study ~~who~~ showed the benefits of being an only child was published last year.

2. Do not omit the relative pronoun in subject relative clauses.

who
Children ∧ have older siblings tend to be somewhat dependent.

3. Remember that the subject and the verb must agree in relative clauses.

have
Children who ~~has~~ siblings often become secure and confident adults.

4. Use *the same as*, not *the same than*.

as
Middle children often have the same level of creativity ~~than~~ youngest children.

Editing Task

Find and correct eight more mistakes in this body paragraph from an essay comparing
trends in families in the past and today.

Families Past and Present

that
    A major way that families have changed is the number of families ∧ have only one child.

The number of families had only one child was low in the United States in the 1950s and

1960s. However, one-child families began increasing in the 1970s and are very common

today. This is especially true in households who have only one parent. One reason families

5 are smaller is the cost of living. It is not the same than it was 40 years ago. For example, it

costs about 10 times more to send a child to college than it did 40 years ago. As a result, many

parents choose to have only one child because they do not have enough money for more

children. In addition, attitudes about only children are also

not the same than attitudes about them in the past. In the

10 1950s and 1960s, people avoided having only one child. At

that time, many people thought that children did not have

siblings had many disadvantages. For example, people

thought that they did not learn good social skills. However,

recent studies who focus on only children show a different

15 picture. These studies show that only children tend to have

the same social skills than children who has siblings.

6 | The Writing Process

In this section, you will write an outline and one body paragraph for a comparison and contrast essay using the block method. Before you start writing, you will learn how to write effective topic sentences.

About Topic Sentences

Topic sentences introduce the main idea of a body paragraph. In academic essays, they often appear at the beginning of body paragraphs. Although not all body paragraphs have topic sentences, it will help you to organize your writing if you always include one.

The following guidelines will help you write effective topic sentences:

1. An effective topic sentence should contain a claim or an opinion that needs to be supported with evidence. It should not be a fact that is widely accepted as true. Notice the difference in the following sentences:
   - Some families are small. (a fact)
   - Small families are better than large families. (a claim that needs to be supported with evidence)

2. The content of the topic sentences should relate back to the thesis statement of the essay.
   - Siblings have different personality traits because of birth order. (thesis statement)
   - Firstborn children are generally leaders. (topic sentence)

3. The topic sentence is usually a general statement. It rarely contains detailed information. The details will come in the rest of the paragraph in sentences that convince the reader that the claim in the topic sentence is valid or true.
   - Middle children can be more solitary. (general statement)
   - Middle children do not always get a lot of attention. (detail to support the topic sentence)

4. Include words and phrases that connect one body paragraph to another.
   - *Unlike* middle children, those born last are often more easygoing.
   - *In addition to* being more easygoing, the youngest are also . . .
   - *Another* common trait of the youngest child is . . .

Exercise

A *Pair Work* With a partner, critique the following topic sentences that support the thesis statement below. Discuss which are strong and which are weak according to the guidelines above.

Thesis statement: *Being brought up in a large family has several advantages and some disadvantages.*

1. One major disadvantage of growing up in a large family is that there is not much privacy.

2. When I was growing up, on the weekends my siblings and I would all go to the park and play soccer together.

3. While there are certainly several disadvantages to being part of a very large family, there are many advantages, too.

4. My next-door neighbor has six siblings.

5. In a study of children growing up in large families, it was found that in 86 percent of the cases, the eldest child had the highest I.Q.

B Read the following thesis statement, and then write topic sentences for the body paragraphs. Use the topic given in parentheses.

Thesis statement: *Being an only child has several benefits: developing independence, encouraging creativity, and creating friendships outside the family.*

1. Body paragraph 1 (independence): *Being an only child provides many opportunities to become independent.*

2. Body paragraph 2 (creativity): _____

3. Body paragraph 3 (friendships): _____

Pre-writing Tasks

Choose a Topic

A Choose one of the essay topics listed below. You will write one body paragraph for a comparison and contrast essay on this topic. This essay will follow the block method.

- The characteristics of large and small families
- Traditions in two different families
- A topic approved by your teacher

B *Pair Work* Share your topic with a partner. Describe the similarities and differences you will write about.

Organize Your Ideas

A For this assignment, you will use the block method of comparison and contrast for organizing your ideas.

Look at the block method outline for the essay on birth order below. Use the blank outline that follows to create an outline for your topic.

Title of Essay: Birth Order

Paragraph 1. Introductory paragraph. Thesis Statement: Experts agree that birth order tends to dictate some basic personality traits in children and adults.

Paragraph 2. Topic Sentence: Firstborn children often share several common traits.
• Traits: responsible, ambitious, authoritarian

Paragraph 3. Topic Sentence: Middle children exhibit unique characteristics.
• Traits: passive, solitary, realistic, creative, insightful

Paragraph 4. Topic Sentence: Youngest children have typical characteristics as well.
• Traits: dependent, controlling, creative, easygoing, social

---

Title of Essay: _____

Paragraph 1. Introductory paragraph. Thesis Statement: _____
_____

Paragraph 2. Topic Sentence: _____
_____

• Details: _____
_____

Paragraph 3. Topic Sentence: _____
_____

• Details: _____
_____

Paragraph 4. Topic Sentence: _____
_____

• Details: _____
_____

B *Pair Work* Share your outline with a partner and discuss your ideas.

Writing Task

Write one of the body paragraphs from your outline. Follow the steps below.

1. Make sure that you have a clear topic sentence that follows the guidelines in About Topic Sentences on page 76.

2. Include the following in your paragraph:
   - identifying relative clauses;
   - *as . . . as*;
   - common patterns that show contrast;
   - at least three of these academic words from the essay in this unit: *adulthood, assumed, author, benefit, creative, environment, exhibit, expert, indicate, individual, insightful, intelligent, maintain, passive, research, role, unique.*

3. After you write your paragraph, review it and make sure that you avoided the mistakes in the Avoid Common Mistakes chart on page 75.

> ### Academic Writing Tip
> **Improving Your Internet Searches**
> When you do an Internet search, use quotation marks around important ideas. For example, "large families" will eliminate results with only "large" or "family" alone.

Peer Review

A Exchange your outline and paragraph with a partner. Answer the following questions as you read your partner's outline and work, and share your responses.

1. Is the outline organized using the block method?

2. Does the topic sentence relate to the thesis statement?

3. Are any identifying relative clauses, *as . . . as*, or common patterns that show contrast used in the paragraph?

4. Is anything confusing? Write a question mark (?) next to it.

5. Provide one compliment (something you found interesting or unusual).

B Use your partner's comments to help you revise your paragraph. Use the Writer's Checklist on page A2 to review your paragraph for organization, grammar, and vocabulary.

Comparison and Contrast 2: Complex Noun Phrases; Parallel Structure; Common Quantifiers

Men, Women, and Equality

1 Grammar in the Real World 🌐

You will read an essay about how men and women are often treated differently in society. The essay is an example of one type of comparison and contrast writing, in which ideas are organized using the point-by-point method.

A *Before You Read* Do you think men and women are treated differently in today's society? Read the essay. According to the writer, what are some ways that men and women are treated differently?

Gender Inequality

Although progress has been made in recent decades, it would be wrong to think that men and women today are treated equally in the United States or in other industrialized nations. Historically, men in the United States have always had more financial, legal, and political power and more job opportunities than women. However, since the 1960s, there
5 has been a progressive increase in the number of women working outside the home, running their own businesses, and participating in political life. Nevertheless, despite women's increasing participation, gender inequality can still be found in the workplace as well as in cultural and social aspects of life.

Women and men are not always treated equally at work. The clearest sign of inequality
10 in the workplace is at the top levels of management. For example, the vast majority of major corporations have male CEOs (Chief Executive Officers), and most of the top positions are filled by men. Another sign of gender inequality is the different expectations employers have of men and women in leadership positions. According to Robinson (2011), men are expected to be assertive, confident, and decisive. When men take a dominant role,
15 they are often rewarded by their employers. Assertive women, on the other hand, are often not well received in the workplace because they are expected to be flexible, cooperative, and deferential.[1] There are also significant differences in salary. According to recent studies (e.g., Sasso, Richards, Chou, & Gerber, 2011), women still make less than men even when they do the exact same job. For example, in 2008, a beginning-level male physician
20 in New York received approximately $17,000 more a year than a beginning-level female physician (Sasso, et al., 2011).

[1]**deferential:** polite and showing respect

Gender differences are found in our cultural and social lives as well. Boys and girls are taught different gender roles and social expectations from birth. For example, in the United States many baby boys still receive blue clothes and blankets, while many girls receive
25 pink ones. Boys are often given cars, trucks, and toy soldiers as presents, while girls often receive dolls, dollhouses, and toy ovens. In terms of behavior, in many cultures people tend to expect boys to be aggressive and dominant, whereas they generally expect girls to be emotional and subordinate.[2] As children grow up and become adults, these behavior patterns are usually reinforced through social interactions.

30 Gender inequality has existed in the United States and other industrialized countries for many years, and it will not disappear overnight. Progress has been made recently regarding the opportunities for women. However, both men and women should continue to work for equality to create a fairer environment for everyone.

[2]**subordinate:** lower in position; following orders

B *Comprehension Check* Answer the questions.

1. According to the writer, what is gender inequality and where can it be found?
2. How does the writer say that women and men are treated differently in the workplace?
3. Give two examples of how boys and girls are treated differently in U.S. society.

C *Notice*

1 **Comparison and Contrast Writing** Complete the chart below with information from the two body paragraphs of the essay. The essay is organized using the point-by-point method, in which aspects of the first topic are presented, and then contrasting aspects of the second topic are presented, and so on.

Point-by-Point Method: Gender Inequality

Body Paragraph 1: Topic: _Women and men at work_
(1)

1. Top positions: _____ _Most of_ _____ the top positions are filled by _____ _men_ _____ .
(2)   (3)

2. Different expectations: Men are expected to be _____ , _____ ,
(4)   (4)

_____ vs. women are expected to be _____ ,
(4)   (5)

_____ , _____ .
(5)   (5)

3. Salary: Women make _____ than men.
(6)

Body Paragraph 2: Topic: _____
(7)

1. Boys and girls are taught different roles from birth: Boys receive _____ ,
(8)

_____ , _____ vs. girls receive _____ ,
(8)   (8)   (9)

_____ , _____ .
(9)   (9)

2. Different expectations: Boys are expected to be _____ , _____
(10)   (10)

vs. girls are expected to be _____ , _____ .
(11)   (11)

---

2 Grammar Follow the instructions below to find ways that the author uses parallel structure to contrast the differences in genders.

1. Find the sentence on lines 13–14 that states how men are expected to behave in the workplace. Then look on lines 15–17 for the sentence that describes how women are expected to behave. How many adjectives describe men's expected behavior? How many adjectives describe women's behavior? What other similarities do the two sentences have?

2. Find the sentence on lines 25–26 in which the author compares the types of toys that boys and girls receive as presents. How many toys are mentioned for boys and how many for girls?

3. Find the sentence in the third paragraph that contrasts how boys and girls are expected to behave. How many adjectives describe boys' expected behavior? How many adjectives describe girls'? What other similarities do the two clauses in the sentence have?

3 The Writing Process In a body paragraph, each main idea is developed by providing supporting information. Read the second paragraph again. Underline the topic sentence and write a number in the margin for each supporting detail that follows it.

2 | Complex Noun Phrases

▶ Grammar Presentation

Noun phrases include a noun and modifiers. Some modifiers, like adjectives, usually come before the noun, but there are other modifiers that can come after the noun. Complex noun phrases can have modifiers both before and after the noun. Complex noun phrases are common in academic writing because adding modifiers is an efficient way to present information.

Noun phrase modified with an adjective and a prepositional phrase:
The **sensitive** issue **of gender inequality** has been discussed for many decades.
Noun phrase modified with an adjective and an identifying relative clause:
Sometimes **professional** women **who start their own businesses** have trouble getting loans.

2.1 Modifiers After Nouns

a. Common modifiers after a noun are:	RELATIVE CLAUSE
relative clauses	New York has the most women **who own businesses**.
	PREP. PHRASE
prepositional phrases	The organization provides advice for women **in business**.

b. Some relative clauses can be shortened by dropping the relative pronoun and the *be* verb.	
-*ing* phrases	The number of women ~~who are~~ **starting their own businesses** is increasing.
-*ed* phrases	Women ~~who are~~ **elected to Congress** are in the minority.

2.2 Using Noun Phrases

a. In academic writing, complex noun phrases can often replace other parts of speech, such as verb phrases. This process makes it possible to pack information into a sentence more efficiently by reducing the number of clauses. Writers also use complex noun phrases to connect ideas between sentences.	VERB PHRASE *Recent research shows that there **are more mothers*** VERB PHRASE ***who are working**. (2 clauses)* NOUN PHRASE *Recent research shows **an increase in the number of working mothers**. (1 clause)* *The **salary** of men and women **differ significantly** for the same job. This **significant difference** in **salary** is one indication of persistent inequality.*
b. A complex noun phrase can often replace a verb (usually *be*) + adjective. The adjective from the verb phrase becomes part of the noun phrase. This makes it possible to include more information in one sentence.	VERB *BE* + ADJ. *The rise of women in business **has been impressive**. This indicates that traditional gender roles are being challenged.* NOUN PHRASE ***The impressive rise of** women in business indicates that traditional gender roles are being challenged.*
c. In comparison and contrast writing, noun modifiers are used to compare and contrast items in detail.	*The boy twin received a **blue blanket with white stripes**, while his twin sister received a **pink blanket with yellow stripes**.*

▶ Grammar Application

Exercise 2.1 Complex Noun Phrases

A Read the sentences about gender and careers. Underline the relative clauses. Circle the prepositional phrases that come after nouns.

1. A couple of decades ago, women <u>who were interested in studying engineering</u> were rare.

2. Today, there are more and more women in the field of engineering.

3. There didn't use to be many men who were attracted to the field of nursing.

4. Now the number of men who are working as nurses is growing.

5. Two fields that were once occupied only by men were law enforcement and firefighting.

6. These are two careers that are attracting many young women today.

7. Because of an increase in demand and services in data communications and home health-care aides, more men and women are choosing professions in these areas.

B *Pair Work* On a separate sheet of paper rewrite each sentence from A that contains a relative clause. Shorten the relative clauses to *-ed* and *-ing* phrases.

1. *A couple of decades ago, women interested in studying engineering were rare.*

Exercise 2.2 More Noun Phrases

Read each sentence or pair of sentences about women in the workplace. Next, write the words in bold as a noun phrase in the sentence that follows. Change the form of the words as necessary.

1. The number of women working outside the home has **increased significantly**.

   There has been a <u>*significant increase*</u> in the number of women working outside the home.

2. It has not been easy for women to **achieve progress** toward equality in the workplace.

   The _____ of _____ toward equality in the workplace has not been easy for women.

3. The **growing** number of women in management **is recent**. This indicates that gender differences are becoming less important.

   The _____ _____ in the number of women in management indicates that gender differences are becoming less important.

4. In many companies the **roles** of men are **dominant**. This is still evident, although it is changing.

   The _____ _____ of men in many companies is still evident, although it is changing.

5. The **struggle** for women in the workplace has been **long** and **difficult**. This has resulted in many more career opportunities in recent years.

   The _____ and _____ _____ for women in the workplace has resulted in many more career opportunities in recent years.

6. Women have **increasingly participated** in the workforce; nevertheless, gender inequality continues.

   Although there is an _____ in the _____ of women in the workforce, gender inequality continues.

7. Current research shows that the number of women going to medical school and law school is **rising steadily**. This is expected to continue.

   The _____ _____ in the number of women going to medical school and law school is expected to continue, according to current research.

8. **Women's enrollment** in college has been **higher** than men's since 2000. This is due in part to the fact that more men drop out.

   _____ _____ _____ in college since 2000 is due in part to the fact that more men drop out.

9. In a recent survey, men **perceive** career advancement more **optimistically** than women. This supports the fact that men hold the majority of middle management positions.

   Men's _____ _____ concerning career advancement supports the fact that men hold the majority of middle management positions.

3 | Parallel Structure

▶ Grammar Presentation

When each item in a list or comparison follows the same grammatical pattern, it is easier for readers to understand complex ideas. This is called *parallel structure*.

*In some cultures, men are expected to be **assertive**, **confident**, and **decisive**.*

*In some cultures, women **spend the day taking** care of the children, while **men spend the day working** outside the house.*

3.1 Parallel Structure

a. Parallel structure applies to series of:
 	
adjectives
 	
noun phrases
 	
verb phrases
 	
clauses
	ADJECTIVE ADJECTIVE ADJECTIVE
	*Boys are encouraged to be **aggressive**, **outgoing**, and **strong**.*
	Many Vietnamese believe that marriage should promote the
	    NOUN PHRASE NOUN PHRASE NOUN PHRASE
	*interests of **the community**, **the family**, and **the couple**.*
	                            VERB PHRASE
	*A Brazilian bride and groom **say their wedding vows**,*
	VERB PHRASE VERB PHRASE
	***kiss**, and **exchange rings**.*
	Many women struggle with cultural expectations
	               CLAUSE CLAUSE
	***when they pursue a career** or **when they decide not to marry**.*

b. Items in a series are often the same length. This makes the ideas easier to understand.	*Receptions for Brazilian weddings involve **delicious food**, **much laughter**, and **constant music**.* (The items listed are all about the same length – each noun is modified by one adjective.)
c. Writers often use parallel structure to compare and contrast items in a series.	*Years ago, men **worked** outside the home, while women **cleaned** the house, **did** the cooking, and **cared for** the children.*

► Grammar Application

Exercise 3.1 Parallel Structure

Choose the best answer to complete the sentences about gender differences below.

1. Men and women working together can reduce inequality slowly, carefully, and *significantly* .
   a. with significance   b. significantly   c. significant

2. Unlike the past, these days women are often encouraged to go to college, have careers,
   and _____ .
   a. invests in her future   b. investing in their future   c. invest in their future

3. Both men and women enjoy going to work, making money, and _____ .
   a. provides for their families   b. providing for their families   c. they provide for their families

4. Traditionally, men have often been encouraged to become competitive, aggressive,
   and _____ .
   a. unemotional   b. they are not emotional   c. they can't show their feelings

5. Companies that attract women tend to offer opportunities for advancement, flexible
   schedules, and _____ .
   a. they have mentors for them   b. mentors   c. women need mentors

6. Unlike women, men are much more likely to ask for raises, bonuses, and _____ .
   a. promote   b. promoting   c. promotions

Exercise 3.2 More Parallel Structure

A Write answers to the questions below about men, women, and careers, using parallel
structure. Use your own ideas or ideas that you have learned in this unit.

1. What are three things that women can do to decrease gender inequality in the
   workplace?

   Women can refuse to accept unfair treatment, make men more aware of
   their behavior, and continue to ask for what they want.

2. What are three skills that many people thought in the past were women's skills?

   _____

   _____

3. What are two professions that men typically did in the past that are now also done
   by women?

   _____

   _____

4. What are three careers that women have traditionally gone into?

   _____

   _____

5. What are two different ways that some women react to having a female boss?

_____

_____

6. What are two possible ways that women are different from men in relationships?

_____

_____

B Write answers to the questions about men, using parallel structure. Use your own ideas.

1. What are three things that men can do to decrease gender inequality in the workplace?

   Men can be more aware of their behavior, honest in their interactions, and accepting of women as their equals.

2. What are three skills that many people believe are more suited to men than women? Why do you think most people have this belief?

   _____

   _____

3. What are three professions that women did in the past that are now also done by men? What are your feelings about having men in these professions?

   _____

   _____

4. What are two professions that people still associate with men rather than women? What are possible reasons for this?

   _____

   _____

5. In your experience, what are two ways that some men react to having a female boss?

   _____

   _____

6. In your opinion, do men in their 20s and 30s have different perceptions of women in the workplace than men who are older? Why or why not? Give two reasons for your opinion.

   _____

   _____

C *Group Work* Share your ideas for each item in A and B in a group. Tell if you agree or disagree and why.

   A   *I say that women can refuse to accept unfair treatment, make men more aware of their behavior, and continue to ask for what they want. Those behaviors would decrease gender inequality.*

   B   *I don't agree with everything you say because first of all, I think that management must change and that change is difficult because it is like changing a culture's values and ideas.*

4 Common Quantifiers

▶ Vocabulary Presentation

Quantifiers indicate the amount or degree of something. They can help a writer be more precise and avoid overgeneralizations. They are common in comparison and contrast academic writing.

Many top positions are filled by men.
Few of the top executives are women.

4.1 Quantifiers

a. Quantifiers are used before nouns. Examples include: *all, almost all, both, few, most, no, several, some.*	*Most toys are gender-specific.* *Several women hold important positions in that company.*
b. Quantifiers also follow the pattern: quantifier + *of* +: *the / this / that / these / those / such* + noun phrase possessive pronoun (*my, your,* etc.) + noun phrase object pronoun (*it, them, us,* etc.) *Note*: Use *none* instead of *no* in this pattern.	*Many of the women in my country have two jobs.* *Most of my friends are aware of traditional gender roles.* *None of us supports inequality in the workplace.*
c. Use these quantifiers only before count nouns: *a few, a great many, both, few, many, several.*	*Only a few presidents of countries are women.* *Both boys and girls learn gender roles from an early age.*
Use these quantifiers only before noncount nouns: *a great deal of, a little, little, much.*	*The article contained a great deal of information about gender roles.* *We have achieved little progress in gender equality.*
d. Some quantifiers compare amounts: *fewer, less,* and *more.*	*Fewer men than women work as nurses.*
Adverbs such as *considerably, significantly, slightly,* and *substantially* are common before the comparative quantifiers.	*In the past, many men felt women could not succeed as executives. Significantly fewer men today believe that.* *In the 1970s, most lawyers were men. Today there are substantially more female lawyers.*
e. Use quantifiers to change overly general statements into qualified, more precise statements in comparison and contrast writing.	*Men are aggressive, and women are passive.* (Too general) *Some men are dominant and some women are passive.* (More accurate)

▶ Vocabulary Application

Exercise 4.1 Common Quantifiers

A The graph below shows the percentage of males and females across some of the major occupational groups in Canada. Write sentences by referring to the graph and using the cues in parentheses.

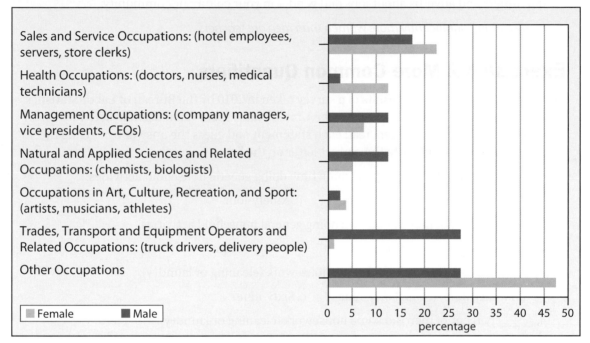

Source: Statistics Canada, Labour Force Survey. (www.statcan.gc.ca)

a great deal of	most of	a slightly higher number of
fewer	significantly fewer	substantially more

1. _A great deal of_ men are in the trades and transport areas.

2. _____ men are in management occupations than in sales and service occupations.

3. There are _____ men than women who are chemists and biologists.

4. _____ women have occupations such as artists, musicians, and athletes than those of truck drivers and delivery people.

5. _____ women than men have jobs in the trades, transport, and equipment operators sector.

6. _____ the women have jobs in occupations not listed in the chart.

B *Pair Work* Work with a partner. Create three sentences using the information in the chart in A. Use the words in the box in A and other quantifiers. Share them with another pair and give a possible explanation for the statement. Do they agree with the statements?

Significantly fewer men are in health occupations. I think this may be because there are usually more women in health-care occupations such as nursing.

C *Pair Work* Using your own knowledge and experience, write four sentences using quantifiers and adverbs about jobs and gender in your culture or community.

In my culture, significantly more women than men are teachers.

Exercise 4.2 More Common Quantifiers

A 🔊 You will listen to the results of a survey taken in 2010 by the Bureau of Labor Statistics on the time that men and women in the United States spent on household activities on an average day. Before you listen, read each statement and guess the answer by circling the letter. Then listen and write the correct letter on the line.

1. _____ percent of women spent some time doing general household activities.

   a. Seventy-four   (b.) Eighty-four   c. Ninety-four

2. _____ percent of men spent time doing general household activities.

   a. Twenty-seven   b. Forty-seven   c. Sixty-seven

3. _____ percent of women did some housework (cleaning or laundry).

   a. Twenty-nine   b. Forty-nine   c. Sixty-nine

4. _____ percent of men did some housework (cleaning or laundry).

   a. Five   b. Ten   c. Twenty

5. _____ percent of women prepared the food and cleaned up.

   a. Fifty-eight   b. Sixty-eight   c. Seventy-eight

6. _____ percent of men prepared food and cleaned up.

   a. Twenty-one   b. Thirty-one   c. Forty-one

Source: www.bls.gov

B Compare the statistics in A. Write statements using the quantifiers in parentheses.

1. (significantly fewer) *Significantly fewer men than women spent time doing housework.*

2. (substantially more) _____

   _____

3. (some) _____

   _____

4. (most) _____

_____

5. (both) _____

_____

C **Group Work** Interview your classmates about men's and women's roles at home. Ask questions such as *Who was mainly responsible for cooking when you were growing up – your mother, your father, or both?* Record the total number of responses on a separate sheet of paper. Write sentences using the results from your survey. Use quantifiers that reflect the results.

Many of my classmates stated that both their mothers and fathers were responsible for cooking when they were growing up.

5 | Avoid Common Mistakes ⚠

1. Remember to use parallel structure with two or more adjectives.

A study showed that elementary school teachers discriminated against children
      inattentive
who were noisy, active, and ~~if they did not pay attention~~.

2. Remember to use parallel structure with two or more noun phrases.

Wedding guests include the friends of the bride, the bride's co-workers, and the bride's family ~~is also invited~~.

3. Remember to use parallel structure with two or more verb phrases.

        to run
The girls loved to play basketball, to wrestle, and ~~running~~ races, just like the boys.

4. Remember to use parallel structure with two or more clauses.

These days most married women feel that they should continue working, have their own bank accounts, and ~~to~~ share household chores with their husbands.

Editing Task

Find and correct nine more mistakes in this body paragraph from an essay comparing women's roles in the past and in the present.

Women's Roles, Past and Present

Roles for women in the United States have changed in terms of the subjects that women
     the careers that they choose
study in college and ~~they choose careers~~. Before the 1970s, most middle-class men were

expected to attend college and pursuing careers that were both professional and they paid

well. Men provided the main financial support for the family. Middle-class women, however,

5　were expected to get married or, if they went to college, preparing for traditionally female

professions, such as teaching or to be a nurse. Women were not expected to support a family.

If a woman worked after college, she was expected to stop as soon as she got married or to

have children. Because they did not expect to support a family or working for a long time,

some women also studied non-career-oriented subjects such as literature or art history.

10　Nowadays, in contrast, most women plan to work for most of their adult lives and they help

support their families. Many women feel that they should prepare for a job, that they should

move forward in their careers, and to find satisfaction in their work. Therefore, today, there

are many more women studying career-oriented subjects such as business, accounting, and

to work in law enforcement. In fact, many fields that were once thought of as for men only,

15　such as law enforcement, now employ women. Although women still do not earn as much

as men, they have come a long way since the 1970s in expanding their college and career

opportunities.

6 | The Writing Process ✒

In this section, you will write an outline and one body paragraph for a comparison and contrast essay using the point-by-point method of organization. Before you start writing, you will learn how to write effective body paragraphs with different types of supporting details.

About Supporting Details

Topic sentences introduce the main idea of a body paragraph. In academic writing, each body paragraph must also include supporting details – often two or three details or examples that explain, or "support," the main idea of the paragraph. The following are four examples that show different ways to support the topic sentence that follows:

Topic sentence: *There have been dramatic shifts for women and girls in sports over the past four decades.*

1. **An example:** *There have been numerous professional sports leagues created for women, such as professional women's basketball and soccer leagues.*

2. **A definition:** *In the United States, Title IX refers to a major law passed in 1972 that prohibited discrimination against women and girls in school-based sports.*

3. **A historical fact:** *In 1972, the passage of Title IX required equal funding for girls' sports.*

4. **Statistical data:** *Prior to Title IX, the ratio of boys to girls participating in sports in schools was over 27 to 1; it is now almost equal.*

There are other ways to support a topic sentence, such as providing a description, making comparisons, or explaining causes and effects. As a writer, you must decide what types of details will best support the main ideas of your body paragraphs.

Exercise

A Match the parts of an essay on the right with the corresponding example of it on the left. Write the letter of the example on the line.

_____ 1. Thesis statement

_____ 2. Body paragraph 1: Topic sentence

_____ 3. A supporting detail for body paragraph 1

_____ 4. Body paragraph 2: Topic sentence

_____ 5. A supporting detail for body paragraph 2

_____ 6. Body paragraph 3: Topic sentence

_____ 7. A supporting detail for body paragraph 3

a. The first major shift has been the increase in the commercialization of sports.

b. Since the 1980s, professional basketball and soccer leagues for women have been formed, creating opportunities for women to earn money playing the sports that they love and excel at.

c. The seasons for many sports have gotten longer, and athletes often train all year with professional trainers.

d. Commercialization refers to the focus on selling the product and making a profit.

e. Over the past 50 years, sports in the United States have become more commercial, competitive, and gender-neutral.

f. Another big change has been the rise of women in sports.

g. As sports have become big businesses, athletes at all levels have trained and played with more intensity.

B Look at your answers in A for items 3, 5, and 7, and write the type of supporting detail for each one: _an example_, _a definition_, or _a historical fact_.

1. The supporting detail for item 3 is _____ .

2. The supporting detail for item 5 is _____ .

3. The supporting detail for item 7 is _____ .

Pre-writing Tasks

Choose a Topic

A Choose one of the essay topics below. You will write one body paragraph for a comparison and contrast essay on this topic. Your body paragraph will use the point-by-point method.

- One aspect of society (sports, business, family) in two different cultures
- One aspect of society (sports, business, family) 50 years ago and now
- A topic approved by your teacher

B _Pair Work_ Share your topic with a partner. Describe the points that you will compare and contrast. Give your partner suggestions about supporting points (comparisons, definitions, examples, facts, etc.) to include.

Organize Your Ideas

A Follow the steps below to develop and organize your ideas before you write.

1. In Unit 5, you outlined a comparison and contrast essay that used the block method. With that method, all the main points and details for one side of an issue are presented together in one "block," and the same main points for the second side of the issue are presented in a second "block."

2. Now outline an essay, using the point-by-point method in which both sides of the first point are presented, then both sides of the second point are presented, and so on. Use the outline in the left column below for an essay on gender inequality to help you complete a point-by-point outline for your topic in the right column.

Title: "Gender Inequality"	Title:
I. Introductory Paragraph **Thesis Statement:** Gender inequality and differences can still be found in the workplace as well as in cultural and social aspects of American life.	**I. Introductory Paragraph** **Thesis Statement:**
II. Body Paragraph 1 – Point 1: Gender role in the workplace **Supporting Details:** • Men's role in the workplace • Women's role in the workplace	**II. Body Paragraph 1** – Point 1: **Supporting Details:** • •
III. Body Paragraph 2 – Point 2: Gender role in the home **Supporting Details:** • Men's role in the home • Women's role in the home	**III. Body Paragraph 2** – Point 2: **Supporting Details:** • •
IV. Body Paragraph 3 – Point 3: Gender role in society **Supporting Details:** • Men's role in society • Women's role in society	**IV. Body Paragraph 3** – Point 3: **Supporting Details:** • •
V. Conclusion	**V. Conclusion**

B *Pair Work* Share your outline with a partner and discuss your ideas.

Writing Task

Write one of the body paragraphs from your outline. Follow the steps below.

1. Include a topic sentence and two or three supporting details about the specific point of comparison or contrast.

2. Include the following in your paragraph:
   - complex noun phrases;
   - sentences using parallel structure;
   - a variety of modifiers;
   - at least three of these academic words from the essay in this unit: *adult*, *approximately*, *aspect*, *cooperative*, *corporation*, *create*, *cultural*, *culture*, *decade*, *despite*, *dominant*, *environment*, *financial*, *flexible*, *gender*, *interaction*, *job*, *legal*, *major*, *majority*, *reinforce*, *role*, *significant*, *subordinate*.

3. After you write your paragraph, review it and make sure that you avoided the mistakes in the Avoid Common Mistakes chart on page 91.

> **Academic Writing Tip**
>
> **Avoid Using the Quantifiers *A Lot Of* and *Lots Of***
>
> The quantifiers *a lot of* and *lots of* are informal expressions. Use *many* or *a great deal of* instead.

Peer Review

A Exchange your outline and paragraph with a partner. Answer the following questions as you read your partner's outline and paragraph, and then share your responses.

1. Is the outline organized using the point-by-point method?

2. Do the supporting sentences adequately support the topic sentence?

3. Are there any noun phrases? Are the sentences with those noun phrases easy to understand? Explain.

4. Are there any sentences that use parallel structure? If not, make suggestions for places to include one or more.

5. Are quantifiers used to make comparisons between main ideas? Suggest other quantifiers if you feel the comparisons overgeneralize.

6. Is anything confusing? Write a question mark (?) next to it.

7. Provide one compliment (something you found interesting or unusual).

B Use your partner's comments to help you revise your paragraph. Use the Writer's Checklist on page A2 to review your paragraph for organization, grammar, and vocabulary.

Comparison and Contrast 3: Comparative and Superlative Adjectives and Adverbs; Articles; Common Expressions That Show Similarity

Family Values in Different Cultures

1 Grammar in the Real World 🌐

You will read an essay about cultural differences between Latino and U.S. families. The essay is an example of one kind of comparison and contrast writing in which the writer compares and contrasts aspects of two cultures.

A *Before You Read* What does the term *family* mean to you? Read the essay. What are some ways that the writer defines *family*?

What Family Means: An Intercultural Perspective

The definition of family differs from culture to culture. These differences become more apparent when families from diverse cultures live in the same area. For example, with the increasing number of Latinos in the United States, contrasts between Latino and U.S. families have become more noticeable. Differences between these two cultures include
5 how family is defined, how children view themselves within the family, and what happens when children reach young adulthood.

Traditionally, in U.S. culture, when people refer to their family, they usually mean their immediate family, that is, their parents and their children. Many of these families follow the basic principles of Dr. Benjamin Spock, a famous pediatrician[1] in the mid-1900s. He wrote
10 a popular book on raising children that changed the style of parenting from strict to more permissive. He believed that children should be free to set their own goals and choose their own career path. In Dr. Spock's view, as children get older they should become more independent ("Dr. Spock: Cultural Differences in Parenting," n.d., para. 4). After finishing high school, American teenagers who go to college often move out of their parents' homes
15 and live in a college dormitory or their own apartment. After college, many live on their own. Children who continue to live with their parents after high school or college might be asked to pay rent. In general, family takes on a smaller role as children enter adulthood.

In contrast, in many Latino cultures, when people refer to their family, they include extended family, such as aunts, uncles, cousins, and grandparents. Latino life centers on
20 family. In fact, the largest component of Latino life is usually the family. Each person in a family "has a moral responsibility to aid other members of the family experiencing financial problems, unemployment, poor health conditions, and other life issues" (Clutter & Nieto, n.d., para. 3). It is common for Latino families to encourage longer visits from relatives,

[1]**pediatrician:** a doctor who treats children

and they expect loyalty, sacrifice, and hard work from family members. Many Latino young
25 adults live with their parents until marriage, and in some cases even after marriage. This is
seen as more acceptable in Latino families than in most U.S. families.

Beliefs about family relationships and expectations differ among U.S. and Latino
cultures. Despite these differences, U.S. culture is similar to Latino culture in terms of
the importance of family. Understanding the cultural background of others is valuable for
30 people living in diverse communities, like in the United States. However, it is wise not to
stereotype cultures. Not all Latino families stick together. Similarly, not all U.S. parents
point to the door when their children turn 18. Cultural background plays a role in
our relationships with family members, but culture is rarely the sole defining element
for anyone.

B *Comprehension Check* Answer the questions.

1. How are the beliefs of Dr. Benjamin Spock related to the way many U.S. families raise
   their children?
2. Who might young Latino adults live with when they finish college? What about college
   graduates in the United States?
3. What does the writer mean when he or she says that "it is wise not to stereotype
   cultures"? Do you think the writer avoids stereotyping cultures in this essay? Explain.

C *Notice*

1 **Comparison and Contrast Writing** Draw a chart like the one below, and complete it with
information from the essay.

U.S. Families' Characteristics	Latino Families' Characteristics
family = parents and children (immediate)	family = parents, children, aunts, uncles, etc. (extended)

Think about where you found the information that you put in the chart. Did the writer
of the essay use the point-by-point method or the block method in his or her comparison
and contrast essay?

2 Grammar Answer the questions below to help you notice the use of comparative adjectives and other ways to describe differences and similarities.

1. Reread lines 12–13 in the second paragraph. What did Dr. Spock believe American children should become as they got older? Notice the two forms of the comparative. What determines which form is used?
2. What two things does the writer compare on lines 23–26?
3. Reread the last paragraph. How are U.S. and Latino cultures the same? Underline the words the writer uses to show similarity.

3 The Writing Process Read this summary of the second paragraph. Then decide if the statements following the summary are true (*T*) or false (*F*).

In the United States, families are defined as the nuclear family: parents and their children. Most families raise their children to be independent. The children often go away for college and live on their own. After college, they usually leave home and are responsible for supporting themselves.

1. _____ The summary is about the same length as the original paragraph.

2. _____ The writer of the summary has included the main ideas of the original paragraph.

3. _____ The writer has included his or her own opinion on the topic of the original paragraph.

4. _____ The writer has not added any new information on the topic of the original paragraph.

5. _____ The writer has not identified the source of his or her summary.

2 | Comparative and Superlative Adjectives and Adverbs

▶ Grammar Presentation

> Comparatives show how two things or ideas are different. Superlatives compare one thing or idea to others in a group. They are both important in comparison and contrast writing.
>
> *In general, Americans are **less relaxed** about time **than** Latinos.*
> *The **largest component** of Latino life is the family.*
> *In general, sports fans in Latin America follow soccer **more intensely than** baseball.*
> *Americans are among the groups who communicate / say things **the most directly**.*

2.1 Comparative Adjectives and Adverbs

a. Comparative adjectives are formed as follows: Add *-er* to one-syllable and some two-syllable adjectives: *easier, greater, older.* Add *more/less* before adjectives with two or more syllables: *more complex, less efficient.*	*Immigrants in the United States often have **larger** families **than** Americans.* *The concept of family is **easier** to define in some cultures **than** in others.* *The extended family is **more important** in Latino families **than** in some other cultures.* *The concept of family in the United States is **less rigid than** in other cultures.*
b. Comparative adverbs are formed as follows: Add *-er* to one-syllable adverbs: *harder, faster.* Add *more/less* before adverbs of two syllables or more: *more quickly, less carefully.*	*Children in the United States usually leave home **earlier than** children in Latino families.* *Some people talk **more quickly than** others.* *In general, the Japanese treat the elderly **more respectfully**.*
c. Do not use *less* with one-syllable words. Use *not as . . . as.*	*The Asian population is **not as** large **as** the Latino population in the United States.* NOT *The Asian population is ~~less large than~~ the Latino population in the United States.*
d. Use a subject pronoun + an auxiliary verb (*be, have,* or *do*) after *than* in formal academic writing. The auxiliary verb is optional. Use an object pronoun in informal writing and speaking.	FORMAL: *My family is more concerned about having dinner together **than I (am)**.* INFORMAL: *My family is more concerned about having dinner together **than me**.*

2.2 Superlative Adjectives and Adverbs

a. Superlative adjectives are formed as follows: Add *the + -est* to one-syllable and some two-syllable adjectives: *easiest, greatest, oldest.* Add *the most/the least* before adjectives with two or more syllables: *most common, least effective.*	*Latinos are currently one of **the largest** ethnic groups in the United States.* *Solidarity is **the most significant** value for people of my culture.*
b. Superlative adverbs are formed as follows: Add *the + -est* to one-syllable adverbs: *hardest, fastest.* Add *the most* before adverbs of two or more syllables: *the most quickly, the most significantly.*	*Researchers often debate about which groups work **the hardest**.* *The Latino population in the United States has increased **the most significantly** of all groups in the country.*

2.3 Using Comparatives

There are two common uses of comparatives: Explicit: Both elements to be compared are included in the sentence.	COMPARED ITEM 1 *Independence is **more valued** in the United States than* COMPARED ITEM 2 *in other cultures.* COMPARED ITEM 1 COMPARED ITEM 2 *My sister and I are close, but my brother and I are **closer**.*
Implicit: The comparison is with something already mentioned in the text, or with something outside the text but known to the reader. As a result, it is not necessary to repeat *"than* + the second element" after the verb.	*If people in the United States knew more about other cultures, they perhaps would be **more understanding** (than they are).*

Data from the Real World

In academic writing, comparatives with *-er* are more common than superlatives with *-est*. Writers tend to avoid making strong claims. Common adjectives include:

best, better, earlier, easier, greater, greatest, higher, highest, larger, largest, lower, older, smaller, wider

*The number of immigrants is **higher** in the United States than in Canada.*

▶ Grammar Application

Exercise 2.1 Comparative Adjectives and Adverbs

A Read each sentence or pair of sentences about North Americans. Then complete the second sentence that is a restatement of the information. Use the comparative form of the adjective or adverb in parentheses. Include *than* when necessary.

1. North American children are very assertive, compared to children from some other cultures.

   North American children are _ *more assertive than* _ (assertive) children from some other cultures.

2. North American parents often allow their teenage children to work while they are in school. Parents from some other cultures want their children to focus only on education until they are out of school.

   Parents from other cultures are much _____ (likely) North American parents to allow their children to work while they are in school.

3. North American children are often permitted to stay out late on weekends. Parents from some other cultures do not allow their children to stay out late.

   North American parents behave _____ (strictly) parents from some other cultures.

4. Children in North American families speak informally to their elders. Children in most Asian families speak politely to their elders.

Children in most Asian families speak _____ (politely) to their elders.

5. In the United States, elderly parents don't often live with their grown children like they do in other countries.

While in many countries elderly parents often live with their grown children, this is much _____ (common) in the United States.

6. In many cultures, grandparents help to raise their grandchildren. This is not normally the case in the United States.

When it comes to their grandchildren's upbringing, grandparents from other countries are often _____ (involved) grandparents in the United States are.

7. In North American culture, the concept of family usually means parents and their children. In other cultures, *family* can mean parents, their children, the children's grandparents, and sometimes aunts, uncles, and cousins.

In North American culture, the concept of family is _____ (complex) in other cultures.

B *Pair Work* Work with a partner. Compare each statement in A to another culture that you are familiar with. Use words from the Data from the Real World chart as necessary. When you are finished, report your ideas to the class.

I would say that Japanese children are less assertive than children from the United States because in Japanese culture it is more desirable to be part of a group.

Exercise 2.2 Superlative Adjectives and Adverbs

Complete the sentences with your ideas about cultural behaviors. Use the superlative forms of the adjectives and adverbs in parentheses.

1. One of _the biggest_ (big) differences between my culture and _North American_ culture is _the way children speak to their parents_ .

2. I think _____ (important) thing to know about my culture is

_____ .

3. The _____ (strange) thing I ever learned about a different

   culture is _____ .

4. I think _____ (difficult) thing to understand about

   _____ culture is _____ .

5. The _____ (significantly) different thing between my culture and

   _____ culture is _____ .

6. The person in my family who works _____ (hard) is

   _____ .

7. The person in my family who behaves _____ (patiently) is

   _____ .

Exercise 2.3 Comparative and Superlative Adjectives and Adverbs

A 🔊 Listen to the lecture about ways that cultures differ. As you listen, check (✓) the correct columns in the chart.

	High-Context	Low-Context	Collectivist	Individualist
1. Communication is direct.		✓		
2. Communication is indirect.				
3. Tone of voice, gestures, and status are important.				
4. The United States and European countries are examples of this type.				
5. Japan and South Korea are examples of this type.				
6. Africa, Latin America, and Asia are examples of this type.				
7. The group is valued.				
8. Family ties are strong.				
9. Merit and expertise are important.				
10. A person's goals are important.				

B Complete the sentences about cultural behaviors with comparatives or superlatives. Use the information from the chart in A and the adjective or adverb form of the words in parentheses. Include *than* when necessary.

1. There are a lot of important things to consider when working with people of different cultures. However, one of _the most important_ (important) topics to learn about is communication style.

2. In high-context cultures like South Korea and Japan, the communication style is _____ (direct) that of people in low-context cultures.

3. In low-context cultures like the United States and England, people communicate _____ (direct).

4. For people in high-context cultures, words are not the only tool of communication. In low-context cultures, words are _____ (essential) thing.

5. Facial expressions, gestures, and tone of voice are often _____ (important) in low-context cultures.

6. Degree of individualism is one of _____ (big) issues to consider when observing cultural differences.

7. In collectivist cultures, the group is valued _____ (high) it is in individualistic cultures.

8. In individualistic cultures, an individual's goals are _____ (valued) a group's goals.

9. Collectivist cultures consider a person's merit or expertise _____ (important) family ties.

10. Communicating effectively with people from other cultures can be difficult. That's why _____ (critical) important thing to do is to learn about cultural differences beforehand.

3 | Articles

▶ Grammar Presentation

> Articles (*a/an, the*) or no article Ø precede nouns. Articles help writers distinguish between general and specific statements and shared knowledge. This is important in academic writing, including in comparison and contrast writing.
>
> *In Latin America, Ø families include **a** mother, **a** father, Ø sisters, Ø brothers, Ø aunts, Ø uncles, and Ø cousins.*
>
> *I have not met **the** family that lives across **the** street from my house.*

3.1 Using the Definite Article

a. Use *the* when both the writer and the reader share common knowledge or information about the noun.	*In American families, it is common for **the** wife and **the** husband to share household duties.* (The writer assumes the reader shares the knowledge that there is usually one wife and one husband in a family.)
b. Use *the* when the noun was introduced earlier in the text and you give more information, or when the noun is related to a noun mentioned earlier.	*Each person in a <u>family</u> has a moral responsibility to aid other members of **the** <u>family</u> experiencing financial problems.*
c. Use *the* when you are writing about "which one" (when there is additional information that identifies the specific noun).	*Mexico is **the** country that is located south of the United States.*
d. Use *the* with superlatives.	***The** <u>strictest</u> family I ever met was from the United States.*
e. Use *the* for: abbreviations (but usually not for acronyms) groups adjectives that refer to a category when there is only one	***the** CIA, **the** UN, **the** FBI Ø NASA, Ø NATO **the** media, **the** military **the** rich, **the** elderly **the** president, **the** queen, **the** United States, **the** Alps, **the** moon, **the** equator*

3.2 Using the Indefinite Article

a. Use *a/an* with a singular count noun when the noun is not specifically identified, or when it is first mentioned and new to the reader.	*A young Latino man is the new student in class.* (The man is not specifically identified.) *The class read **an** article about cultural values.* (The reader does not know this article.)
b. Do not use *a/an* with noncount or plural nouns. Use *some* or Ø.	*My cousin borrowed **some money** from me, but he has not paid me back yet.* *Ø Large **families** can be enjoyable but complicated.*
c. Use *a/an* when introducing a count noun.	*A young Latina woman is the new student in my class. I found out that she is from Colombia.*

3.3 Using Articles in Discourse

a. In academic writing, paragraphs and essays often begin with generalizations. Use the indefinite article when making generalizations: Ø for noncount nouns and plural nouns *a/an* for singular nouns	*"Ø Advertising is about Ø norms and Ø values, Ø aspirations and Ø prejudices."* –Anil Ambani *In some cultures, **a** teenager is expected to move out of their parents' home and live in **a** college dormitory.*
b. Use the definite article if it refers to a specific noun that is known to the reader. The reference may be: direct clear from context	*Teens leave their parents' homes to live in a dormitory.* ***The** parents are often sad to see their children leave.* (*Parents* were already mentioned.) *Although **the** rooms are often very small, most teenagers do not seem to mind.* (Readers know that dormitories have rooms.)

▶ Grammar Application

Exercise 3.1 Indefinite and Definite Articles

A Read the article about how relationships are affected by the mobility of American society. Choose the best article (*a/an*, *the*, or Ø) for each item. Sometimes more than one answer is possible.

Mobility in the United States

The United States is a very mobile society. People frequently do not live in the same town

for their entire lives. Often ____Ø____ large corporations require their employees to move

(1)

if they want to advance in _____ company. Students typically do not go to _____

(2)   (3)

college near their families. As a result, it is not uncommon

for _____ extended families to be separated by
     (4)

hundreds, if not thousands, of miles.

This mobility is probably one of _____ most
                                   (5)

significant factors influencing _____ relationships
                                    (6)

in the United States. For example, people tend to be very

friendly on a casual basis and open to meeting many new

individuals, but these interactions do not always result in

_____ close, lasting relationships. There is _____
   (7)   (8)

common tendency of people in _____ United States
                                 (9)

to say things like, "Let's get together sometime," or "Let's

have lunch," and then not follow through with _____
                                                 (10)

invitation.

People who are not from _____ United States
                            (11)

sometimes see this informal style as superficial, and it can

be confusing. If someone says, "Let's get together," _____ visitor to the United States
                                                        (12)

might expect the person to make _____ call and suggest _____ meeting time and
                                    (13)   (14)

place. This doesn't always happen. However, _____ visitor who has this experience
                                                (15)

shouldn't be offended because _____ expression "Let's get together" has almost
                                  (16)

_____ same meaning as "hello" to many Americans.
   (17)

B *Group Work* Take turns explaining why you chose each answer in A.

*I chose no article for item 1 because corporations is plural and here the writer is referring
to all large corporations, not specific large corporations.*

Exercise 3.2 More Indefinite and Definite Articles

A Write sentences about cultural differences with the cues in parentheses. Use your own
ideas. Use the correct articles.

1. (a definition of *family*) *A family can consist of parents and children, or it can
   consist of parents, children, grandparents, and others.*

2. (a definition of *values*) _____

   _____

3. (a generalization about cultural differences – what they are) _____

   _____

4. (a description of one cultural difference concerning time, family, relationships, etc.)

_____

_____

5. (a detail about your difference in item 4) _____

_____

6. (a statement about a cultural difference that you think is more confusing than any other)

_____

_____

7. (a generalization about groups and individuals in your culture) _____

_____

B *Pair Work* Talk with a partner about your sentences in A. Which sentences are
generalizations? Which contain specific nouns? Share your sentences with another pair.
Ask the other pair to identify the reason why each article or no article is appropriate.

*You used "a family" in this sentence because here you are using a singular count noun to
make a generalization.*

4 Common Expressions That Show Similarity 🌐

▶ Vocabulary Presentation

Some words and phrases are commonly used to show similarity in comparison and
contrast writing.

*There are many **similarities** between Turkish and Brazilian cultures.*

*Japanese and South Koreans **have something in common**: they tend to avoid directly
looking into someone's eyes while speaking.*

4.1 *Similar to, Similarities, Similarly, Likewise, Like*

a. Use *be similar to* to compare two noun phrases.	*Mexican culture **is similar to** Spanish culture in many ways.*
b. Use *the similarities between _____ and _____ to* compare two noun phrases.	*Many people believe that **the similarities between** the United States **and** Canada outweigh the differences.*
c. Use *similarly* and *likewise* as transition words to connect sentences with shared features. Use a comma after the words.	*In Nigeria, social recognition is achieved through extended families. **Similarly,** a family's honor is influenced by the action of its members.* *Chinese children enjoy playing video games. **Likewise,** American children find this an enjoyable activity.*

d. Use _____ *and* _____ *have* + *something/ one thing/a lot* + *in common* to introduce shared features of two nouns.	*Germany **and** Spain **have something in common**: their people love coffee.*
e. Use *Like* _____, before a clause to show how a noun is similar in one way to the subject of the clause.	***Like** bedtime stories in the United States, the stories that Chinese parents tell their children send a strong message about values.*

▶ Vocabulary Application

Exercise 4.1 Words That Show Similarity

A Complete the sentences about culture and online media with the appropriate word or expression from the box. Use each word or expression only once.

in common	like	similarities between
is similar to	~~likewise~~	similarly

1. A person who does business with people from different cultures should be aware of how cultures differ in communication styles. _Likewise_ , website designers should be aware of how people from different cultures will respond to their designs.

2. People from different cultures communicate in different ways, but most have one important thing _____ . People in most cultures use the Internet on a daily basis.

3. Years ago, there were many _____ paper-based media and online media. Both included simple text and images that people read from top to bottom. Now, however, online media is much more interactive.

4. _____ a person engaging in face-to-face communication, a website designer must take into account another person's expectations and assumptions. Some users may expect direct communication, while others may want more indirect messages.

5. In terms of cultural expectations, face-to-face interaction _____ Internet interaction. Some cultures may expect a website to communicate information directly with headlines and clear text. Others may respond better to less text and more images.

6. In some cultures, the relationship between speakers is important in face-to-face communication. _____ some Internet users may respond better to websites that have animation or interactivity that imitates human interaction.

B *Pair Work* With a partner, think of other ways that face-to-face communication and online communication are similar. On a separate sheet of paper, write five sentences using the expressions in A. Next, trade papers with another pair. Read their sentences. Share examples that illustrate their ideas.

5 | Avoid Common Mistakes ⚠

1. **Remember to use *more* or *-er* in comparisons. Do not use both.**
   Middle Eastern families tend to be ~~more~~ closer than American families.

2. **Remember to use *best*, not *most*, before nouns.**
   In the 1960s, the ~~most~~-selling child-rearing book in the U.S. was Raising an Independent Child. *(best written above)*

3. **Do not use the definite article *the* with title/position + name.**
   ~~The~~ Dr. Benjamin Spock wrote Baby and Child Care in 1946.

4. **Remember to use *the* in the expression *the same* as.**
   Child-rearing beliefs in one culture are rarely ˄ same as child-rearing beliefs in another culture. *(the inserted at ˄)*

Editing Task

Find and correct eight more mistakes in the body paragraphs from an essay comparing the celebration of the new year in different cultures.

The celebration of the New Year in South Korea is not ˄ same as in the United States. First *(the inserted at ˄)* of all, South Koreans celebrate the Lunar New Year (the second new moon in winter), so the date is not same as in the United States, where the New Year is celebrated on the first day of the Gregorian Calendar (January 1). The New Year is more later in South Korea, usually in February.

5 In addition, the South Korean New Year celebration lasts for three days and involves the entire family. According to the Dr. Sook-Bin Woo, this is because South Korean families tend to be more closer than U.S. families. For example, South Korean families play special games with each other during this holiday. This family closeness may be the reason that many South Koreans report that their most childhood memories are of New Year's celebrations.

10 In the United States, the celebration of the New Year begins on the evening of the last day of the year and continues into the following day; it is therefore more shorter than the South Korean celebration. Traditionally, it tends to be primarily an adult celebration for many people. On New Year's Eve, many adults hire a babysitter for their children and go out to a restaurant or to a party to celebrate with other adults. Because U.S. celebrations often do not

15 include children, most Americans are unlikely to say that their most childhood memories are of the celebration of the New Year. Sociologist the Dr. George Lee notes that this tradition is changing in the United States as more adults stay home and celebrate with their children.

6 | The Writing Process

In this section, you will write a comparison and contrast essay using either the point-by-point or the block method. You will use information from outside sources to make your essay stronger. Before you start writing, you will learn about summarizing.

About Summarizing

When academic writers support their ideas, they often include information and ideas by experts to sound convincing. They will not want to include everything that was written or said, so they summarize the information. The following is a summary of the essay "What Family Means: An Intercultural Perspective" on pages 96–97 of this unit with guidelines for summarizing appropriately and effectively.

1. Identify the source of the information. Use reporting verbs.

2. Include all the main ideas from the text. The main ideas are in **bold**.

3. Omit less important ideas and specific details that are not really necessary.

4. Use paraphrasing strategies. For original text, see the essay on pages 96–97.

5. Do not include your own ideas when summarizing.

6. Do not add any new information that is not in the text.

> In the text "What Family Means: An Intercultural Perspective," Smith (2012) **points out** that the United States and many Latino cultures have different concepts of family. First, **the definition of family is different.** In the United States, *immediate family* refers to parents and
> 5 children, while in many Latino cultures, *immediate family* includes grandparents, uncles, aunts, and cousins. **Family expectations are also different in the two cultures.** In Latino cultures, most children are expected to live with their parents until they get married. ~~I believe this can bring many problems to the family dynamic.~~ They are also expected
> 10 to take care of their family members when they are sick or when they need help. In contrast, in the United States, children are raised to be more independent. After high school, most teenagers are expected to get a job and support themselves. ~~Once a person has graduated, they might be expected to pay rent if they live at home.~~ The concept of extended
> 15 family does not play as big of a role in the United States as it does in Latino cultures. ~~Also, in Latino cultures, people tend to get married at a much younger age than in the United States.~~ Even though it is beneficial to understand cultural differences and expectations, it is important to bear in mind that culture is only one factor in determining the dynamics
> 20 of a family.

Exercise

A Interview someone about the differences between two cultures that he or she is familiar with. Use the following categories about culture to help you think of questions to ask:

- **Physical aspects** – what people eat, what they wear, what sort of transportation they use, and so forth
- **Customs** – marriage, dating, etc.
- **Celebrations** – holidays, social events
- **Education** – what age children begin school, how formal or informal classes are

B Write a summary of the interview, using the summarizing guidelines listed above.

Pre-writing Tasks

Choose a Topic

A Choose one of the topics below or the topic of your interview in the previous section. You will write a comparison and contrast essay using either the block method or the point-by-point method of writing.

- Wedding customs of two cultures
- Coming-of-age celebrations / rituals in two cultures

B *Pair Work* Share your topic with a partner. Discuss whether the block method or the point-by-point method would be most suitable for your topic.

Organize Your Ideas

A Complete the chart below with the two or three aspects you are going to write about. Include a brief summary on each aspect from a source (either the interview conducted earlier or an additional source). Indicate the source.

	Topic 1: Culture A _____	**Topic 1: Culture B** _____
Aspect 1	Summary: Source:	Summary: Source:
Aspect 2	Summary: Source:	Summary: Source:
Aspect 3	Summary: Source:	Summary: Source:

B Create an outline using either the block or the point-by-point method. See pages 78 and 94 for sample outlines of each method.

Writing Task

Write your comparison and contrast essay. Follow the steps below.

1. Use your chart and outline to decide how many aspects of comparison and contrast to include.

2. Make sure if you use the block method of organization that each paragraph presents all of the points from one side of an issue. If you are going to use the point-by-point method, be sure to include information from both sides for each point in a paragraph.

> ### Academic Writing Tip
>
> **Make Personal Stories More Academic**
> In academic writing, personal examples may sometimes be considered too informal. Instead, make the comments more general. Instead of "My family is large" say "Families in the Dominican Republic are generally large."

3. Plan your thesis statement, making sure that it gives the reader a preview of what you will be comparing.

4. Include the following in your essay:

   • comparatives and superlatives;

   • common expressions of similarity;

   • summaries of information and ideas from either written or spoken text;

   • acknowledgment of the sources of the summaries;

   • at least three of the academic words from the essay in this unit: *adult, adulthood, aid, apparent, area, component, contrast, cultural, culture, define, definition, diverse, element, financial, goal, issue, principle, role, sole, style, traditionally.*

5. After you write your essay, review it and make sure you avoided the mistakes in the Avoid Common Mistakes chart on page 109.

Peer Review

A Exchange your essay with a partner. Answer the following questions as you read your partner's essay, and then share your responses.

1. What is the thesis statement? Underline it.

2. Does the essay use the point-by-point or the block method?

3. Does the writer use any comparative or superlative adjectives?

4. Circle any expressions of similarity that the writer uses.

5. Has the writer included any summaries of information in the essay and cited the sources for them?

6. Is anything confusing? Write a question mark (?) next to it.

7. Provide one compliment (something you found interesting or unusual).

B Use your partner's comments to help you revise your essay. Use the Writer's Checklist on page A2 to review your essay for organization, grammar, and vocabulary.

Comparison and Contrast 4: Adverb Clauses of Contrast and Concession; Transition Words and Phrases That Show Contrast and Concession

Intercultural Communication

1 Grammar in the Real World

You will read an essay about misunderstandings that can happen when people from different cultures attend business meetings together. The essay is an example of one kind of comparison and contrast writing.

A *Before You Read* What are two cultural differences that might cause misunderstandings when people from different cultures attend business meetings together? Read the essay. What are some assumptions that may cause misunderstandings?

International Business Etiquette

Large companies want to remain competitive in today's global markets. To reach their goals, they are often required to take their businesses beyond the boundaries of their home countries. Consequently, they need to interact with individuals from other cultures. Cross-cultural business transactions can be challenging since the rules about what is
5 considered appropriate and acceptable and what might be seen as rude vary across cultures. Some aspects of culture are likely to cause misunderstandings in multicultural business situations.

One aspect of culture that may be problematic during business interactions is the perception of time. People from cultures such as the United States or Germany commonly
10 pay close attention to schedules and meeting agendas. In those cultures, it is impolite if someone habitually arrives late to meetings. In contrast, in cultures such as Mexico and Brazil, people tend to see schedules simply as guidelines. They often see deadlines as being more flexible. A Brazilian businessperson, for example, might find it strange that a U.S. business meeting has an ending time that is nonnegotiable. In Brazil, the length of a
15 meeting is generally dictated by the needs of its participants, while in the United States, a predefined length is often the norm.

The amount of emotion expressed during business interactions can be the cause of other potential cross-cultural problems. This can differ significantly from culture to culture. In some cultures, such as in parts of Italy, people express feelings more openly and argue

20 more passionately about their points of view. For this reason, they may readily show emotion during critical parts of a negotiation, whereas this practice can come across as unprofessional in more emotionally neutral cultures, such as in Sweden. People in these cultures are generally more careful in controlling the feelings they display.

Understanding local customs can also be problematic for businesspeople. Some

25 customs may seem inappropriate in some countries even though they are perfectly acceptable in others. For example, exchanging gifts between the parties involved in a business deal is a common practice in many parts of the world. However, this practice could be seen as inappropriate in other places, such as the United States or Britain. In those cultures, it could even be interpreted as being unethical since gift-giving may be

30 seen as improperly influencing the outcome of the negotiation.

Doing business with people from different cultures can be challenging. When someone is conducting business abroad, it is important not to assume that what is considered polite in one culture is universal. Instead, it is essential to understand and respect other traditions and business practices. Being aware of those differences can give business professionals a

35 competitive edge when conducting business abroad. It might make the difference between a deal's success or failure.

B *Comprehension Check* Answer the questions.

1. According to the essay, what are three main problems that businesspeople might have when they do business with individuals from different cultures?
2. Why do some cultures perceive the exchange of gifts as inappropriate in a business transaction?
3. According to what you have read in this essay, who would businesspeople from your culture possibly have misunderstandings with: Americans, Germans, Brazilians, Italians, Swedes, or the British? Explain.

C *Notice*

1 Comparison and Contrast Writing Complete the following outline of the body paragraphs of the essay on a separate sheet of paper. Then discuss with a partner whether the essay follows the point-by-point or block method.

Body Paragraph 1: Time in different cultures

1. _____

2. Mexico and Brazil – schedules and agendas not so important

Body Paragraph 2: _____

1. Parts of Italy – express feelings more openly

2. _____

Body Paragraph 3: Local customs can be problematic

1. Gift-giving – common practice in many business cultures

2. _____

---

2 Grammar Answer the questions below to help you notice sentences in which two things are contrasted.

1. In the second paragraph, find the words *in contrast* and the word *while* that both signal a contrast. Which one can only come at the beginning of a sentence? Which one is followed by a comma?
2. Find a word on line 21 that signals a contrast. Is it similar to *in contrast* or *while*?
3. Compare the use of the words *even though* and *however* in the fourth paragraph. Which word is similar to *while*? Which one is similar to *in contrast*?
4. *Even though* on line 25 signals concession. This means that the information that follows is not only different from the preceding information, but is also unexpected. Explain why *even though* is more appropriate than *while* in this case.

3 The Writing Process Reread the conclusion (the last paragraph) of the essay. Which of the following describes what the writer does in the conclusion? Check (✓) all that apply.

_____ 1. Links back to the hook in the first paragraph

_____ 2. Summarizes the main ideas of the essay

_____ 3. Challenges the reader by asking a provocative question or questions

_____ 4. Gives a warning, a call for action, or a recommendation for the future

_____ 5. Gives a thought-provoking quotation

2 | Adverb Clauses of Contrast and Concession

▶ Grammar Presentation

Adverb clauses can show many different relationships. Adverb clauses of contrast and concession are common grammatical constructions in academic writing and are especially useful in comparison and contrast writing.

In some cultures punctuality is important, **while in other cultures**, *people arrive at events quite late.*
Even though most companies train their executives, *cross-cultural problems still arise.*

2.1 Adverb Clauses of Contrast

a. Adverb clauses of contrast are used mainly to contrast two things or ideas.	*The official language of Brazil is Portuguese,* **while** *in Colombia it is Spanish.*
b. Adverb clauses of contrast are introduced by the subordinators *while* and *whereas*. 🌐 *While* is much more common than *whereas*. *Whereas* appears in academic writing, but it is rare in spoken English.	*In Mexico, the length of a meeting varies according to the needs of its participants,* **while** *in the United States, the time is generally set and unchanging.* *Women in the United States work an average of 41 hours per week,* **whereas** *women in Europe work about 30 hours per week.*

2.1 Adverb Clauses of Contrast (continued)

c. An adverb clause of contrast can come before or after the main clause. If it comes first, it is followed by a comma. However, it is more common for an adverb clause of contrast to appear second. Unlike other adverb clauses, a comma can come before an adverb clause of contrast when it appears second to emphasize contrast.	*While some countries are open to immigration, other countries have strict policies against it.* *Some customs may be perceived as inappropriate in some countries, **whereas** they are perfectly acceptable in others.*

2.2 Adverb Clauses of Concession

a. Adverb clauses of concession express a special kind of contrast. They show that the idea in the main clause is surprising or unexpected.	ADVERB CLAUSE OF CONCESSION ***Although** businesspeople are careful about cultural differences,* UNEXPECTED INFORMATION *misunderstandings sometimes occur during business transactions.*
b. Adverb clauses of concession are introduced by subordinators: *although*, *even though*, *though*, and *while*. A comma can precede an adverb clause of concession to emphasize the contrast. *Note: While* can express general contrast as well as concession.	***Even though** face-to-face communication is preferred, sometimes business has to be conducted virtually.* ***The company is doing more business with South America, though / while** in the past, it conducted business more frequently with Europe.*

▶ Grammar Application

Exercise 2.1 Adverb Clauses of Contrast

A ◀)) Listen to an interview about possible differences between North American (U.S. and Canadian) and Mexican businessmen. Check (✓) the correct column for each opinion expressed by Dr. Julio Sanchez.

	Most North Americans	Most Mexicans
1. They are strict about time.	✓	
2. They often arrive up to 30 minutes late for business meetings.		
3. It's polite to arrive on time to a dinner party.		
4. They share personal information in business meetings.		
5. They call each other by their first names as soon as they meet.		
6. They have a direct communication style.		
7. They may not tell you immediately when they can't attend an event.		

B Use the information from the chart in A and the interview to write sentences using *while* or *whereas*. Sometimes more than one answer is possible.

1. While _most Mexicans are flexible about time, people from the United States are very strict._

2. Whereas _____

   _____

3. _____, whereas

   _____

4. _____, while

   _____

5. While _____

   _____

6. _____, while _____

7. Whereas _____

   _____

C *Pair Work* Discuss with a partner your opinions of different behaviors of two cultures that you are familiar with. Write sentences that contrast these behaviors using adverb clauses of contrast, and then report your ideas to the class.

A *In Brazil, people are flexible about time.*

B *In my opinion, it's different in India. There, it's very important to be on time to meetings.*

People are flexible about time in Brazil, while it's very important to be on time in India.

Exercise 2.2 Adverb Clauses of Concession

A Combine each pair of sentences about Chinese business culture using the subordinator in parentheses to show relationships of concession. Sometimes more than one answer is possible.

1. a. It is not appropriate to treat a Chinese business colleague informally.
   b. Doing business in China often involves informal social gatherings where business is not discussed.

   (even though) _It is not appropriate to treat a Chinese business colleague informally even though doing business in China often involves social gatherings where business is not discussed._

2. a. Rank is very important.
   b. Gender bias is not common.

   (though) _____

   _____

3. a. This lack of gesturing does not mean a lack of responsiveness.
   b. The Chinese do not gesture or show much body language.

   (while) _____

   _____

4. a. It is important to send written information about your company well before your arrival in China.
   b. Chinese businesspeople like to meet face-to-face rather than over the phone or by e-mail.

   (although) _____

   _____

5. a. Chinese business meetings are very formal affairs.
   b. The meetings may frequently be interrupted by the ringing of cell phones.

   (even though) _____

   _____

6. a. Chinese businesspeople are hardworking and serious.
   b. Chinese businesspeople have a great sense of humor.

   (though) _____

   _____

7. a. Some companies may be very successful in their own countries.
   b. Their success in China depends on a solid understanding of Chinese culture.

   (although) _____

   _____

B *Group Work* On a separate sheet of paper, write sentences about the customs of another culture. Use the subordinators of concession in A. Share your sentences with a group. Tell your group members about information that surprised you.

Even though Brazilian people are not very strict about time, it is necessary to schedule an appointment.

Although most business meetings in Morocco are conducted in French, sometimes English is used. Find out which language will be used before your meeting so that you can hire an interpreter if necessary.

3 | Transition Words and Phrases That Show Contrast and Concession

▶ Grammar Presentation

> Another important way to signal differences or unexpected results in comparison and contrast writing is with transition words and phrases.
>
> *Nodding means yes in some countries;* **however**, *this is not universal.*
> *U.S. executives prefer time limits for meetings.* **In contrast**, *Greeks see them as less necessary.*
> **Despite** *their significant cultural differences, Mexico and China are strong trade partners.*

3.1 Transition Words and Phrases That Signal Contrast and Concession

a. Use transition words and phrases such as *conversely, however, in contrast, instead, nevertheless, nonetheless, on the contrary,* and *on the other hand* to signal differences.	*In some Asian cultures, it is impolite to arrive late at a meeting without an explanation.* **In contrast**, *in some European cultures, it is more natural to view schedules and start times as guidelines.*
b. Transition words and phrases often begin a sentence and are followed by a comma and an independent clause. Sometimes they are preceded by a semicolon, but this use is not as common.	*North Americans usually smile when they greet other people.* **On the other hand,** *they don't always shake hands.* *Some African cultures do not use the firm handshake common in the United States;* **instead**, *they prefer a gentle, slightly longer touching of hands.*
c. Transition words and phrases can also come between the subject and the verb. In this case, commas go before and after it.	*In some Asian cultures, it is impolite to arrive late at a meeting without an explanation. In some European cultures,* **in contrast,** *it is more natural to view schedules and start times as guidelines.*

3.2 Transition Words and Phrases: Differences in Meanings

a. *However* is the most common transition word that shows direct contrast. It is similar in meaning to *but.*	*In India, gift-giving is common.* **However**, *the gifts do not need to be expensive.*
b. *On the contrary* rejects the statement that precedes it and then introduces an opposing idea.	*Adapting to another culture's customs is not a weakness;* **on the contrary**, *it builds stronger relationships and is simply good business.*
c. *In contrast* presents two ideas that are different in some way.	*Table manners are informal in Canada.* **In contrast**, *Moroccan dining usually requires an understanding of a complex set of rules. (These two cultures contrast in their table manners.)*

3.2 Transition Words and Phrases: Differences in Meanings *(continued)*

d. *On the other hand* presents contrasting aspects of one idea. Note: Sometimes *in contrast* and *on the other hand* are used interchangeably.	*It is not common for people in Turkey to give gifts in a business relationship. **On the other hand**, they give gifts freely among family members. (Giving gifts in Turkey contrasts in business and personal settings.)*
e. *Nevertheless* and *nonetheless* show unexpected facts or ideas.	*Learning about a new culture can be frustrating. **Nevertheless**, a little effort will lead to both personal and professional rewards.* *Students may be anxious about studying abroad. **Nonetheless**, it is a once-in-a-lifetime chance that should be considered.*

3.3 Prepositions That Show Contrast and Concession

a. Prepositions can also signal contrast or concession. Unlike transition words, prepositions are followed by a noun phrase. Often the noun phrase begins with a verb + *-ing*. *Despite* and *in spite of* express an unexpected fact or idea.	NOUN PHRASE ***Despite / In spite of*** <u>their cultural differences</u>, *international students usually create close friendships.* NOUN PHRASE (VERB + *-ING* PHRASE) ***Despite / In spite of*** <u>coming from different cultures</u>, *international students usually become very close friends.*
Instead of replaces one idea or thing with another. Note: Don't confuse *instead* with *instead of*.	REPLACEMENT IDEA *Some African cultures prefer shaking hands gently* IDEA BEING REPLACED ***instead of*** *shaking hands firmly like in the United States.*

▶ Grammar Application

Exercise 3.1 Transition Words and Prepositions That Show Contrast and Concession

Read the e-mail. Complete the sentences about cultural behaviors in different countries. Choose the correct transition words and prepositions.

Send　Attach　Save Draft　Spelling ▾　Cancel

Dear Professor Jones:

I am in your Anthropology 101 class. I really enjoyed your lecture today. I was not aware of how different other cultures can be. You asked us to e-mail the most interesting things we learned in Chapter 5. The aspects that really caught my attention were:

1. In many countries, shaking the head from side to side is used to indicate *no*. **Nonetheless, / However,** in India, individuals move their head from side to side to acknowledge what another person has said.

2. In many places, people greet by shaking hands. **In contrast, / Despite** people hug and kiss in informal circumstances in Latin America.

3. In Japan, the *OK* hand sign does not mean "fine" or "all right" as it does in the United States. **On the other hand, / Instead,** it means "money."

4. It's fairly common knowledge that bowing is a common practice in some Asian countries. **However, / Despite** this knowledge, not many people are aware that the way people bow depends on the social situation and the reason they are bowing.

5. Many businesses spend millions on cross-cultural training. **On the other hand, / Nonetheless,** embarrassing mistakes continue to occur.

6. North Americans can be very direct when sharing their opinions. **On the other hand, / In spite of** they can be vague when making social plans.

7. North Americans' tendency for direct communication is not a sign of unfriendliness. **Nevertheless, / On the contrary,** they are very friendly people.

8. **In spite of / Instead,** the many opportunities for cultural misunderstandings, people continue to conduct business successfully across cultures.

   I am looking forward to reading the next chapter.

   Thank you,

   Maria Yolanda Tavarez

Exercise 3.2 More Transition Words and Phrases and Prepositions That Show Contrast and Concession

Group Work Write six sentences about differences in cultural behaviors that you have noticed. Use these transition words and phrases and prepositions to show contrast and concession: *despite*, *however*, *in contrast*, *instead of*, *nevertheless*, *on the contrary*, *on the other hand*, *in spite of*. Then present your sentences to another group or to the class. Do the listeners agree with your statements? Why or why not?

In Italy, the expression of emotions during negotiations does not imply that someone is unprofessional. On the contrary, showing emotions is just a normal part of negotiating in that country.

4 | Avoid Common Mistakes ⚠

1. Use the correct preposition with *on the other hand*.

In the United States, it is appropriate to send a thank-you letter after an interview. ~~In~~ *On* the other hand, a thank-you e-mail is also acceptable in some situations.

In some cultures, it is important to ask co-workers about their families. Asking too many personal questions, ~~at~~ *on* the other hand, could seem offensive.

2. Use *the other*, not *another* in *on the other hand*.

On ~~another~~ *the other* hand, many young American business people speak Chinese.

3. Remember to use a comma when transition words and phrases such as *on the contrary* and *in contrast* come at the beginning of a sentence.

Business meetings usually begin and end at specific times in North America. In contrast‸ meeting times in some cultures are not always exact.

4. Do not use *but* in sentences with adverb clauses of concession.

Although many people in the United States have studied foreign languages, ~~but~~ most international business meetings are conducted in English.

Editing Task

Find and correct seven more mistakes in the body paragraph from an essay comparing website differences in different cultures.

Although the use of corporate websites is universal, ~~but~~ corporate website design is

another aspect of doing business that differs from culture to culture. The different website

designs for Good Foods are one example. The company operates globally. It wants to appear

as though it sells the same quality products everywhere in the world. On another hand, the

5 company wants to appeal to the consumers in each country where it does business. Therefore,

the look of its sites differs from country to country. For example, the website for Good Foods

in the United States tends to use a limited number of colors. In contrast the company site in

India tends to use a great deal of color. The Indian version uses bright colors, such as pink, red,

orange, and purple, while the U.S. version of the site uses only shades of blue and gray. This is

10 because the way people interpret colors is cultural. Bright colors suggest "fun" to people in the

United States, while blue and gray suggest "importance." In another example, the Good Foods

site in Switzerland shows the company's products; however it rarely shows people using or enjoying them. In the other hand, when it does show people, they are usually alone. In contrast the Good Food site for Mexico shows families shopping together and large groups of people

15 enjoying the products. This is because people in Mexico tend to prefer being with others. However people in Switzerland value independence and solitude. Although the main purpose of a company's website is to present important information about the business, but the site must also address the cultural values of the people who view it.

5 The Writing Process

In this section, you will write a comparison and contrast essay using either the point-by-point or the block method. Before you start writing, you will learn how to write effective conclusions.

About Conclusions

The conclusion is the final paragraph of an essay. The conclusion is the writer's last opportunity to make an impact on the reader.

The following are different techniques to end an essay in a way that makes an impact:

1. **Link back to ideas from the first paragraph of the essay.** For example, the writer could link to the "hook" from the introduction or restate the main idea of the essay. In the conclusion below, the writer refers to the hook in the introductory paragraph in which there is an anecdote about a businessperson who inappropriately arrived "on time" in a culture with which he was unfamiliar.

   In conclusion, successful international businesses must train their executives to be aware of cultural differences. The businessperson who arrived "on time" for the social event did not realize how impolite his actions could be. Learning a few key facts about the target culture can lead to greater success in business.

2. **Ask a thought-provoking question.** The writer can add a question about one of the main points in the essay as a way for readers to continue to think about the topic. However, the writer should not include questions that were not addressed in the essay.

   In conclusion, successful international businesses must train their executives to be aware of cultural differences. If it is known that there is no universal agreement on what is considered polite, shouldn't people be more willing to respect cultural differences when conducting businesses with other countries?

3. **Discuss potential consequences.** The conclusion may include a prediction for the future, sometimes by giving a warning, a recommendation, or a call for action.

   In conclusion, successful international businesses must train their executives to be aware of cross-cultural issues. When someone is doing international business, it is important to never assume that what is considered polite in one culture is universal. Instead, it is essential to understand and respect other traditions.

4. **Include a relevant quote.** Including a quote from an expert on the essay topic can help create a powerful conclusion. The quote should be closely related to the ideas in the essay.

> *In conclusion, successful international businesses must train their executives to be aware of cultural differences. Of course, knowing individuals is as important as knowing the culture. As Geri-Ann Galanti (2000), a noted professor at UCLA, stated recently, "The danger in considering cultural differences is that of stereotyping people" (p. 335).*

Exercise

A *Pair Work* Look at the outlines of the following essays. With a partner, discuss ways to write a concluding paragraph for each one.

An Essay Comparing Venezuelan and U.S. Cultures	An Essay Comparing Nelson Mandela and Bill Gates
I. Introductory Paragraph **The Hook:** *A description of an American's daily life in Caracas, Venezuela* **Thesis Statement:** *While there are some differences, Venezuela and the United States are similar in several important ways.*	**I. Introductory Paragraph** **The Hook:** *"Overcoming poverty is not a task of charity, it is an act of justice," a quote from Nelson Mandela* **Thesis Statement:** *These two influential people of the recent past achieved their goals in very different ways.*
II. Body Paragraph 1: *A comparison and contrast of baseball in Venezuela and the United States*	**II. Body Paragraph 1:** *A description of Mandela's contributions to politics, the economy, and fighting poverty*
III. Body Paragraph 2: *A comparison and contrast of dating and family life in Venezuela and the United States*	**III. Body Paragraph 2:** *A description of Gates's contributions to politics, the economy, and fighting poverty*
IV. Conclusion _____ _____ _____	**IV. Conclusion** _____ _____ _____

B Choose one of the essays outlined above and write a concluding paragraph. Include one of the four techniques for writing an effective conclusion.

Pre-writing Tasks

Choose a Topic

A Choose one of the topics below. You will write a comparison and contrast essay using either the block method or the point-by-point method.

- Three or four aspects of two different cultures, for example, art, music, religion, and family life
- Two important and influential people
- A topic of your own approved by your teacher

B *Pair Work* Share your topic with a partner. Describe the aspects you are going to compare and contrast. Give each other suggestions about ideas or facts to include.

Organize Your Ideas

Follow the steps below to develop and organize your ideas before you write.

A Complete both outlines below with information for your essay on a separate sheet of paper before you decide which method you will use. There is no "right" choice. The best method depends on what you want to emphasize and how you think your audience will most easily grasp what you are trying to say.

Point-by-Point Method	Block Method
Point 1:	First culture / person:
First culture / person:	Point 1:
Second culture / person:	Point 2:
Point 2:	Point 3:
First culture / person:	Second culture / person:
Second culture / person:	Point 1:
Point 3:	Point 2:
First culture / person:	Point 3:
Second culture / person:	

B *Pair Work* Look at your outline and your partner's outline, and decide which method will best present the information that you are planning to include in your essays.

Writing Task

Write your comparison and contrast essay. Follow these steps.

1. Write an introduction that includes a hook and a thesis statement.
2. Follow the correct format for either the point-by-point or block method essay pattern.
3. Write your body paragraphs. Do not forget to include topic sentences.
4. Write your conclusion. Use one of the techniques on pages 124–125.

5. Include the following in your essay:
   - adverbial clauses of contrast and concession;
   - transition words and phrases that show contrast and concession;
   - at least three of these academic words from the essay in this unit: *appropriate, aspect, assume, aware, challenging, conduct, consequently, contrast, cultural, culture, display, flexible, global, goal, guideline, inappropriate, individual, interact, interaction, interpret, involved, neutral, norm, outcome, participant, perception, potential, professional, require, schedule, significantly, tradition, unethical, vary.*

> **Academic Writing Tip**
>
> **Academic E-mail Messages**
> When you e-mail your professors, make sure your message is clear, concise, and respectful. Start your e-mail with a greeting and the professor's name: *Dear Professor Khan.* End your message with a closing such as:
> *Thank you,*
> *Your name*

6. After you write your essay, review it and make sure you avoided the mistakes in the Avoid Common Mistakes chart on page 123.

Peer Review

A Exchange your essay with a partner. Answer the following questions as you read your partner's essay, and then share your responses.

1. Does the essay have a thesis statement? Underline it.

2. Do the body paragraphs have topic sentences? Underline them.

3. Do the body paragraphs have details that support the topic sentences? Number them.

4. Does the essay use the point-by-point or the block method?

5. How does the writer conclude the essay? What technique did the writer use in the conclusion?

6. Did the writer include transition words of contrast or concession? Circle any that you can find.

7. Is anything confusing? Write a question mark (?) next to it.

8. Provide one compliment (something you found interesting or unusual).

B Use your partner's comments to help you revise your essay. Use the Writer's Checklist on page A2 to review your essay for organization, grammar, and vocabulary.

Narrative 1: Past Perfect;
Past Modals; Common Time Clauses

The American Dream

1 Grammar in the Real World

You will read an excerpt from *The Pact: Three Young Men Make a Promise and Fulfill a Dream* (2003), a book about how three men raised in poverty achieved success. The excerpt is an example of narrative writing. Following that you will read a writer's response to the excerpt.

A *Before You Read* In your opinion, what is the American Dream? Do you believe the American Dream is something that is worth aiming for? Read the essays. According to the writer, are people confident today that they can reach the American Dream? Why or why not?

Drs. Davis, Jenkins, and Hunt

Excerpt from *The Pact: Three Young Men Make a Promise and Fulfill a Dream* (2003)

"We treat them in hospitals every day. They are young brothers, often drug dealers, gang members, or small-time criminals, who show up shot, stabbed, or beaten after a hustle[1] gone bad. To some of our medical colleagues, they are just nameless thugs,[2] perpetuating crime and death in neighborhoods that have seen far too much of these things. But when we look into
5　their faces, we see ourselves as teenagers, we see our friends, we see what we easily could have become as young adults. And we're reminded of the thin line that separates us – three twenty-nine-year-old doctors (an emergency-room physician, an internist, and a dentist) – from those patients whose lives are filled with danger and desperation.

"We grew up in poor, broken homes[3] in New Jersey neighborhoods riddled with crime,
10　drugs, and death, and came of age in the 1980s at the height of a crack epidemic[4] that ravaged communities like ours throughout the nation . . . Two of us landed in juvenile-detention centers[5] before our eighteenth birthdays. But inspired early by caring and imaginative role models, one of us in childhood latched on to[6] a dream of becoming a dentist, steered clear of[7] trouble, and in his senior year of high school persuaded his two best friends to apply to a college program
15　for minority students interested in becoming doctors. We knew we'd never survive if we went after it alone. And so we made a pact:[8] we'd help one another through, no matter what" (Davis, Jenkins, & Hunt, 2003, pp. 1–2).

---

[1]**hustle:** the act of tricking people to cheat them out of money | [2]**thug:** a violent person, often a criminal | [3]**broken home:** a family where one parent has left | [4]**crack epidemic:** the widespread drug addiction to crack cocaine in some neighborhoods in the United States during the 1980s | [5]**juvenile-detention center:** a form of prison for young people who are not yet considered adults | [6]**latch on to:** grasp or hold on to | [7]**steer clear of:** avoid | [8]**pact:** a promise or an agreement to do something together in the future

Writer's Response

The excerpt from *The Pact: Three Young Men Make a Promise and Fulfill a Dream* might
be described as a contemporary version of the American Dream. Simply stated, the American
20 Dream is the belief that if people work hard and play by the rules, they will have a chance to
get ahead. The American Dream is based on the belief that people have the same opportunity
regardless of their race, creed, color, national origin, gender, or religion.

For middle-class Americans, the American Dream typically means that each generation will
have more material possessions than the last. For some, achieving the American Dream means
25 having a secure job and owning a home. For others, it is the promise that anyone may rise from
poverty to wealth with hard work.

For many years, people had considered the American Dream to be achievable. Several
decades ago, things changed. A number of events damaged the idea of the American Dream
for the American middle class. In the late 1980s and early 1990s, housing costs increased
30 dramatically, and job security, which had been assured for previous generations, became much
less certain. As a result, many people believed that they would be worse off than their parents.
The Great Recession of 2008 further shook people's confidence about the likelihood of reaching
the American Dream.

For some, it appears that the dream may have died, but does it really matter? Gregory
35 Rodriguez (2010) would say yes. As he states, "The dream is the glue that keeps us all together . . .
it's the fabled dream that fuses hundreds of millions of separate, even competing individual dreams
into one national collective enterprise" (para. 2). Thus, it is the dream that reassures Americans
that the factors for success – ability, strong work ethic, and education – will be rewarded. Like the
three doctors who had grown up in such poverty before they achieved success, many people rely
40 on the dream for encouragement as they work hard to create their own versions of the American
Dream.

B *Comprehension Check* Answer the questions.

1. Why is the story of the three doctors remarkable?
2. What are some events that have negatively impacted or affected the American Dream?
3. According to Rodriguez, why is the American Dream important?

C *Notice*

1 Narrative Writing Discuss the reasons why the writer chose this narrative to illustrate the
American Dream.

2 Grammar Follow the instructions below to help you notice how the essay writer shows a
sequence of past events.

1. Read the two sentences on lines 27–28 again. Which came first: (a) people had
considered the American Dream to be achievable or (b) the idea of the American Dream
was damaged? What form of the verb gives you the answer?
2. Reread the sentence on lines 29–31 beginning with "In the late 1980s . . . " Which came
first: (a) less job security for Americans or (b) more job security? What form of the verb
does the writer use to show this?

3 The Writing Process Notice the way writers can add impact to their writing.

1. Underline the shortest sentence in the first paragraph (just seven words) of the personal narrative. What impact does the writer create by this short sentence?
2. Reread the second paragraph of the personal narrative. Notice how the writer varies the types of sentences. Circle a simple sentence, and double underline a complex sentence in the paragraph. Underline the three main verbs in the sentence starting with "But inspired early . . ."
3. Reread the two paragraphs from *The Pact*. Notice the use of sentences starting with *And* and *But*. In more formal academic writing, this is generally discouraged. Underline the words. For each instance of them, decide on a transition word or phrase that could replace the word to make the writing reflect a more academic style.

2 | Past Perfect and Past Perfect Progressive

▶ Grammar Presentation

In academic writing, the past perfect and the past perfect progressive can be used to contrast earlier background events and information with other later events and information in the past.

*By the 1990s, housing costs **had increased** dramatically, and job security **had become** much less certain than for previous generations.*

*When Bob got his first job, his brother **had** already **been working** for several years.*

2.1 Using Past Perfect

a. Use the past perfect to describe the first of two completed events in the past. Use the simple past for the later event.	EARLIER EVENT *By midnight, he **had finished** most of his work,* LATER EVENT *so he **decided** to go to bed.*
b. You can use the past perfect in sentences with time clauses with *when*, *by the time*, and *while*. The past perfect is often used in the main clause. The use of the past perfect in sentences with time clauses with *before* and *after* is not necessary since the words indicate a clear time relationship. *Note:* The use of the simple past in both the main clause and time clause with *when* shows a different time relationship. Choose the past perfect to emphasize that one action was completed before the other.	LATER EVENT EARLIER EVENT <u>*When she arrived*</u>, *the class **had** already **started**.* <u>*By the time she registered for classes*</u>, *the semester **had** already **begun**.* *She started college after she **earned** / **had earned** enough money to pay for the first year.* FIRST EVENT SECOND EVENT *When she <u>arrived</u>, the class <u>started</u>.*

2.1 Using Past Perfect (continued)

c. Use the past perfect to go back to an earlier time in a narrative or description.	*Nesreen was nervous on her first day of work. She'd never **had** a job before.*
d. Use the past perfect in narrative writing, and in academic writing in general, to give background reasons and explanations for later past events.	*For years, many people **had considered** the American Dream to be achievable. Then the economy changed.*

2.2 Past Events with Adverbs and Frequency Expressions

Use adverbs of time with the past perfect to emphasize the earlier time period in the past: *after, before, earlier* *already, not . . . yet, still . . . not* *ever, just, never, recently*	*No one in her family **had** ever **attended** college <u>before</u>. She'd <u>already</u> **talked** to a few colleges, but she **hadn't applied** <u>yet</u>. She needed to find a way to pay the tuition. They'd <u>recently</u> **applied** for a grant and were waiting for a final response.*

2.3 Using Past Perfect and Past Perfect Progressive

a. Like the past perfect, the past perfect progressive can give background reasons or describe past events.	PAST PERFECT *They **had experienced** many challenges, so they **decided** to make a pact.* PAST PERFECT PROGRESSIVE *They **had been experiencing** many challenges, so they **decided** to make a pact.*
Note: As with other progressive forms, don't use past perfect progressive with stative verbs, such as *be, know,* and *seem.*	*She **had known** that she wanted to be in education since she was a young girl.* NOT *She ~~had been knowing~~ that she wanted to be in education since she was a young girl.*
b. Use the past perfect progressive to emphasize an ongoing past action leading up to a point in the past. This action may have been occurring when another past action took place. The past perfect progressive form is much less common than the past perfect.	*He'**d been talking about** applying to medical school for a long time. Finally, last January, he applied.* FIRST EVENT *They'**d been working** for about an hour* SECOND EVENT *when the bell rang.*

▶ Grammar Application

Exercise 2.1 Simple Past and Past Perfect

A Complete the sentences about an immigrant who came to the United States. Use the simple past or past perfect form of the verbs in parentheses.

1. Naresh _had studied_ (study) English for three years in his native country, India, before he _came_ (come) to the United States.

2. Naresh _____ (arrive) in the United States six months ago to study. He _____ (never / be) here before.

3. At first, he _____ (stay) in a motel because he _____ (neglect) to look for a place to live before arriving.

4. Naresh's parents _____ (be) worried about him because after a month, he still _____ (not find) an apartment.

5. They _____ (contact) their friend Sam who was living in the United States. Naresh's parents _____ (help) Sam 25 years earlier to adjust to living in India.

6. Sam and his wife, Lea, _____ (be) good friends with Naresh's parents. They _____ (go) to visit Naresh's family several times.

7. Naresh _____ (hope) to live on his own, but after struggling so much, he _____ (be) happy to accept Sam and Lea's offer to stay with them.

8. Sam and Lea _____ (give) Naresh as much help as they could, just like Naresh's parents _____ (assist) Sam 25 years earlier.

B *Pair Work* Explain your answers in A to a partner. Do you agree?

First, Ali studied English and second, he came to the United States. So we need to use the past perfect form had studied *and the simple past form* came.

Exercise 2.2 Past Perfect and Past Perfect Progressive

A Complete the sentences about a South Korean woman who moved to the United States. Circle the past perfect or past perfect progressive form of the verbs. For some items, both forms are possible.

1. Mi Young's mother **had planned** / **had been planning** to visit her daughter in the United States for several years, but by Mi Young's fifth year in New York, her mother still **hadn't visited** / **hadn't been visiting** her.

2. Mi Young's mother **had gone** / **had been going** to Los Angeles once before to visit her sister when she was much younger, and she **had wanted** / **had been wanting** to return ever since then.

3. At one point, it seemed as if Mi Young might come home because she **had lost** / **had been losing** her job and she **had looked** / **had been looking** for a new job for several months.

4. Mi Young **had thought** / **had been thinking** about moving back to South Korea when she got a job offer in Los Angeles. It was a company that a friend of hers **had just started** / **had been starting** to work for.

5. Mi Young's mom **had worried** / **had been worrying** about traveling all the way to New York, so she was happy when Mi Young moved to Los Angeles. The flight was a lot shorter!

6. Also, her mother **had had** / **had been having** a nice time in Los Angeles on her first trip, so she **had hoped** / **had been hoping** since then that Mi Young might get a job there.

B *Pair Work* Think of a major change in your life or in the life of someone you know, such as a move, a marriage, or a new job. Describe the events leading up to the change. Use the past perfect and the past perfect progressive where necessary.

My boyfriend and I'd been talking about getting married for over a year when he proposed to me. We'd been together for three years by that time. I'd known soon after we met that I was going to marry him, but I was still nervous about making the commitment. When I told my parents, they weren't surprised at all, but they thought I was too young. I was 21 at the time . . .

3 Past Modals and Modal-like Expressions

▶ Grammar Presentation

Past modals and modal-like expressions are used to give a perspective on events (whether the speaker or writer saw the event as possible, necessary, desirable, and so on).

*I **should have studied** French when I was in high school.*
*Joanna **could not finish** college in four years because she **had to** work full-time.*

3.1 Past Modals and Modal-like Expressions

a. Use these modal-like expressions for past necessity and lack of necessity: *had to* to say something was necessary in the past *did not have to* to say something wasn't necessary in the past	*The three friends came from poor families, so they **had to** find a way to pay for their education.* *They **did not have to** pay for their college education because they got scholarships.*
b. Use these modals for past permission and prohibition: *could* to say something was allowed or permitted in the past *could not* to say something was not allowed or permitted in the past	*In the past, minority students **could apply** for special college grants.* *Nonminority students **could not apply** for these special college grants.*

3.1 Past Modals and Modal-like Expressions *(continued)*

c. Use these modals for disapproval or regret over an action taken or not taken: *should have*, *should not have*, and *could have*	***I should have applied*** *for a work study job.* (But I didn't, and I regret it.) *She **shouldn't have missed** so many classes.* (But she did and now she's failing.) *We **could have asked** for help.* (But we didn't and now we're sorry.)
d. Use these modals for possibility or impossibility of a past action: *could / might have* to show possibility *could not have* to show impossibility	*He **could / might have found out** about the job opening through the school's career center.* (It's possible because I know he went there.) *We **could not have predicted** that the number of college applications would increase so much this year.* (It was impossible to predict.)

3.2 *Would* and *Used To* for Past Habits

a. Use *would / used to* + base form of the verb to describe habits or routines that happened regularly in the past, but don't happen now. With *would*, a past time reference – such as a past time clause – must be used or understood. *Would* is more common than *used to* in academic writing.	*While I was living in my country, I **would go** for long walks.* *I **used to study** on the bus to school every day. Now I drive my car to school, so I can't study then.*
b. Use *used to* with stative verbs (verbs like *have* or *be*) that describe states or conditions in the past. Do not use *would* to describe states or conditions in the past.	*I **used to be** a manager at a hotel, but now I work at a bank.* *My brother **used to have** a bike. Now he has a car.* *I **used to like** long walks in the country.* NOT *I ~~would~~ like long walks in the country.*

3.3 *Was / Were + Supposed To* and *Was / Were Going To* for Past Expectation

Use *was / were + supposed to* and *be going to* + base form of the verb to describe required or planned actions in the past that did not take place. They are often followed by *but* and a clause that explains why the action was not completed.	*The foundation **was supposed to provide** full funding for 30 students.* *The students **were going to get** part-time jobs, **but there were none available**.* *She **was supposed to start** classes this fall, **but she didn't have enough money for tuition**.*

▶ Grammar Application

Exercise 3.1 Past Modals and Modal-like Expressions

Complete the sentences about a woman who found success because of her hard work. Use the verbs in parentheses and a modal (*could, could have, had to, might have, should have*). Use the cues at the beginning of the sentences to decide on the appropriate modal.

1. [necessary] Sarah _had to work_ (work) when she was young because her father's salary wasn't enough for the family.

2. [not necessary] Every day, Sarah went to school and then went to work at a pizza shop. Her school and the pizza shop were close to home, so she _____ (drive) or take the bus.

3. [possible] When Sarah finished high school, she wanted to go to college, but she didn't have enough money. She _____ (win) a scholarship because she had high grades, but she never applied for one.

4. [regret] Later she realized that she _____ (apply) for every possible scholarship.

5. [not necessary] Sarah decided that she could be a success even without a college education. Because she _____ (go) to school anymore, she began working full-time.

6. [possible] She worked 60 hours a week at the pizza shop and made a lot of money, yet she hardly spent any. Her thriftiness _____ (be) the result of growing up in a poor household.

7. [not permitted] After a few years, the owner of the pizza shop decided he wanted to sell the shop. Sarah wanted to buy it. She didn't have enough money, so she tried to take out a loan at the bank, but she _____ (get) a loan.

8. [allowed] The pizza shop owner really liked Sarah because she was such a hard worker. He told her that she _____ (buy) the shop from him and pay him over five years.

9. [disapproval] The owner's friends thought it was a bad idea. They told him he _____ (loan) her the money, but he knew he had made the right decision.

10. [possibility] Once Sarah had bought the shop, she made it more successful than it had ever been. No one _____ (predict) how successful Sarah would be.

11. [impossibility] Sarah continued to work hard, and after 10 years, she bought five more shops. She herself _____ (guess) that she would one day become such a successful businesswoman.

Exercise 3.2 *Used To* and *Would*

A 🔊 Listen to the story about Rita and Edwin, a couple from the Dominican Republic. Write *T* if the statement is true or *F* if the statement is false.

1. __F__ Rita and Edwin used to live in New York.

2. _____ Every semester, they would enroll in the free English classes offered at schools.

3. _____ In his English classes, Edwin would always sit next to Spanish-speaking students.

4. _____ When she started classes, Rita wouldn't speak when the teacher called on her.

5. _____ She used to always start crying when she got nervous in class.

6. _____ Rita would often talk to her classmates.

7. _____ When he got a job at a hotel, Edwin would take a bus to get there.

8. _____ Rita and Edwin used to dream of a better life.

B *Pair Work* Tell your partner about your past habits, and contrast them with your current life. Explain to your partner why your past habits have changed.

I used to work as a waiter in a restaurant, but now I'm a full-time student. I realized that it was difficult to work and study at the same time, so I quit my job.

Exercise 3.3 *Was / Were Supposed To* and *Was / Were Going To*

A The chart below shows expectations and plans that John and people who knew him had about his life and the reasons why the plans did not come true. Write sentences about John using the information in the chart and *was / were supposed to* and *was / were going to*.

Expectations	Reasons Why the Plans Did Not Come True
1. Everyone expected John to become a doctor.	Nobody knew that he couldn't stand the sight of blood.
2. John planned to major in biology.	He changed his mind and decided to major in business instead.
3. John and his friends planned to go into business together after college.	They didn't have enough money.
4. John planned to move to California to find a job.	He was offered a job in Japan.
5. Everyone thought John would marry his high school sweetheart.	He fell in love with a girl in Japan.
6. John's parents planned to visit him this month.	His father broke his leg, so they postponed the trip.

1. *John was going to be a doctor, but nobody knew he couldn't stand the sight of blood.*

2. _____

3. _____

4. _____

5. _____

6. _____

B *Pair Work* Tell your partner about plans that you and others had that changed. Explain why they changed. Then tell your partner about plans that people you know had that changed and why they changed.

I was going to major in computer science, but I decided I was more interested in history. My brother has always loved animals. We always thought he was going to be a veterinarian, but he ended up majoring in business. He said that he changed his mind when he started working at a bank. He really wants to own his own business some day.

4 | Common Time Clauses

▶ Vocabulary Presentation

Time clauses show time or sequence. It is common to use these constructions in longer, more complex sentences in a narrative.

***After** I finished high school, I had to find a job.*
*I started practicing interview skills **when** I heard that I had a job interview.*

4.1 Common Time Clauses

a. Dependent clauses that show a time relationship begin with subordinators such as *after*, *as*, *before*, and *while*. They are sometimes called adverb clauses of time.	*Life in the U.S. was difficult at first. I did my English homework **while** my baby was sleeping.*

4.1 Common Time Clauses *(continued)*

b. Use these subordinators to show different aspects of time and sequence:

after to show that the event in the time clause happened first

FIRST   SECOND

After *he started working on campus, it was very difficult to keep up with his classes.*

before to show that the event in the time clause happened second

SECOND   FIRST

Before *I moved to this country, I did not know how to cook.*

every time to show repeated events that are connected in either the past or present

Every time *they moved, the children had to adjust to a new school.*

since (often using the present perfect or past perfect in the main clause) to show when an action or state started in the past

*He's been working **since** he left high school.*

once, *when*, and *as soon as* to show that one event quickly followed another event

Once *I finished college, I started looking for a job.*

when, *while*, and *as* to show that both events happened at the same time

*He worked full-time at a grocery store **while** he was going to college.*

until to show a time frame that continues up to a certain time or event

*I had to work night shifts **until** I found a better job.*

🌐 *Before*, *when*, *until*, and *after* are the most frequently used subordinating conjunctions in academic writing.

▶ Vocabulary Application

Exercise 4.1 Common Time Clauses

Combine the sentences about the author Stephen King using the subordinator in parentheses.

1. Stephen King struggled a lot in his life. Then he became a famous author.

   (before) *Stephen King struggled a lot in life before he became a famous author.*

2. He was two years old. His father left.

   (when) _____

   _____

Stephen King

3. His father left. Then his mother struggled to take care of him and his brother.

(after) _____

_____

4. He was 12. He became interested in writing horror stories.

(when) _____

5. He was in school. He wrote many stories.

(while) _____

6. He sold stories to his classmates. Then the teachers asked him to stop.

(until) _____

7. His first short story was published. Then he graduated college.

(before) _____

8. His mother died. Then his first novel, *Carrie*, was published.

(after) _____

Exercise 4.2 More Common Time Clauses

A Complete the paragraph about the life of Dr. Martin Luther King, Jr. Circle the correct subordinators using information from the time line of events in his life.

1955 – Rosa Parks arrested on December 1 for refusing to give up her seat on a bus to a white passenger in Montgomery, Alabama; started a boycott on December 5 to stop segregation on Montgomery buses
1956 – In June, segregation law declared unconstitutional; in December, bus segregation stopped
1963 – King delivered "I Have a Dream" speech at the Lincoln Memorial in Washington, D.C.
1968 – King assassinated at the Lorraine Motel in Memphis, Tennessee
1986 – Birthday of Dr. Martin Luther King, Jr. declared a national holiday
2011 – Memorial statue of King put up in Washington, D.C.

August, 1963, at the March on Washington

Dr. Martin Luther King, Jr. was an influential leader in the 1950s and 1960s in the Civil Rights movement, a movement that ended segregation and discrimination of African Americans in American society. **After /(While)** other leaders were considering violence as the way to bring
(1)
about social changes in the early 1950s, King was urging people to use nonviolent means, such as boycotts and demonstrations. The movement did not become energized **until / as soon as** Rosa
(2)
Parks, a social activist, refused to give her seat on a bus to a white man. On December 1, 1955, black residents in Montgomery, Alabama, boycotted the buses and elected King as their leader. **Once / As** the boycott continued into 1956, King's reputation as a courageous leader grew, and
(3)
his outstanding speaking skills inspired many to join the movement. **Before / After** the U.S.
(4)

Supreme Court declared Alabama's segregation laws unconstitutional in June, segregation on Montgomery buses finally ended that following December. **Once / Since** the Supreme Court made its decision, King ended the boycott. In 1963, King delivered his famous "I Have a Dream" speech. Just five years **since / after** he delivered that speech, King was assassinated in Memphis, Tennessee. **Since / Until** the Civil Rights Act of 1964 was passed, many people have benefited from it. Among other provisions, the act made it illegal to discriminate against someone based on race, religion, and gender. Dr. Martin Luther King, Jr. continues to be an icon for the civil rights movement.

(5) (6) (7)

As / Until more and more people recognized King's significant contribution to civil rights and equality over time, political figures began to ask for a day of remembrance. The first Martin Luther King Day of Service was observed in 1986. In 2011, a memorial was dedicated to King on the National Mall in Washington, D.C.

(8)

B Make a time line similar to the one in A with important events in your life or the life of someone that you admire on a separate piece of paper. Explain the events on your time line to a partner. Use time clauses.

Since I was young, I've wanted to go to college to study math. Before I started college, I spent two years in the army. As soon as I got out of the army, I sent out applications for college.

5 | Avoid Common Mistakes ⚠

1. Remember to use the past participle after *had* when forming the past perfect.

He had ~~went~~ ^{gone} to college, so he already had a degree.

Blanca's family had ~~came~~ ^{come} to the United States when she was still a child.

2. Remember to use the past perfect progressive, not the past progressive, in the main clause for an action that happens in an earlier time frame than the action in the *when* clause.

She ~~was taking~~ ^{had been taking} care of children for many years when she realized she needed an A.A. degree.

Ahmet ~~was working~~ ^{had been working} in a restaurant for a long time when he decided to go to college.

3. Remember to use the simple past, not the past perfect, for a single completed action or state. The past perfect is often used to describe a previous time before another past time.

I ~~had graduated~~ ^{graduated} from college last year.

Editing Task

Find and correct nine more mistakes in the use of the past perfect and past perfect progressive in the narrative paragraphs on changing careers.

Changing Careers

   Jessica had always loved photography, even as a child. She ~~was asking~~ *had been asking* for a camera for a long time when her father had gave her one on her tenth birthday. She would take her camera everywhere and record the small moments of everyday life that caught her eye: a cluster of leaves on the sidewalk, or a spider web on a garden fence. Jessica had always see photography

5 as a hobby. Moreover, since she had came from a family that had endured economic hardships when she was growing up, she had always know that she had to choose a career that paid well and was secure. Therefore, after high school, she got a degree in landscape design. She was considering a job with the city during her last year of college, but when her uncle, the owner of a landscape company, asked her to work for him, she changed her mind. She had

10 joined his landscaping business right after graduation. However, Jessica never lost her love of photography. She eventually bought herself a higher quality camera and continued to take pictures whenever she had the opportunity.

   Jessica was working at the landscaping company for about two years when her uncle decided to build a website to advertise the business. He needed images of the company's

15 best work to publish on the site and immediately thought of Jessica. She was taking photos of the company's projects the entire time that she had worked there. The website had been a success. More importantly, other companies saw it and wanted to know who the great photographer was. Soon, Jessica was working full-time as a photographer. Her uncle missed Jessica's presence, but everyone was pleased that she was now earning a living doing

20 something that she truly loved.

6 The Writing Process ✏️

In this section, you will write an introductory paragraph for an essay. This paragraph will contain a narrative. Before you start writing, you will learn how to use a range of sentence structures in narrative writing to add impact to your writing.

About Sentence Variety

There are several ways to add impact to your writing, such as by using precise vocabulary and by including clear and convincing examples. Another way is by using a variety of sentence structures:

1. **Alternate short and long sentences.** While academic writers often use compound and complex sentences, short sentences are an effective way to emphasize important information. In a narrative, a short sentence may contain the climax or the turning point of the story.

   When William Jefferson Blythe III was born in 1946, his father had died in a car crash three months earlier. Billy, as he was known as a child, was a good student and loved to play the saxophone. While he excelled in school, Billy's family life was troubled. His stepfather, a man named Roger Clinton, was an abusive alcoholic who was difficult to live with. As a teenager, Billy took his stepfather's name and continued to protect his mother and younger brother from his stepfather's drunken rage whenever he could. This boy certainly did not have an easy time in his early life, but it did not stop him from going on to do great things. In fact, in 1992 he achieved what very few people have ever done. Bill Clinton was elected president of the United States.

2. **Use a variety of words and phrases and vary their position in the sentence.** Do not always start sentences the same way. Find different ways to connect ideas between sentences. Use a variety of connectors.

Original	Variety of Words and Phrases
The American Dream consists of many factors. For example, it includes personal wealth and job satisfaction. When one considers personal wealth, it is measured in many ways. For example, wealth can be measured in salary, property, and investments. Job satisfaction is complex. For example, some people measure it by how happy a person is while doing the job, while other people measure it by how important or relevant the work is.	*The American Dream consists of many factors such as personal wealth and job satisfaction. When one considers personal wealth, it is measured in many ways, including salary, property, and investments. Job satisfaction is complex. Some people, for example, measure it by how happy a person is while doing the job, while other people measure it by how important or relevant the work is.*

3. **Place key ideas in the main clause of a sentence.** It is usually a good idea to put the most important idea in the main clause of a sentence. In addition, it adds more impact to put that clause at the end of the sentence, especially if you are going to write more about that idea in the next sentence.

Two Ideas:	Emphasizing Idea 1	Emphasizing Idea 2
Idea 1: Many people know what the American Dream means to them. **Idea 2**: Few people can clearly define the American Dream.	*While few people can clearly define it,* ***many people know what the American Dream means to them***.	*Although many people know what the American Dream means to them,* ***few people can clearly define it***.

4. **Avoid using too many words to explain an idea.** The more concise, the better.

   Wordy: *Maria thought, but was not really sure, that life in the United States would be better for her than the life she had in her country.*

   Better: *Maria assumed that life in the United States would be better than life in her country.*

Exercise

A Read the paragraph below. Then rewrite the sentences as indicated to improve the writing and give it more impact.

(1) The night before my first job interview, I was so nervous I could not sleep. (2) Having eaten a large supper earlier as well as being nervous, it wasn't surprising that with my full stomach and nerves that I found myself having a great deal of trouble when I tried to fall asleep. (3) When I finally fell asleep, my alarm clock turned off as a result of a power outage. (4) The next morning, as a result of oversleeping, I had to move very fast to get to the interview on time. (5) I arrived at the interview very hungry since I hadn't had time to eat breakfast. (6) During the interview, the manager offered me a piece of candy. (7) I ate it and, after a few moments, I felt something strange in my mouth. (8) I realized that a filling in my tooth had come out! (9) I ran from the office covering my mouth, and I learned that I should never eat anything at a job interview.

1. Make sentence 2 more concise and write it below.

   _____

   _____

2. Sentences 3 and 4 contain the same connector. Replace one with a different connector.

   _____

   _____

3. Change the order of ideas in sentence 5 so that it ends with the idea of arriving hungry.

   _____

   _____

4. Revise sentence 9 so that it is three sentences. Make the last sentence the shortest.

   _____

   _____

   _____

B *Pair Work* Compare your revised sentences with a partner's. Did you make the same changes? Read your sentences aloud. Whose sentences make more of an impact?

Pre-writing Tasks

Choose a Topic

A Choose one of the topics below. You will write one paragraph that contains a narrative to illustrate your topic.

- A narrative about job hunting that illustrates the topic sentence: *Job candidates need to be well-prepared for anything during the interview process.*

- A narrative about interviewing that illustrates the topic sentence: *Every interview shows something important about the interview process.*

- A narrative about a trait that is considered to be necessary to be an excellent student or employee and that illustrates the topic sentence: *One important trait that many students / employees display is _____ .*

B *Pair Work* Share your chosen topic with a partner. Provide suggestions about ideas or facts to include. Make a list.

Organize Your Ideas

A Write down as many events and details for your story as you can. This is a brainstorm, so don't worry about the order of the events. Just write down words and phrases that remind you of the story.

B *Pair Work* Share your brainstorm with a partner and together choose which events and details should be included in the story. Write out the events that you chose to include in the order that they happened. Use these notes to help you write the story.

Writing Task

Write your narrative paragraph. Follow the steps below.

1. Review your notes.

2. Write your narrative. Remember to include a topic sentence.

3. Include the following in your paragraph:
   - the past perfect and past perfect progressive;
   - past modals and modal-like expressions;
   - common time clauses;
   - a variety of sentence lengths and structures to add impact;
   - at least three of these academic words from the essay in this unit: *achieve, adult, assure, colleague, contemporary, create, decade, dramatically, ethic, factor, gender, generation, job, medical, minority, previous, rely, secure, security, survive, version.*

> **Academic Writing Tip**
>
> **Avoid the Simple Present in Narratives**
> Use past forms of verbs rather than the present forms to describe events in narratives. The use of the simple present is often considered more informal.

4. After you write your paragraph, review it and make sure you avoided the mistakes in the Avoid Common Mistakes chart on page 140.

Peer Review

A Exchange your paragraph with a partner. Answer the following questions as you read your partner's story, and then share your responses.

1. Does the writer's story illustrate the topic sentence well?

2. Did the writer include any verbs in the past perfect tense when contrasting two events in the past to show that one occurred before the other? Circle any verbs in the past perfect tense.

3. Did the writer appropriately include any past modals?

4. Are there any time clauses? Do they help make the order of events in the narrative clear?

5. Which is the shortest sentence in the narrative? Underline it. Does this sentence deserve to receive the emphasis it does?

6. Are there any overly long sentences? How could they be improved?

7. Is anything confusing? Write a question mark (?) next to it.

8. Provide one compliment (something you found interesting or unusual).

B Use your partner's comments to help you revise your paragraph. Use the Writer's Checklist on page A2 to review your paragraph for organization, grammar, and vocabulary.

UNIT 10

Narrative 2: Demonstratives; Common Time Signals

Immigration

1 | Grammar in the Real World 🌐

You will read an essay about the history of immigration in the United States. The essay is an example of a historical narrative.

A *Before You Read* Why do people immigrate to the United States? What are some of the problems that immigrants encounter? Read the essay. How has the United States benefited from immigration throughout the years?

Immigration and the United States

Since the seventeenth century, immigrants from all over the world have come to the United States in search of safety, freedom, and economic opportunities. Immigration patterns have varied over time, with distinct periods of immigration from different countries. In each of these periods, immigrants helped shape U.S. society and the economy. However, the flow of
5 immigrants has also brought challenges that continue into the present.

The period from the seventeenth century through the early nineteenth century is the first and longest U.S. immigration wave. During this time, most immigrants came from Europe, including France and the Netherlands. The number of immigrants was small, and most of the newcomers became farmers (Diner, 2008). By the 1820s, this pattern started to change. From
10 the 1820s to 1880s, approximately 15 million immigrants settled in the United States. Even though some of these immigrants decided to work in agriculture in the Midwest and Northeast, many more moved to big cities, such as New York City and Boston.

The immigration wave that took place between the 1890s and the beginning of the twentieth century is often referred to as the flood of immigrants. During that period, nearly
15 25 million immigrants arrived in the United States (Diner, 2008). They were mainly young Europeans from countries such as Italy, Greece, Hungary, and Poland.

Each group of immigrants presented distinct characteristics. Some groups were less formally educated and some were mostly young, for example. However, they all contributed to the growth of many industries, including steel, automobile, and textile. Because of them, the
20 United States turned into one of the world's most powerful countries ("Economic Impact of Immigration in the Twentieth Century," 2011, para. 3).

Over the course of the late nineteenth and early twentieth centuries, protests over immigrants grew. Many people were troubled by the new religions and customs that immigrants brought to the United States (Diner, 2008, p. 3). As a result, in 1921 the government passed laws limiting the number of immigrants allowed to enter each year. Even though immigrants contributed to the
25 economic growth of the United States, the country made it difficult for them to enter.

In the early 2000s, the immigration debate was reignited due to high numbers of immigrants, legal and illegal. Opponents argued that immigrants took jobs away from people and that the cost of maintaining their welfare was a drain on the education and health care systems. (Diner, 2008, p. 4). Although the arguments continue to this day, it is important to
30 remember that the country was and will continue to be built with the help of immigrants.

B *Comprehension Check* Answer the questions.

1. Describe the immigrants who traveled to the United States in the seventeenth century.
2. When and why did the U.S. government start to restrict entrance into the United States?
3. Why does the writer say that the United States will continue to be built with the help of immigrants?

C *Notice*

1 Narrative Writing Draw the time line below on a separate sheet of paper, and complete it with the information from the essay that describes each wave of immigrants.

First wave of immigrants

| 1600s | 1820s | 1880s | 1890s | 1900s | 2010s |

2 Grammar Follow the instructions below to help you understand the use of demonstratives and time words to define different periods of time.

1. On lines 10–12, notice the use of the word *these* in the sentence "Even though some of these immigrants . . .". What does *these* refer to?
2. On lines 14–15, notice the use of *that* in "During that period . . .". What does *that* refer to?
3. In the second paragraph, underline the words the writer uses to define two different periods of time.

3 The Writing Process Answer the following questions.

1. Who do you think is the audience (the main readers) of this essay? Circle all that apply.
   a. college students
   b. readers who are interested in immigration issues
   c. middle school students
   d. readers of a fashion magazine

2. What is the purpose of this essay? Circle all that apply.
   a. to inform readers about immigration issues
   b. to compare immigration in two countries
   c. to show readers that immigrants have always played an important role in the United States

2 | Demonstratives

▶ Grammar Presentation

Demonstratives (*this, that, these, those*) are used in all kinds of writing to connect ideas or give coherence.

*In my neighborhood, there are people from all over the world. Most of **these** people have good jobs.*

*The article is about recent immigration. **That** topic always generates interesting conversation.*

2.1 Demonstratives

Use demonstratives (*this, that, these, those*) to show physical distance from the speaker or distance in time. Use *this/these* to refer to people or things close in time and space to the speaker. Use *that/those* to refer to people or things in a more distant time and space.	***This** unit is about immigration. Let's look at the first page.* *I remember **those** days when I'd been in this new country for only three weeks and didn't speak any English.*

2.2 Demonstratives That Connect Ideas

a. Use demonstratives to connect ideas that are close to each other and to make the text cohesive. These are also called demonstrative adjectives.	*Immigrants came from all over Europe. Most of **these** immigrants opted for farming. (These immigrants refers to the immigrants from all over Europe.)* *The flood of immigrants occurred between the 1890s and the beginning of the twentieth century. During **that** period, nearly 25 million immigrants arrived in the United States.*
b. You can use demonstratives without a noun. When they stand alone, they are pronouns. You can also use *it* for the same purpose.	*Climate change affects everyone. Indeed, **this** is the most important environmental issue of our time. (This refers to climate change.)* *Climate change affects everyone. Indeed, **it** is the most important environmental issue of our time. (It refers to climate change.)*
c. Use demonstrative pronouns to summarize or refer to a previously mentioned idea in the same paragraph.	*Economic disparity is widespread and increasing. **This** is an especially significant problem for developing countries. (This refers to the fact that economic disparity is increasing.)*

2.2 Demonstratives That Connect Ideas *(continued)*

d. Use a demonstrative with a noun that summarizes or clarifies what it refers to, for example: *approach, aspect, development, experience, factor, reason, phenomenon, topic*	*Nearly 25 million Europeans traveled to the United States at the end of the nineteenth century and early twentieth century. **That development** changed the demographics of the country. (That development refers to the idea of the previous sentence.)*
e. The summary word or phrase that follows demonstratives can reflect the writer's opinion about a previously described topic, for example: *controversial argument, indisputable fact, questionable claim, undisputed fact*	*Some people believe immigration leads to increases in crime. **This controversial argument** has been challenged by many.* *Millions of people have immigrated to the United States. **This undisputed fact** constitutes one of the central elements in the country's development.*

▶ Grammar Application

Exercise 2.1 Demonstratives

A Read the sentences about immigration in Europe. Complete the sentences with the correct demonstratives. Sometimes more than one answer is possible.

1. The European Union has expanded in recent years to include over two dozen countries. ___This___ has contributed to increased immigration all over Europe.

2. In 2004, ten countries joined the European Union. _____ countries included Hungary, Poland, Lithuania, and Slovakia.

3. For the most part, citizens of European Union member nations have permission to work in other member nations. _____ makes it fairly easy for people to move from one EU country to another.

4. In recent years, immigration to Norway has increased significantly. _____ increase is responsible for more than half of Norway's population growth.

5. There are about five to six million immigrants living in Italy. _____ people make up nearly 10 percent of the population.

6. In 2010, 32,000 people wanted to immigrate to Sweden for asylum.[1] _____ was 30 percent more than in 2009.

[1]**asylum:** protection or safety

B *Pair Work* Take turns with a partner explaining what each demonstrative refers to in the sentences.

In sentence 1, This refers to the expansion of the European Union.

Exercise 2.2 More Demonstratives

A Choose the correct word or words to complete the paragraphs that explain one writer's view of the challenges of immigration.

Millions of people move to new countries every year. This (**phenomenon**)/ reason can
_(1)_
cause challenges for both the residents of the host country and for the immigrants. Often,
the people from the host country and the immigrants have difficulty relating to each other
and understanding each other's customs. Also, the language of the host country and the
immigrants' language are sometimes very different. If people cannot speak to each other, they
cannot begin to understand each other. This **fact** / **argument** may be the underlying cause
_(2)_
of most misunderstandings between residents and immigrant groups. People often fear what
they do not understand.

However, people disagree about which language immigrants should speak. This
development / **controversial issue** can produce very different responses. Some people
_(3)_
believe that immigrants should stop speaking their native language and speak the host
country's language, even in their homes. They feel that immigrants will be able to assimilate
better if they adopt the host country's language. This **questionable claim** / **aspect** is directly
_(4)_
opposed to the opinion of those who believe that it is important for immigrants to continue to
speak their own language while they learn the host country's language. Many believe that this
second **aspect** / **approach** is the best one for young children. These **people** / **factors** argue
_(5)_   _(6)_
that individuals who have a strong command of their own language are better able to learn
a new language. This **argument** / **topic** seems to have some validity since research shows
_(7)_
that immigrant children who cannot read and write in their parent's language have trouble
learning to read and write their adopted country's language.

B _Pair Work_ Discuss your answers in A with a partner. What do you think the writer's
opinion is about immigrants and language? How do you know? Do you agree or disagree
with the writer's opinion? Write a response of four to five sentences to the writer's opinions
using demonstratives and the words in A. Present it to another pair or to the class.

The writer believes that immigration can cause problems for countries and immigrants.
We understand that there are sometimes issues that need to be resolved, but we strongly
feel that this phenomenon is actually, in the long run, good for both the countries and the
immigrants because . . .

3 | Common Time Signals 🌐

▶ Vocabulary Presentation

Time signals are important to use in narrative writing to make the sequence of events or ideas easier to follow.

Over the past twenty years, *immigration has become a controversial issue in many European countries.*

*This is not **the first time** in U.S. history that immigrants have been criticized.*

3.1 Common Time Signals

a. The most common time signals are prepositional phrases such as:	
by + specific time	*The immigration situation changed **by** the mid 1800s.*
from + specific time + *through/to* + specific time	*The first and longest immigration era stretched **from** the seventeenth century **to** the early nineteenth century.*
after/since + specific time	***After** the end of World War I (from 1914 to 1918), Congress changed the nation's basic policy about immigration.*
over/during the course of + specific time	***Over the course of** the late nineteenth and early twentieth centuries, the government took measures to slow down immigration.*
over the past/next/last + time period	***Over the last/past** 20 years, immigration has increased.*
in the past/next/last + time period	***In the next** 10 years, immigration is likely to decrease.*
for + time period	*The high rate of immigration continued **for** almost one hundred years.*
b. Time adverbs are also considered time signals:	*We've **always** lived in this neighborhood.*
already, always, ever, just, lately, never, now, recently, since, yet, the first/last time.	*I will **never** again feel so helpless.*
	*I **now** work in a clinic that serves immigrants.*
	*It felt great **the first time** I realized I could make my own choice.*
	*The debate over immigration has heated up **recently**.*
Note: Use the present perfect with the expression *this is the first time.*	INCORRECT: ***This is the first time** I ~~read/am reading~~ about immigration issues.*
	CORRECT: ***This is the first time** I've read about immigration issues.*

3.1 Time Signals (continued)

c. Use *every day*, *once (once more / once again / once or twice)*, and *twice* to indicate frequency.	***Every day***, I'm amazed by how far I've gone. *By 2000, the United States had **once again** become a nation of immigrants.*
d. Use time + *later / earlier* to indicate when something happened in relation to another event.	*I left my neighborhood when I was just 11. <u>Years **later**</u>, I returned to Boston to go to medical school.*

▶ Vocabulary Application

Exercise 3.1 ◄» Time Signals

You will listen to an essay written by a Vietnamese immigrant to the United States. Listen and write the missing words. Then listen and check your answers.

I was born in Vietnam. My family moved to the United States _*when I was eight*_ .
(1)

Vietnamese American Tet Festival in San Jose, California

_____ , I lived in San Jose,
(2)
California. All our neighbors were immigrants.

_____ a new immigrant family
(3)
arrived, we helped them settle. We lived there

_____ .
(4)

_____ , I studied very hard
(5)
in school. My parents taught me to value education even though they were poorly educated. Then

_____ , I went to college and _____ to medical
(6)   (7)
school. I _____ work in a hospital in the same neighborhood that I grew
(8)
up in, and _____ I feel happy that I can give back to my community.
(9)

I am very grateful for the life I have now. Even though it is _____
(10)
that I arrived, sometimes that first day here seems like yesterday. _____
(11)
I still remember how terrified I felt _____ I took the
(12)
bus to school. _____ I wait for my young son's school bus
(13)
to arrive and watch him get on the bus. The freedom that I still cherish is normal for him.

_____ I intend to teach my son about the values of hard
(14)
work and the sacrifices that his grandparents made so that he can enjoy the world he lives in.

Exercise 3.2 More Time Signals

A Complete sentences about yourself. Write about your life, for example, important events in your past and present and your hopes for the future.

1. I _____ for the first time in

   _____

2. By the time I was _____

   I _____

3. Years later, I _____

4. After I _____

   I _____

5. Over the past few years, I _____

6. I recently _____

7. Every day, I _____

8. In the next few years, I hope to _____

B *Pair Work* Share your sentences with a partner. Give more details.

I flew in a plane for the first time in 2002. I was 16 years old. I flew from Taiwan to Australia to see my aunt who had immigrated there. We spent a few days at a beach. It was so beautiful. We also went to a national park, and I saw koalas and kangaroos.

4 Avoid Common Mistakes

1. **Remember to use *this / that* with singular nouns and *these / those* with plural nouns.**

   These
   ~~This~~ *ideas about immigrants are common.*

2. **Remember to use *the* in time signals such as *over the past year* and *in the next five years*.**

   the
   In ‸ last five years, our neighborhood has become less diverse.

3. **Remember that frequency adverbs are usually placed before the main verb but after the verb *be*.**

   never
   He ~~never~~ has ‸ seen so much traffic.
   always
   The traffic ~~always~~ is ‸ bad.
   He usually
   ~~Usually he~~ arrives late.

Editing Task

Find and correct eight more mistakes in the paragraph about an innovative device for the developing world.

      The lack of clean drinking water is a problem in many parts of the world, but even

when people have a source of water, collecting it can be arduous. Every morning, Isha gets

water for her family. ~~Always it~~ *It always* takes her 30 minutes to get to the well and about an hour to

walk back with a heavy clay container of water balanced on top of her head. By time she

5 returns, her body is aching from the weight of the water. She has been bringing water home

like this for last 20 years. Isha lives in Niger, a country in West Africa. In Africa, women, and

sometimes children, often are the ones responsible for collecting their family's water, and

these responsibility takes a toll on their bodies. For some women, the journey to a water

source is very long. This women have to walk up to 18 miles (30 kilometers) a day for water.

10 Hans Hendrikse, a native South African, wanted to do something about this problem. Working

with his engineer brother, Pieter, he created a new way of transporting water. It is called the

Q-Drum. The Q-Drum is lightweight, durable, and affordable, and it can hold 50 liters of water.

While this features alone make the product appealing, the most groundbreaking feature is its

doughnut shape. When a rope is looped through the hole in the Q-Drum, the container can be

15 rolled along the ground like a wheel. The Q-Drum's unique design allows even a young child

to pull water for several miles, so the women never will have to carry the water solely on their

heads. Over next decade this invention will have a major impact on the lives of the people of

Africa, especially the women.

5 | The Writing Process ✒

In this section, you will write a narrative essay. You will use a time line to organize your ideas. Before you start writing, you will learn about audience and purpose in narrative writing.

About Audience and Purpose

Whenever you write, you should always take into account who is going to be reading what you write. In other words, you should consider your audience. When you are writing an e-mail to friends to tell them about a recent trip, for example, you will probably use very informal language, such as contractions and slang. You probably won't worry about spelling and punctuation. However, the audience for a paper written for a college class would be very different. You would be much more careful about the kind of language that you use, the information that you provide, and your spelling and punctuation.

Here are some questions about audience for you to consider when you are planning your writing for a college class:

1. Who is my audience? Do I have multiple audiences (for example, a classroom teacher and an advisor)?

2. What do I want my audience to gain from reading the essay?

3. Am I writing for an audience who is likely to agree or disagree with my point of view? How does this affect the amount of detail I will provide and the type of language I use?

After deciding on the audience, a writer will need to determine the purpose of the writing. For an e-mail to friends about a recent trip, for example, the writer's purpose is likely to tell a story and entertain.

The purposes of writing for an audience could be:

- to entertain them;
- to teach them something new;
- to change their opinion;
- to change their behavior;
- to lead them to consider alternative options;
- to show your knowledge of a topic.

Exercise

A Match the texts to the appropriate audiences in the box. Write the number of the audience next to each text.

Audiences

1) a teacher   3) readers of an online magazine
2) classmates   4) a group of friends and relatives

Text 1
    Are you considering moving to another country? If so, do your homework first. Here are two points you need to keep in mind:

1. Talk to as many people who live in the country as possible. They will be able to give you different perspectives of what life is like in the country.

2. Learn about actual costs. How much does it cost to rent an apartment or go food shopping? You need to know if you can afford living there.

Audience: _____

Text 2
    Sorry I can't make this afternoon's meeting. Do you think it would be OK if we scheduled it for later in the week?

Thanks,

Audience: _____

> **Text 3**
>
> "Migration is a difficult concept to define because it includes people who move for different reasons across different spaces. A migrant can be a person who moves to another city or town within a nation; a refugee who crosses an international border to escape religious or political persecution; a jobseeker who moves to another country for better economic opportunities; a slave who is forcibly moved; or a person displaced by war or natural disaster. Demographers lack a single operational definition for migration because it occurs under different conditions" ("Migration – Types of Migration," n.d.).
>
> Audience: _____

> **Text 4**
>
> I'm having lots of fun in Australia. I can't believe it's been six months already! I've made tons of friends. Sometimes I'm homesick, but oh, well . . . who isn't? I'll keep you updated about all the cool stuff I'm doing. Miss you all!
>
> Audience: _____

B *Pair Work* Work with a partner and discuss the purpose of each of the texts in A. Share your ideas with another pair. Do you agree or disagree?

Pre-writing Tasks

Choose a Topic

A Choose one of the topics below. You will write an essay that contains a narrative that describes events that happened over several years.

- A success story
- A person who overcame difficulties
- A topic of your own approved by your teacher

B *Pair Work* Make a list of the main ideas and events to include in your essay. Share your ideas with a partner. Give each other suggestions about ideas to include.

Organize Your Ideas

A Creating a time line can help a writer organize the key events or information in the essay's narrative. On a separate sheet of paper, draw a time line similar to the one below and sequence the events that you will include in your essay.

born in Ecuador	came to U.S.	B.S. in Mechanical Engineering	moved to Texas	first job with company
1984	2003	2008	2010	2011

B *Group Work* Share your completed time line with a group. Encourage your group to ask you questions to help you explain and sequence the events in your story.

Writing Task

Write your essay. Follow the steps below.

1. Make sure you understand who your audience is.

2. Make sure that you understand the purpose of your paper before you start writing.

3. Include the following in your essay:
   - *this / that / these / those* to connect ideas;
   - common prepositional phrases and adverbs that signal time and sequence;
   - at least three of these academic words from the essay in this unit: *approximately, challenge, contribute, distinct, economic, economy, immigrant, immigration, period, vary.*

> **Academic Writing Tip**
>
> **Avoid Vague References**
> Make sure the noun referents of your demonstratives are clear.
>
> *Some scholars claim that economic disparity results in increased immigration.* **This** *is a significant problem for many countries.*
>
> "This" is vague. What does "this" refer to? Economic disparity? Immigration? The claim?

4. After you write your essay, review it and make sure you avoided the mistakes in the Avoid Common Mistakes chart on page 153.

Peer Review

A Exchange your essay with a partner. Answer the following questions as you read your partner's essay, and then share your responses.

1. Who is the audience for the essay?

2. What is the purpose of the essay?

3. Did the writer use demonstratives?

4. Did the writer use time signals? Underline the ones the writer used.

5. Is anything confusing? Write a question mark (?) next to it.

6. Provide one compliment (something you found interesting or unusual).

B Use your partner's comments to help you revise your essay. Use the Writer's Checklist on page A2 to review your essay for organization, grammar, and vocabulary.

11

Classification and Definition 1: The Passive; Common Words and Phrases Used to Classify

Job Interviews

1 Grammar in the Real World

You will read an essay describing different types of job interviews. This essay is an example of a classification essay, which classifies information into groups or categories.

A *Before You Read* Have you ever gone on a job interview? What was the experience like? Read the essay. How does the writer classify different types of job interviews?

Job Interviews

Interviews are a familiar process for anyone entering the job market. They are by far the most common method used by companies to recruit new employees. All job interviews have the same goals – getting to know the job candidate better and giving the candidate a chance to learn about the job. However, they can take several different forms depending on geographic
5 location and format.

Depending on the geographic location of the candidates, interviews can be divided into two types: remote[1] and face-to-face. In remote interviews, candidates are geographically separated from the interviewers. This type of interview is usually the preferred method for initial screening,[2] as it eliminates traveling expenses. These interviews can be conducted over
10 a teleconferencing system or over the phone. Face-to-face interviews, in contrast, require the physical presence of the candidate. They are normally reserved for candidates who have already gone through a first round of remote screening.

Face-to-face interviews can be classified as either collective or sequential, depending on the number of people interacting with the candidate. Collective interviews can have two
15 possible structures: team interviews and group interviews. In a team interview, multiple interviewers interact with the candidate. In a group interview, multiple candidates are screened by a single interviewer. Sequential interviews, on the other hand, involve private, one-on-one conversations between the candidate and several interviewers, one after another.

As far as the format is concerned, interviews can be divided into two categories: structured
20 and unstructured. In a structured interview, the same list of questions is rigidly followed with all candidates. Companies sometimes use this format to ensure equal treatment among interviewees. It also makes it easy for recruiters to directly compare how two candidates responded to the

[1]**remote:** not near, at a distance, far away | [2]**screening:** the process of sorting something into different groups

same question. Conversely, unstructured interviews have a less strict format. Candidates might be asked more open-ended questions that encourage them to lead the discussion. For example, 25 the interviewer could start by asking candidates to talk about themselves. Interviewers could also ask them to describe their professional experience.

Finally, there are a few less conventional types of interview formats. One example is an audition. In this type of interview, recruiters might ask candidates to perform a task that simulates the actual duties of that job. For example, a candidate for a computer programming 30 position could be required to write a small piece of computer code. Candidates for a marketing job might be asked to persuade their interviewers to buy a fictitious product, and interviewees applying for a teaching job may be invited to prepare and deliver a mini-lesson.

Despite their possible variations, interviews should be seen as almost always having two main objectives. First, they are a way for the employer to test the potential employee. Second, 35 but equally important, they are an opportunity for candidates to learn more about the company and to evaluate their interest in the job. Being aware of the different types of interviews will help job seekers to be more prepared to accomplish those goals.

B *Comprehension Check* Answer the questions.

1. According to the writer, what are the main differences between remote and face-to-face interviews?
2. Why is an audition considered a less conventional type of interview?
3. Do you agree with the writer's conclusions in the final paragraph? Why or why not?

C *Notice*

1 Classification and Definition Writing Write the definitions of the terms below. Why is it important for the writer to define these terms?

1. Remote interviews _____

2. Face-to-face interviews _____

3. Collective interviews _____

4. Sequential interviews _____

5. Structured interviews _____

6. Unstructured interviews _____

2 Grammar Find sentences in the essay that mean the same as the sentences below and write the number of the line on which each sentence is located. Compare the underlined verbs below with the verbs in the sentences in the essay. What do you notice about the form of the verbs the writer used? Why do you think the writer uses this form?

1. It is possible to divide interviews into two types. _____

2. You can classify face-to-face interviews as either collective or sequential. _____

3. A single interviewer screens multiple candidates in a group interview. _____

4. Interviewers might ask a candidate for a marketing job to persuade them to buy a fictitious product. _____

3 The Writing Process Draw the chart below on a separate sheet of paper and complete it with the information from the essay.

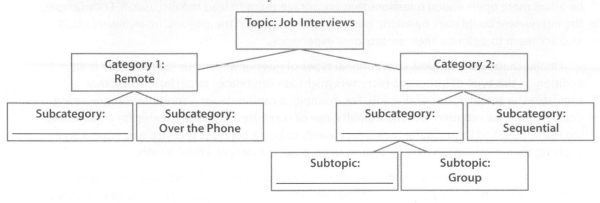

2 | The Passive

▶ Grammar Presentation

The passive focuses on the action rather than the person or thing that receives the action. In academic writing, the passive can also improve text cohesion by making connections across sentences.

*Candidates **are asked** several questions during the interview. The interview questions **are created** by a hiring committee.*

2.1 Forming the Passive

AGENT   OBJECT

The committee presented the results of the survey at the meeting. (Active).

The results of the survey were presented by the committee at the meeting (Passive).

2.2 The Passive

a. Passive and active sentences have similar meanings, but a different focus.

In active sentences, the subject is the agent – the person or thing that performs the action of the verb.

In passive sentences, the subject is the receiver – the person or thing that receives the action of the verb.

         AGENT   RECEIVER

Active: *HR **screens** the candidates.*

         RECEIVER   AGENT

Passive: *Candidates **are screened** by HR.*

2.2 The Passive *(continued)*

b. Passive sentences consist of a form of *be* and the past participle.	Simple present: *Remote interviews **are considered** to be effective.* Present progressive: *The candidate **is being interviewed**.* Present perfect: *The final candidates **have** already **been selected**.* Simple past: *Candidates **were expected** to send a thank-you note after the interview.* Past progressive: *The candidate **was being interviewed** when his cell phone rang.* Past perfect: *Several candidates **had** already **been interviewed** when I arrived for my interview.*
c. The passive can also be used with modals.	*By Friday, several candidates **will have been chosen**.* *Candidates **may be asked** difficult questions.* *The candidates **should have been asked** more questions about their problem-solving skills.*
d. Some verbs that usually occur in the passive are followed by prepositions: *associated with, based on, compared to / with, involved in, linked to, related to*	*Interview questions **should be based on** job requirements.*
e. The passive is often followed by infinitives with verbs for speaking and thinking. Common verbs are: *ask, believe, expect, find, know, say, think, understand*	*Approximately 100 people **are expected to apply** for the job.* *Auditions **are known to be** effective job interview tools.*

Data from the Real World

The following verbs are commonly used in the passive in academic writing:

analyze, argue, carry out, conduct, consider, discuss, estimate, examine, explain, find, illustrate, include, note, observe, perform, present, study, suggest

*Personal questions about age and marital status **are** never **included** in the interview process.*

*Job responsibilities **are discussed** with the candidates at the interview.*

2.3 Using the Passive

a. Use the passive when the agent is not known, not obvious, or not important.	*Many types of interview formats **have been used** at the research lab.* *Some candidates **are required** to perform a task.*

2.3 Using the Passive (continued)

b. Use the passive to improve the flow of ideas across sentences.	*In the group interview, multiple candidates **are screened** by a single interviewer. The interviewer asks a set of questions on standard topics. These questions **have been chosen** by the managers.*
c. Use the passive to describe a process. Common verbs are: *classify, compare, develop, examine, measure, study, test*	*In many community colleges, interview questions **are** carefully **developed** and **tested** before they are used. Face-to-face interviews **can be classified into** several different types.*
d. Use the passive to report news events.	*According to a government report, fewer people **were hired** by companies in June than in May.*

▶ Grammar Application

Exercise 2.1 The Passive

Rewrite the tips and information about job interviews by changing the parts of the sentence in bold from active to passive. Leave out the agent when it is not important, is unknown, or is obvious.

1. Occasionally **a member of the human resources staff will observe an interview**.

   Occasionally an interview will be observed by a member of the human resources staff.

2. **A company may not even consider you** for the job if you arrive late to the interview.

3. During the interview, **the interviewer will ask you questions** about your résumé.

4. **Interviewers may conduct interviews** over the phone.

5. One question you could ask is "What **training programs does the company offer**?"

6. **Employers often base the decision to employ someone on** a person's behavior during an interview.

7. **Federal and state laws prohibit employers** from asking certain questions about race, religion, and age.

8. **People have known some employers** to give tests during interviews.

9. If you do well, **an interviewer might ask you** to come in for a second interview.

_____

10. Interviewers often see more than one candidate in a day, so **they will probably compare you** with other candidates.

_____

Exercise 2.2 More on the Passive

A Complete the e-mail below about recent interviews at a software company. Use the correct passive form of the verbs and, where appropriate, modals in parentheses.

| Send | Attach | Save Draft | Spelling ▾ | Cancel |

From: Peter Campbell

Date: October 14

To: Kim Chen

Subject: The search for project managers

Hi Kim,

Our search for new project managers is going very well so far. Ten interviews _have been conducted_ (conduct) this week so far. The following procedures
(1)
_____ (follow) each time. First, the interviewees all had individual interviews
(2)
during which they _____ (ask) about their previous work experience.
(3)
Then the interviewees _____ (divide) into two groups: those with project
(4)
management experience and those without that experience. After that, each interviewee

_____ (give) a problem-solving test. The test items _____
(5)   (6)
(base) on the kinds of problems that project managers might encounter. My experience has

shown me that a lot _____ (can / learn) about a candidate through
(7)
a problem-solving test.

   Then the interviewees _____ (give) a short writing test. They
(8)
_____ (tell) when they applied that they might have to do some writing.
(9)
After the writing test, the interviewees went home. The tests _____
(10)
(should / evaluate) by Friday, and three interviewees _____ (will / choose)
(11)
to come in for second interviews.

   Let me know if you have any questions.

   Peter

B *Pair Work* Discuss with a partner your experiences or experiences of people you know with job or college interviews. Use the passive where possible.

When I went to the interview for my current job, I was interviewed by my manager first. Then I was asked to take a test. After that, they told me they would call me if they were interested. They called, and I went in, and I talked to someone in the personnel department.

3 | Common Words and Phrases Used in Classification Writing

▶ Vocabulary Presentation

There are common words and phrases that writers use to organize or classify ideas in classification writing.

Colleges **can be classified** into different types.
Most colleges offer the most popular majors, which **include** business administration and psychology.

3.1 Classification Words and Phrases

a. Use the following common verbs and phrases (listed from most to least frequent) to classify ideas: *involves* _____ *involves not only* _____ *but also* _____ *can be classified into* _____ *is a combination of* _____ , _____ , *and* _____ *consists of* _____ *is made up of* _____ *can be / is / are divided into* _____ *is composed of* _____	*The job **involves** a lot of traveling.* *Preparing for an interview **involves not only** physical preparation **but also** mental preparation.* *Interviews **can be classified into** two types.* *A strong cover letter is **a combination of** confidence, preparation, **and** curiosity.* *A typical job application **consists of** a cover letter and a résumé.* *A résumé **is divided into** several key sections.*
b. Use the following common nouns to describe groupings: *categories, classifications, divisions, factions, groups, kinds, parts, sections, sets, types, units*	*Job interviews can be divided into two **categories**.* *Interviews can be divided into two **kinds**: remote and face-to-face.* *There are two main **types** of interviews.*

3.1 Classification Words and Phrases *(continued)*

c. Use these common phrases to develop topics:

TOPIC, *which are* A *and* B.

TOPIC, *which include* A *and* B.

TOPIC, *such as* A *and* B.

TOPIC: A, B, *and* C.

TOPIC, *including* A, B, *and* C.

TOPIC. *These are* A, B, *and* C.

Notice the use of commas in these structures.

> TOPIC
> *There are two main types of interviews,*
>   A   AND   B
> ***which are** remote **and** face-to-face.*
>
> TOPIC
> *The field of health care provides many opportunities:*
>   A   B   AND   C
> *therapy, outpatient care, **and** home health care.*

d. Use these common phrases to introduce the criterion (method) for classification:

according to, based on, depending on, on the basis of

> TOPIC   PHRASE
> *Job interviews can be classified **according to***
> CRITERION
> *their structure.*
>
> PHRASE   CRITERION
> ***Depending on** the number of participants,*
> TOPIC
> *job interviews can be divided into two categories.*

▶ Vocabulary Application

Exercise 3.1 Classification Words and Phrases

Choose the best word or words to complete the sentences about work.

1. A successful job search _____ determination, networking, and luck.
   a. can be divided into   b. involves   c. can be classified

2. Job descriptions on websites often _____ job titles, salaries, and benefits.
   a. are divided into   b. can be classified into   c. consist of

3. Succeeding in an interview _____ both preparation and an ability to adapt quickly to a situation.
   a. involves   b. is composed of   c. is made up of

4. Some companies prefer interviewing people in _____ .
   a. types   b. parts   c. groups

5. Most people want a job that _____ interesting opportunities, challenging tasks, and nice co-workers.
   a. is a combination of   b. can be divided into   c. can be classified into

6. Most businesses _____ several divisions.
   a. can be classified into   b. are composed of   c. involve

7. There are three _____ of a small business owner's job: managing employees, handling the finances, and marketing the business.
   a. kinds   b. sets   c. parts

8. Data Technician and Social Worker I are two _____ of government jobs listed online.
   a. classifications   b. sections   c. sets

Exercise 3.2 ◄)) More Classification Words and Phrases

Read the questions below. Then listen to a lecture about higher education in the United States. Take notes as you listen. Then write the answers to the questions in complete sentences. Use the classification nouns and phrases in parentheses in your answers.

1. How many categories can higher education in the United States be divided into?

   (can be divided) _Higher education in the United States can be divided into five_ _categories, which are universities, community colleges, liberal arts colleges,_ _vocational-technical and career colleges, and special interest colleges._

2. What are the main criteria for determining whether an institution of higher education is a community college or a university?

   (classified / according to) _____

   _____

3. What are the three degree programs in a university?

   (is composed of / generally) _____

   _____

4. What is another way that schools can be divided?

   (can be divided by) _____

   _____

5. How many funding classifications of schools are there?

   (which are) _____

   _____

6. What are the types of publicly supported schools?

   (can be subdivided into) _____

   _____

7. What are the advantages of attending a community college?

   (including) _____

   _____

Exercise 3.3 More Classification Words and Phrases

A Write sentences about job interviews using the words below and your own ideas.

1. a job interview involves

   I think a job interview involves not only talking about your experience but also making a good impression on the interviewers.

2. interviews can be classified into

3. a successful job search is a combination of

4. the perfect job involves

5. a good résumé consists of

6. I answer job advertisements on the basis of

B *Pair Work* Share your ideas with a partner. Decide which of your answers are the best. Report your best answers to the class.

I said that a job interview involves talking about your experience and making a good impression. My partner said that it involves finding out about job requirements. We agreed that my answer was probably the better answer because it's very competitive, so people need to sell themselves very well.

4 | Avoid Common Mistakes ⚠

> **1. Remember to place the adverb after the modal in passive sentences.**
>
>   *often*
> Leadership skills can be ~~often~~ determined in group interviews.
>
> **2. Remember to use the correct preposition in the phrase *based on*.**
>
>   *on*
> The company's hiring decisions are based ~~in~~ candidates' interview behavior.
>
> **3. Remember to use the correct preposition in the phrase *involved in*.**
>
>   *in*
> The company vice presidents are rarely involved ~~on~~ hiring decisions.

Editing Task

Find and correct seven more mistakes in the introduction and body paragraph from an essay on ways to pay for a college education.

Funding Options for Higher Education

                                   in
There are many issues involved ~~on~~ choosing an institution of higher education. A prospective student's choice might be based in the location of the institution, or it might be based in the reputation of the academic programs and the faculty. However, for many students, the process of choosing a university may be often determined by economics. A

5 college education may be one of the greatest expenditures an individual will make in his or her lifetime. If money is an issue in a student's choice, there are several funding options.

       One funding option available to low-income college students is a grant. A grant is a sum of money that does not have to be paid back. Government programs are the primary source of education grants. In addition to government sources, grants may be sometimes

10 awarded by private organizations and companies. The main factor involved on the awarding of government grants is income level. Private grants may often be based in additional factors, such as ethnicity, grades, or other academic achievements. As reporting one's income is always involved on the process of applying for a grant, a good place to begin is with the U.S. Department of Education's Free Application for Federal Student Aid (FAFSA). The FAFSA

15 application simplifies the income reporting process and matches the applicant's income with several grant opportunities. Grants are often the first and best choice for students who cannot afford a college education on their own.

5 | The Writing Process ✏

In this section, you will write an introductory paragraph and one body paragraph for a classification essay. Before you start writing, you will learn how to classify things into categories and subcategories.

About Classifying

When you are classifying ideas or things in an essay, it is important to identify the categories into which you are placing things. You should explain carefully what criteria you used as the basis for each category, so that you clearly differentiate one category from another. Often, as in the sample essay at the beginning of this chapter, you will further divide things into subcategories. Again, you should clearly show why the subdivision was necessary and what the differences are between the subcategories.

Your introductory paragraph should contain a thesis statement that states the categories that will be presented in the body of the essay.

Exercise

A In the box below are different ways to classify jobs. Match each classification type to one of the thesis statements below. Write the letter on the line.

> a. Jobs classified by the types of industries they are in
> b. Jobs classified by whether the salaries are low or high
> c. Jobs classified by what level of education is required

1. _____ New professions have developed in the past several decades; some of them require extensive educational training, while others require only a high school diploma.

2. _____ Explosive new growth in jobs can be divided into the areas of transportation, health care, and tourism.

3. _____ Perhaps not surprisingly, in some parts of the country, new jobs are available in two main areas: unskilled low-paying positions and high-risk positions in start-up companies that have the potential to be extremely well paying.

B *Pair Work* Classification writing contains elements of comparison and contrast writing. After identifying categories, academic writers often explain how the categories are different from or similar to each other. With a partner, explain how you might compare and contrast the different categories in each thesis statement in A.

Pre-writing Tasks

Choose a Topic

A Choose one of the topics below. You will write an introductory paragraph for this topic and one body paragraph.

- Types of majors
- Types of employers
- A topic of your own approved by your teacher

B *Pair Work* Share your chosen topic with a partner. Provide suggestions about ideas or facts to include. Make a list.

Organize Your Ideas

A Draw the chart below on a separate sheet of paper to help you organize your ideas. First, write the topic you chose in the top box. Then choose two of the ideas from your list and write them in the Category boxes. Write information about each of those categories in the subcategory boxes. Add more boxes if you need to.

B *Pair Work* Explain your chart to a partner. Ask your partner whether your categories are clear, and whether there are other ways you could divide your topic.

Writing Task

Write an introductory paragraph and a body paragraph for a classification and definition essay. Follow the steps below.

1. Using the information from your chart, write a thesis statement for the essay.

2. Include in the thesis statement the criteria you will use to classify your topic.

3. Write a hook that will work well for your topic.

4. Provide any necessary background information about the topic in the rest of the introductory paragraph.

5. In your body paragraph, discuss one of the categories mentioned in the thesis statement. Divide the category into its subcategories.

> **Academic Writing Tip**
>
> **Irregular Plurals in Academic Writing**
> Remember to use the correct plural forms of the following academic words: *appendix / appendices; criterion / criteria; fungus / fungi; hypothesis / hypotheses; phenomenon / phenomena; stimulus / stimuli.*

6. Include the following in your paragraphs:
   - the passive;
   - common words and phrases that can be used to classify;
   - at least three of these academic words from the essay in this unit: *aware, category, code, computer, conduct, contrast, conventional, definition, despite, eliminate, ensure, evaluate, finally, format, goal, initial, interact, involve, job, location, method, normally, physical, potential, process, professional, require, respond, rigidly, sequential, simulate, structure, task, team, topic, unstructured.*

7. After you write your paragraphs, review them and make sure you avoided the mistakes in the Avoid Common Mistakes chart on page 168.

Peer Review

A Exchange your paragraphs with a partner. Answer the following questions as you read your partner's paragraphs, and then share your responses.

1. Does the introductory paragraph introduce the topic and explain the criteria used to organize the topic? Do the criteria used relate well to the topic?

2. In the body paragraph, is one of the categories presented in the introductory paragraph described well?

3. Do the subcategories support the main category?

4. Has the writer used the passive in the essay? Is it used correctly?

5. What common words and phrases does the writer use to classify?

6. Is anything confusing? Write a question mark (?) next to it.

7. Provide one compliment (something you found interesting or unusual).

B Use your partner's comments to help you revise your paragraphs. Use the Writer's Checklist on page A2 to review your paragraphs for organization, grammar, and vocabulary.

12 Classification and Definition 2: The Language of Definition; Appositives

Your Ideal Job

1 Grammar in the Real World

You will read an essay that examines the theories of vocational psychologist John Holland. The essay is an example of classification and definition writing that shows how Holland categorizes people according to their personalities.

A *Before You Read* How would you describe your personality? Do you think that your personality influences your decision in careers? Read the essay. What are the six personality types?

Matching Personality Type and Work Environment

Most people spend over a third of their waking hours at work. Because work is such an enormous part of people's lives, their career choices are critical for personal and professional success. Vocational[1] counselors, who are trained to help with these choices, use many tools to help people find the best jobs. One tool is the use of personality tests to suggest job choices
5 that could lead to greater job satisfaction. The most popular of these tests was created by John Holland, a leading researcher in vocational psychology. He developed six categories of personality type – *Artistic, Investigative, Realistic, Social, Enterprising,* and *Conventional* – which are used to help identify the best job choices (Holland, 1997). Understanding these personality types can help identify an appropriate job for one's personality.

10   Each personality type has defining characteristics. An Artistic personality type refers to a person who enjoys creative activities like art, dance, or creative writing, and who generally avoids highly structured or repetitive activities. A person with an Investigative personality type, on the other hand, is defined as someone who likes to study and solve math or science problems. People who fall into the Investigative personality type generally see themselves as

[1] **vocational:** relating to a job, career, or profession

15 scientific and intellectual. Having a Realistic personality type means valuing practical work, such as jobs that require technical or manual skills and are productive. A person with a Realistic personality type particularly values environments where they produce goods or use machines. Other people have good skills at teaching, counseling, nursing, or giving information. They are referred to as Social personalities. People with Enterprising personalities are good at leading

20 people and selling things or ideas. Many entrepreneurs fall into the Enterprising category. Finally, people who have a Conventional personality type are able to work with written records and numbers in a systematic way. These people are usually very detail-oriented and value structure and planning.

Holland's personality types can provide insights into compatible jobs and work

25 environments where people can best use their abilities. For example, Realistic personality types would look for environments that allow them to use tools or machines and generally avoid those that require a lot of interaction with people. Artistic people are more likely to find satisfaction and success in an artistic environment, such as an arts center or theater. Someone with an Investigative personality type would be best suited for a job in an investigative

30 field, such as medicine or mathematics. Figure 1 provides examples of jobs that match each personality type. Holland believed that people who look for jobs that suit their abilities are more likely to find environments in which they can succeed and be satisfied.

Figure 1. Holland Personality Types and Career Examples

ARTISTIC	INVESTIGATIVE	REALISTIC	SOCIAL	ENTERPRISING	CONVENTIONAL
Architect	Mathematician	Auto Mechanic	Nurse	Flight Attendant	Accountant
Dancer	Professor	Cook	Teacher	Lawyer	Cashier
Musician	Scientist	Electrician	Therapist	Salesperson	Secretary

Matching someone's personality type with a work environment is actually a more complicated process because people are often a combination of two or three personality

35 types. This means that the range of suitable jobs can actually be quite diverse. For example, a person may have a Realistic personality type but also have characteristics of an Enterprising personality type and a Social personality type. This person would likely be suitable for a job as an electrician, a salesperson, or a nurse. Discovering one's major personality types involves using assessment tools that identify skills and strengths.

40 For many people, it is often a difficult task to decide on a career. Realizing that much of one's life will be spent doing a certain kind of work can make the decision stressful. Many people use tools like Holland's personality types to help make their decisions. Information about personality types can be interesting and useful. Holland's theory is a valuable guide for people in choosing satisfying jobs and careers.

B Comprehension Check Answer these questions.

1. Why are people's career choices so important for success?
2. According to the essay, how will understanding one's vocational personality type be helpful?
3. Based on this essay, what is your personality type? Why?

C Notice

1 Classification and Definition Writing In the chart below, write a definition of each personality type, based on information from the essay.

Personality type	Definition
1. Social	
2. Enterprising	
3. Realistic	

2 Grammar Find the sentences that contain the definitions of the personality types that follow to notice the grammar the writer uses to introduce the definitions. Underline the verb phrases used in each definition.

1. Artistic personality type on lines 10–12.
2. Investigative personality type on lines 12–14.
3. Realistic personality type on lines 15–16.
4. Social personality type on lines 18–19.

3 The Writing Process Complete the tasks below to notice how the writer creates cohesion by linking back to previous words and ideas in the essay using different ways:

1. Find *their* on line 2. Who does this pronoun refer to?
2. On lines 15–17 in the sentence beginning with "Having a Realistic personality . . . " the writer uses the word "valuing." In the sentence that follows, the writer uses a different form of the word to connect the ideas. What word does the writer use?
3. What pair of synonyms does the writer use in the sentences on lines 29–31? Why?

2 | The Language of Definition

▶ Grammar Presentation

Definitions are very common in academic writing. Writers define key terms in the text so that readers will understand the exact meaning of the concepts being described. Definitions usually use the simple present form of *be*, the verb *means,* or the passive of certain verbs.

*Having a Conventional personality type **means** being good at working with written records and numbers in a systematic way.*
*A person with an Investigative personality type **is defined as** someone who likes to study and solve math or science problems.*

2.1 Definitions

a. A definition generally follows the pattern: term + *be* + general noun + defining details	TERM *IS / ARE* GENERAL NOUN *Realistic personality types* **are** *people* DEFINING DETAILS *who value practical work.*
A general noun names a larger category for the term being defined. It is more general than the term being defined.	DEFINED TERM GENERAL NOUN *A Realistic person is a* **person** *with practical skills.* *Visual learning means* **learning** *by seeing.*
The defining details are often in the form of an identifying relative clause or a prepositional phrase.	IDENTIFYING RELATIVE CLAUSE *A headhunter is a person* **whose job is to find qualified people to take high-paying jobs.** PREPOSITIONAL PHRASE *A chief executive officer is the person* **with the most important position in a company.**
b. You can also use the verb *mean* to define terms.	*Conventional* **means** *standard, predictable, or normal.*
c. Avoid gender-specific singular pronouns in definitions.	SINGULAR NOUN: GENDER-SPECIFIC *A general practitioner is a doctor who provides basic medical services to* **his** *patients.* (This assumes the doctor is a man, not a woman.)
Make the noun plural and use *their*. OR Keep the noun singular and use *his or her* or *his / her*.	PLURAL NOUN: GENDER NEUTRAL *General practitioners are doctors who provide basic medical services to* **their** *patients.* SINGULAR NOUN: NEUTRAL *A general practitioner is a doctor who provides basic medical services to* **his / her** *patients.*

2.2 The Passive in Definitions

You can use the verbs *call*, *define*, *know*, and *refer* in the passive when defining a term.
With *is / are defined as*, the definition comes last.
With *is / are known as*, *is / are called*, and *is / are referred to as*, the definition comes first.
	TERM
	A certified public accountant (CPA) **is defined as**
	DEFINITION
	a person who has passed a state accounting exam.
	DEFINITION
	A person who has passed a state accounting exam
	        TERM
	is known as *a certified public accountant (CPA).*
	DEFINITION
	A person who instructs or trains others, especially in a
	        TERM
	school, **is called** *a teacher.*

2.3 Using Definitions

a. Place the term being defined at the end of the sentence to make a stronger connection to the subject of the next sentence.	*People who are skillful at occupations such as nursing, teaching, and counseling are known as Social types.* *The types of people in this group like to work in social environments.* (The link between the term *Social types* and the next sentence is stronger.)
b. Break more complex definitions into two sentences. Use a pronoun in the second sentence to create cohesion.	*Some people are good at jobs that require working with numbers and following strict procedures.* ***They*** *are called Conventional personality types.* (The definition of *Conventional personality types* is in the previous sentence.)

▶ Grammar Application

Exercise 2.1 Identifying the Parts of Definitions

A Unscramble the sentences below and find definitions of different types of jobs.

1. who repairs / water pipes, baths, / is / a person / a plumber / and toilets

   A plumber is a person who repairs water pipes, baths, and toilets.

2. who designs / is a person / certain that they / new buildings and makes / an architect / are built correctly

   _____

3. sell merchandise / who work / are sometimes referred to / people / as sales associates / in stores and

   _____

4. is called / a musician / who / someone / is skilled / in playing music

   _____

5. out of materials / sculptors / make art / are artists / like clay, marble, and metal / who

   _____

6. as stylists / fashionable clothing, / who / hairstyles, and makeup / are known / people / help their clients choose

   _____

B Rewrite items 1–6 in Part A using the cues below.

1. (is called) _A person who repairs water pipes, baths, and toilets is called_
   a plumber.

2. (is referred to as) _____

   _____

3. (are people who) _____

   _____

4. (is defined as) _____

   _____

5. (are known as) _____

   _____

6. (are people who) _____

   _____

C *Pair Work* Think of definitions for other jobs. Ask questions and test your partner to see if he or she knows the name of the job. Use different defining language in your questions.

A *What do you call someone who flies an airplane?*

B *A person who flies an airplane is called a pilot.*

Exercise 2.2 Writing Definitions

A 🔊 Listen to two students who are studying for a criminal justice test. As you listen, match the terms with the correct definition.

Field	Noun	Noun	Verb	Verb	Adjective + Noun
law	testimony	bankruptcy	to appeal	to sentence	~~admissible evidence~~

1. _admissible evidence_ : the kind of evidence that juries or judges can consider in civil and criminal cases

2. _____ : a system of rules that a community recognizes as regulators of behaviors and actions of people

3. _____ : evidence presented orally by witnesses during trials or before grand juries

4. _____ : to ask a higher court to review a decision after a trial to determine if it was correct

5. _____ : to announce a punishment to someone convicted of a crime

6. _____ : a legal procedure for dealing with debt problems of individuals and businesses

B Write definitions for the terms in A using the verbs in parentheses.

1. (define) _Evidence that juries or judges can consider in civil and criminal_
   cases is defined as admissible evidence.

2. (be) _____

   _____

3. (know) _____

   _____

4. (means) _____

   _____

5. (call) _____

   _____

6. (refer) _____

   _____

3 | Appositives

▶ Grammar Presentation

> To provide additional information about a noun or noun phrase in academic writing,
> you can use an appositive: a noun phrase that either defines, restates, or gives important
> additional information about the noun phrase it follows.
>
> *John Zappa,* **president of Sylvania Community College,** *believes that instructors*
> *should always be aware of different learning styles.*
>
> *People with Enterprising personalities,* **personalities that have leadership traits,**
> *are good at leading people and selling things or ideas.*

3.1 Appositives

a. An appositive is a noun phrase that refers to the same person or thing as the noun it follows.	MAIN NOUN APPOSITIVE *John Holland,* **a leading researcher in vocational psychology,** *developed a theory about career choices.* (*John Holland* and *a leading researcher* refer to the same person.)
A sentence with an appositive is similar in meaning to one with a nonidentifying relative clause. The only difference is the relative pronoun and *be* verb are left out.	NONIDENTIFYING RELATIVE CLAUSE *John Holland,* **who is a leading researcher in vocational psychology,** *developed a theory about career choices.*

3.1 Appositives *(continued)*

b. You usually set off an appositive with commas.

You can also use dashes or parentheses to set off an appositive.

> MAIN NOUN   APPOSITIVE
> *Enterprising personalities, **personalities that hold leadership traits**, are good at leading people and selling things or ideas.*

> MAIN NOUN   APPOSITIVE
> *Kinesthetic learners – **people who learn through moving, doing, and touching** – prefer actively exploring the physical world around them.*

> MAIN NOUN
> *Workers with the Enterprising personality type*
> APPOSITIVE
> ***(people who are energetic, ambitious, and sociable)** often work in real estate agencies and law firms.*

c. You can also place an appositive before the noun that it refers to.

> APPOSITIVE
> ***A leading vocational psychologist,** John Holland developed a well-known list of personality types.*

3.2 Using Appositives

a. You can use an appositive to provide a definition or description of a proper noun.

> APPOSITIVE ADDING DESCRIPTION
> *Ben Cohen, **co-founder of Ben & Jerry's Ice Cream**,*
> APPOSITIVE PROVIDING A DEFINITION
> *is a good example of a "Healer," **a business leader who provides nurturing harmony to a business**.*

b. You can use an appositive to refer to tables or figures and citations, or when you use an acronym (a word formed from the first letters or parts of other words) or an abbreviation.

References to tables and acronyms are usually in parentheses.

These uses are very common in academic writing.

> *To illustrate his theory, Holland created a model of*
> APPOSITIVE
> *personality types **(Figure 1)**.*

> *Federal data are now collected using the North*
> APPOSITIVE
> *American Industrial Classification System **(NAICS)**.*

▶ Grammar Application

Exercise 3.1 Appositives

The items below contain information about remarkable people and organizations. Rewrite each sentence or pair of sentences to make a sentence containing an appositive.

Michael Pollan   Bono   Howard Gardner

1. Michael Pollan is the author of *Food Rules* and *The Omnivore's Dilemma*. Michael Pollan believes we should all examine our eating habits.

   Michael Pollan, the author of Food Rules and The Omnivore's Dilemma,
   believes we should all examine our eating habits.

2. Steve Jobs, who was a driving force in technology, had an enormous impact on the way we use technology on a daily basis.

   _____

   _____

3. One supporter of the nonprofit housing organization Habitat for Humanity is Jimmy Carter. Jimmy Carter is a former U.S. president.

   _____

   _____

4. Desmond Tutu is a Nobel Peace Prize laureate and retired South African archbishop. Desmond Tutu has promoted peaceful conflict resolution for many years.

   _____

   _____

5. Dr. Douglas Schwartzentruber and Dr. Larry Kwak are cancer researchers. Dr. Douglas Schwartzentruber and Dr. Larry Kwak are both working separately to find a vaccine against cancer.

   _____

   _____

6. Bono is a famous singer with the band U2. Bono works to improve health and nutrition throughout the world.

_____

_____

7. Howard Gardner proposed nine types of intelligences. The nine types of intelligences are in Table 1.

_____

_____

8. The Ronald McDonald House Charities help families of children who are receiving medical treatment for serious diseases. The abbreviation for the organization is RMHC.

_____

_____

Exercise 3.2 More Appositives

On a separate sheet of paper, write five sentences about people, places, or organizations that you know about, using appositives. Try to use different punctuation – commas, dashes, and parentheses – in your answers.

Jules Yakakao, an expert in English language learning, works at a major university in Côte d'Ivoire.

Human Rights Watch – an organization dedicated to defending human rights – is well respected.

4 Avoid Common Mistakes ⚠

1. Remember to use singular and plural nouns correctly in definitions.

Artistic types are ~~a person~~ who ~~enjoys~~ creative activities.
(people / enjoy)

2. Remember to use the correct verb form in the passive when giving definitions.

Sometimes, emergency medical technicians are ~~refer~~ to as paramedics.
(referred)

3. Remember to use the correct pronoun in relative clauses. Specifically, remember to use *who* only with animate nouns.

A résumé ~~who~~ does not include dates is called a functional résumé.
(that)

People ~~which~~ are energetic and sociable often work in sales.
(who)

4. Make sure your pronoun use is clear so that it can only refer to one preceding noun. Otherwise, use more precise words, not pronouns, to refer to previously mentioned nouns.

Julio and Luis are creative people. They work in an art studio making large murals. The murals are very expensive. Many people come to see ~~them~~ to learn about ~~them~~.
(the artists / their work)

Editing Task

Find and correct seven more mistakes in the introduction and body paragraph from an essay about a personality test.

The Myers-Briggs Personality Type Indicator

        The Myers-Briggs Type Indicator, MBTI, is a personality assessment tool ~~who~~ *that*

has increasingly gained popularity in the workplace. It is based on a psychological theory

developed by Carl Jung. Jung proposed that there are two basic categories of thinking styles:

rational and irrational. Rational functions involve thinking and feeling. Irrational functions

5 involve sensing and intuition. Jung further proposed that there are two basic types of people,

introverts and extroverts. While there are several personality qualities who psychologists

associate with each type, introverts are usually define as people who are more interested in

ideas and thinking. In contrast, extroverts are define as people who are more action-oriented.

The MBTI has taken these four basic Jungian personality categories and types and established

10 four sets of opposing pairs: extrovert/introvert, sensing/intuition, thinking/feeling, and

judgment/perception. While individuals use all of these thinking styles, their MBTI results

indicate their thinking-style preferences. They can help match individuals to careers and help

managers understand how to best work with these employees.

        One of the MBTI personality types, ISTJ (Introvert, Sensing, Thinking, Judgment),

15 illustrates the way in which the MBTI assessment tool can match individuals to

appropriate working environments. ISTJ personality types are a person who tends to

be quiet. They prefer to be alone. They attend to details rather than to the Big Picture.

They prefer thinking to feeling. This means that they use logic when making decisions. ISTJ

personality types like controlled, organized environments. They are concrete, ordered, and

20 predictable. They are more in tune with facts than with other people's feelings. ISTJs do well as

accountants and in law enforcement. Managers of ISTJ types who are having difficulty getting

along with others need to take action. They can be placed in situations where they can work

alone, for example. Other remedies for unhappy ISTJs might include moving them to a more

organized work group.

5 | The Writing Process ✏

In this section, you will write an essay that will involve classifying topics and writing definitions of key terms. Before you start writing, you will learn how to use a variety of cohesive devices.

About Cohesive Devices

In academic writing, a writer often connects back to previously stated ideas or information. To help their readers see that connections are being made to these previously mentioned ideas and information, writers make use of several different devices, known collectively as *cohesive devices*. When writers use these devices, the text is more cohesive. This literally means it "sticks together" well.

Here are some different types of cohesive devices that you can use to make your writing more cohesive:

1. **Pronouns** refer back to previously mentioned nouns (e.g., *it, she, they*).
2. **Demonstratives** also refer back to previously mentioned nouns (e.g., *this, that, these, those*).
3. **Repetition of words and phrases** remind readers of what they have already read.
4. **Different word forms** of previously mentioned words also remind readers of what they have read (e.g., *resolve → resolution*).
5. **Synonyms** can also help create cohesion in a text by reminding readers of previously mentioned topics (e.g., *reduce → diminish*).
6. **Signal words and transitional expressions** clearly help readers see connections between different parts of a text (e.g., *so, because, then, for example*).

Exercise

Write the number of the cohesive device used above each word in bold.

| 1. Pronoun | 2. Demonstrative | 3. Repetition |
| 4. Different word form | 5. Synonym | 6. Signal/Transitional word or phrase |

According to Neil Fleming, a professor at Lincoln University, learning styles can be classified into several categories. Visual learners are defined as people who **learn** *(4)* through *(1)* seeing. **For this reason** **these** **learners** need to see the teacher's facial expressions to fully *(2)* *(3)* *(4)* understand the content of a lesson. **Students** who learn through listening are called Auditory *(5)* learners. **They** learn best through lectures and discussions. Finally, Kinesthetic **learners** refer *(6)* *(7)* to people who learn through moving, doing, and touching.

Pre-writing Task

Choose a Topic

A Howard Gardner is a psychologist who developed the theory of Multiple Intelligences. He divided intelligence into different categories that the brain uses in learning. Every individual uses these Intelligences in a unique way and often uses some Intelligences more than others. Read about Gardner's Multiple Intelligences.

Linguistic Intelligence is the ability to express your ideas and communicate well with other people through the use of language. Writers, lawyers, and others who value effective communication usually have linguistic intelligence.

Logical / Mathematical Intelligence is the ability to understand the principles and complex ideas of cause / effect systems, the way a scientist does, or to work well with numbers, the way a mathematician does.

Musical Rhythmic Intelligence is the ability to hear patterns in music, recognize them, and work with them. People with musical intelligence have music as a main part of their lives. In fact, some feel like life revolves around music.

Bodily / Kinesthetic Intelligence is the ability to be physical and use the body to solve problems or to perform in some way. Good examples are athletes, firefighters, and dancers.

Spatial Intelligence is the ability to understand space and where things are in relationship to each other – the way a sailor can navigate on the ocean, or the way a sculptor creates a work of art from a piece of stone or wood. Spatial intelligence can be either artistic or scientific.

Naturalist Intelligence is the ability to see differences in living things – plants and animals – and to be aware of the natural world around us, like geographical forms and climate. This ability was essential long ago when people were hunters; it is still important for people who work in fields like botany.

Intrapersonal Intelligence is the ability to honestly know yourself: your abilities and desires, likes and dislikes, and your reactions to different things. Many people like to be around these people who really seem to know themselves well.

Interpersonal Intelligence is being able to understand others. This ability is especially important for anybody who must deal with other people frequently, such as teachers, counselors, politicians, or people in sales.

Existential Intelligence is the ability to ask difficult questions about life, death, and spirituality.

Adapted from *Great performances online: Howard Gardner's multiple intelligences.* (n.d.) Used by permission of WNET New York Public Media. Retrieved from PBS online www.pbs.org

B *Pair Work* Discuss these questions with a partner:

1. Which Intelligences do you tend to use in learning? Give examples.

2. Think of people that you know and their jobs. What assumptions can you make about the types of Intelligences that are dominant?

3. What jobs might people with Existential and Intrapersonal Intelligences be good at?

C *Pair Work* Choose two types of Intelligences to write about in an essay. Explain to your partner why you chose them. Did you pick the same Intelligences?

Organize Your Ideas

A Use the chart below to organize information about the two types of Intelligences you chose. You may need to do some additional research in order to complete the chart.

Type of Intelligence		
Definition		
Skills		
People you know who have / don't have this type		
Suitable and unsuitable jobs		
Other characteristics		
Sources used in your research		

B *Pair Work* Share your chart with a partner who chose at least one different type of Intelligence. Help each other add to or modify the information in your charts.

Writing Task

Write a classification and definition essay about the two Intelligences you have chosen. Follow the steps below.

1. Using the information from your chart, write a thesis statement that previews what your essay is going to be about.

2. Write an introductory paragraph with a hook that introduces the topic and includes your thesis statement.

3. Write several body paragraphs that define your chosen intelligences and classify jobs and skills that work best with these Intelligences.

> ### Academic Writing Tip
> **Use Thought-Provoking Questions**
> Writers sometimes use thought-provoking questions in an introductory or concluding paragraph. For example:
> *How can students learn new information through ways that are unique to each individual?*

4. Write a concluding paragraph that restates the thesis statement and gives some suggestion or prediction for the future.

5. Include the following in your essay:
   - at least two definitions of key words and appositives to describe experts or writers from your sources;
   - a variety of cohesive devices to connect paragraphs as well as ideas within paragraphs;
   - at least three of these academic words from the essay in this unit: *appropriate, assessment, category, compatible, conventional, create, creative, define, definition, design, diverse, enormous, environment, finally, identify, insight, interaction, investigative, involve, job, major, oriented, process, professional, psychology, range, require, researcher, stressful, structure, task, technical, theory.*

6. After you write your essay, review it and make sure you avoided the mistakes in the Avoid Common Mistakes chart on page 181.

Peer Review

A Exchange your essay with a partner. Answer the following questions as you read your partner's essay, and then share your responses.

1. Does the introductory paragraph have a thesis statement that previews the content of the essay?

2. Does the rest of the essay match your expectations from reading the thesis statement? If not, explain.

3. Has the writer included any definitions? Put brackets around any definitions and underline any words or phrases used to introduce the definitions.

4. Has the writer used appositives? Has the writer used correct punctuation with the appositives?

5. Has the writer used any cohesive devices? Place a check mark (✓) next to three of them.

6. Is anything confusing? Write a question mark (?) next to it.

7. Provide one compliment (something you found interesting or unusual).

B Use your partner's comments to help you revise your essay. Use the Writer's Checklist on page A2 to review your essay for organization, grammar, and vocabulary.

Problem–Solution 1: Present Perfect and Present Perfect Progressive; Noun Phrase Structures

Food and Technology

1 | Grammar in the Real World 🌐

You will read an essay about genetically modified food. The essay is an example of problem–solution writing, in which the writer poses a problem and then suggests some possible solutions.

A *Before You Read* Do you worry about the safety of the food you buy from supermarkets? What information do you think should be on the labels of packaged foods? Read the essay. What information does the writer want to see on food labels?

Genetically Modified Foods

Any time humans make technological advances, they have the potential to do great harm and great good. Genetically modified (GM) foods, which are foods that have had changes made to their DNA, are no exception. Many people believe that there are possible advantages to genetically modifying plants, for example, to improve their nutritional value or protect them
5 from pests as they grow. Recently, scientists have added a growth hormone to salmon for faster growth (DeNoon, 2010) and high starch to potatoes so that they absorb less oil when fried ("GM Crops: Costs and Benefits," n.d.). Despite these alleged[1] benefits, there are some scientists and consumer groups that fiercely question the safety of these foods for human consumption and the environment. Peter Katel (2010), a writer for CQ Researcher (a publication
10 that reports on congressional news) claims that more independent tests are needed in order to conclude whether GM foods are suitable for consumption by the general public. Researchers must continue to thoroughly test GM foods to verify their safety, and consumers need to educate themselves and demand that food companies be more open in their identification of food sources.

15   According to The Center for Food Safety, GM foods have entered nearly every sector of the food market (n.d.). This shift means that a majority of the public is consuming GM foods as part of their regular diet. Statistics detailed in 2010 by Patrick Byrne, a professor at Colorado State University, revealed a little known fact: From 60 to 70 percent of all prepared foods in a typical supermarket in the United States contain GM ingredients. However, little research
20 has been done concerning the existence of any short- or long-term side effects. Larry Trivieri, author of several books on alternative medicine, cites the fact that the U.S. Food and Drug Administration does not require independent safety tests on GM foods (2011). Because of the lack of conclusive research, Neal Barnard (2011), as well as other researchers, has been warning us that potential health risks may be associated with the consumption of these foods.

[1]**alleged:** said to be true, but without proof that it is true

As consumers, we must make informed choices in the food we buy for the sake of our
25 families. To do that, we need to educate ourselves on the issues surrounding GM foods so that
we can choose whether to buy this "enhanced" food or not. Even though research has been
inconclusive as to the effects of eating GM foods, we have the right to know their presence in
the food we buy. Currently, foods with genetically modified ingredients are not labeled as such.
One way to address the problem is by systematically labeling foods. People have the right to
30 know what they are consuming. In 2001, Eli Kintisch, a writer for *The New Republic*
(a well-known magazine of politics and arts), suggested that the few remaining
products should be simply labeled "GM-free." Since then, some manufacturers
have added these labels. Consumers should pressure food manufacturers to
continue to add them.

35　　More research on the effects of GM foods must be done promptly. People
have already consumed a significant amount of these foods throughout the world,
and that amount is increasing, yet there is concern that we do not understand
the possible side effects on humans, other living things, and our environment.
Consumers must educate themselves and make wise choices. While there
40 appear to be advantages to this technological advance, we must make sure
that the good that GM foods do for society far outweighs any potential harm.

B *Comprehension Check* Answer the questions.

1. According to the writer, what is the problem with GM foods?
2. Give two reasons why food is genetically modified, according to the essay.
3. In the third paragraph, the word "enhanced" is in quotation marks. Why do you think the writer used quotation marks around this word?

C *Notice*

1 Problem–Solution Writing Look at the second paragraph, which states the problem. In that paragraph, the writer offers information from four different sources to convince the reader that GM foods may be a problem. Complete the chart below with the information described in each of the sources.

Source	Information
The Center for Food Safety	GM foods have entered nearly every sector of the food market. A majority of the public is consuming GM foods as part of their regular diet.
Patrick Byrne	
Larry Trivieri	
Neal Barnard	

2 Grammar Follow the instructions below to help you notice and understand how the writer uses the grammar to explain the problem.

1. Read the second paragraph again.
   a. Do the verbs *have entered* and *has been done* describe a period of time up to now or a specific time in the past?
   b. How does the meaning of the verb *has been warning* differ from the meaning of the verbs in a.? Which form of the verb emphasizes that the action is potentially still continuing, the present perfect or present perfect progressive?

2. Reread the sentence starting on line 17 beginning with "Statistics detailed in . . ." Why do you think the writer used the past form of the verb "reveal" (*revealed*) instead of the present perfect form (*has revealed*) in this sentence?

3 The Writing Process The writer uses the four strategies in the box below to try to convince the reader of the seriousness of the problem. Write the name of each strategy next to the sentence below that illustrates it.

| emotional appeal | fact | statistic | strong opinion |

1. People have a right to know what they are consuming. _____

2. The FDA does not require independent safety tests on GM foods. _____

3. From 60 to 70 percent of all prepared foods in supermarkets contain GM ingredients. _____

4. We must make informed choices in the food we buy for the sake of our families. _____

2 | Present Perfect and Present Perfect Progressive

▶ Grammar Presentation

In problem–solution writing, the present perfect is used to describe situations, recent research, or trends that have an impact on a problem. The present perfect emphasizes a time in the past up to now. The time period may or may not be completed but in both cases there is a connection to the present. The present perfect progressive describes an action that started in the past and emphasizes that it is still going on.

*Genetically modified food **has been** available in grocery stores for many years.*
*Researchers **have been studying** the impact of GM foods on our health.*

2.1 Using Present Perfect

a. Use the present perfect to describe an event that started at an unknown or unspecified time in the past. This event may be completed, or it may continue into the future.

Note: Do not use the present perfect for events that happened at a specific time in the past.

*Some researchers **demonstrated** that genetically modified foods may cause damage to humans.* (completed event)

*The consumption of GM foods **has increased** significantly in the last ten years.* (the event may continue)

SIMPLE PAST

*Sales of GM foods **increased** dramatically between 2001 and 2011.*

b. Use the present perfect to indicate that a past event relates to the present – it is still important *now*. These are often recent events.

These events may include general experiences up to now.

*Researchers **have discovered** recently that some GM foods may not cause health problems.* (The discovery is important and relevant now.)

*It is true that most people **have not noticed** any difference after eating GM foods.*

*The research team **has received** several grants for GM food research.*

c. Use the present perfect to introduce general ideas and provide background information about a problem.

Then use the simple past to fill in the details that led to the problem.

*The farming of GM foods **has increased** in recent years.*

*In 2010, Brazil dramatically **increased** the use of land for farming GM crops.*

d. The adverbs *already, ever, never,* and *yet* often occur with the present perfect.

*Many farmers **have already seen** enormous gains in productivity using GM crops.*

***Has** any technological advance **ever been accepted** immediately?*

*They **haven't finished** the research **yet**.*

e. Use the present perfect in academic writing to refer to earlier parts of a text.

You can also use the present perfect to refer to other research.

***As we have seen**, there is no easy answer to the problem of our nation's food shortage.*

***Swanson (2010) has argued that** labeling foods may be the only short-term solution to the problem of GM foods.*

***Critics have examined** the situation carefully but have not proposed any definitive solution to the problem.*

2.2 Using Present Perfect Progressive

a. Use the present perfect progressive to describe actions that started in the past and to emphasize that they continue to the present and may continue in the future.

As with other progressive forms, do not use the present perfect progressive with stative verbs.

*Researchers **have been warning** us for many years that GM foods have potential health risks.*

*This group **has been studying** the effects of GM foods since 2001.* (They are still studying them.)

*Some scientists **have believed** for years that GM foods are unsafe.*

NOT

Some scientists have been believing for years that GM foods are unsafe.

b. Use the present perfect progressive with time expressions to emphasize how long an action has been going on: Use *all (semester), for (years), in (months), not . . . in (a long time)*, to show the duration of the action or event. Use *since (2010)* to show the starting point of the action or event.	He**'s been collecting** data <u>all semester</u>. They**'ve been interviewing** consumers <u>for three months</u>. Stores **have not been carrying** that product <u>since 2010</u>.
c. The present perfect progressive often has no time expression associated with it.	What **has** your research group **been working on**? We**'ve been studying** GM crops.
d. The present perfect and the present perfect progressive can often have the same meaning and can be used interchangeably.	The number of farms that grow GM foods **has increased** <u>since 2005</u>. The number of farms that grow GM foods **has been increasing** <u>since 2005</u>.

▶ Grammar Application

Exercise 2.1 Present Perfect Forms or Simple Past?

A Complete the paragraph about one farmer's story about switching to organic farming. Use the passive where appropriate. Sometimes more than one answer is possible.

Since 1979, <u>*I've been farming*</u> (farm) using conventional methods and
$\qquad\qquad$ (2) (get) good results. However, after my first granddaughter

$\qquad\qquad$ (3) (be) born, I $\qquad\qquad$ (4) (start) to think of the world that
she would live in and to consider organic farming. It means making a lot of changes, though.

I $\qquad\qquad$ (5) (always / apply) chemical fertilizers to promote plant growth, but
that will change. For years, I $\qquad\qquad$ (6) (spray) insecticides to reduce pests and
disease, but that will change, too. Starting next year, I will use birds, insects, and traps to

do that. For the entire time I $\qquad\qquad$ (7) (live) on the farm, chemical herbicides

$\qquad\qquad$ (8) (use) to kill weeds. Once in 1992, I $\qquad\qquad$ (9) (use) natural
herbicides, but they $\qquad\qquad$ (10) (not work) well, so I $\qquad\qquad$ (11) (stop)
using them, and I $\qquad\qquad$ (12) (go) back to using chemical herbicides. However,
starting next year, I will rotate crops to manage weeds.

B *Pair Work* Role-play a discussion between two people with different views on genetically modified foods. Use the present perfect and present perfect progressive forms where appropriate.

Student A You are skeptical about the farming of GM foods and think that not enough research has been done. You do not trust food companies and you wish that more information about GM foods were available. You believe that the use of the foods may harm the ecosystem. Your solution: There should be more research done on GM foods.

Student B You are enthusiastic about GM foods. You have read some research on the foods and are convinced that they are not harmful and that our bodies will adapt to eating them. You think that the use of technology to create new foods will allow people to be healthier and potentially reduce starvation worldwide. Your solution: There should be more GM foods.

A *The farming of GM foods is a problem. The research on GM foods has suggested that they could be harmful, so I don't feel confident that the foods are good for society.*

B *I disagree. We've been eating these foods for years now with no ill effects, and it seems the advantages outweigh the disadvantages. . . .*

Exercise 2.2 More Present Perfect Forms or Simple Past?

Complete the sentences. Use the present perfect, present perfect progressive, or simple past of the verbs in parentheses. Use the passive forms when necessary. Circle any time markers that help you decide which form is correct. Sometimes more than one answer is possible.

1. From 2000 to 2007, the value of GM crops *increased* (increase) considerably.

2. For the past 20 years, researchers _____ (track) the areas used to grow GM crops in the world.

3. Over the past 15 years, the number of GM crops _____ (grow) significantly.

4. Over 309 million acres of land _____ (use) for GM crops in 2008 compared to 282 million in 2007.

5. Many people are not even aware that farmers _____ (begin) growing GM crops in the mid-nineties.

6. Statistics show that the global area of GM crops _____ (increase) steadily since the mid-nineties.

7. In 2010, farmers from 29 countries, including Brazil, Argentina, and India, _____ (plant) GM crops.

8. The effects of GM foods on people _____ (not / determine), and scientists continue to do research.

9. Research _____ (not / show) yet that GM foods have a negative effect on our health and environment.

10. Until there is definite proof that GM foods are not harmful, some people _____ (decide) to avoid them.

Source: Genetically modified plants: Global cultivation on 134 million hectares. (2010).
GMO Compass. Retrieved from www.gmo-compass.org

Exercise 2.3 ◄)) More Present Perfect Forms and Simple Past

Read the statements below. Then listen to the radio program about urban gardening. As you listen, decide if the statements are true or false. Circle *T* or *F*.

T/Ⓕ   1. Residents of urban areas such as Los Angeles grow vegetables in their apartment.

T / F   2. Mark Johnson started a rooftop garden five years ago.

T / F   3. Mark Johnson no longer has a rooftop garden.

T / F   4. The neighborhood swap in Mark's neighborhood started four years ago.

T / F   5. Emily Ling regularly brought cooked food to the neighborhood swap.

T / F   6. Emily Ling goes every week to the neighborhood swap.

T / F   7. Emily and her neighbors never buy vegetables from stores anymore.

T / F   8. Neighborhood gardens have been popular for a while in Emily's city.

T / F   9. Annie Suarez started to grow food in her local neighborhood garden in 2010.

T / F 10. Annie Suarez currently writes a gardening blog.

3 | Common Noun Phrase Structures 🌎

▶ Vocabulary Presentation

In academic writing, certain noun phrase structures (sometimes called *shell nouns*) are used to identify and restate more complex ideas. They generally refer to information already mentioned or that will follow in the text. In problem–solution writing, these structures can be used to define a problem and explain its importance.

*It is important to identify **the causes of** famine.*

*Research needs to be done because of **the fact that** more and more people are consuming GM foods.*

3.1 Noun Phrases with *Of*

a. Some noun phrases with *of* explain, label, or define a concept. For example: *the basis of, the concept(s) of, the definition of, the essence of, the idea of, the meaning(s) of, the notion of*	*It is important that the public understands **the concept of** genetic engineering and its implications.* ***The definition of** organic farming is agriculture that relies on natural methods and limits the use of chemical fertilizers and pesticides.*

3.1 Noun Phrases with *Of* (continued)

b. Some noun phrases with *of* express consequences and outcomes. For example: *the cause(s) of, the consequence(s) of, the effect(s) of, the result(s) of*	*Consumers need to be aware of **the potential consequences of** GM foods on their health.* *No one has studied **the effects** of GM foods on babies.*
c. Some noun phrases with *of* express goals. For example: *the aim of, the benefit(s) of, the goal(s) of, the purpose(s) of*	***The aim of** the program is to reduce reliance on pesticides.* ***The purpose of** food labeling is to help consumers make more informed decisions.*
d. Some noun phrases with *of* express the importance of a concept. For example: *the core of, the heart of, the importance of*	*Sustainability is **the heart of** organic farming.* ***The importance of** organic farming is sustainability – not harming the environment and managing it well.*
e. Some noun phrases with *of* indicate measure and quantity. For example: *the amount of, the frequency of, the majority of, a number of, the number of, the rest of* Note: *A number of* means "several" or "many" and is followed by the plural form of a verb. *The number of* refers to a specific number and is followed by the singular form of a verb.	*Consumers need to be aware of **the amount of** GM foods that they eat.* ***The majority of** GM products come from crops such as soybeans, corn, and cotton.* ***A number of** people **have asked** about the benefits of organic farming.* ***The number of** consumers who buy GM foods **is increasing**.*

3.2 Noun Phrases with *That* Clauses

a. Noun phrases with *that* clauses are used to: express a fact: *conclusion, fact* express an idea: *claim, idea, notion* express a view: *belief, doubt, sense, view* express a claim that is not yet proven: *assumption, hope, hypothesis, impression, observation, possibility, suggestion*	***The fact that** the population continues to increase makes efficient food production essential.* *New research may support **the notion that** modifying food has a negative impact on health.* *Many governments hold **the view that** genetically modified food has successfully fed many hungry people.* *Many people are concerned about **the possibility that** GM foods can be dangerous.*
b. Noun phrases with *that* clauses can appear anywhere noun phrases appear (for example, as a subject or object).	SUBJECT ***The claim that GM foods can be beneficial** is true.* SUBJECT ***The fact that conventional agricultural products can have an "organic" label** has created skepticism in consumers.* OBJECT *I support **the idea that GM foods should be labeled**.*

3.2 Noun Phrases with *That* Clauses *(continued)*

c. *The fact that* and *the idea that* are especially common expressions in academic writing. *The fact that* often introduces ideas that are generally accepted. You can use *the fact that* to persuade. A reader is less likely to challenge a statement that follows *the fact that*. It suggests that the information is not an opinion.	The writer cites **the fact that** no long-term studies have been done on the effects of GM foods. Not all consumers agree with **the idea that it is necessary to label foods**.

▶ Vocabulary Application

Exercise 3.1 Noun Phrases with *Of*

A Complete the sentences about genetically modified foods with an appropriate noun phrase from the box. Sometimes more than one answer is possible.

the aims of	the basis of	the benefits of	~~the concept of~~	the effects of
the heart of	the majority of	a number of	the number of	

1. _The concept of_ genetic modification is not new.

2. One of _____ modifying food genetically is to produce enough food, especially corn, rice, and soybeans, for people all over the world.

3. However, _____ genetic modification of food are still not completely understood.

4. In a recent study, _____ people surveyed were uncomfortable with the idea of GM foods. In fact, _____ them avoided the foods.

5. At _____ their concern is the fact that researchers don't really know whether GM foods are completely safe.

6. _____ GM foods produced every year is steadily growing.

7. Proponents of this technology talk about what _____ this technology will be; however, only time will tell if they are correct to be so optimistic.

8. Opponents of GM foods do not think that the government should allow more GM foods on _____ inconclusive findings.

B *Group Work* Work in a group to answer the questions about GM foods. Use the noun phrases from the word box in A in your answers. Then present your answers to the class.

1. What are some reasons why scientists created GM foods?

2. What are some advantages and disadvantages of GM foods?

3. What do you think the majority of people know about GM foods? What do they base their understandings on? What are some of their concerns?

Exercise 3.2 Noun Phrases with *That* Clauses

A Read about the benefits of eating locally grown food and circle the correct phrases to complete the sentences.

Among the many current food trends, one is based on **the belief that** / **the fact that** it is better to
(1)
eat locally grown food than food exported from far away. **The doubt that** / **The notion that** local food is
(2)
better for you is based on a few facts.

First, **the idea that** / **the fact that** food has only
(3)
traveled a few miles to get to your supermarket means that the food is probably fresher than meat or produce that has been shipped from the other side of the world. There is **a conclusion that** / **possibility that** produce
(4)
that has traveled a long way may have lost some of its nutrients or begun to deteriorate during the trip.

Second, people who prefer local food might hold **the view that** / **the conclusion that**
(5)
eating locally grown food is good for the community. For example, buying this food supports local farmers and other food producers, like cheese manufacturers and bread bakers.

Third, **the doubt that** / **the hope that** eating locally grown food will help protect the
(6)
environment – because less fuel is required to transport the food – might motivate some people to follow this trend.

Ironically, locally grown food can sometimes be more expensive than exported food even though it doesn't have to travel very far. This is often due to **the impression that** / **the fact that** local food producers usually consist of small businesses
(7)
with high overhead costs and low levels of production.

B *Pair Work* What is your opinion of eating locally grown foods? What are the benefits? What are some possible disadvantages? Talk with a partner and explain your opinion. Use nouns phrases with *that*.

The possibility that exported food may be less nutritious is surprising to me. I didn't realize that food could lose nutritional value like that. I think the fact that locally grown food might be more nutritious is a strong argument for eating food that is produced near my home.

4 | Avoid Common Mistakes ⚠️

1. **Remember that noncount nouns such as *advice*, *equipment*, *evidence*, *information*, *knowledge*, and *research* do not have plural forms.**
   information
   We do not have enough ~~informations~~ on the health effects of GM foods.

2. **Remember to use *the fact that*, and not *this fact that*.**
   the
   Many people are not aware of ~~this~~ fact that many snack foods contain GM ingredients.

3. **Remember that a *number of* takes a plural count noun and plural verb.**
   experts agree
   A number of ~~expert agrees~~ that GM foods may help solve world hunger.

Editing Task

Find and correct eight more mistakes in the body paragraph from an essay on environmental problems associated with food production.

Engineered Food and the Environment

activists think
A number of animal rights ~~activist thinks~~ that laboratory-generated meat, also known

as cultured meat, provides a solution to the negative environmental effects of food production.

Cultured meat is grown in a laboratory from animal tissue cells. There are many benefits

of cultured meat. First, animals do not have to be killed for food. According to the animal

5 rights organization People for the Ethical Treatment of Animals (PETA), "More than 40 billion

chickens, fish, pigs, and cows are killed every year for food in the United States" (as cited in

Harder, 2008, para. 1). This fact that cultured meat would virtually eliminate animal suffering

is not in dispute. Additionally, most people are aware that raising animals for food is harmful

to the environment. This is because processing meat requires large amounts of resources such

10 as land and water. There is also a great deal of informations on this fact that raising animals for

meat contributes to greenhouse gases and pollutes water, air, and land. Recent researches on

the environmental impact of cultured meat is very promising. A number of environmentalist

agrees that cultured meat would greatly reduce greenhouse gas emissions. There is also

evidences that cultured meat might be healthier and safer. A number of scientist is continuing

15 to do researches on cultured meat. Many of these experts predict that we will see cultured meat

in supermarkets within five to ten years. It seems clear that relying more on engineered food

products may someday help to solve some of the environmental problems that we face today.

5 | The Writing Process

In this section, you will write two paragraphs describing a problem and explaining its importance. Before you start writing, you will learn strategies for emphasizing the significance of a problem.

About Emphasizing the Significance of a Problem

When you are presenting a problem in problem–solution writing, it is important to use strong arguments and strong language to convince the reader that the problem is significant and worthy of discussion and analysis.

The following are strategies you can use to emphasize the significance of the problem:

1. **Use facts.**

   Sixty to seventy percent of all prepared foods in a typical supermarket in the United States contain GM ingredients and yet these foods are not labeled as such. Thus, a majority of the public are consuming these foods without their knowledge of it.

2. **Use examples.**

   For example, the FDA is considering the approval of genetically altered animals, such as cattle and pigs.

3. **Use strong opinions.**

   Unless we take immediate action now, it may well be too late to reverse what is happening.

4. **Use an emotional appeal.**

   We must ensure that our children and our grandchildren have a safe and healthy world to live in.

5. **Use statistics and, if possible, data from charts and graphs.**

   As shown in Figure 1, the percentage of planted acres of corn has risen significantly since 2005.

Figure 1

Growth in adoption of genetically engineered crops in the U.S.
Percent of planted acres

Data for each crop category include varieties with both HT and Bt (stacked) traits.
Sources: 1996 –1999 data are from Fernandez-Cornejo and McBride (2002). Data for 2000 –11 are available in the ERS data product. Adoption of Genetically Engineered Crops in the U.S. tables 1–3

Exercise

A Write two arguments about each of the problems below, emphasizing the significance of the problem. In each sentence, use a different strategy.

1. As the world population grows, we need more and cheaper sources of food.

2. Foods that contain genetically modified organisms are not labeled in the United States.

3. The supply of fish worldwide is becoming depleted.

B *Pair Work* Share your arguments with a partner. Identify the strategies your partner uses – facts, statistics, emotional appeal, strong opinions.

Pre-writing Tasks

Choose a Topic

A Choose one of the topics below. You will write two paragraphs explaining the problem and giving two or three reasons for its significance.

- The demand for and the production costs of food are rising, while global population is increasing.
- The effects of climate change – increased frequency of droughts, floods, and extreme temperatures – have affected food production.
- A topic of your own approved by your teacher

B *Pair Work* Share your topic with a partner. Describe some of the reasons you believe the topic is significant. Give each other suggestions about reasons for the problem, why the problem is significant, and where to do research to find additional facts.

Organize Your Ideas

A Draw the chart below on a separate sheet of paper and complete it to organize your ideas. Describe the problem and write three reasons why the problem you chose is significant. If possible, give the source of your information.

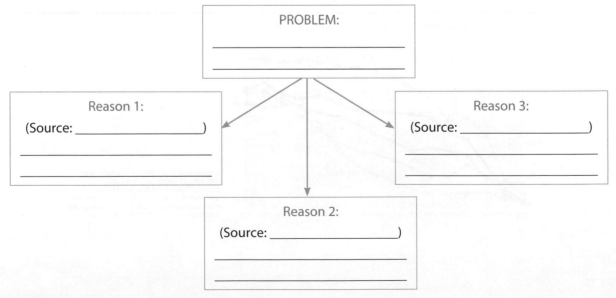

B *Group Work* In a small group, take turns presenting your ideas. Try to convince your classmates that your problem is more significant than theirs. After everyone has finished presenting, choose the most convincing presentation and explain why you chose that presentation.

Writing Task

Write two paragraphs that describe the problem and explain why the problem is significant using the ideas that you wrote in your chart. Follow the steps below.

1. Introduce and describe the problem, providing any historical or factual information that the reader may need to understand the background to the problem.

2. State two or three reasons why the problem is significant. Use strategies that you learned on page 199 to emphasize the significance of the problem.

3. Include the following in your paragraphs:

   • the present perfect and present perfect progressive to describe past situations that have an impact on present events;

   • noun phrases with *of* and *that* clauses;

   • at least three of these academic words from the essay in this unit: *alternative, benefits, challenging, cite, conclude, conclusive, consume, consumer, consumption, enhance, environment, identification, inconclusive, intensive, issue, label, labor, majority, modify, percent, potential, require, research, researcher, reveal, sector, shift, significant, source, statistics, technological.*

4. After you write your paragraphs, review them and make sure you avoided the mistakes in the Avoid Common Mistakes chart on page 198.

Peer Review

A Exchange your paragraph with a partner. Answer the following questions as you read your partner's paragraphs, and then share your responses.

1. Does the writer explain the problem clearly?

2. Do the paragraphs contain facts, statistics, opinions, and emotional appeals to convince the reader that the problem is significant?

3. Do the paragraphs include the present perfect and present perfect progressive? Underline any instances of these tenses.

4. Do the paragraphs include noun phrase structures with *of* and *that* clauses? Put brackets [ ] around any instances of these noun phrase structures.

5. Is anything confusing? Write a question mark (?) next to it.

6. Provide one compliment (something you found interesting or unusual).

B Use your partner's comments to help you revise your paragraphs. Use the Writer's Checklist on page A2 to review your paragraph for organization, grammar, and vocabulary.

Problem–Solution 2: Reporting Verbs; Adverb Clauses and Phrases with *As;* Vocabulary for Describing Information in Graphics

Children and Health

1 Grammar in the Real World 🌐

You will read an essay that focuses on the problem of childhood obesity. The essay is an example of problem–solution writing, in which the writer describes the problem and the reasons why the problem exists. At the end of the essay, the writer voices a need to find a solution to the problem.

A *Before You Read* In what ways have the lifestyles of children changed in the past 20 years? How have these changes affected their health? Read the essay. According to the author, what are the main causes of childhood obesity?

Fighting Childhood Obesity

Childhood obesity is a major concern in the United States and in many other countries around the world. As shown in Figure 1, obesity in U.S. children has increased dramatically since the late 1980s. The Centers for Disease Control and Prevention (2011) state that an overweight or obese child has a Body Mass Index (BMI, a measure of weight in relation to the child's age,
5 sex, and height) above the 85th percentile for his or her age and sex. As an example of this, a second grader whose weight is above the 85th percentile would weigh 95 pounds or more. While it appears that the rates of obesity are falling for younger children, this trend is still likely to persist and perhaps worsen in the future for older children.

Former President Bill Clinton, a supporter of stronger policy on childhood obesity, asserts
10 that the causes of this health crisis range from overworked parents, with no time to prepare healthy food, to a lack of sidewalks and safe outside play areas for children (2010). Clinton also recognizes that a contributing factor is the marketing of inexpensive large-portion meals at fast-food restaurants. Companies make these meals for children even more attractive by giving away small toys and prizes with each meal.

15 Doctors are concerned about increased childhood obesity because of its health-related consequences. One consequence of obesity is cardiovascular disease.[1] Certain risk factors, such as high blood pressure, high cholesterol, and high blood sugar, are present in people who develop this disease. A study of obese children and adolescents has shown that approximately 60 percent of the participants had at least one risk factor for cardiovascular disease (A Change
20 of Pace Foundation, n.d.).

[1]**cardiovascular disease:** heart disease

There are additional health risks associated with being overweight or obese. Though less common, they are serious health issues. They include asthma, sleep apnea (when breathing stops during sleep for at least 10 seconds), and Type 2 diabetes. While Type 2 diabetes has been a common health consequence of adult obesity, in recent years it has become a problem among 25 children and adolescents (Bellows & Roach, 2011). Finally, other studies of obese children and teens have indicated that these young people are more likely to be obese when they are adults (American Academy of Child & Adolescent Psychiatry, 2011, para. 2).

Apart from physical issues, childhood obesity can also generate social problems. Puhl (2011) notes that overweight and obese children are often discriminated against socially, and that this 30 can cause stress and low self-esteem. These feelings are likely to have an impact on children's academic and social lives.

Figure 1.

Parents, doctors, scientists, and policy makers all believe that childhood obesity is a critical issue. It is clear that the reasons 35 for the rise in childhood obesity are complex. Therefore, the solution must involve everyone – parents, doctors, the media, as well as the community. A committed response now will ensure that the obese 40 child of today will not grow up to be an obese adult.

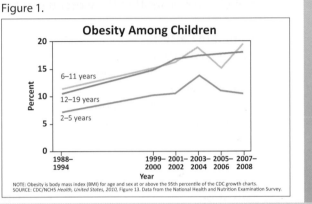

SOURCE: CDC/NCHS *Health, United States, 2010,* Figure 13. Data from the National Health and Nutrition Examination Survey.

B *Comprehension Check* Answer the questions.

1. According to the essay, what are some health issues that result from children being overweight or obese?

2. What are the social concerns for children who are overweight or obese?

3. Why does the author say, "It is clear that the reasons for the rise in childhood obesity are complex"?

C *Notice*

1 Problem–Solution Writing Notice how the writer not only states the problem, but also explores the reasons for and consequences of the problem. Draw the chart below on a separate sheet of paper and complete it with information from the essay.

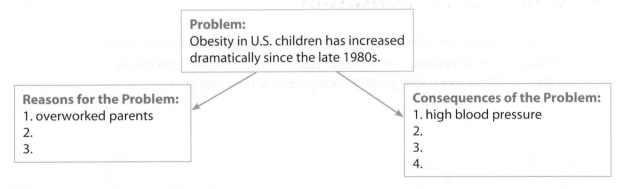

Problem:
Obesity in U.S. children has increased dramatically since the late 1980s.

Reasons for the Problem:
1. overworked parents
2.
3.

Consequences of the Problem:
1. high blood pressure
2.
3.
4.

2 Grammar Find the verbs that the writer uses to report ideas and information from sources. Write them on the blank lines.

1. The Centers for Disease Control and Prevention (2011) *state that* ...

2. Former President Bill Clinton _____ ...

3. Finally, other studies of obese children and teens _____ ...

4. Puhl (2011) _____ ...

5. Parents, doctors, scientists, and policy makers all _____ ...

3 The Writing Process The writer of this essay brainstormed seven different reasons for childhood obesity; however, he or she chose not to include them all in the essay. Draw a line through the reasons that the writer did not include in the essay.

Homelife Patterns
- unsupervised children, parents allow children too much freedom
- parents always at work, no time to fix healthy meals

Lack of Physical Activity
- watching TV
- playing computer games and handheld games
- less outdoor activity – no safe places

Childhood Obesity

Nutrition
- cheap fast food, young children want prizes
- not enough vegetables and fruit
- too much processed food
- soda or high-sugar juices instead of water

2 | Reporting Verbs

▶ Grammar Presentation

Academic writers use reporting verbs to report ideas or findings from a source.

*Bill Clinton (2010) **provides** several reasons for the increase in childhood obesity.*
*The study **illustrates** several possible consequences of childhood obesity.*

2.1 Reporting Verbs

a. Reporting verbs have the pattern:

the source + a reporting verb + *that* + clause with source's information.

SOURCE   REPORTING VERB
Puhl (2011) **points out that**
                    CLAUSE WITH SOURCE'S INFORMATION
obese children are targets of social discrimination.

b. In less formal writing, *that* can be omitted after a reporting verb.

It is better to keep *that* in academic writing.

INFORMAL: *Many parents **believe** children should avoid junk food.*

FORMAL: *Doctors **believe that** children should avoid junk food.*

c. Many reporting verbs, such as *illustrate, point out, show,* and *suggest,* can also be followed by a noun phrase.

                    NOUN PHRASE
*Figure 1 **illustrates** the three levels of influence on children's health.*

d. Some reporting verbs can only be followed by noun phrases and never by *that* clauses, for example:

describe, display, evaluate, give, investigate, present, summarize

*Chart 1 **describes** seven parental influences on children's health.*

NOT *Chart 1 describes that there are seven parental influences on children's health.*

*Figure 1 **gives** eight community influences on children's health.*

Data from the Real World

Common reporting verbs that take *that* clauses are (in order of frequency):

say, show, assume, suggest, complain, announce, argue, add, declare, explain, imply, mention, point out, propose, recommend, remark, report, state, write, warn

*A recent government report **suggests that** obesity is a problem for all ages, but it is most significant among children.*

2.2 Using Reporting Verbs

a. Most reporting verbs are neutral in tone. Use them to report facts.

*Research by Johnson (2009) **demonstrates that** the consumption of fast food has increased in the last 10 years. The authors of the study **conclude that** childhood obesity can be very harmful.*

b. Use certain reporting verbs to report a point of view, for example:

believe, emphasize, predict, recognize, recommend, suggest

*The U.S. Department of Health and Human Services **believes that** people should read food labels carefully when shopping.*

*Doctors **recommend that** people get 30 minutes of exercise daily.*

c. Use certain reporting verbs to report results, for example:

conclude, demonstrate, estimate

Note: The verbs *demonstrate* and *estimate* can also be followed by a noun phrase, but the meaning is different.

*The U. S. Department of Health and Human Services **concluded that** consumers should read ingredient lists carefully.*

*The workshop **demonstrated** ways for children to improve their health.*

2.2 Using Reporting Verbs (continued)

d. Use *allege* and *claim* when you doubt or are unsure of the truth of the original author's statement.	*Ramirez (2007)* **claims that** *the number of fast-food restaurants in the world has increased.* *The attorney general* **alleges that** *the problem started with a complaint from parents in the public schools.*
e. Use *propose* and *suggest* when the author presents information as likely but still uncertain.	*Davidson (2010)* **suggests that** *the consumption of fast food has increased.*

▶ Grammar Application

Exercise 2.1 Reporting Verbs

Underline the reporting verbs in the letter to a newspaper about the problem of childhood obesity.

> Dear Editor,
>
> I want to bring your readers' attention to the issue of childhood obesity in the United States. Recent studies <u>show</u> that 32 percent of children and adolescents in the United States are overweight. Doctors claim that unhealthy childhood weight can affect adult weight. Some reports estimate that children who are overweight before the age of 15 are
> 5 80 percent more likely to be obese at 25 than children with healthy weights.
>
> Experts suggest that some of the main causes of childhood obesity are a lack of parental influences, a lack of nutritious foods available in the home, and availability of fast-food restaurants. However, we should also consider the role that school plays in influencing a child's diet and weight. Because students spend a large part of their day at
> 10 school, that is where they do much of their eating. Research indicates that children get about 40 percent of their daily calories while they are at school. This statistic suggests a link between school lunches and childhood obesity. In addition, most students these days have to do a lot of homework. Some parents estimate that their children have to do more than three hours of homework a night. This keeps them from spending their after-school
> 15 time engaging in physical activities. I don't want to blame schools for childhood obesity, but I do think we should all work together to help our children be healthy.
>
> Sincerely,
>
> A concerned parent

Exercise 2.2 More Reporting Verbs

A Complete the sentences with the appropriate reporting verbs. Remember to write *that* after the verb.

1. A report from the Dietary Guidelines for Americans (2005) _suggests that_ people should "eat fewer calories, be more active, and make wiser food choices" (p. vi).

   (a. suggest)   b. complain   c. demonstrates

2. The Centers for Disease Control and Prevention (CDC) _____ one way to fight childhood obesity is to remove high-calorie, low-nutrition snacks.

   a. emphasizes   b. illustrates   c. warns

3. Former President Bill Clinton (2010) _____ many parents are overworked and don't have time to prepare healthy food for their children.

   a. describes   b. believes   c. estimates

4. A report by the Centers for Disease Control and Prevention (2011) _____ a child whose body mass index is above the 85th percentile is overweight.

   a. states   b. recommends   c. warns

5. The Dietary Guidelines for Americans (2005) _____ people can reduce the risk of many chronic diseases, including cancer, through better nutrition.

   a. assumes   b. predicts   c. points out

6. A spokesperson from the American Academy of Pediatrics _____ it is unhealthy to allow children age two or younger to watch television.

   a. recommends   b. mentions   c. claims

7. The results of studies by Puhl (2011) _____ overweight children are often bullied and teased by their peers.

   a. evaluate   b. demonstrate   c. believe

8. Several states have had court cases in which the state _____ childhood obesity is a form of child abuse.

   a. has emphasized   b. has alleged   c. has recommended

B *Pair Work* Talk with a partner and explain your choices in A.

> *I think suggest is the best answer for item 1 because the Dietary Guidelines are not forcing people to do anything, but telling people what might be a good thing for them to do. The guidelines are certainly not complaining about anything or demonstrating something.*

Exercise 2.3 Using Reporting Verbs

Pair Work Talk with a partner about one of the topics below or a topic approved by your teacher. Take notes on your partner's answers, and then report your partner's ideas to the class. Use reporting verbs in your report.

- At what age should children have cell phones?
- At what age should children be allowed to join social networks?
- At what age should children have their own computers?
- At what age should children have TVs in their rooms?

Monica argues that children under 10 should not have cell phones. She points out that cell phones are expensive and young children could easily break them. She also believes that children under 10 should always have an adult present, so they wouldn't need their own phones.

3 | Adverb Clauses and Phrases with *As*

▶ Grammar Presentation

Use adverb clauses and phrases with *as* to refer to a source of information.

As seen in Figure 1, *the number of fast-food restaurants in the country has increased significantly.*

As Smith and Jones (2005) point out, *there is a variety of reasons related to the increase in childhood obesity.*

3.1 Adverb Clauses and Phrases with *As*

a. Use adverb clauses with *as* to refer to information from a chart, graph, or other sources. Common verbs in *as* clauses are: *demonstrate, illustrate, point out, and show*	***As Figure 1 illustrates***, *eating habits have changed recently.* ***As Puhl (2011) points out***, *a key issue is the stigma of obesity.*
Use a comma after the clause.	***As Dr. Jarolimova illustrates,*** *there are many things that children can do every day to become healthier.*
b. You can also use adverb phrases with *as* in the passive, for example: *as demonstrated in / by _____, as illustrated in _____, as seen in _____, and as shown in / by _____*	***As demonstrated in Table 1***, *there is a positive trend in the results.* ***As shown by Professor Green***, *there are actions that can effectively address the problem.*
c. You can use the passive with modals, for example: *as can / may be seen in _____*	***As can be seen in Graph 1***, *a higher percentage of boys has become overweight in the past several decades.*

▶ Grammar Application

Exercise 3.1 Using Adverb Clauses with *As*

A Answer the questions about the results of the Virginia Childhood Obesity Survey (2010). Use adverb clauses with *as* and the correct form of the verb in parentheses. Use the passive with modals where appropriate.

Chart 1

Body Mass Index (BMI) for Age

Chart 2

During the past 7 days, on how many days were you physically active for a total of at least 60 minutes per day?

1. What percentage of Virginia youth are physically active at least twice a week?

   (demonstrate) *As demonstrated in Chart 2, / As Chart 2 demonstrates, 88 percent of Virginia youth are physically active at least twice a week.*

2. What percentage of Virginia youth are obese?

   (show) _____

3. Are the majority of Virginia children overweight?

   (illustrate) _____

4. Are most Virginia youth active at least four days a week?

   (point out) _____

5. What percentage of Virginia youth are not at a healthy weight?

   (demonstrate) _____

6. What percentage of Virginia youth are physically active less than two days per week?

   (see) _____

B *Pair Work* Compare your answers with a partner. Then create two more questions and answers with the information in the chart.

Exercise 3.2 Using Adverb Phrases with As

Answer questions about the information from the Virginia Childhood Obesity Survey (2010). Use adverb phrases with *as*.

Chart 3

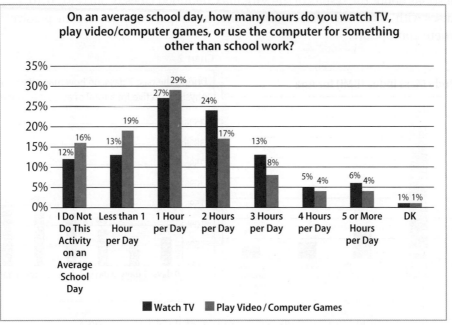

1. Compare the percentage of Virginia youth who watch TV for two or more hours per day with those who spend two or more hours playing video games.

   As Chart 3 shows, Virginia youth spend more time watching TV than playing video and computer games.

2. Compare the percentage of Virginia youth who don't watch TV with those who don't play video / computer games.

   _____

3. Compare the percentage of Virginia youth who spend one hour or less watching TV per day with those who spend one hour or less playing video / computer games.

   _____

4. Compare the percentage of Virginia youth who spend three hours per day playing video games with those who spend one hour playing video games.

   _____

5. Compare the percentage of Virginia youth who don't watch TV or play video / computer games with those who spend five or more hours watching TV and playing video / computer games.

   _____

4 Common Vocabulary for Describing Information in Graphics 🌐

▶ Vocabulary Presentation

Graphics (tables, charts, graphs) provide helpful visual support for ideas in writing. There are common words and phrases that are used to introduce the graphic and direct readers to specific information in it.

It can be seen from Figure 1 that *the number of girls and young women in sports has* ***increased dramatically*** *in recent decades.*

Chart 2 shows *that overall participation in physical education has* ***declined***.

4.1 Common Vocabulary for Describing Information in Graphics

a. Refer to a graphic by first identifying it and then highlighting specific information that you want readers to notice. *Chart 1 shows _____.* *The graph shows (that) _____.*	IDENTIFY GRAPHIC HIGHLIGHT INFORMATION ***Chart 1 shows that*** *most students watched one hour or less of TV per average school day.* ***The graph shows*** *how many hours a day individuals from certain countries spend watching television.* ***The graph shows that*** *there is a relationship between weight and amount of exercise.*
b. You can use passive forms to identify a graphic. *From _____, it can be concluded/estimated/inferred/seen that _____.*	*From the chart,* ***it can be concluded that*** *individuals in the United States are getting much less exercise than a few decades ago.* *From the chart,* ***it can be inferred that*** *individuals in Switzerland maintain active lifestyles and healthy weights.*
c. You can use these nouns to describe change: ↑ *increase, rise* ↑↓ *fluctuation* ↓ *decline, decrease, drop, fall*	*There was* ***an increase*** *in girls' participation in team sports from 2002 to 2010.* *Figure 1 shows* ***the fluctuation*** *in funding for physical education in the last three decades.* *There was* ***a decrease*** *in students' participation in physical education between ninth grade and tenth grades.*

d. You can use the following adjectives to describe the intensity of a change:	
slight, slow	*There was a **slight rise** in physical activity among ninth graders between 2007 and 2010.*
gradual, steady	*There was a **gradual decline** in physical education participation during high school.*
dramatic, rapid, sharp, steep, sudden	*There was a **sharp drop** in physical education participation between ninth and tenth grades.*

e. You can use the following verbs to describe a change: *decline, drop, fall, increase, reduce, rise*	*Participation in sports **fell** in three grades in the last few years.* *Participation **has increased** only for ninth graders.*
f. You can use the following verbs to indicate no change: *remain, stay, maintain*	*The hours students spent in physical activity each week has **remained** steady for the past few years.*

▶ Vocabulary Application

Exercise 4.1 Vocabulary to Describe Chart Information

A 🔊 The principal at Cascades High School developed a program last year to address students' low energy levels. As you listen to the principal describe the program and its results, fill in the missing information in the line graph below.

B *Pair Work* Describe the information in the chart in A using the common vocabulary to describe chart information.

Exercise 4.2 More Vocabulary to Describe Chart Information

On a separate sheet of paper draw a chart similar to the one in Exercise 4.1. Imagine one year of reports of flu or colds among schoolchildren and create a line graph similar to the one in A. Describe your chart to a partner. Use the common vocabulary to describe charts.

As shown in the chart, the number of colds remained low from September through October. Then in November there was a sharp rise. This was probably a result of the fluctuation in temperature during the day and cold winds…

5 | Avoid Common Mistakes ⚠

1. **Remember to use the base form of *be* after modals in the passive.**

   be
   From the chart, it can ∧inferred that simple lifestyle changes result in major health gains.

2. **Remember that reporting verbs such as *demonstrate*, *illustrate*, and *show* can be followed by a *that* clause or by a noun phrase. Be careful to use these two correctly.**

   there is
   Table C shows that ∧an increase in weight loss.
   Figure 8 illustrates ~~that~~ the results of increased exercise over a three-week period.

3. **In general, when referring to a numbered chart, graph, figure, or other source with *As . . .*, do not use an article.**

   As ~~the~~ Chart 1 shows, the number of hours participants engaged in physical activity per week had a direct effect on their body weight.

Editing Task

Find and correct eight more mistakes in the body paragraph from an essay on the problem of obesity.

Genetics and Obesity

Several studies have shown ~~that~~ a connection between genetics and obesity. As the Smith's 2009 study shows, people who have access to exactly the same foods will use those calories differently. Figure A demonstrates that the differences. It shows how a controlled diet and exercise program affected a group of 50 participants: some people in the group gained

5 weight, others maintained their weight, and a small percentage even lost weight. From this study, it can inferred that these different responses to the same situation are primarily genetic. Wu's research (2009) provides further support for the genetic connection to obesity. Her 2010 long-range study on body weight and family history clearly demonstrates that a genetic link to obesity. As the Figure B illustrates, there was very little variation in body weight among three

10 generations of ten families. Finally, several studies have shown that a connection between a gene called FTO and obesity. These studies also demonstrate that a relationship between FTO and diabetes and other diseases. From these and other studies, it can argued that genetics plays a role in body weight.

6 | The Writing Process

In this section, you will write two paragraphs that give the reasons for and consequences of a problem. Before you start writing, you will learn how to narrow down a topic for an essay.

About Narrowing Down a Topic

As a writer, you probably have lots of ideas that you could include in your essay. However, part of your job as a writer is to narrow down the ideas to the few most important ones that you want to emphasize.

The following steps can help you decide what to emphasize:

1. **Brainstorm ideas.** Make a list of ideas about a topic.

2. **Narrow down the ideas.** Cross out ideas that are less important.

3. **Prioritize the ideas.** Put the remaining ideas in the order of importance.

Look at the chart below that a writer created for the topic "Factors at home that affect children's health." First, in column A she brainstormed the factors at home that can affect children's health. Next, in column B she narrowed down her ideas by crossing off three ideas that seemed less important. Finally, in column C she rearranged the remaining items in order of importance.

Topic: Factors at home that can affect children's health

A. Original Brainstorm List	B. Narrowed List	C. Prioritized List
Parents' knowledge about nutrition	~~Parents' knowledge about nutrition~~	Kind of food available at home
What parents actually eat	~~What parents actually eat~~	Parents' control of TV hours, video games
Do parents encourage physical / outdoor activity?	Do parents encourage physical / outdoor activity?	Do parents encourage physical / outdoor activity?
Kind of food available at home	Kind of food available at home	
Parents' exercise and eating habits	~~Parents' exercise and eating habits~~	
Parents' control of TV hours, video games	Parents' control of TV hours, video games	

Exercise

A *Pair Work* With a partner, brainstorm a list of factors that can affect children's performance at school. Use the chart above as a model. Then narrow the list down and prioritize the items.

Topic: Factors that can affect children's performance at school

A. Original Brainstorm List	B. Modified List	C. Prioritized List

B *Group Work* Compare your final list with other classmates and discuss your choices.

Pre-writing Tasks

Choose a Topic

A Choose one of the topics below. You will write two body paragraphs on your topic for a problem–solution essay. The first paragraph will explain the reasons for the problem, and the second paragraph will explain the consequences of the problem.

- The high dropout rate of U.S. high school students
- The drop in sports programs in high schools because of budget cuts
- A topic of your own approved by your teacher

B *Pair Work* Work with a partner to brainstorm a list of reasons for and the consequences of the problem. Then narrow down the topic. Finally, help each other search online for a table or chart that supports one or more of your ideas.

Organize Your Ideas

A Use the outline below to plan your paragraphs. Refer to your prioritized list of ideas. The topics of your body paragraphs should be in the same order as they appear in the list. Decide where to put the table or chart that you found that illustrates one of your points.

Topic:
Body paragraph 1: [the reasons for the problem]
Topic sentence:
Main points:
Body paragraph 2: [the consequences of the problem]
Topic sentence:
Main points:

B *Pair Work* Discuss your outline with a classmate and explain your choices.

Writing Task

Write two body paragraphs that belong in a problem–solution essay using the ideas in your outline above. Follow the steps below.

1. Write the first body paragraph focusing on the reasons for the problem.

2. Write the second body paragraph focusing on the consequences of the problem.

3. Use a chart or table in one of your paragraphs and refer to it.

4. Include the following:
   - appropriate reporting verbs;
   - adverb clauses with *as* and common vocabulary for describing graphics;

Academic Writing Tip

Citing Sources in Academic Writing
Academic institutions require writers to follow a certain style of writing. APA (American Psychological Association) and MLA (Modern Language Association) are common styles in academic writing. Student writers should ask their professors which style to follow.

- at least three of these academic words from the reading in this unit: *academic, adult, approximately, area, committed, community, complex, consequence, contribute, discriminate, dramatically, ensure, factor, generate, impact, indicate, involve, issue, major, media, normal, percent, persist, physical, policy, portion, range, response, stress, trend*

5. After you write your paragraphs, review them and make sure you avoided the mistakes in the Avoid Common Mistakes chart on page 213.

Peer Review

A Exchange your paragraphs with a partner. Answer the following questions as you read your partner's paragraphs, and then share your responses.

1. Has the writer included topic sentences in both paragraphs? Underline them.

2. What are the reasons for and consequences of the problem? Number them.

3. Is there a graph or chart that relates to the problem described in one of the paragraphs?

4. Are there any adverb clauses with *as* that refer to the graphic? Double underline them.

5. Are there reporting verbs? Circle them.

6. Is anything confusing? Write a question mark (?) next to it.

7. Provide one compliment (something you found interesting or unusual).

B Use your partner's comments to help you revise your paragraph. Use the Writer's Checklist on page A2 to review your paragraph for organization, grammar, and vocabulary.

Problem–Solution 3: Adverb Clauses and Infinitives of Purpose; Reduced Adverb Clauses; Vocabulary to Describe Problems and Solutions

Health and Technology

1 Grammar in the Real World 🌐

You will read an essay about people who use the Internet to diagnose themselves and find information about illnesses. The essay is an example of problem–solution writing.

A *Before You Read* How often do you or people you know use the Internet to diagnose symptoms? Read the essay. According to the writer, what are some concerns that doctors have?

Patient–Doctor Relationships in the 21st Century

There was a time when a person with a medical problem would ask a family member, friend, or neighbor about their symptoms before visiting a doctor. Now, many people gather a great deal of information before their first visit. Their first source for this information is now the Internet. In fact, a survey by Pew Research Center's Internet & American Life Project (2011)
5 found that 80 percent of American adults use the Internet for health-related information. This increased use of the Internet for health purposes has led to a new phenomenon, *cyberchondria*. Cyberchondria is a situation in which people with no medical background diagnose themselves by reviewing symptoms and other information online and determine that their situation is worse than it really is. Educating patients about using online information,
10 identifying changes doctors could make, and using online medical information more effectively are all necessary in order to solve this problem of cyberchondria.

The term *cyberchondria* is based on the term *hypochondria*, a belief that one has a serious disease even though there is no medical confirmation. After gathering information online, cyberchondriacs often conclude that they have a disease or health issue that is worse than
15 the one that their doctor diagnoses (Torrey, 2009, para. 2). While not being a real physical condition, cyberchondria can lead to problems. For example, patients often find it difficult to accept their doctor's diagnosis, causing friction[1] between patients and doctors.

With patients self-diagnosing more often, a shift has occurred in the patient–doctor relationship. For example, patients may challenge doctors more aggressively and spend
20 more time discussing topics that they had researched online. Another concern is that patients do not always use credible websites. As a result, they may find information that is based on out-of-date research. Most importantly, doctors are concerned that patients will

---

[1]**friction:** unpleasant feelings caused by differences of opinion

scare themselves when reading symptoms online. As Brazilian cardiologist Dr. Fernando Botelho explains, "Patients read non-contextualized information and do not know how to process it.
25 This situation can bring anxiety" (personal communication, October 29, 2010).

While acknowledging these concerns, many doctors also see the benefit of having more actively engaged patients. Dr. Igor Barrios, a surgeon in Venezuela, believes that these changes will lead to better care. He feels that doctors will have to become more effective communicators (personal communication, October 29, 2010). Doctors should become more
30 sensitive to patients' more active role and learn to accept that they will have to be able to provide explanations for patients' questions about information they find on the Internet.

Using medical information available on the Internet wisely can also address the problem of cyberchondria. Health-care websites must state clearly that their information should be in addition to, rather than a replacement of, a consultation with a doctor and medical treatment.
35 For doctors, while it may be difficult, they need to acknowledge that the old rules have changed – they are no longer the only source of information. They should educate their patients on how to evaluate the health information they find on the Internet so that the process of diagnosing becomes collaborative rather than adversarial.[2] Finally, the last part of the solution involves patients. When searching for information on the Internet, patients should
40 remember that no website can replace a doctor's physical exam. Before approaching their doctor, they should check that the information they have is up-to-date and credible. In this way, they can avoid wasting time during appointments.

This cooperation will not be easy to implement. It will be difficult to persuade health-care website
45 providers to change information online. It will also be challenging for doctors and patients to change their roles, especially without additional training about these new relationships. However, when health-care website providers, doctors, and patients all realize that
50 these changes will benefit health care, they will be more likely to collaborate. This cooperation will help create a stronger twenty-first-century model for patient–doctor relationships.

[2]**adversarial:** opposing each other, like enemies

B *Comprehension Check* Answer the questions.

1. What is cyberchondria?

2. What concerns do doctors have when patients use the Internet to self-diagnose?

3. What is the solution suggested in the essay?

C *Notice*

1 Problem–Solution Writing Draw a chart like the one on page 220. Use the information in the essay to complete the chart, which shows that the proposed solution has three parts. Write the proposed solution for each part.

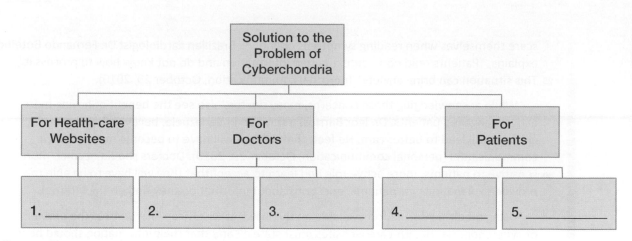

```
                    ┌─────────────────┐
                    │  Solution to the │
                    │    Problem of    │
                    │  Cyberchondria   │
                    └─────────────────┘
```

For Health-care Websites	For Doctors	For Patients

1. _____ 2. _____ 3. _____ 4. _____ 5. _____

2 Grammar Follow the instructions below to notice how the author uses adverb clauses and phrases to express purpose or reason.

1. Find the last sentence in the first paragraph. Which phrase in the sentence explains the purpose of the parts of the solution.
2. Find the sentence that starts with *while* in the second paragraph. What form of the verb follows *while*? What is the understood subject of the phrase with *while*?
3. Find the sentences that contain *when* on lines 39–40 beginning with "When searching . . . " and on lines 48–51 beginning with "However, when health-care website providers . . . " How is the use of *when* in these two sentences different in structure?

3 The Writing Process What is the function of the concluding paragraph of the essay? Check (✓) all that apply.

_____ a) It restates the background to the problem.

_____ b) It summarizes the main parts of the solution.

_____ c) It considers problems that may arise from the solution.

_____ d) It suggests a couple of new solutions to the problem.

2 Adverb Clauses of Purpose and Infinitives of Purpose

▶ Grammar Presentation

Adverb clauses of purpose and infinitives of purpose express the purpose, or reason, for an action or idea. They usually follow the main clause and are often used in problem–solution writing to explain the reasons for a proposed solution.

*Some clinics have computer stations **so that** patients can go online in the waiting room.*
*She researched the disease on the Internet **in order to** learn more about it.*

2.1 Adverb Clauses of Purpose

a. An adverb clause of purpose is a dependent clause that answers the question *why?*	*Doctors should educate their patients about how to evaluate medical information on the Internet **so that the process of diagnosing becomes collaborative rather than adversarial**.*
b. *So that* is the most common way to introduce clauses of purpose. Sometimes it is reduced to *so*.	*He cut down on fatty food **so that** he could lose weight.* *He cut down on fatty food **so** he could lose some weight.*
c. The adverb clause of purpose usually comes after the main clause.	COMMON: *The clinic provided training for using online medical reference information **so that patients would feel less anxious**.* LESS COMMON: ***So that patients would feel less anxious**, the doctors provided training for using online medical reference information.*

2.2 Infinitives of Purpose

a. When the subject of the main clause and the adverb clause of purpose are the same, you can use *in order* or *so as* with an infinitive (*to* + verb) of purpose. For example: *in order to* + verb You can omit the words *in order* when the meaning is clear. *so as to* + verb	*Doctors place brochures on medical conditions in their waiting rooms (**in order) to provide** patients with valuable information.* *Doctors should discuss treatment options with patients **so as to address** any concerns.*
b. You can also use these forms in the negative. The *not* comes before the infinitive: *in order not to* + verb *so as not to* + verb	*A patient might not say anything about what he or she reads on the Internet **in order not to make** the doctor angry.* *Patients should avoid the use of unqualified medical websites **so as not to make** false assumptions about their medical issues.*
c. When an infinitive is followed by an infinitive of purpose, you should use *in order to* or *so as to* for clarity.	UNCLEAR: *Some patients write a list of questions to ask to use time efficiently during medical appointments.* CLEAR: *Some patients write a list of questions to ask in order to use time efficiently during medical appointments.*

The 10 most common verbs that follow *in order to* are (in order of frequency):

be, make, get, obtain, keep, determine, avoid, see, protect, provide
Why can't we e-mail our doctor **in order to make** an appointment?

The 10 most common verbs that follow *so as to* are (in order of frequency):

avoid, be, make, provide, have, create, form, maintain, preserve, give
Ari made his next appointment before he left the doctor's office **so as to avoid** having to do it later.

▶ Grammar Application

Exercise 2.1 Adverb Clauses and Infinitives of Purpose

Read the magazine article about how a mother used the Internet to diagnose a disease. Underline seven more examples of adverb clauses and infinitives of purpose.

Before the invention of the Internet, people would visit their doctors in order to find out what was wrong with them. These days, when people begin to feel ill, they often turn to the Internet to diagnose themselves. Many medical professionals agree that self-diagnosis by the Internet can often cause unnecessary and unwarranted fears. However, once in a while, the
5　patient's hunches are correct.

Take the case of Alison Chambers. Alison has a 10-year-old son named Miles. When Miles was about two years old, he began getting fevers on a regular basis. She took him to a doctor to get help, and her doctor told her that children often get fevers and it was nothing to worry about. The doctor told Alison that Miles should stay home from day care when other children
10　were ill so as not to get sick. He also said that Miles should wash his hands often so that he would not pick up other children's germs as readily. Although Alison was very careful to follow the doctor's advice, Miles continued to get a fever about once a month. She took Miles to three more doctors so that she could get other opinions, but they all agreed with her doctor's diagnosis.

15　　Alison began to get very frustrated and started researching Miles's symptoms online so as to find out some information for herself. She read about a rare disease whose symptoms sounded like Miles's symptoms. She visited Miles's doctor to ask his opinion. He thought it was unlikely that Miles had the disease, but he agreed to test him for it. The test showed that Miles did have the rare disease. Alison was scared but relieved to know what was wrong with her
20　son. Miles received treatment and stopped getting fevers soon after. It can be dangerous to rely on the Internet for medical information, but in Alison and Miles's case, it paid off.

Exercise 2.2 More Adverb Clauses and Infinitives of Purpose

A 🔊 Listen to the podcast interview about using digital tools for health. Then write answers to the questions using adverb clauses of purpose and infinitives of purpose.

1. Why did Cindy interview people?

   Cindy interviewed people to understand how they used digital tools to monitor and improve their health.

2. Why did a writer for the *New York Times* use Twitter?

   _____

   _____

3. Why does Pam use an app to take pictures of her food?

   _____

   _____

4. Why does Pam use a running app?

   _____

5. Why do people need to commit to using digital resources?

   _____

6. Why do we need to arrive at the doctor's office armed with knowledge?

   _____

7. Why might doctors have to change their relationships with patients?

   _____

8. Why does Jeff want Cindy to tell one more piece of advice?

   _____

B *Pair Work* With a partner discuss the apps that people used in the interview. Would they work for you? Why or why not? Which app seemed the most helpful to you? Why? What other apps have you heard about to improve health or break bad habits? What kind of app would you invent to improve your health and your life?

I liked the app that calculated calories based on pictures. I'd use it with my boyfriend so that I could persuade him to make better choices too. I don't run, but I'd like an app to motivate me and to remind me of my goals. I'd love someone to invent an app that I could easily use to describe symptoms and conditions in English so as to make it easier to communicate with doctors.

3 | Reducing Adverb Clauses to Phrases

▶ Grammar Presentation

> You can reduce adverb clauses to adverb phrases. The adverb phrase modifies the subject of the main clause. Adverb phrases can describe problems and solutions.
>
> *Sometimes patients become frightened **when they read symptoms online**.*
>
> → *Sometimes patients become frightened **when reading symptoms online**.*

3.1 Adverb Phrases

a. You can reduce adverb clauses to phrases when they begin with *when*, *while*, *before*, and *after* and when the subject of the main clause and the adverb clause are the same.	ADVERB CLAUSE *Joanna tried various home remedies **before she saw the doctor**.* ADVERB PHRASE *Joanna tried various home remedies **before seeing the doctor**.*
b. If a clause contains a present progressive or past progressive verb, you can reduce the adverb clause by deleting the subject and the form of *be*.	***When I am dieting**, I never eat sugar or red meat.* ***When dieting**, I never eat sugar or red meat.* ***While Tran was searching** the Internet, he found positive reviews about his doctor.* ***While searching** the Internet, Tran found positive reviews about his doctor.*
c. If a clause contains a simple present or simple past verb, delete the subject and change the verb form to the *-ing* form.	***Before they see** a doctor, many patients use the Internet to find information about their symptoms.* ***Before seeing** a doctor for an appointment, many patients use the Internet to find information about their symptoms.* *In the past **before they saw** a doctor, people would ask for advice from family and friends.* *In the past **before seeing** a doctor, people would ask for advice from family and friends.*
d. If a clause contains a verb in the present perfect or past perfect, delete the subject of the adverb clause and change *have* or *had* to *having*.	***After you've read** multiple articles online, you'll have a better understanding of your doctor's diagnosis.* ***After having read** multiple articles online, you'll have a better understanding of your doctor's diagnosis.* ***After he'd read** multiple articles online, he had a better understanding of his doctor's diagnosis.* ***After having read** multiple articles online, he had a better understanding of his doctor's diagnosis.*

▶ Grammar Application

Exercise 3.1 Reducing Adverb Clauses

A Complete the excerpt from a blog entry for evaluating the information in health-related websites. Reduce each adverb clause to an adverb phrase. Remember to use commas.

A few months back I was plagued with headaches and fatigue.

<u>*Before going to the doctor,*</u> I decided to read up on possible diagnoses.
(1. before I went to the doctor)

_____ I was frantic. My long list of ailments included
(2. after I'd visited a few sites)

migraines, Lyme disease, and one deadly disease. _____
(3. while she was looking at the list)

my wife kept shaking her head and frowning. She asked me where I found the information.

I didn't remember. Then she e-mailed a friend of hers who is a nurse practitioner and we got

the following advice on how to use the Web wisely for research:

- _____ look for websites with the domains .gov and .edu,
  (4. when you do research)
  which tend to be more credible.

- Also, _____ look for websites that are operated by
  (5. when you consider which websites to go to)
  hospitals, universities, and recognized medical institutions.

- _____ search for the name of the author (if there is one)
  (6. after you've read an article that interests you)
  to find out his / her credentials.

- Be extra critical _____ . A lot of advertising might
  (7. when you visit websites that try to sell you products)
  mean that the objective of the website is really to sell merchandise.

- _____ make a list of questions about it to ask your
  (8. after you collect all the information)
  doctor.

- _____ if something doesn't feel right, you should tell
  (9. after you've been diagnosed)
  your doctor and continue your research because you never know when you'll come across

  important new therapies and medicines for you and your doctor to discuss.

B *Pair Work* With a partner, explain how you or someone you know uses the Internet for medical or health purposes. Use adverb phrases.

After hearing or reading about some new research on health that I'm interested in, I'll look it up on the Internet and find out more about it. While searching, I try to go to a variety of sites so that I can find out a few opinions of the information.

Exercise 3.2 Adverb Phrases

Combine each pair of sentences about online support groups. Use the appropriate adverb phrase with *when*, *while*, *before*, and *after*, depending on the sequence of the actions.

	First Action	Second Action	Simultaneous Actions
1.	Some people discover they have a serious illness.	Some people find help through online support groups.	
2.			• People go through treatment. • People find it comforting to communicate with others diagnosed with their disease.
3.	People talk with others about their illness.	People don't feel so alone.	
4.	People should read the messages that members post to make sure the group is supportive.	People choose a group to join.	
5.			• Leaders monitor members' messages. • Leaders should encourage positive participation.
6.	Members notice that a member is going through a difficult time.	The members of good groups offer encouragement and advice.	
7.	Members of good groups receive the support they asked for.	Members of good groups stay with the group and give others support.	

1. *After discovering they have an illness, some people find help through online*
   support groups.

2. _____

   _____

3. _____

   _____

4. _____

   _____

5. _____

   _____

6. _____

   _____

7. _____

   _____

4 Common Vocabulary to Describe Problems and Solutions 🌐

▶ Vocabulary Presentation

There are several common words and phrases that are useful in problem–solution writing.

The most important problem is finding the right doctor to treat your illness.

There are several ways to address the problem of cyberchondria.

One solution for cyberchondria **would be to** avoid unreliable websites.

4.1 Phrases to Introduce Problems

Use the following phrases to introduce a problem: *The key / main / primary / most important problem is* _____ . *A / The secondary issue / problem is* _____ . *While* _____ *are issues / problems / factors,* *the most important / urgent / pressing / critical issue / problem is* _____ .	For doctors, **the main problem is** the extra time they spend arguing with ill-informed patients. **A secondary issue is** the patients' increased stress. **While** wasted time and patient stress **are factors, the most urgent issue is** misinformation on the Internet.

4.2 Phrases to Introduce Solutions

a. Use the following phrases to introduce solutions: *The solution to the problem lies in* _____ . *There are several ways to address the problem of* _____ . *One solution to / for* _____ *would be to* _____ . *The problem of* _____ *can be solved by* _____ . _____ *is a possible solution to the problem of* _____ .	**The solution to the problem lies in** medical websites, doctors, and patients. **There are several ways to address the problem of** cyberchondria. **One solution to** cyberchondria **would be to** educate patients. **The problem of** cyberchondria **can be solved by** reorganizing information on medical websites. Educating patients **is a possible solution to the problem of** cyberchondria.
b. Use the following phrases to make recommendations for possible solutions: *is needed* *is necessary* *should be / may be / might be / must be considered*	A definite decision by the government **is needed**. Based on the results, it **will be necessary** to make changes to the treatment. An individual's caloric needs **should be considered** before starting any diet.

▶ Vocabulary Application

Exercise 4.1 Phrases to Introduce Problems and Solutions

Complete the sentences about the patient–doctor relationship using phrases to introduce problems and solutions.

a secondary issue	one solution for the first problem	the problem of
can be solved by	~~the most important problem~~	

The most important problem when communicating with doctors
                (1.)
is that sometimes they don't understand exactly what a patient is feeling.

_____ is the fact that patients don't always ask
             (2.)
the right questions. _____ would be to require
                   (3.)
doctors to use checklists when discussing symptoms so that there is more discussion

of feelings. _____ asking the right questions
              (4.)
_____ providing patients with frequently asked questions
         (5.)
about their illness to help them come up with questions.

is necessary	there are several ways to address the problem of
the most urgent issue is	are issues
while	

     The patient–doctor relationship has changed in recent years and new issues have arisen.

Patients come to appointments with a great deal of information and strong opinions. Doctors

can feel uncomfortable with their patients' new assertiveness, and patients can feel mistrustful

and even skeptical of their doctor's opinions. _____
                                   (6.)
patients' mistrust and skepticism _____ ,
                           (7.)
_____ the antagonistic relationship that can develop.
        (8.)
_____ antagonism. One way is for doctors to help their
        (9.)
patients use the Internet more discerningly and discuss findings. In sum, a change in the

patient–doctor relationship _____ in order to adapt to the
                        (10.)
current information age.

Exercise 4.2 Phrases to Introduce Problems and Solutions

A *Pair Work* With a partner, rank the three problems below that doctors have with patients from 1 (the most serious) to 3 (the least serious).

- Some patients believe inaccurate information.
- Some patients don't follow advice.
- Some patients are unwilling to admit the seriousness of their health issues.

Next, decide on a possible solution for doctors to each problem. Use the phrases below or others in Chart 4.2 on page 227. Then share your ideas with another pair.

The primary issue with patients is . . .	*One solution to the problem might be . . .*
The secondary issue with patients is . . .	*. . . is a possible solution to the problem of . . .*
The last issue with patients is . . .	*The problem of . . . can be solved by . . .*

In my opinion, the primary issue with patients is that they don't follow their doctor's advice. I think that one solution to the problem might be for doctors to ask the patient to follow up and call after a week or two to report how he or she is doing. This will motivate the patient to follow the advice and avoid getting sicker.

B *Group Work* Work with a group and choose one of the problems concerning health issues below. Brainstorm possible solutions to the problem. Write one sentence describing the problem and three to four sentences describing possible solutions. Use the common phrases to introduce problems and solutions. Present your ideas to the class.

- You are sick and you disagree with your doctor's diagnosis.
- You have insomnia.
- You have a friend who is a cyberchondriac.
- A problem approved by your teacher.

There are many things you can do if you feel sick and you disagree with your doctor's diagnosis. One solution would be to . . .

5 | Avoid Common Mistakes ⚠️

1. Remember that *for example* is always singular, even when several examples follow.

There are many solutions to the problem of cyberchondria. For ~~examples~~, using credible ⟨example⟩
websites or avoiding the Internet altogether are ways to solve cyberchondria.

2. Remember that the phrase *The problem of* is not followed by *the*.

The problem of ~~the~~ Internet addiction can be solved by limiting time spent online.

3. Remember not to confuse *so that* (to express purpose) and *so* (to express result). Do not use a comma before *so that*.

The physician provided her patients with a list of credible medical ~~websites, so~~ they would ⟨websites so that⟩
stop arguing with her about their symptoms. (purpose)

The patient stopped consulting medical ~~websites so that~~ he argued much less with his ⟨websites, so⟩
physician. (result)

Editing Task

Find and correct eight more mistakes in the body paragraph from an essay on the problem of cyberchondria.

Cyberchondria

A solution to the problem of ~~the~~ cyberchondria is to help individuals become informed

Internet users. The Internet can be a useful source of information, but only if people use it

wisely. Individuals need to know how to evaluate search results, so they can avoid misleading

information. For examples, a website may be out of date, or it may not be published by a

5 credible medical source. Users should look for a date somewhere on the site, so they know that

content is updated regularly. The solution to the problem of the unreliable medical websites

is to establish the validity of sites. For examples, users should avoid sites with URLs ending in

".com" and sites that do not have scientific or medical sponsors. A commercial website that

looks like a medical source may actually be a business selling products. However, medical sites

10 with URLs ending in ".gov" or ".edu" tend to have credible content so that users can be more

confident of the information they contain. Physicians can also help solve the problem of the

cyberchondria by directing their patients to their own preferred sites. This will reduce patient

anxiety and frustration, so physicians can use their consultation time more productively.

6 | The Writing Process ✏️

In this section, you will write two paragraphs for a problem–solution essay. The paragraphs will include a solution to a problem and an evaluation of the solution. Before you start writing, you will learn different ways to evaluate a possible solution.

About Evaluating Proposed Solutions

When you propose one or more solutions to a problem, evaluate the solutions by mentioning any limitations. This will show the reader that you have considered the limitations and that despite any drawbacks to a solution, you still believe it is worth recommending. This will make your proposal stronger.

The following are ways to write about the limitations to a solution:

1. **The solution is not easy to implement.**
   The proposed solution will not be easy to implement because it will require changing longstanding habits and behavior. However, no important change happens overnight.

2. **The solution will not solve all aspects of the problem**.
   The proposed solution for addressing the problem of cyberchondria has some limitations. It will not completely prevent patients from consulting unreliable websites.

3. **The solution requires that certain conditions be met.**
   Before this solution is implemented, doctors need to accept the fact that they may no longer be the source of all the information.

4. **There are other solutions that can be beneficial.**
   Although this is not the only way to address the problem of Internet addiction, it is an effective way to obtain short term results.

Exercise

A Match each solution to a limitation.

Possible Solution	Limitation
1. __e__ Hire more police.	a) A more attractive neighborhood may discourage vandalism, but it's not clear that it will lower other types of crime.
2. _____ Create neighborhood watch groups.	b) Monitoring the streets is a good start, but without a stronger police presence it will not be effective.
3. _____ Install video surveillance on dangerous streets.	c) Sports programs for bored teenagers are good. Other programs should be considered for them, too.
4. _____ Tidy up and beautify the neighborhood.	d) Neighbors will have to work together to create a schedule, and they have never been willing to work together.
5. _____ Provide afternoon sports programs for bored teenagers.	e) The cost of more officers on the street will not be possible without raising taxes or laying off other city employees.

B *Pair Work* Tell your answers to a partner. Identify each limitation as one of the four types in About Evaluating Proposed Solutions.

Hiring more police is a good solution. The problem is that this will mean that a city government will have to spend less money on some other city employees, like firefighters. This is limitation type 3: Certain conditions must be met.

Pre-writing Tasks

Choose a Topic

A Choose one of the topics listed below. You will write two paragraphs related to solutions for a problem–solution essay.

- People put off regular checkups at the doctor's office to save money.
- There is an increase in crime in your neighborhood.
- A topic of your own approved by your teacher

B *Pair Work* Share your topic with a partner. Brainstorm one or more solutions to your problem and then evaluate them. Think of possible limitations to your solutions.

Organize Your Ideas

A Do some research and reflect on your topic. Draw the chart below on a separate sheet of paper. Using the information from your research, complete your chart with possible solutions, supporting details, and any limitations to the solutions.

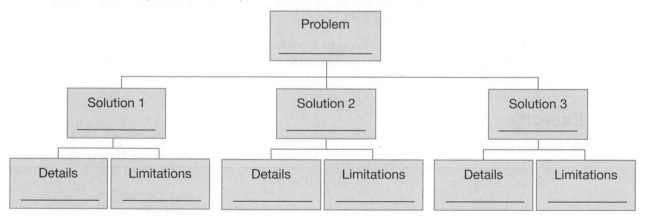

B *Pair Work* Share the information in your chart with a partner. Give each other suggestions about ideas or facts to include.

Writing Task

Write your two paragraphs for a problem–solution essay using your chart. Follow the steps below.

1. Choose one of the solutions in your chart and describe it in the first paragraph.

2. In the second paragraph, evaluate that solution and write about any limitations that it has.

3. Include the following in your paragraphs:

   - adverb clauses of purpose;
   - reduced adverb clauses with *when*, *while*, *before*, and *after*;
   - vocabulary that deals with problems and solutions;
   - at least three of these academic words from the essay in this unit: *acknowledge*, *adult*, *approach*, *available*, *benefit*, *challenge*, *challenging*, *communication*, *conclude*, *confirmation*, *consultation*, *contextualize*, *convince*, *cooperation*, *create*, *evaluate*, *identify*, *implement*, *involve*, *issue*, *medical*, *occur*, *percent*, *phenomenon*, *physical*, *process*, *research*, *role*, *shift*, *source*, *topics*.

4. After you write your paragraphs, review them and make sure you avoided the mistakes in the Avoid Common Mistakes chart on page 230.

> **Academic Writing Tip**
>
> **Use a Thesaurus to Build Your Vocabulary**
>
> A thesaurus can help you be more precise in your ideas, paraphrase ideas, and add variety to your writing.
>
> Doctors should ~~say that they don't know~~ *acknowledge that they* ~~everything.~~ *have limitations.*

Peer Review

A Exchange your paragraphs with a partner. Answer the following questions as you read your partner's paragraphs, and then share your responses.

1. Are there topic sentences in both paragraphs? Underline them.

2. Did the writer identify just one solution in the solution paragraph? What was it?

3. How many limitations were there in the second paragraph? Number them.

4. Does the writer use any adverb clauses of purpose or reduced adverb clauses? Underline any that you can find.

5. Does the writer use the vocabulary of problems and solution? Circle any words or phrases that you can find.

6. Is anything confusing? Write a question mark (?) next to it.

7. Provide one compliment (something you found interesting or unusual).

B Use your partner's comments to help you revise your paragraphs. Use the Writer's Checklist on page A2 to review your paragraphs for organization, grammar, and vocabulary.

UNIT 16

Problem–Solution 4: *It* Constructions; Transition Words to Indicate Steps of a Solution

Leading a Healthy Life

1 Grammar in the Real World

You will read an essay about changes that people can make in their lives in order to have a healthier lifestyle. In this problem–solution essay, the writer describes the process of implementing the solutions.

A *Before You Read* What are some things a person can do in order to live a healthy life? Why is it sometimes difficult in our modern world to do what is necessary to live a healthy life? Read the essay. What solutions to this problem does the writer suggest?

Leading a Healthy Life

In the last few decades, the average person's life has become increasingly unhealthy. The rules of modern society seem to have forced many into a stressful lifestyle. As individuals strive to meet the demands of their lives, they often overlook the multiple sources of stress and unhealthiness in their lives. Even though the task is challenging, it is not impossible to make
5　some changes that can lead to a healthier lifestyle.

Many factors can contribute to creating tension in everyday life. For most people, a busy work schedule usually prevents them from dedicating time to other stress-relieving activities. Lack of exercise and not enough sleep are only two of the consequences of such a lifestyle. Also, as time is consumed by work-related responsibilities, individuals tend to have less time to eat well. Many
10　people end up eating fast food as a strategy to save time, which adds to unhealthy practices.

Contrary to what many people may think, living a healthy life does not have to be difficult; nor does it have to be time-consuming. In terms of eating habits, a few changes can go a long way. First, individuals need to be committed to the challenge. Next, in order to have a healthier diet, they should buy low-calorie and low-fat foods that are easy to cook, such as
15　broccoli, cauliflower, carrots, chicken, and fish. Then they can cook more quantities of food over the weekend and freeze the leftovers in small containers so that the food can be consumed throughout the week. It has been argued that freezing the food destroys some of the nutrients. This may be true. However, this solution is certainly better than the fast-food option.

Just as with eating habits, it is a common belief that exercising takes away many hours of an
20　average person's week. However, first, it is important to find an activity that is enjoyable, such as playing a sport or hiking. Even simple activities, like taking the stairs, raking leaves, or

234

sweeping the floor, contribute to keeping someone active. Next, after finding an enjoyable activity, people need to commit to it. This means that people need to exercise regularly and make it part of their routine, just like brushing their teeth or combing their hair. Many people
25 will agree that their level of stress tends to decrease once exercising becomes part of their daily lives.

Maintaining a healthy lifestyle does not have to be challenging but can be accomplished with a series of small steps. Setting a few reachable goals can make a huge difference. Drastic diets, fasting,[1] or very demanding exercise routines are not that likely to generate permanent
30 improvements (as cited in Wong, 2010). On the contrary, it is essential to take a holistic approach[2] to good health. Such an approach starts with healthy food and regular exercise. When these items are part of someone's life, lack of time becomes just an excuse for not adopting a healthier lifestyle.

[1]**fasting:** intentionally eating no food for a long period of time | [2]**holistic approach:** a way of solving a health problem by looking at the social, psychological, and physical aspects of the problem

B *Comprehension Check* Answer the questions.

1. According to the essay, what is the main reason that people are prevented from leading a healthy life?
2. What are some of the beliefs that people have when it comes to healthy eating and exercising?
3. Do you think the writer would think that you have a healthy lifestyle? Why or why not?

C *Notice*

1 **Problem–Solution Writing** Reread the third and fourth paragraphs. Draw the chart and complete it with the missing information.

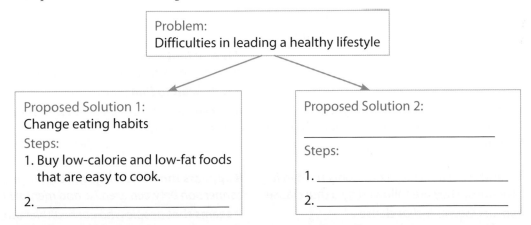

2 **Grammar** Follow the instructions below to help you notice how the writer uses *it* constructions:

1. Reread the sentence with the word *it* on lines 4–5 in the first paragraph and the sentence with the word *it* on lines 11–12. One *it* refers to a previously mentioned noun, but the other one doesn't. Which one doesn't refer to a previously mentioned noun?

2. Reread the sentence on line 17 with the word *it*. The writer uses the passive. Does the use of the passive and *it* make the sentence more subjective or objective?

3. Reread the sentence on lines 30–31 that begins with "On the contrary, . . . " Notice how the writer uses the word *it* to introduce his proposal. What adjective does the writer use after *it* to make the proposal stronger?

3 The Writing Process Label the different parts of the problem–solution essay in the margin of the essay. Note that each part may not be a whole paragraph.

- background information
- description of the problem
- solution
- steps of the solution
- limitations of the solution
- conclusion

2 | *It* Constructions

▶ Grammar Presentation

It constructions are commonly used in academic writing to make the text more impersonal and objective. In problem–solution writing, *it* constructions are often used when a solution to a problem is being proposed and evaluated.

It is important to *find an exercise that is enjoyable, such as playing a sport or hiking.*
It has been argued that *freezing the food destroys some of the nutrients.*

2.1 *It* Constructions

a. *It* constructions are formed in the following ways: it + *be* + adjective + *that* clause	**It is true that** *people who exercise usually have more energy than people who do not.*
it + *be* + adjective + infinitive *It* is not the subject. To provide a specific subject with infinitives, you can add *for* + noun phrase to the sentence.	**It is difficult to find** *time to exercise every day.* **It is difficult** <u>*for many adults*</u> **to find time** *to exercise every day.*
b. *Appear* and *seem* are verbs commonly used in *it* constructions. They are followed by a *that* clause: it + *appears* / *seems* + *that* clause	**It appears that** *researchers have made the connection between exercise and mental health.* **It seems that** *people who eat healthier are frequently in a good mood.*
it + *appears* / *seems* + adjective + *that* clause *Appear* and *seem* are used when the writer is almost certain, but not completely certain of the truth of the statement.	**It appears unlikely that** *the government will issue new guidelines for healthy eating within the year.*

2.1 *It* Constructions *(continued)*

c. You can use *it* constructions with a modal:
may, might, could
These modals soften claims that follow them.

It may be true that people who eat healthier are always in a good mood.
It might seem that people are not losing weight when they start a new diet program.
It could be that genetics plays the main role in obesity.

Data from the Real World

Adjectives that frequently occur after *It is* to show evaluation are (in order of frequency):

important to, clear that, difficult to, possible that, possible to, necessary to, better to, impossible that, likely that, true that, essential to, common to, doubtful that, easy to, evident that, unlikely that
It is important to eat a healthy diet and exercise every day.

It seems is twice as common as *It appears*. Adjectives that frequently occur after *It seems* are:

likely, unlikely, clear, possible, reasonable, obvious, certain, impossible, logical, probable
It seems reasonable that many people would make the connection between nutrition and physical health.

Adjectives that frequently occur after *It appears* are:

possible, unlikely, plausible
It appears possible that health insurance companies will provide more guidance on nutrition issues.

2.2 *It* Constructions in the Passive

You can use *it* constructions in the passive with reporting verbs. This allows the writer to emphasize the idea without stating (or restating) the source.

It has generally been accepted that people who exercise frequently have more energy.
It was found that certain fruits and vegetables can help with weight loss.

Data from the Real World

Verbs that frequently occur in *it* + the passive form of the present perfect are:

shown, suggested, reported, proposed, demonstrated, determined, linked, observed, documented, called, estimated, used, recognized, known, found, argued, applied, approved, associated
It has been shown that drastic diets are less likely to generate permanent health improvements.

Modals that frequently occur with passive *it* constructions are:

can, should, could, and *must*
It can be argued that schools should be more involved in teaching about healthy living.
Note: Will, would, and *shall* are very infrequent in passive *it* constructions.

2.3 Using Adjectives in *It* Constructions

a. In problem–solution writing, certain adjectives can be used with *it* constructions to emphasize the importance of a problem and the effectiveness of the solution.

These adjectives include:

accepted, certain, clear, evident, important, indisputable, obvious

It is clear that exercising is good for children.

From the results of the study, **it is obvious** *that children are healthier if they watch only one hour of TV a day.*

b. Use the following adjectives to show the strength of the ideas or claims:

To show that something is certain, use *accepted, certain, indisputable,* or *true.*

To show that something is possible, use *likely* or *possible.*

To show that something is not likely, use *unlikely* or *unusual.*

To show that something is not possible, use *impossible.*

It is true that children are heavier, but the causes are not clear.

It is likely that genes also play a big role in health.

It appears unlikely that cell phone use will decrease.

It is impossible to address health without including exercise.

Use these adjectives to show the degree of difficulty:

difficult, easy, hard

It is difficult to imagine restaurants eliminating desserts.

Use these adjectives to show the writer's perspective:

clear, curious, evident, important, obvious, strange

It seems curious that fruit and vegetables are not emphasized.

It is evident that people's lifestyles contribute to their stress.

2.4 Using *It* Constructions

You can use an *it* construction instead of a statement that directly attributes the idea to someone.

Use *it* constructions as a more formal way of presenting information.

STATEMENT

Doctors and health officials agree that *people should exercise at least three times a week.*

IT CONSTRUCTION

It is important to exercise at least three times a week.

INFORMAL: **She argued that** exercising is very time consuming.

MORE FORMAL: **It has been argued** that exercising is very time consuming.

▶ Grammar Application

Exercise 2.1 *It* Constructions

A Choose the appropriate adjective to describe the idea in each sentence about health information. Then complete the new sentence with an *it* construction with the adjective. Use *that* or an infinitive. Use *for* and *not* where necessary.

1. People need to find time to prepare a healthy dinner every night.
   a. difficult   (b. important)   c. unusual

   It is important for people to find time to prepare a healthy dinner every night.

2. Everyone can eat good food by planning meals ahead of time.
   a. accepted   b. likely   c. easy

3. Young people don't usually pay attention to their dietary habits.
   a. possible   b. impossible   c. unusual

4. There is a good chance that meditation or yoga can reduce stress.
   a. possible   b. unlikely   c. obvious

5. Doctors agree that people should focus on their exercise and eating habits.
   a. clear   b. unlikely   c. strange

6. There is no doubt that moderate exercise results in fewer diseases such as diabetes.
   a. unlikely   b. indisputable   c. strange

7. There is a good chance that working out regularly improves mood.
   a. may be impossible   b. could be obvious   c. might be true

8. We can't really say why some people like to exercise and some don't.
   a. evident   b. impossible   c. reasonable

9. There is little evidence that regular exercise can cause physical harm.

    a. unlikely   b. impossible   c. important

_____

10. Everyone knows that good support systems have a positive impact on one's health.

    a. curious   b. likely   c. evident

_____

B *Pair Work* Think of four ideas that you have heard that have a positive or negative impact on health. Discuss them with a partner and give your opinion of the ideas. Then share them with another pair. Include statements that state something is certain, possible, not possible, or difficult.

From what we have read, it is accepted that vitamins can be beneficial for one's health. I personally don't think that people need vitamins if they eat well. I have also read that it appears unlikely that cell phone use is harmful to one's health. No one's really sure about this, though.

Exercise 2.2 Passive *It* Constructions

A Unscramble the sentences that compare medical beliefs today with medical beliefs in the past in the United States.

1. a. your health / accepted / cigarettes / bad for / it is / that / are

    It is accepted that cigarettes are bad for your health.

   b. the body / that tobacco / believed / was / it was / good for / in the 60s,

   _____

   c. thought / a person's life / and were good for / that cigarettes / might lengthen / years ago, / it was / his or her teeth

   _____

2. a. been recently / that sugar / one's health / it has / is bad for / shown

   _____

   b. a good source / argued / of energy for children / it was / that sugar was / years ago,

   _____

3. a. generally been / is bad for children / accepted / it has / that watching / too much television / now,

   _____

   b. suggested / that too much / it / from doing physical activities / has been / television keeps children

   _____

   c. children's grades / that watching television / could improve / it was / believed / in the 60s,

   _____

B *Group Work* As a group, compare medical beliefs of today with medical beliefs in the past. Share your ideas using passive *it* constructions.

It was once accepted that eggs were one of the causes of high cholesterol, but I think that it is evident from current research that they are not a primary cause.

3 Common Transition Words to Indicate Steps of a Solution

▶ Vocabulary Presentation

> Transition words and phrases are commonly used to guide readers through the steps in a solution or process.
>
> *First, it is important for people to find an activity that is enjoyable, such as playing a sport or hiking. Next, they need to commit to doing it.*

3.1 Using Transition Words to Indicate Steps of a Solution

a. Use transition words such as *first* and *to begin* to introduce the first step of a proposed solution. Use a comma after them when they appear at the beginning of the sentence.	*First, one needs to acknowledge that a problem exists.* *To begin, put the problem into words.*
b. Use *after that, following that, next, second, third, subsequently,* and *then* to introduce the next steps. Use *at the same time* to introduce a step that happens or needs to happen at the same time.	*Following that, ways to address specific aspects of the problem should be developed.* *Next, key terms should be clearly defined.* *At the same time, the scope and effects of the problem need to be identified.*
c. Use *finally, in the end, last,* and *lastly* to conclude the steps.	*Finally, the set of strategies should be implemented.*
d. You can also place transition words such as *next* and *then* in the middle of a sentence, before the verb. You can also use *next* at the end of a sentence.	*The scope and effects of the problem then need to be identified.* *The people associated with the problem need to be contacted next.*
e. You can also use phrases like *the first step, the second step, the third step,* and so forth, to indicate steps of a solution. These phrases are usually followed by *be* + infinitive.	*First, one needs to acknowledge that a problem exists.* *The first step is to acknowledge that a problem exists.*

3.2 Using Transition Words in Problem–Solution Writing

Use transition words to link the steps of a solution. This makes writing more cohesive.	***First**, one needs to acknowledge that a problem exists. The scope and effects of the problem **then** need to be identified. **Next**, key terms and ideas should be clearly defined. **Following that**, ways to address specific aspects of the problem should be developed. **Finally**, the set of strategies should be implemented.*

▶ Vocabulary Application

Exercise 3.1 Transition Words to Indicate Steps of a Solution

A 🔊 Listen to part of a lecture about how companies can address specific health problems that occur on the job. Complete the steps of the solution, using the transition words you hear to identify the steps.

Notes:

Problem: For data-entry workers, sitting at a computer for hours every day leads to weight gain, back pain, neck pain, and wrist pain.

Solution: Set up a plan to address the specific problems that workers have.

Steps:

1. _____*The first step is to*_____ identify _____*the health issues*_____ .

2. _____ determine _____ .

3. _____ implement _____ .

4. _____ evaluate _____ .

B *Pair Work* Work with a partner and discuss one of the problems below. Using A as a model, write the problem, the solution, and possible steps for the solution. Include at least three transition words. When you have finished, report your problem and solutions to the class.

- Smokers who want to give up smoking
- Students who don't study enough
- People who worry too much

Exercise 3.2 More Transition Words to Indicate Steps of a Solution

Read the steps below about ways to make health a focus in your life. Number the sentences in the correct order.

_____ Next, keep a journal for a week and write down what you eat every day and how you spend your time.

_____ At the same time, substitute at least one hour of the time that you spent watching TV or doing some other unnecessary activity with one hour of exercise. Do this for 21 days because some experts claim that it takes 21 days to make or break a habit.

_1_ To begin, acknowledge that you need to focus on your health.

_____ Subsequently, look at your journal and circle the unhealthy foods that you ate during the week.

_____ At the same time, circle the things that you did during the week that were unnecessary or could be cut down. For example, did you spend your lunch break surfing online, or did you watch three hours of TV after dinner?

_____ Finally, evaluate how you feel after three weeks of eating better and exercising one hour a day. You should feel great and have more energy.

_____ Also, hopefully you'll have created a new, healthy habit for yourself!

_____ After you examine your journal, substitute each unhealthy food with a healthy food like fruit, vegetables, or lean proteins.

4 | Avoid Common Mistakes ⚠️

1. **Remember to use *It is important to* and not *It is import to* or *It is importand to*.**

   It is ~~import~~ *important* to admit that the problem exists.

   It is ~~importand~~ *important* to find an exercise routine that is convenient.

2. **Remember to use *to* or *for* after *impossible*.**

   For many people, it is impossible ⌄*to* find the time for exercise.

   It is impossible ⌄*for* some people to slow down and relax.

3. **Remember to use *then*, not *than*, when introducing next steps.**

   First, one needs to identify the sources of the stress. ~~Than~~ *Then*, ways to eliminate them should be considered.

Editing Task

Find and correct six more mistakes in the body paragraph from an essay on ways to improve health.

It is ~~importand~~ *important* to get an adequate amount of sleep in order to maintain a healthy lifestyle. For many people, it is almost impossible get a good night's sleep. Stress and the demands of work have a tremendous effect on one's ability to sleep. Lack of sleep can also result from certain lifestyle habits. However, it is virtually impossible people to function well without adequate

5 sleep. Studies have shown that lack of sleep can lead to a variety of physical and emotional problems. Therefore, it is import to get at least seven to eight hours of sleep at night because getting the recommended amount of sleep means optimal health and energy, more acute mental faculties, and a better memory. It also means getting sick less and being better able to deal with the stresses and strains of everyday life. Although at times it may seem impossible get

10 enough sleep, there are a few simple strategies for improving one's chances. First, one needs to determine the causes of sleeplessness, such as lack of exercise or consuming too much caffeine. Than, one needs to commit to making a few small lifestyle changes. People who have difficulty sleeping should increase their daily exercise, but not exercise too late in the day. They should avoid consuming too much caffeine and eating close to bedtime. It is also important to have a

15 regular bedtime and to get the same number of hours of sleep each night. These small changes to one's daily routine can lead to a better night's sleep and improved health.

5 | The Writing Process ✎

In this section, you will write a problem–solution essay in which you describe in detail how to implement the solution you propose. Before you start writing, you will learn about describing the steps of a solution.

About Describing the Steps of a Solution

When you describe a solution in problem–solution writing, it is important to develop a plan of action, or process, to implement the solution. All the steps involved in the planning and implementation of the solution should be explained.

The following guidelines can help you when writing about the steps in a solution:

1. **Reduce the steps to three or four major steps.** It can be very confusing for a reader to try to follow six, seven, or eight steps in a process. If you find that there are that many steps necessary to implement your solution, combine some steps into one so that your reader only perceives three or four, which should usually be the maximum.

2. **Use signal words or phrases.** To help your reader realize that you have finished writing about one step in the process and started writing about another, use transition words and phrases such as the following: *first; the first thing to do; second; next; after that; finally; the last step to take is . . .*

3. **Put the steps in a logical order.** Sometimes the steps in the solution will be in chronological order. In this case, it is obvious that you should write about the step that comes first in time, then second in time, and so on. In other cases, you may want to order the steps in order of importance. Often, this will mean writing about the most important step first. Later steps may be introduced by using such phrases as: *It is also important to . . .*

Exercise

A Read one student writer's solution to the problem of teenagers having a poor body image, and then answer the questions below.

An issue that is very important to young people is understanding and accepting their own bodies. Many young people, especially women, can develop unrealistic expectations about how they should look. This can cause a great deal of unhappiness and can lead to eating disorders and worse. Parents and teachers can take several practical steps to help young
5 people create a healthier sense of self. First, it is essential that parents and teachers learn about the warning signs of eating disorders and other body-image issues. When they have this information, they can act quickly and decisively to help young people who are in crisis. Next, parents and teachers should think about how they compliment girls. It is not unusual for girls to receive compliments only about their looks. Instead, parents and teachers should notice
10 what girls do, not how they look. Finally, parents and teachers should give young people a place where they can talk openly about how they feel when comparing themselves to thin girls or models they may see in fashion magazines. If young people realize that others have

similar feelings and issues, they may not feel alone. Young people are surrounded by media images of unrealistic body types that can make them feel insecure. However, following these
15 practical steps can help address avoidable suffering.

1. How many steps are there in the solution?

2. Did the writer use signal words to show where a new step begins? If so, what are they?

3. Are the steps organized in order of importance or in chronological order?

4. What are the steps described by the writer?

B *Pair Work* Discuss your answers with a partner.

Pre-writing Tasks

Choose a Topic

A Choose one of the topics listed below. You will write a problem–solution essay in which you propose at least one solution to your problem and describe the steps necessary to implement the solution. You will also note any limitations or drawbacks to your solutions and tell how you would address them.

- The park in your neighborhood is unsafe and unkempt. As a result, families don't use it for recreation and exercise.
- A social problem that is worldwide
- A topic of your own approved by your teacher

B *Pair Work* Share your topic with a partner. Then brainstorm some possible solutions to your problem.

Organize Your Ideas

A Draw the chart below on a separate sheet of paper. Write your problem, your suggested solution or solutions, the steps that need to be taken to implement your solution(s), and any limitations of your solution(s).

```
Problem:
_____

```

Proposed Solution 1:	Limitation or Drawback to the Solution:
_____	_____
Steps:	How Will You Address It?
1. _____	1. _____
2. _____	2. _____
3. _____	

B *Pair Work* Share your chart with a partner. Discuss whether the steps to your solution(s) are logically ordered. Discuss the limitation you see and how you will address it. Does your partner agree?

Writing Task

Write a problem–solution essay in which you describe a problem and propose at least one solution and describe the steps necessary to implement the solution. Follow the steps below.

1. Write an introductory paragraph that describes the problem (including a hook) and includes the solution in your thesis statement.

2. In the second paragraph, explain the importance of the problem you chose.

3. In the next paragraph(s), propose a solution(s). Use the chart you filled out to guide you. Present the solution(s) and explain the steps necessary to implement each solution.

4. Acknowledge possible limitations or drawbacks to the solution(s) and how to address them.

> **Academic Writing Tip**
>
> **Keep an Error Log**
>
> Keep an error log with the mistakes you make and an explanation. Review the log as you write. For example:
>
> 1. ~~I think~~ it is important to eat healthily. (Avoid "*I think*" where possible.)
>
> 2. *It is* ~~Is~~ essential for people to spend time relaxing. (Remember to include subjects.)

5. Write a concluding paragraph that restates your thesis statement and includes either a prediction or recommendation about your solution to the problem.

6. Include the following in your essay:

   - *it* constructions;

   - transition words and phrases that signal the different steps of a solution;

   - at least three of these academic words from the reading in this unit: *approach, challenge, challenging, cite, commit, committed, consequence, consume, contrary, contribute, create, decade, factor, generate, goal, individual, item, maintain, option, schedule, series, source, strategy, stress, stressful, task, tension.*

7. After you write your essay, review it and make sure you avoided the mistakes in the Avoid Common Mistakes chart on page 244.

Peer Review

A Exchange your essay with a partner. Answer the following questions as you read your partner's essay, and then share your responses.

1. Is there a thesis statement? Does it mention the solution to the problem?

2. Does the essay contain an effective description of the problem? What is the problem, and does the writer make the reader feel that it is important?

3. Does the essay contain a clear description of the steps necessary to implement the solution? Does it address any limitations or drawbacks to the solution? Does it consider other possible solutions?

4. Does the writer use any *it* constructions? Underline any that you find.

5. Does the writer use any transition words or phrases to signal steps in the process? Circle any that you find.

6. Is anything confusing? Write a question mark (?) next to it.

7. Provide one compliment (something you found interesting or unusual).

B Use your partner's comments to help you revise your essay. Use the Writer's Checklist on page A2 to review your essay for organization, grammar, and vocabulary.

Summary–Response: Past Unreal Conditionals; Phrases Used in Summary–Response Writing

Privacy in the Digital Age

1 | Grammar in the Real World

You will read an article that discusses the issue of privacy and computers. You will then read an essay that summarizes and responds to the article.

A *Before You Read* What are some possible dangers of surfing the Internet? What can people do to protect themselves from these dangers? Read the article. Then read the response to the article below it. What do the two writers suggest as ways Internet users can protect themselves?

Privacy and Computers
by Robert Erani

In an era of online social media, people can announce any event to their virtual network of friends, family, and acquaintances within moments. From birthday celebrations to baby pictures, friends get news about each other from texts, tweets, or social networks. In addition, many people use credit cards to purchase products and complete numerous online forms with
5 personal information for a variety of purposes. As a result, personal information is ending up in the hands of other people. There are critics who are concerned by the lack of privacy. Despite such concerns, by following a few common-sense measures, people can use the Internet enjoyably and safely.

In our fast-paced world, social networking sites are, for many people, an important way to
10 keep up with friends and family. The issue now is how open one should be with sharing private information since the information could be stolen by criminals. For example, some people have had their homes broken into because they had posted the details of their vacation online. If they had not posted those details, the thieves would not have known that they had gone away. One way to reduce the risk of this happening is to activate the privacy controls on social
15 networking sites and smartphones. In other words, think about who will see your information and consider how they might use it.

Another important step is to shop only on secure websites so that one's accounts, passwords, and financial records are protected. Some experts recommend that people should treat their online information like they would treat the contents of their wallets. For example, a
20 man bought merchandise on a website that did not have a security padlock, and as a result of this transaction, his bank accounts were emptied. If he had paid attention to the security on the site, he would not have lost his money. However, it appears that people are becoming more aware of the risks of fraud and taking steps to avoid them since the total percentage of

incidences of fraud remained steady in 2011 (Campana, 2012). It may be that people who have
25 grown up using the Internet understand its risks as well as its strengths.

The ease of sharing information provides opportunities for crimes and abuses. While it may
be impossible to entirely eliminate the risks, if people followed reasonable guidelines to protect
important data, they could greatly reduce these risks. The benefits of being able to do such
things as bank online, keep medical records updated almost instantly, and share the thrills both
30 big and small of everyday life with friends outweigh these concerns.

Summary–Response Essay on "Privacy and Computers"

Robert Erani, in the article "Privacy and Computers," explains the issues
concerning the sharing of personal information online. According to Erani,
one area of concern is that people may sometime share details of their lives
online without thinking about the consequences. As the author points out,
5 "The issue now is how open one should be with sharing private information
since the information could be stolen by criminals" (para. 2). The author
describes a situation in which people were robbed after revealing their
vacation plans online. The author further states how important it is for
consumers to protect their personal information when they purchase
10 products online. Erani concludes the article by stating that, despite the
concerns about privacy, one can still use online services safely by using
common sense and privacy controls.

In sum, the author provides a general introduction to the issues of privacy online
and offers some advice on how to avoid problems. I agree that insecure websites are
15 a problem, but I disagree with the author's contention that people who have grown
up using the Internet are more savvy about using it. Hackers and scammers continue
to come up with more sophisticated and convincing schemes. The consumer needs
to constantly be wary of them. In addition, the article fails to address the more
controversial issues concerning the consequences of posting information regarding
20 health issues, job dissatisfaction, or even political views. This is an oversight because
these issues impact individuals every day. It is becoming increasingly common for
employers, for instance, to view the online profiles of potential employees as part
of their selection process. Despite these shortcomings, the author rightly states that
the concern around privacy issues seems to be an acceptable exchange for many
25 people for the benefits of sharing their lives with others.

B *Comprehension Check* Answer these questions.

1. What two suggestions does the writer of "Privacy and Computers" make for being safe on the Internet?
2. What important issues does the summary–response writer believe are missing from the original article?
3. What other privacy concerns do you have concerning the use of your personal information? What do you do to keep your information safe?

C Notice

1 Summary–Response Writing Find the following sentences in the summary–response essay and fill in the missing words to notice how the writer refers back to the first essay.

1. _____ _____ _____ , one area of concern is that people may sometimes share details of their lives online without thinking about the consequences. (para. 1)

2. _____ _____ _____ _____ , "The issue now is how open one should be with sharing private information since the information could be stolen by criminals." (para. 1)

3. _____ _____ _____ _____ how important it is for consumers to protect their personal information when they purchase products online. (para. 1)

2 Grammar Follow the instructions to notice how the author of "Privacy and Computers" uses unreal conditionals.

1. Reread the second paragraph of the article. What happened to the people who went on vacation? Underline the unreal conditional on lines 13–14. How does using an unreal conditional help the writer?

2. Reread the third paragraph of the article. What happened to the man who bought merchandise on a website that did not have a security padlock? Underline the unreal conditional on lines 21–22. How does using an unreal conditional help the writer?

3. Reread the last paragraph of the article. Find the sentence with the *if* clause. Compare this sentence with the sentence with the *if* clause in 2. Which one refers to an imagined past result? Which one refers to an imagined present result? What do you notice about the forms of the verbs?

3 The Writing Process Match the excerpts from the summary–response essay to the lines in the "Privacy and Computers" essay that it summarizes. Write the paragraph number and the line numbers in which the information appears.

1. Robert Erani, in the article "Privacy and Computers," explains the issues concerning the sharing of personal information online. Para. _____ Lines _____ to _____

2. The author describes a situation in which people were robbed after revealing their vacation plans online. Para. _____ Lines _____ to _____

3. Erani concludes the article by stating that, despite the concerns about privacy, one can still use online services safely by using common sense and privacy controls. Para. _____ Lines _____ to _____

2 | Past Unreal Conditionals

▶ Grammar Presentation

Past unreal conditionals allow the writer to discuss hypothetical situations – untrue or unreal situations in the past – and the consequences of the situations. Effective academic writers use this form to contrast what happened (the "real") with what was possible but did not happen (the "unreal").

*If the author **had discussed** education in his article, the text **would have been** stronger.*
*If this information **had been taught** years ago, we **would not have had** so many problems.*

2.1 Past Unreal Conditionals

The past unreal conditional is formed as follows: *if* clause (past perfect) + main clause (*would / could / might* + *have* + past participle) The *if* clause can come first or last in a sentence. Use a comma when it comes first.	IF CLAUSE (PAST PERFECT) ***If** I **had read** the privacy policy on the company's website* MAIN CLAUSE (*WOULD / COULD / MIGHT* + *HAVE* + PAST PARTICIPLE) *carefully, I **would have avoided** the problem.* MAIN CLAUSE IF CLAUSE *I **would have avoided** the problem **if** I **had read** the website's privacy policy carefully.*

2.2 Using Past Unreal Conditionals

a. The *if* clause gives the untrue condition in the past. The main clause expresses the imaginary past result.	IF CLAUSE: PAST UNREAL CONDITION ***If** she **had used** separate accounts for work and personal* MAIN CLAUSE: IMAGINARY PAST RESULT *e-mail, she **would have avoided** trouble.* (The real situation: She used the same e-mail account for personal and work e-mail. She got into trouble.) UNREAL PAST CONDITION ***If** he **hadn't made** his passwords difficult,* IMAGINARY PAST RESULT *the thieves **would have been able to access** his accounts.* (The real situation: His passwords were difficult. The thieves did not access his accounts.)

2.2 Using Past Unreal Conditionals *(continued)*

b. As with other forms and uses of modals, *would have* expresses a more certain (but still imaginary) past result. *Could have* and *might have* express less certain results.	*If I had noticed the lack of security on that website, I **wouldn't have ordered** merchandise from it.* *If I had ordered merchandise from that website, I **might have had** my information stolen.*
c. Use past unreal conditionals to express regrets about past situations or actions.	*If I **had insured** my laptop, the insurance company **would have reimbursed** me when it was stolen.* (I regret that I did not have insurance for my laptop.)
d. Past unreal conditionals can also express an imaginary present result. Use *would / could / might* + the base form of the verb in the main clause.	UNREAL PAST CONDITION *If the author **had mentioned** his sources,* IMAGINARY PRESENT RESULT *the article **would be more** compelling.*

▶ Grammar Application

Exercise 2.1 Past Unreal Conditionals

Read the story about identify theft. Complete the sentences with the appropriate modal and the correct form of the verb in parentheses. Sometimes more than one answer is possible.

I know that thieves have ways to steal people's identities online, so I'm always

careful about the e-mails I read and the links that I click on. However, I didn't realize

that thieves sometimes go through people's garbage to look for personal information.

I *'d have been* (be) more careful if I *'d known* (know) that.
　　　　(1)　　　　　　　　　　　　　　　(1)

Last year, I put a letter that had my Social Security number on it in the garbage.

Normally, I shred important documents, but I was in a hurry that day. If

I _____ (not be) in a hurry, I definitely _____ (shred) it.
　　　　(2)　　　　　　　　　　　　　　　　　　　　　　(2)

A few days later, there was no money in my checking account. I realized that if someone

_____ (take) the letter out of the garbage, he or she _____ (have)
　　　(3)　　　　　　　　　　　　　　　　　　　　　　　　　　　(3)

my Social Security number now. I knew that if someone _____ (find) my Social
　　　　　　　　　　　　　　　　　　　　　　　　　　　　(4)

Security number, they _____ (have) the ability to access my bank accounts,
　　　　　　　　　　　(4)

use my credit cards, and get new credit cards in my name.

By the time I realized that my identity had been stolen, the thief had taken all my money

and applied for 10 new credit cards. If I _____ (realize) sooner that a thief had
　　　　　　　　　　　　　　　　　　　(5)

found my Social Security number, I _____ (be) able to stop him or her from
　　　　　　　　　　　　　　　　(5)

using it. The identity theft has caused all kinds of problems for me. I can't get a loan to buy a car, and I can't get a new credit card. If someone _____ (not steal) my identity,

(6)

I _____ (not have) all these problems now.

(6)

   I shred all my important documents now before I throw them away. Last week, I told my neighbor what had happened to me. She was going to put some important mail in her garbage without shredding it. She immediately shredded the mail. If I _____ (not warn)

(7)

her, she _____ (have) the same problems that I do now.

(7)

Exercise 2.2 More Past Unreal Conditionals

A Combine the pairs of sentences describing an unfortunate event. Use past unreal conditionals. Sometimes more than one answer is possible.

1. I visited my friend Eric for the weekend. I lost all my credit cards and my cell phone.

   If I hadn't visited my friend Eric for the weekend,
   I wouldn't have lost all my credit cards and my
   cell phone.

2. Eric wasn't ready to go swimming on Saturday morning. I went to the beach alone.

   _____

   _____

3. Eric wasn't with me. I left my wallet and phone on the beach while I went swimming.

   _____

4. I went swimming. Someone stole my credit cards and my phone.

   _____

5. I forgot the address of Eric's house. I couldn't find the house.

   _____

6. I didn't have my cell phone. I couldn't call Eric.

   _____

7. My cell phone wasn't password-protected. The thief was able to use my phone.

   _____

8. I had personal information on my cell phone. The thief got my bank account numbers.

   _____

9. I also forgot to wear sunscreen. I have a terrible sunburn.

   _____

B *Pair Work* With a partner, take turns describing mistakes you have made and ways that you could have avoided making the mistakes.

Someone stole my wallet from my purse at a restaurant last weekend. I'd hung my purse on the back of my chair. If I hadn't put it on the back of my chair, no one would have stolen my wallet. If I had put my purse closer to me, I'd have my wallet now.

3 | Common Phrases Used in Summary–Response Writing 🌐

▶ Vocabulary Presentation

> Good academic writers use phrases appropriate to introducing and identifying ideas in summary–response writing.
>
> *The article **provides** a thorough introduction to the issues of privacy.*
> *The author **fails to address** more controversial concerns.*

3.1 Common Phrases in Summary–Response Writing

a. You can use these common subject + verb combinations to introduce the main idea of a summary. They are listed in order of frequency: *The article + say, state, note, describe, mention, quote, report* . . . *The author + claim, explain, call, say, write, argue, cite, establish, start* . . . *The article* is used much more frequently than *the author* in summary–response statements. Note: Do not use *believe* or *think* in summary–response statements that begin with the words "*The author* . . . "	***The article describes*** *the problem of privacy and computers.* ***The article mentions*** *ways that education can prevent problems with technology.* ***The author starts the article by saying that*** *technology is part of everyone's lives.* ***The author claims*** *that the experts he interviewed for this article were well-known.* NOT *The author ~~thinks~~ that the experts he interviewed for this article were well-known.*
b. The common subject + verb combinations in (a) are usually used in the present but sometimes also appear in the simple past or present perfect. (See Unit 14 on reporting verbs.)	***The article quoted*** *many well-known sources.* ***The author has argued*** *that individuals are responsible for protecting their own privacy.*

3.1 Common Phrases in Summary–Response Writing *(continued)*

c. Use these phrases to identify ideas by the author of the original text:

discuss	***The article discusses*** *identity theft in detail.*
go on to say	***The article goes on to say*** *that the problem is being addressed.*
further state / explain	***The author further states*** *that regulations may be necessary in the future.*
also state	***The author also states*** *that consumers need to become proactive on this issue.*
according to the author	***According to the author***, *the government has an important role in this debate.*

d. Use these phrases to conclude the summary–response:

In conclusion, *In sum,* *The author concludes* *Summing up,*	***In conclusion***, *the author predicts that Internet privacy will become one of the most important issues of the next decade.* ***Summing up***, *the author calls for people to be cautious when giving their personal information online.*

e. Use these phrases in the response part of summary–response writing to indicate what the author omitted or did not consider:

fail to address / mention	*The author* **fails to address** *the idea that users are also to blame for identity theft.*
not address / mention	*The author* **does / did not mention** *that we are all responsible for protecting privacy.*
Note: Phrases that use the first person, such as *In my opinion*, are rare in academic writing. They are more common in informal texts like magazines.	~~*I think that*~~ *the author . . .* ~~*In my opinion*~~, *the author could have . . .*

► Vocabulary Application

Exercise 3.1 Summarizing Information

Read the summary of an article about privacy on the Internet.
Circle the correct words or phrases to complete the summary.

John M. Eger, Chair of Communications and Public

Policy at San Diego State University, (addresses)/ claims
(1)

the issue of privacy in the Internet age in his article

"Growing Concerns Over Internet Privacy" (2010). He

starts the article / further states by explaining the historical context of the right to privacy
(2)

in the United States and **cites / describes** how in 1928, a Supreme Court decision was
(3)

made to protect the right to privacy. However, he **concludes that / notes that** our online
(4)

lives are today being monitored in ways that most people do not even realize. He then

claims / goes on to explain how websites use cookies to follow an Internet user's every move.
(5)

The author **acknowledges that / thinks that** some sharing of information may provide us with
(6)

advertisements for things that may be beneficial to us, but then he **argues that / sums up that**
(7)

data collectors might collect and share health and financial information, and even connect

our names to our data. In addition, **according to the article, / the article quotes** there
(8)

are currently no laws that adequately protect our right to privacy. Then, while the author

goes on to show / concludes by saying that we need to do something about this problem,
(9)

he **does not mention at all / further states** what we can do to protect ourselves.
(10)

Exercise 3.2 🔊 More Summarizing Information

Read the sentences below. Then listen to two people talk about an article on Internet
passwords. Make notes as you listen. Listen again and complete the sentences.

1. _The author starts the article by saying that a website_ was recently hacked.

2. _____ when they create their passwords.

3. _____ can break one password a second.

4. _____ shouldn't use the same password
   for multiple accounts.

5. _____ says, "I always use the same
   password for everything because otherwise I can't remember them."

6. _____ is abc123.

7. _____ is 123456.

8. _____ can do to create strong passwords.

4 Avoid Common Mistakes ⚠️

1. Remember to use the past participle form of the verb after the modal in past unreal conditionals.

avoided
If the company had installed secure systems, it would have ~~avoid~~ data theft.

2. Remember to use academic, precise words rather than multi-word verbs or idioms such as:

find out → discover / learn
put up with → tolerate
start off / out → start / begin
look into → investigate

discovering
Social media users enjoy ~~finding out~~ what products and services their friends recommend.

tolerate
Older users will not ~~put up with~~ further invasions of privacy.

The article starts ~~off~~ with a presentation of both sides of the issue.

investigates
The author ~~looks into~~ recent developments in Internet security.

Editing Task

Find and correct five more mistakes in the summary paragraph from a summary–response essay on privacy issues and social networking.

investigates
In his article "Privacy and Security Issues in Social Networking" (2008), Brendan Collins ~~looks into~~ the security and privacy problems associated with social networks. He starts off by making the distinction between security issues and privacy issues, pointing out that social networking sites (SNSs) provide ideal opportunities for both types of violations to take place

5 because they are so popular. As an example of a security violation, Collins cites the case of a hacker who shut down a social networking site a few years ago just for fun. It was fortunate that the attack was harmless. If the attack had been committed with a malicious intent, the personal data of millions of users would have be stolen. According to Collins, SNSs provide ideal opportunities for break-ins because they process so much information, and because so

10 many people have access to them. As an example, he describes the case of Adrienne Felt, a PhD candidate at U.C. Berkeley, who found out that there was a security flaw in a major social networking site. In other words, the same program that allowed people to share photos and send invitations also exposed their information to theft. If Felt had not looked into the

social networking site, a large proportion of users could have get their information stolen.

15 Collins goes on to recommend ways users can limit the possibility of security and privacy violations. Because SNSs are getting so big, he says, it is becoming impossible to monitor the activity that takes place on them. It is therefore the responsibility of users to take precautions as they share information about themselves. Collins concludes that there probably will never be a solution to these issues and implies that we will have to put up with threats to our privacy

20 and security. Collins adds, however, that the less one uses SNSs, the lower the chance one has of getting their identity stolen.

5 | The Writing Process ✏

In this section, you will write a two-paragraph summary–response to an article about a topic on technology. Before you start writing, you will learn about summary–response writing.

About Summary–Response Writing

Being able to create strong summary–response writing is an important skill for academic writers. Academic writers have to be able to show that they understand the ideas put forward by others and how those ideas fit into their own worldview.

The following are guidelines for writing a summary–response of an article:

1. **Identify the writer's main ideas.** While reading the original text, use a highlighter or take notes that show what the writer's main ideas are.

2. **Make notes about your own ideas.** Review your highlighted text and notes and then make more notes indicating which points you agree or disagree with.

3. **State your source at the beginning of the summary–response.** Begin your summary by giving the name of the author and the article. In your opening statement, also state as briefly as possible the writer's main point or purpose in writing the article.

   Robert Erani, in the article "Privacy and Computers," explains the issues concerning the sharing of personal information online.

4. **Refer to main ideas in the same order as in the original text.** As you summarize the article, choose the main ideas that you want to refer the reader to and identify them in the same order in which they appear in the original text. Use examples that are essential for understanding the main ideas, but only use examples from the original text – do not include your own examples.

5. **Paraphrase and use short quotations.** Use your paraphrasing skills to review the writer's ideas. Also include short quotations from the original text to give your reader a clear sense of how the writer expressed key points.

6. **In the response section, present your views clearly.** Discuss aspects you agree and disagree with. Identify ideas that the writer either missed entirely or did not develop completely. Before offering your own suggestions, it can be a good strategy to find at least one positive thing to say about the original writer's ideas. In this way, you can sound thoughtful, balanced, and reasonable.

Exercise

A Reread "Patient–Doctor Relationships in the 21st Century" in Unit 15 on pages 218–219 or "Leading a Healthy Life" in Unit 16 on pages 234–235. Then complete the following:

Summary

1. Write a sentence that identifies the source and the main point or purpose of the essay.

_____

_____

2. List the main ideas in the same order as in the original essay.

_____

_____

_____

3. Choose one short quotation that illustrates one of the writer's key points.

_____

_____

Response

1. Write your overall opinion about the essay.

_____

_____

_____

2. Write one point that you agree with and one point you disagree with.

_____

_____

_____

3. Write one point that you believe is missing and that expresses your own idea on the topic.

_____

_____

B *Pair Work* Explain your ideas to a partner. Discuss any disagreements that you have. Try to convince your partner of your idea by using information from the article, your knowledge of the topic, and your experiences.

Pre-writing Tasks

Choose a Topic

A Find a short article about one of the topics listed below. You will write a two-paragraph summary–response of the article.

- Plagiarism in the digital world
- Social media and privacy
- A topic of your own approved by your teacher

B *Pair Work* Share the main ideas and details of the article you read with a partner. Express your own views on the topic of the article, noting where you agree or disagree with the writer.

Organize Your Ideas

Complete the following outline using information from the article you found.

Summary–Response Outline
Paragraph #1: Summary Source:
Main ideas:
Examples:
A short quotation:
Paragraph #2: Response Your overall view:
Ideas that you agree with:
Ideas that you disagree with:
Ideas that are missing:

Writing Task

Write your summary–response paragraphs using your outline above.
Follow the steps below.

1. In your summary paragraph, start by giving the source information, the writer's overall purpose, and main idea. Then restate the writer's main ideas in their original order without giving your own opinion.

2. In your response paragraph, find an idea or ideas of the writer's that you can agree with, and then present your own ideas on the topic.

3. Include the following in your paragraphs:

   - a quotation from the original article;
   - common summary–response phrases, such as noun / verb combinations like *the article says / states / notes* and *the author claims / explains / argues*;
   - past unreal conditionals to express what could have happened but did not;
   - at least three academic words from the essays in this unit: *area, author, aware, benefit, conclude, consequence, consumer, controversial, data, despite, eliminate, expert, financial, guideline, issue, job, media, medical, network, networking, percentage, potential, process, purchase, reveal, secure, security, selection, site, text, virtual.*

4. After you write your paragraphs, review them and make sure you avoided the mistakes in the Avoid Common Mistakes chart on page 257.

> ## Academic Writing Tip
>
> ### In fact
> Use the phrase *in fact* to add strong support – especially surprising information – to a preceding statement.
>
> *Deleting information from a computer is not always as secure as it seems.* **In fact,** *specialists can easily retrieve "deleted" files from a hard drive.*

Peer Review

A Exchange your paragraphs with a partner. Answer the following questions as you read your partner's paragraphs, and then share your responses.

1. Does the writer include the source and topic of the original article in the opening section of the summary paragraph?

2. What main points from the original article does the writer emphasize? Does the writer use the common summary–response phrases to introduce these points?

3. Does the writer avoid including his or her own opinion in the summary paragraph?

4. Does the writer include a short quotation from the original article? Underline it.

5. In the response paragraph, does the writer praise any elements from the original source material before disagreeing and offering new ideas?

6. Does the writer use any past unreal conditionals? Circle them.

7. Is anything confusing? Write a question mark (?) next to it.

8. Provide one compliment (something you found interesting or unusual).

B Use your partner's comments to help you revise your paragraphs. Use the Writer's Checklist on page A2 to review your paragraphs for organization, grammar, and vocabulary.

UNIT 18

Persuasion 1: Nonidentifying Relative Clauses; Phrases That Limit Overgeneralization

Violence in the Media

1 | Grammar in the Real World

You will read an essay about violence on television. In the essay, the writer argues that violence on TV should be regulated by the government. The essay is an example of one type of persuasive writing.

A *Before You Read* Do you think there is too much violence shown on TV? Who do you think should be responsible for controlling the amount of violence that children watch on TV: parents, the government, or both? Read the essay. What is the writer's main argument?

TV Violence: Who Is Responsible?

Should violence on TV be regulated? This question has long been debated. Opponents defend the right to freedom of speech. Proponents believe that some restriction is essential to protect young people from too much exposure to violence. In 2007 in a controversial report, the Federal Communications Commission (FCC), which is the government agency that regulates
5 radio, TV, and Internet communications, advised the government to regulate violence on television to protect children. A report in 2010 by Brocato, Gentile, Laczniak, Maier, and Ji-Song states that children who watch violent TV shows and play violent video games are likely to exhibit more aggressive and violent behavior (para. 2). It is clear that the government should take immediate action and control violence on TV through regulations.

10   Regulation by the government should protect the public, especially children, from overexposure to violence. In the past, courts have protected violent speech and depictions[1] of violence under the First Amendment.[2] Nonetheless, the government regulates TV and film indecency.[3] According to the FCC, the Supreme Court allows these restrictions so that children are not so easily exposed to indecency. The parallel with violence in the media is obvious.
15 Limiting media violence is much like limiting indecency in the media (FCC, 2007, p. 11–12).

[1]**depiction:** an image | [2]**First Amendment:** an amendment in the United States Constitution that allows for freedom of speech in most situations | [3]**indecency:** behavior that upsets popular moral standards, usually as they relate to sexual behavior and nudity

Government regulation will also help parents monitor their children's exposure to violence. FCC Chairman Kevin Martin explained that while parents should always be the decision makers on how to best protect their children from violence, they alone cannot be responsible (FCC, 2007, p. 25). The main problem is that television violence seems to have a strong presence
20 in most children's lives. TV rating and program-blocking systems, which are both tools to help parents control viewing, are "not effective," according to the FCC, since networks may not consistently monitor TV shows for violent content (FCC, 2007, p. 25). In fact, the Parents Television Council, which monitors TV shows for violent content, states that networks are not doing a good job of rating TV shows. As a result, children have access to inappropriate content.

25 Congress has resisted addressing this issue. However, not addressing it could put children, who have young minds that are easily impressionable,[4] at risk. It could also put society at risk for aggressive acts committed by people influenced by violent media. Therefore, the government must act now to regulate media; otherwise, society will have a difficult road ahead trying to control the negative effects of violent media on our children.

[4]**impressionable:** readily or easily influenced

B *Comprehension Check* Answer the questions.

1. What evidence is given in the essay that violence on TV may negatively affect children's behavior?

2. Why might it be difficult in the United States for the government to regulate TV violence?

3. Do you agree with the writer that violence on TV should be regulated? Why or why not?

C *Notice*

1 Persuasive Writing Check (✓) the two arguments to regulate violence on TV that are emphasized in the essay.

Government regulation of the television industry will:

_____ generate tax revenue

_____ protect the public from overexposure to violence

_____ protect free speech

_____ reduce indecency

_____ help parents limit their children's exposure to violence

2 Grammar Answer the questions below to notice how the writer uses relative clauses to explain and support his ideas.

1. Compare the two sentences concerning children on lines 6–8 and 25–26. In which sentence does the writer refer to *all* children? In which sentence does the writer identify a particular group of children?

2. Read the two sentences on lines 20–24, starting with "TV rating and blocking systems . . ." Look at the relative clauses in these sentences. Are these relative clauses essential to understanding the sentences? What information do these clauses provide the reader?

3 The Writing Process

Pair Work Work with a partner to analyze the introduction to the persuasive essay by answering the questions below.

1. Which sentence contains the hook – a sentence that serves to create interest and motivate readers? (See Unit 2 page 30 to review the four types of hooks.) Why is this sentence an effective hook?

2. What controversial issue does the writer introduce?

3. What evidence does the writer introduce to support his or her position?

4. What is the writer's thesis?

2 | Nonidentifying Relative Clauses

▶ Grammar Presentation

Nonidentifying relative clauses provide additional information about a noun phrase. Writers often use nonidentifying relative clauses to describe or identify the proper noun or organization they are citing. The relative clause can add credibility to the expert or organization.

The Federal Communications Commission (FCC), **which regulates radio, TV, and Internet communications,** *has condemned violence in children's programming.*
Parents, **who one could argue have the most influence on young children,** *must limit their children's exposure to violence.*

2.1 Nonidentifying Relative Clauses

a. Nonidentifying relative clauses add more details about a noun or noun phrase. They begin with a relative pronoun: *who, which, whose,* or *whom.* Use a comma before and after these clauses.	*The National Institute of Mental Health,* NONIDENTIFYING RELATIVE CLAUSE **which is a government agency,** *conducts research on the effects of violence on children.*
b. The information in a nonidentifying relative clause can be omitted and the sentence will still make sense.	*Brad J. Bushman and Craig A. Anderson,* **who are on the faculty of Iowa State University**, *have written extensively on violence in the media.* *Brad J. Bushman and Craig A. Anderson have written extensively on violence in the media.*

2.1 Nonidentifying Relative Clauses (continued)

c. Nonidentifying relative clauses are more common in writing than in speaking.	*L. Rowell Huesmann, PhD,* **whose research on the effects of media violence on children is well-regarded,** *argues that there is a correlation between watching violent shows and aggressive behavior.*
d. Do not use *that* or omit the relative pronoun in a nonidentifying relative clause.	*The American Academy of Pediatrics,* **which is a prominent group of medical professionals**, *has several suggestions about television violence.* NOT *The American Academy of Pediatrics,* ~~that~~ *is a prominent group of medical professionals, has several suggestions about television violence.* NOT *The American Academy of Pediatrics,* ~~is a prominent group of medical professionals~~*, has several suggestions about television violence.*
e. You can use nonidentifying relative clauses after proper nouns, such as the name of a person or an organization. This adds credibility to the source.	*Susan P. Leviton,* **who is the president of the Advocates for Children and Youth**, *is on the faculty of the University of Maryland School of Law.* *The National Violence Survey,* **which has examined violence on TV for many years**, *released its report today.*
A shorter way to indicate an expert's credentials is to use an appositive. (See Unit 12 for more information on appositives.)	*Adam D. Thierer,* **a senior fellow at the Progress & Freedom Foundation**, *believes that parents should decide whether their children play violent video games.*

▶ Grammar Application

Exercise 2.1 Nonidentifying Relative Clauses

A Underline the names of the experts in the sentences. Next, write new sentences by adding the additional information about the expert using nonidentifying relative clauses.

1. <u>Jason Edwards</u> reports that the effect of violent content on adolescents depends on how it is portrayed.

   Additional information: Jason Edwards is an assistant professor of communication at Bradford College.

   Jason Edwards, who is an assistant professor of communication at Bradford College, reports that the effect of violent content on adolescents depends on how it is portrayed.

2. A child who watches two hours of TV a day is exposed to approximately 10,000 acts of violence a year, based on research by the Philips Family Foundation.

Additional information: The Philips Family Foundation is a nonprofit organization that focuses on health-care issues.

_____

_____

3. Parents should discuss the content of TV advertising with their children, according to Joanna Moore.

Additional information: Joanna Moore is the mother of five teenagers.

_____

_____

4. According to Pablo Silva, the best way for children to be active is to turn off the TV set.

Additional information: Pablo Silva studies the effects of TV on children's development.

_____

_____

5. In 2006, the American Academy of Child & Adolescent Psychiatry determined that children with excessive exposure to violence on television may "become 'immune' or numb to the horror of violence" (p. 1).

Additional information: The American Academy of Child & Adolescent Psychiatry provides resources about children's mental health.

_____

_____

6. Gerard Jones believes that effective use of media violence can help children vent their anger.

Additional information: Gerard Jones is a well-known comic book writer and the author of the article "Violent Media Is Good for Kids."

_____

_____

B *Pair Work* Find the sentences in A in which the relative clauses can be turned into appositives. Say each sentence with the appositive. Then give your opinion of the information.

Jason Edwards, an assistant professor of communication at Bradford College, reports that the effect of violent content on adolescents depends on how it is portrayed. I think I agree. When violence is portrayed as something heroic or admired, then I think it is harmful because children always want to imitate their heroes.

Exercise 2.2 More Nonidentifying Relative Clauses

A 🔊 Listen to a talk show on the effects of media violence on children. Take notes about the speakers on their credentials or information about their background and their opinion on the issue. Finally, write statements about each person. Use nonidentifying relative clauses.

1. Dr. Marc Richards

   Marc Richards, who is a school psychologist, believes that exposure to violence in the media encourages young children to react violently when they're upset.

2. Kevin McDonald

   _____

   _____

3. Dr. Marcia Chan

   _____

   _____

4. Catherine Wong

   _____

   _____

5. Dr. Eric Lopez

   _____

   _____

6. Barbara Cramer

   _____

   _____

7. Noah Friedman

   _____

   _____

B *Group Work* Take turns choosing a speaker in A, summarizing the speaker's opinion, and sharing your opinion of the speaker's ideas. Include the credentials of the speaker. After you give your opinion, ask your group members to respond with their opinions.

> *A* *Marc Richards, who is a school psychologist, says that exposure to violence in the media causes children to react violently when they get upset. I'm not sure I agree with him. It's true that young children are impressionable, so they may think that the violent behavior on video games, for example, is appropriate, but I think family and friends are more influential.*
>
> *B* *I think I agree with Dr. Richards more. When children see violent images over and over, I think it might make them more likely to use violence when they get angry.*

3 Phrases That Limit Overgeneralization 🌐

▶ Vocabulary Presentation

> Writers of persuasive essays need to provide facts to support their arguments and points. However, it is important to be careful about the language used to express these ideas. Some phrases can help limit overgeneralizations and make claims more accurate and therefore more credible. Limiting claims is also called "hedging."
>
> *This statement **is likely to** cause arguments.*
>
> *Television violence **seems to** be everywhere.*
>
> ***In most cases**, parents try to control what their children watch on television.*

3.1 Words and Phrases That Limit Overgeneralization

a. Use *seem / appear / tend / be likely* + infinitive to indicate something that is possible but not certain, or to indicate something may not be true all the time. *Seem* is the most common verb in this construction.	*Experts who study violence **seem to / appear to** disagree with one another's conclusions.* (We do not know all the experts who study violence, but from what we have read, they do not agree with one another.) *Children who watch many hours of TV every day **are likely to / tend to** be exposed to violent programs.* (We do not know that all children will be exposed to violent programs, but we suspect that it is true most of the time.)
b. Use *it* constructions like *It seems that* and *It appears that* when you believe that something is a trend, but do not have enough evidence to support it strongly.	***It seems that** parents are becoming more cautious about what programs their children should watch on TV.*
c. Use these phrases to express limits on your general claims: *in most cases, mainly, typically.*	***In most cases**, children can tell the difference between cartoon violence and real violence.* *Children will **typically** show higher levels of aggression after watching violence on TV.*
d. *According to* is the most common way to identify a specific source.	***According to** the report, the television industry is not policing itself to the satisfaction of parents.*

▶ Vocabulary Application

Exercise 3.1 Words and Phrases That Limit Overgeneralization

A Rewrite each sentence about the possible positive effects of media violence. Use the word or phrase that best fits the description of the limitation in parentheses: *according to*, *appears*, *in most cases*, *likely*, *seems*, *tend*, *typically*. Use each word or phrase once. In some cases, you may need to change some of the wording of the sentence.

1. Many parents and teachers believe children should not be exposed to any kind of violence in the media. (This is a trend, but there is not enough evidence to support this.)

   It appears that many parents and teachers believe children should not be
   exposed to any kind of violence in the media.

2. Children are taught to deny their feelings of violence. (This is true of some children, but not all children.)

   _____

3. Adults attempt to repress any violent reactions they have. (This seems to be true of many, but not all adults.)

   _____

4. Media violence allows people to fantasize about releasing their aggression in a safe, nonthreatening environment. (Some experts believe this claim.)

   _____

5. Violent video games provide players with an outlet for feelings of anger and frustration. (This is possible, but there isn't enough research to back this up.)

   _____

6. Constant denial of violent feelings, rather than exposure to media violence, makes people react to problems with aggression. (It is very possible, but it is not certain that this is true.)

   _____

7. Video games portray heroes as violent. (It is possible, but not true all the time.)

   _____

B *Pair Work* Work with a partner. Take turns making overgeneralizations about the topics below. Your partner will ask you to limit your generalization.

   • The effects of violent video games on teenagers
   • Reasons that children like to play violent video games
   • The effects of violence in cartoons and movies on children

   A *Violent video games always make children act violently.*
   B *I think you're overgeneralizing. In some cases, some violent video games may make some children act violently, but you can't say that is true for all violent video games and all children unless you have research to back up your claims.*

4 Avoid Common Mistakes ⚠

> **1. Remember to include the relative pronoun in nonidentifying relative clauses.**
>
> *which*
> *"Violent Video Games: Myths, Facts, and Unanswered Questions,"* ∧ *was published by the American Psychological Association, establishes the connection between violence in games and violent behavior.*
>
> **2. Remember not to use *that* as a relative pronoun in nonidentifying relative clauses.**
>
> *which*
> *The National Institute of Mental Health, ~~that~~ published the article, is an excellent source of recent studies on the effects of violence in the media.*
>
> **3. Remember to use the singular form of the verb *seem* with *it*.**
>
> *seems*
> *It ~~seem~~ that not enough parents take responsibility for monitoring their children.*

Editing Task

Find and correct eight more mistakes in the body paragraph from an essay on violence in the media.

Government's Role in Violence in the Media

There is a major reason that the government should not be involved in solving the

problem of violence in the media. Government control of the media is unconstitutional.

seems
It ~~seem~~ that some people feel that the Federal Communications Commission (FCC), is

the government agency that regulates media such as TV and the Internet, is the best tool

5   for protecting children. However, many experts disagree. For example, the American Civil

Liberties Union (ACLU), that focuses on constitutional rights, believes that government

control of the media is a form of censorship. The First Amendment to the U.S. Constitution,

guarantees freedom of speech, gives us the right to media that are not controlled by the

government. A free and open media is the foundation of democracy in the United States.

10   However, it is important to protect children from violence. According to the ACLU, protecting

children is the responsibility of parents, although it seem that many parents are unwilling

to take on this responsibility. Caroline Fredrickson, is a director of the ACLU's Washington

Legislative Office, points out in her article, "Why Government Should Not Police TV Violence

and Indecency," was published in *The Christian Science Monitor* in 2007, that parents "already

15   have many tools to protect their children, including blocking programs and channels,

changing the channel, or simply turning off the television" (p. 2). She adds that the Parents Television Council, that is a nonprofit media monitoring organization, provides information on their website about television programs that are appropriate for children. It seem that if parents take responsibility for monitoring their children's television viewing, then we will be

20 able to have free and open media and protect children at the same time.

5 | The Writing Process ✏

In this section, you will write an introductory paragraph and two body paragraphs of an essay about a controversial topic. Before you start writing, you will learn about introductory paragraphs to persuasive essays.

About the Introductory Paragraph to a Persuasive Essay

The introductory paragraph of a persuasive essay should arouse the reader's interest in a controversial topic, explain the nature of the controversy, and provide the writer's position.

The following three elements are required in an introductory paragraph to a persuasive essay:

1. A hook

2. A clear explanation of the controversy

3. A thesis statement containing the writer's position on the controversy

Exerclse

A Read this introductory paragraph to a persuasive essay and answer the questions on a separate sheet of paper.

Video Games Are Being Unfairly Targeted

There is a war out there, but it is not in any video game. It is an attack on teenagers who enjoy playing video games that include warfare and violence. There is a growing number of adults who believe that video games are turning their children into mindless, heartless killing machines. They believe that violent video games must be censored, for the good of

5 teenage players and society as a whole. While their arguments seem valid at first glance, upon reflection, this attack on video-game violence and youth is both exaggerated and unnecessary.

1. What is the topic of the essay?

2. What is the controversy?

3. What is the hook?

4. What is the writer's position on the controversy?

B *Pair Work* Share your answers in A with a partner. Then answer the questions below together.

1. Was the hook effective? Why or why not?

2. Did the writer express the controversy clearly? Why or why not?

3. Based on the writer's thesis statement, what arguments do you think might be in the body of the essay?

4. What is your position on this controversy? Do you agree with the writer or do you have another point of view?

Pre-writing Tasks

Choose a Topic

A Choose one of the topics listed below. You will write an introductory paragraph and two body paragraphs on your topic.

- Are there any benefits to violent entertainment?
- Should children go to school year-round?
- A topic of your own approved by your teacher

B *Pair Work* Share your topic and position with a partner, and together brainstorm a list of arguments that support your position.

Organize Your Ideas

A Choose your two strongest arguments and complete the chart below.

Your thesis statement:
Argument 1:
Supporting information:
Argument 2:
Supporting information:

B *Pair Work* Share your chart with a partner. Ask your partner to "play devil's advocate," that is, to think of reasons why your arguments are weak. By thinking of weaknesses in your arguments, you will be able to strengthen them.

Writing Task

Write an introductory paragraph and two body paragraphs for your essay, using the information in your chart from above. Follow the steps below.

1. In the introductory paragraph, include a hook, a clear explanation of the controversy, and a thesis statement that expresses your point of view.

2. In the two body paragraphs, develop your arguments. Use the opinions of experts if possible.

3. Include the following in your paragraphs:

   - nonidentifying relative clauses;

   - phrases that limit overgeneralizations;

   - at least three academic words from the essay in this unit: *access, amendment, commission, committed, consistently, controversial, debate, exhibit, expose, exposure, federal, inappropriate, issue, media, monitor, negative, network, obvious, parallel, regulate, regulation, restriction.*

4. After you write your paragraphs, review them and make sure you avoided the mistakes in the Avoid Common Mistakes chart on page 270.

> **Academic Writing Tip**
>
> **Use Adverbs to Avoid Overgeneralizations**
> You can also use the following adverbs to avoid generalizing:
>
> *apparently, generally, occasionally, often, probably, regularly, reportedly, usually*
>
> Video games **generally** portray heroes as violent.

Peer Review

A Exchange your paragraphs with a partner. Answer the following questions as you read your partner's paragraphs, and then share your responses.

1. Does the writer's introductory paragraph contain an effective hook, a clear explanation of the controversy, and a strong thesis statement?

2. Are the arguments in the body paragraphs well supported?

3. Does the writer include nonidentifying relative clauses? If there are few or none, indicate places where the writer could add one or two.

4. Does the writer use words or phrases that limit overgeneralizations? Underline them.

5. Is anything confusing? Write a question mark (?) next to it.

6. Provide one compliment (something you found interesting or unusual).

B Use your partner's comments to help you revise your paragraphs. Use the Writer's Checklist on page A2 to review your paragraphs for organization, grammar, and vocabulary.

Persuasion 2: Noun Clauses with *Wh-* Words and *If/Whether*; Phrases for Argumentation

Living in an Age of Information Overload

1 | Grammar in the Real World

You will read an essay that discusses the easy availability of information online. The essay is an example of a type of persuasive writing in which the writer chooses to present opposing views.

A *Before You Read* How do you find most of your information: in printed sources or online sources? Read the essay. What concerns does the writer have about relying on the Internet for information?

So Much Information, So Little Time

　　We live in an amazing time, with access to almost unlimited information, entertainment, and opinions. Digital technology offers us new information whenever we are "plugged in." Just the other day, I watched a baseball game on TV, texted a friend, and kept track of the details of my other friends' lives online. I also kept an eye on all the other sports scores as they were
5　happening. I did all this while also having a conversation with my brother. While it is true that digital technology has many benefits, they come at a cost, producing citizens who have fewer critical-thinking skills and weaker social skills.

　　According to the proponents[1] of technology, easy access to information is one way that people benefit from new technology. When doing research, you do not have to walk to a library,
10　search for books, and read words on paper. Obviously, finding what we need from the Internet is faster, and online searches provide a broader range of sources. Often, however, when people are faced with search-engine results in the thousands or more, their critical-thinking skills may be overwhelmed by the sheer volume of material to read. One study in the UK showed that students skimmed over most information they found. According to this study, they rarely read
15　more than a page or two when completing academic research (Carr, 2008, para. 7).

　　Proponents also point out that technology has increased social connections. People can stay in touch with friends more easily now, sending them birthday greetings, sharing complaints, and keeping each other informed, all online. Naturally, e-mail and social networking websites have facilitated[2] communication. Ironically,[3] though, the tools designed for increased online
20　interaction may actually lead to people being less social. Students rarely need to engage in

---

[1]**proponent:** supporter │ [2]**facilitate:** make easier │ [3]**ironically:** in a way that is different from what was expected

face-to-face interactions these days either with their professors or their fellow students. Lonely librarians remember when students used to ask them questions in person. Now they more often respond to students' text queries via website help centers. At the end of the day, workers come home exhausted by so much online interaction. Having made themselves accessible
25 online 24 hours a day, they end up sacrificing family time at home as they prepare for the next round of virtual interaction.

Clearly, increased access to information results in added benefits, but it is also true that there is a cost. People who embrace new technology should reflect on what they lose as well as what they gain. There is a choice between touching and smelling a flower grown in my garden
30 and sharing it with one or two friends in the neighborhood, and instead photographing the flower, putting that image online, and reading the responses of my worldwide set of "friends." Perhaps the touch of the real flower should rule.

B *Comprehension Check* Answer the questions.

1. What are the two main points in favor of new technology mentioned by the writer?

2. Why does the writer believe that ease of access to information may not be such a good thing?

3. The writer offers readers a choice in the concluding paragraph. What point do you think the writer is making by offering a choice?

C *Notice*

1 Persuasive Writing

Pair Work Find examples in the essay where the writer presents views that oppose his or her own thesis, and then discuss the following question with a partner: Why do writers include opposing points of view in persuasive writing?

2 Grammar Find the answers to the following questions in the essay to notice how the writer uses grammar in her arguments:

1. Read the sentence on lines 28–29 beginning with "People who embrace . . ." to notice how the writer uses a clause with a *wh-* word to help present the different sides of the argument. What are the two sides of the argument?

2. Find the sentence in the first paragraph in which the writer states the opponent's view and then responds. What phrase does the writer use to introduce the opponent's view before refuting it?

3 The Writing Process Check (✔) which order the writer uses to organize the ideas in each of the two body paragraphs in the essay.

_____ a. Presentation of opposing viewpoint → Presentation of writer's viewpoint

_____ b. Presentation of opposing viewpoint → Refutation of (finding fault with) opposing viewpoint → Presentation of writer's viewpoint

_____ c. Presentation of writer's viewpoint → Presentation of opposing viewpoint

2 Noun Clauses with *Wh-* Words and *If/Whether*

▶ Grammar Presentation

> Noun clauses with *wh-* words and *if/whether* are useful in persuasive academic writing, especially to present different viewpoints and then critique those viewpoints.
>
> *Experts disagree on* **what the benefits and drawbacks of Internet use are for students**. *Nobody really knows* **if children today have more difficulty with concentration**.

2.1 Noun Clauses with *Wh-* Words

a. *Wh-* noun clauses start with a *wh-* word (*who, what, where, when, why,* and *how*) and function as nouns. They can act as subjects, objects, or objects of prepositions. In academic writing, they are more frequent as objects and objects of prepositions.	WH- NOUN CLAUSE *Readers have to decide* **which expert they trust**. *Readers are concerned about* **who seems the most credible**.
Wh- noun clauses use statement word order (subj + verb). Do not put an auxiliary or modal before the subject.	*Students have to learn* **how they can evaluate sources**. NOT *Students have to learn how* ~~can they~~ *evaluate sources.*
b. Noun clauses with *wh-* words often come after the following verbs: Thoughts and opinions: *agree, consider, disagree, know, remember* Learning and perception: *see, understand, wonder*	*We need to* <u>consider</u> **who our main market is.** *I don't* <u>remember</u> **where I read that**.

2.2 Noun Clauses with *If/Whether*

a. *If/whether* noun clauses function as nouns. They start with *if* or *whether* and show an alternative choice or a *yes/no* choice. As in *wh-* clauses, these clauses are in statement word order. *Whether* is more commonly used when alternatives are presented or implied.	*Students need to check* **whether their online sources are current or out-of-date**. (Alternative choice: Are they current or are they out-of-date? The answer is one or the other.) *I don't know* **if that website has accurate information.** (*Yes/no* choice: Does that website have accurate information? The answer is *yes* or *no*.)
b. The verbs *know, see,* and *wonder* are commonly used with *if/whether* noun clauses.	*Let's* **see** *if we can find an answer on this website.* *Some students* **wonder** *whether they should do research online or in the library.* *I don't* **know** *if there are computers available to do the research online.*

▶ Grammar Application

Exercise 2.1 Noun Clauses with *Wh-* Words and *If/Whether*

Combine each pair of sentences about the effects of information overload on workers and the workplace. Use a noun clause with a *wh-* word, *if*, or *whether*. Sometimes more than one answer is possible.

1. How does information overload affect the workplace? Researchers are studying this.

   Researchers are studying how information overload affects the workplace.

2. Does information overload make an employee more or less efficient? Researchers are trying to determine this.

   _____

3. What do employees do when they are overwhelmed by too much information? Employers want to know this.

   _____

4. Do employees ignore important facts or absorb more when they are overloaded with information? Employers wonder this.

   _____

5. Do overloaded employees waste time? Corporations want to find this out.

   _____

6. How does information overload affect employees' decision-making skills? Studies may determine this.

   _____

7. When do employees feel overwhelmed by information? Researchers wonder this.

   _____

8. Does information overload increase or decrease productivity? Researchers want to learn this.

   _____

Exercise 2.2 More Noun Clauses with *Wh-* Words and *If/Whether*

A 🔊 Listen to a lecture about information overload. Number the questions in the order that the speaker mentions them as noun clauses with *wh-* words and *if/whether*.

_____ 1. What is the daily volume of new web content?

_____ 2. What can we do about information overload?

_____ 3. Do you really need to send out e-mails to people who don't need them?

_____ 4. Does each recipient of information really need the information that he or she receives?

__1__ 5. How does information overload impact us?

_____ 6. Do you have to look at that video that your friend sent you?

_____ 7. What are some of the causes of information overload?

_____ 8. What can you do to avoid being overwhelmed by information?

_____ 9. Can you spend a portion of your day disconnected from technology?

B *Pair Work* Complete the summary below of the lecture in A with a partner. Use the answers in A written as noun clauses with *wh-* words and *if/whether*. Then share your paragraph with another pair.

First, the lecturer says that he wonders *how this information overload impacts us*

and _____ . Then he says he is going to examine

        (2)

_____ . Next, he tells us that people tend to distribute

    (3)

information without considering _____ . The

        (4)

lecturer also wonders _____ . Then he moves on to

      (5)

consider _____ . His first suggestion is that people

    (6)

should see _____ . Second, he tells his audience

    (7)

to focus on one source of information at a time. Third, he asks people to consider

_____ . Finally, he tells people to ask themselves

   (8)

_____ .

   (9)

3 | Phrases for Argumentation

▶ Vocabulary Presentation

> Writers use particular words to present an opposing view, to acknowledge that an opposing view has some merit, and to refute, or disprove, the opposing view.
>
> ***It has been argued that*** *the Internet has caused groups to form more quickly than in the past.*
>
> ***Clearly****, the Internet offers access to a wealth of information.*
>
> ***However****, some students need more guidance than others in using online resources.*

3.1 Phrases That Present an Opposing View

a. Use the following phrases to present opposing documented views: *It has been argued that . . .* *It is argued that . . .* *It has been claimed that . . .* *Some researchers disagree that . . .* *Argue* and *claim* are the most common.	***It has been argued that*** *young people handle information in a much different way.* ***It has been claimed that*** *it is important for adolescents to spend time away from electronic devices.*
b. Use these phrases to present potentially opposing views when you do not have sources for your claim. Modals make the claim less strong. *It might / could / may be argued that . . .* *It might / could / may be claimed that . . .* *Might* and *could* are more common than *may*. (See Unit 16 for more practice with *it* constructions.)	***It could be argued that*** *video games allow children to develop critical-thinking skills.* ***It might be claimed that*** *cell phone use can be addictive.*

3.2 Logical Connectors That Show a Point of View

Use these adverbs as logical connectors to acknowledge a specific point of view or an opposing argument: *clearly, naturally, obviously, of course*	***Clearly****, increased access to information results in a benefit.* ***Obviously****, few want to return to the old system of information gathering.* *Internet research is different,* ***of course****, and it requires specific strategies to get proper results.*

3.3 Phrases That Introduce a Refutation

Use these phrases to introduce a refutation or to dispute an argument:

However, . . .

It is not true that . . .

That may be so, but . . .

(Unfortunately,) this is (simply) not true.

While it is true that . . .

This is (simply) not true is the most common of these phrases.

OPPOSING VIEW

Some claim that violence on TV leads to violence at

REFUTATION

*school. **However, this is simply not true**.*

OPPOSING VIEW

*While it is true that well-designed video games can help children think creatively, **they do not replace***

REFUTATION

***physical interaction with others**.*

▶ Vocabulary Application

Exercise 3.1 Phrases for Argumentation

Complete the paragraph below about some drawbacks of easy access to information. Circle the correct word or phrase.

(While it is true that)/ However, it has been argued that easy access to information
                 (1)

allows people to learn almost anything they want at any time, there are some downsides

to this accessibility. Some people believe that individuals are more productive when they

multitask. **Naturally / Unfortunately**, this is simply not true, according to recent studies.
              (2)

Attempting to do several things at once is less efficient than doing one thing at a time. People

should attempt to focus on one source of information at a time and one piece of information

at a time. **Clearly, / It has been claimed that** people want to receive a lot of information,
                  (3)

though. Otherwise, they wouldn't access so many different sources of information at once.

    Also, **while it is true that / it has been claimed that** social networks allow people to
                   (4)

stay updated on their friends' activities, they also create a big distraction. The vast amount of

information that we have to sift through cuts into time we could actually be

spending with friends. **It is not true that / Obviously**, individuals have to decide on
               (5)

their own priorities, but spending time with friends face-to-face might be more valuable

than communicating with them online. A person would probably benefit greatly from

trading time spent learning unimportant information for some time spent with friends.

It could be argued that / Of course, people will not remember the 20 status updates and 5
           (6)

e-mails they read after work, but they will very likely enjoy and remember a dinner

with a friend.

Exercise 3.2 More Phrases for Argumentation

On a separate piece of paper, write a short paragraph for the thesis statement in item 2. Use the example in item 1 as a model. Include the opposing view, an agreement, and a refutation. Use the phrases for argumentation to connect the ideas.

1. Thesis Statement: The college should provide more on-campus child care for students.

Opposing view: The college should not provide more on-campus child care.

Agreement with the opposing view: There are enough day-care facilities in the community to serve the students who need them.

Refutation: The majority of day-care centers do not have evening hours, and most students attend school at night.

Supporting information: Many students miss school because they do not have anyone to care for their children while they are at school.

Body Paragraph: _Some college personnel may argue that the college should not provide more on-campus child care. Clearly, they believe that there are enough day-care centers in the community to serve the students who need them. However, the majority of day-care centers do not have evening hours, and most students attend school at night. Therefore, many students miss school because they do not have anyone to care for their children while they are at school._

2. Thesis Statement: Students should turn off their electronic devices during class.

Opposing view: Students should be allowed to have their devices on during class.

Agreement with the opposing view: Students may need to be in contact with family members or their jobs.

Refutation: Electronic devices can be a distraction in the classroom.

Supporting information: Students can become easily distracted by their devices and miss important information.

Exercise 3.3 More Phrases for Argumentation

Pair Work Work with a partner and choose a topic from the list below or a topic approved by your teacher. Choose opposing sides and, individually, write sentences to argue for your side. Use vocabulary that addresses opposing views. Then role-play a debate about the topic.

- Are parents who allow their children to spend all day using electronic devices negligent?
- Should people turn their cell phones off when they're out with friends?
- Is it acceptable to surf the Internet and check text messages during class?

A *It has been claimed that too much television is not good for young children. However, children can learn a lot from watching television. They can learn about cultures and families that are different from their own. And they can learn practical information like reading and numbers by watching educational shows.*

B *That may be so, but it is also true that children can learn even more by interacting with humans rather than with an "electronic babysitter."*

4 | Avoid Common Mistakes ⚠

1. **Remember to use *if*, and not *whether*, to express a condition.**

   E-books will be popular ~~whether~~ they are less expensive than print books. (*if*)

2. **Remember that *or not* can immediately follow *whether*, but it can only appear at the end of a sentence with *if*.**

   Experts can't decide ~~if~~ or not students retain enough information with online reading. (*whether*)

   Experts can't decide if ~~or not~~ students retain enough information with online reading. (*or not*)

3. **Remember to spell *whether* correctly.**

   The instructors decide ~~weather~~ students bring laptops or smartphones to class. (*whether*)

   They have not decided ~~wether~~ laptops are helpful or a distraction. (*whether*)

Editing Task

Find and correct six more mistakes in the body paragraph from an essay on information overload.

Information Overload

Opponents of online technology often point to the negative effects of the information age. They claim that ~~weather~~ (*whether*) individuals use the Internet for research or for social networking, they suffer from information overload. They believe that easy access to information has a negative effect on users' critical-thinking skills. They also cite the fact that online readers

5 understand and retain less than print readers. The fact is, however, that experts have not yet determined if or not there is a difference between reading online and reading print material. There haven't been enough studies to determine if or not there truly are negative effects of information overload. Furthermore, it is important for proponents of this argument to identify wether they are referring to the effects of technology on older people or younger people.

10 For example, their arguments may not be valid whether they consider how digital natives respond to technology. Digital natives are people who were born since the 1990s. They were born into a digital world, and they have been using technology since childhood. According to Tapscott (2009), digital natives process information differently than digital immigrants (people who were born before the 1990s and learned how to use the Internet later in life than

15 digital natives did). Tapscott cites a study designed to show whether digital natives retained more information from a traditional newscast or an interactive webcast. The study showed that digital natives remembered more from the interactive news source. Tapscott also points out that intelligence and aptitude test scores are rising, which further indicates that digital natives' thinking styles have not suffered. Some wonder wether digital natives should adapt

20 to traditional ways of processing information. However, if or not we like it, the information age is here to stay. Therefore, digital immigrants are going to have to adapt to digital ways of interacting with technology.

5 | The Writing Process

In this section, you will write two body paragraphs for a persuasive essay that will include two opposing views and refutations of those views. Before you start writing, you will learn about opposing views and refutations.

About Presenting and Refuting Opposing Views

In persuasive essays, writers often include views that oppose their own, and then refute them (show why those views are not as valid or strong). In doing this, writers provide support for their own viewpoints. The following steps can be used when writing body paragraphs in a persuasive essay:

1. **State the opposing view.** Good persuasive writers often start to argue a position by recognizing that other people have points of view that should be considered. A reader is more likely to be persuaded by a writer who presents opposing views than by a writer who puts forward only his or her own viewpoint without acknowledging the existence of other viewpoints.

2. **Partially agree with the opposing view.** Persuasive writers can make their own case even stronger when they then state that the opposing view has some merit. A reader will believe that a writer is very reasonable if that writer is prepared to agree that his or her opponent has made some good points.

3. **Refute the opposing view.** Once the opposing position has been stated and shown to have some good qualities, the persuasive writer can now show his or her own position by showing the weaknesses in the opponent's viewpoints. The change in tone from one of reasonableness to one of refutation is usually marked by *However, . . .* or such phrases as *While it may be true that. . . .*

4. **Support the refutation.** Finally, persuasive writers need to provide evidence to support their own positions, not just point out the weaknesses in others' viewpoints. They do this by presenting supporting data and examples, citing research, and providing quotations from experts.

Exercise

Match the views below to the example sentences.

Views	Example Sentences
_____ 1. Presentation of opposing view	a. However, we must also consider the fact that individuals in a society have an important right to privacy.
_____ 2. Partial agreement with opposing view	b. There have been many cases over the years in which the police have been given great powers and then have used those powers in a corrupt way.
_____ 3. Refutation and presentation of own view	c. Many people argue that the police should be able to locate anyone's cell phone at any time and be given the power to listen in to cell phone conversations whenever they want.
_____ 4. Support for own view	d. It is true that this particular use of technology could indeed give the police a tremendous tool in solving crimes quickly and efficiently.

Pre-writing Tasks

Choose a Topic

A Choose one of the topics listed below. You will write two body paragraphs of a persuasive essay and argue for or against the topic. In each paragraph you will present and refute the opposing viewpoints and then argue a position.

- The use of technology in our daily lives is making our lives too complicated.
- Virtual friendships are as genuine as face-to-face friendships.
- A topic of your own approved by your teacher

B *Pair Work* Share your viewpoint on the topic with a partner. Have your partner brainstorm opposing viewpoints. Then find arguments to refute the opposing viewpoints that your partner raises. Take notes.

Organize Your Ideas

A Draw the chart below on a separate sheet of paper and complete it. Write your thesis statement, two viewpoints that oppose your thesis, your refutation of the opposing viewpoints, and support for your own position.

Thesis Statement:		
	Opposing Viewpoint 1	**Opposing Viewpoint 2**
Presentation of the opposing viewpoint		
Refutation of the opposing viewpoint		
Support for your own viewpoint		

B *Pair Work* Share your chart with a partner. See if your partner agrees that you have presented the opposing viewpoints fairly and presented the best refutations possible.

Writing Task

Write two body paragraphs that contain persuasive writing that supports the thesis statement that you wrote in the chart above. Follow the steps below.

1. Start each paragraph by presenting an opposing point of view and acknowledging one aspect of that view.

2. Continue the body paragraphs with a refutation and support for your own point of view.

3. Include the following in your essay:
   - noun clauses with *wh-* words and *if/whether*;
   - phrases to present, acknowledge, and refute an opposing view;
   - at least three academic words from this unit: *academic, access, accessible, benefit, communication, design, facilitate, image, interaction, networking, obviously, range, research, response, source, technology, text, via, virtual, volume.*

> ### Academic Writing Tip
>
> **Using Scare Quotes**
> Scare quotes are quotation marks used for purposes other than quoting sources. Writers use scare quotes to:
> 1. Alert the reader to a nontraditional or new use of a word / phrase (e.g., "plugged in" in the essay on p. 274).
> 2. Show that they disagree in some way with the meaning of a term used in a source.
> 3. Show irony or sarcasm.

4. After you write your paragraphs, review them and make sure you avoided the mistakes in the Avoid Common Mistakes chart on page 282.

Peer Review

A Exchange your paragraphs with a partner. Answer the following questions as you read your partner's paragraphs, and then share your responses.

1. Does the writer present two opposing viewpoints? What are they?

2. Does the writer agree that the opposing viewpoints have some merit?

3. Does the writer refute the opposing viewpoints and provide support for his or her own viewpoint? Mark the point in the paragraphs where this occurs.

4. Does the writer use noun clauses with *wh-* words or *if* and *whether*? Underline any you find.

5. Is anything confusing? Write a question mark (?) next to it.

6. Provide one compliment (something you found interesting or unusual).

B Use your partner's comments to help you revise your essay. Use the Writer's Checklist on page A2 to review your essay for organization, grammar, and vocabulary.

Persuasion 3: Expressing Future Actions; Common Words and Phrases in Persuasive Writing

Social Networking

1 Grammar in the Real World 🌐

You will read an essay about the impact that social networking websites may be having on college students' academic performance. In this persuasive essay, the writer argues for banning social networking sites from college campuses.

A *Before You Read* What social networking sites are popular among you and your friends? What are some possible negative aspects of social networking sites? Read the essay. Does the writer think of social networking sites as having a positive or negative impact on students? Why?

Social Networking on College Campuses

Social networking sites (SNSs) have revolutionized the way we communicate with friends, colleagues, classmates, and even family members. It is now possible to interact and maintain a relationship with someone without ever meeting in person. There are many positive aspects of these new types of interactions. However, the excessive use of such websites has created a
5 distraction[1] for some users. Some college students spend hours a day "networking" instead of focusing on their studies. To help these students be more successful, colleges and universities should block access to SNSs in most areas of their campuses.

SNSs have been growing in popularity at an astonishing rate. According to the Pew Research Center's Internet & American Life Project, it is estimated that at least 85 percent of college
10 students in the United States use some type of online social network on a daily basis (Smith, Rainie, & Zickuhr, 2011). In fact, according to many instructors, college students are growing dependent on such networks. While there is no doubt that SNSs have created valuable new ways to communicate and share information, they have also become a distraction for college students who spend time online instead of preparing for their future careers.

15 Some proponents claim that the networking phenomenon[2] can be positive. Students can join online groups in which everyone shares the same interest, and they can learn how to communicate effectively in this digital age. It has been further argued that, when online, students will discuss current events and issues that they are less likely to discuss in "real life" interactions. In an ideal world, this could indeed be a beneficial way to promote interaction with people from different cultures and backgrounds. Opponents argue that, in reality, some

---

[1]**distraction:** something that takes your attention away from where it should be focused | [2]**phenomenon:** something that is noticed because it is unusual or new

20 discussions provide a less rigorous platform for ideas because of the lack of monitoring and the informal nature of the format. It is therefore difficult to argue that these postings would add significantly to the students' knowledge base.

Colleges and universities should consider strong policies on the use of SNSs on campus because students waste valuable study time on them. In fact, some studies report a link 25 between time on SNSs and grades. For example, an Ohio State University survey indicates that students who regularly use SNSs study less than five hours per week and have an average GPA between 3.0 and 3.5. In contrast, students who do not use these websites study 11 hours or more per week and have an average GPA between 3.5 and 4.0 (Grabmeier, n.d.). In addition, teachers are increasingly concerned about social networking use in class. They complain that 30 students are "messaging friends or posting . . . status updates from their laptops instead of paying attention to lectures" (Hamilton, 2009, para. 7). Based on these concerns, establishing clear policies for use of these websites on campus is likely to help students focus on their studies. They would spend more time studying, and their grades should improve as a result.

Social networking sites present a new way to find, organize, and share information and 35 contacts. These visually stimulating, highly interactive websites attract many college students. However, their addictive nature can potentially disrupt[3] student life to the degree that colleges and universities have to take action and ban access to social networking sites in some areas on campuses.

[3]**disrupt:** change the normal direction and create disorder

B *Comprehension Check* Answer the questions.

1. What positive things does the writer say about social networking sites?

2. Why does the author want to limit or ban social networking sites on campuses?

3. Do you agree or disagree with the writer's point of view? Why?

C *Notice*

1 Persuasive Writing Match the excerpts from the essay on the left with the type of argument they represent on the right.

_____ 1. It is estimated that at least 85 percent of college students in the United States use some type of online social network on a daily basis (Smith, Rainie, & Zickuhr, 2011).	a. opinion from respected authorities or experts
_____ 2. In addition, teachers are increasingly concerned about social networking use in class. They complain that students are "messaging friends or posting . . . status updates from their laptops instead of paying attention to lectures" (Hamilton, 2009, para. 7).	b. connection between presented information and recommendations c. facts, statistics, trends
_____ 3. Based on these concerns, establishing clear policies for use of these websites on campus is likely to help students focus on their studies. They would spend more time studying, and their grades should improve as a result.	

2 Grammar Complete the tasks below to notice the grammar that the writer uses to talk about possible future events and opposing views.

1. Compare the use of the word *should* on lines 7 and 33. How are the meanings of *should* different?

2. Read the sentence on lines 31–33 beginning with "Based on these concerns . . ." Look at the verb phrase. Does the verb phrase refer to present or future time? What words in the phrase help you to determine this?

3. Look at the use of *would* on lines 21 and 33. Does the meaning of *would* refer to present time or a likely result in the future?

3 The Writing Process The writer included findings from research in the essay. Complete the table below with the authors, sources, and the information or opinion that was taken from those sources.

Name of Source	Information/Opinion Retrieved from Source
Smith, Rainie, Zickuhr	At least 85 percent of college students in the United States use online social networks daily.
Grabmeier	
Hamilton	

2 | Expressing Future Actions

▶ Grammar Presentation

> To express plans, predictions, and expectations, writers use *will*, *be going to*, modals, and a variety of words and phrases.
>
> Students **will not** be able to access social networking websites if colleges ban them.
>
> Blocking social networking websites on campus **would** help students focus on their studies.

2.1 Using *Will*, *Be Going To*, and Modals to Express Certainty and Make Predictions

a. Use *will* and *be going to* to write about a plan or prediction in the future. *Will* is more common in academic writing than *be going to*.	The Internet **will continue to allow** for a greater exchange of ideas. Some colleges **are going to ban** access to social networking sites on campuses.

2.1 Using *Will*, *Be Going To*, and Modals to Express Certainty and Make Predictions *(continued)*

b. Use modals *could*, *might*, and *may* to express possibility in the future.	*The use of social networking sites by recruiters for jobs **could increase** in the next few years.*
c. Use *should* to express an expectation.	*New technology **should make** communication more efficient.*
d. Use *would* to express an expectation based on either a stated or unstated condition.	*Banning note-taking on laptops **would prevent** students from using the Internet during classes.* *If the school implements the ban now, it **would see** major benefits within the next few months.*

2.2 Using Other Expressions to Express Future Action

a. Use these phrases to write about something that will likely happen in the near future:	
is due to	*The new version of the phone **is due to come** out by next year.*
is about to	*The company **is about to introduce** a new app.*
b. The following phrases can be used to talk about possible future events:	
it is / seems / looks likely that + clause	***It seems likely that** younger teachers will be more comfortable with educational technology.*
something / someone is / seems / looks likely to + verb	*Younger teachers **are likely to be** more comfortable with using technology.*
is / are considering + verb + *-ing*	*The school **is considering prohibiting** all unauthorized Internet access on campus.*
anticipate + verb + *-ing* (suggests that the event is very likely)	*We **anticipate focusing** only on student performance scores, not other factors.*
c. The following verbs, usually in the present tense, show plans for the future:	
hope to: not definite but preferable	*The students **hope to maintain** their high school friendships online.*
intend to: not definite but preferable	*The university **intends to investigate** the effects of technology on student performance.*
plan to: scheduled to happen	*Large technology companies **plan to move** many applications to phones and other digital devices.*

▶ Grammar Application

Exercise 2.1 Future Possibilities

A The managers of a design magazine have noticed an increase in the number of employees who use social networking sites at work. Read the blog post and employee comments about the issue. Circle the correct words and phrases to complete the sentences.

Friday, May 8

It has been noted that some employees are spending a lot of time on social networks during work hours, and productivity has gone down. We really need everyone to be focused right now because we **are about to**/ **are considering** launch our new website,
(1)
and we **plan to get**/ **anticipate getting** a lot of new business as a result. Because of this,
(2)
management **is likely to block**/ **is considering blocking** social networking websites from the
(3)
office. However, we'd like to hear what you all think about this. We welcome your comments.

We **anticipate having**/ **will have** a meeting next Friday at 2:00 to discuss this issue. All
(4)
employees are welcome. We **plan to**/ **hope to** see all of you there.
(5)

COMMENTS:

Marta G.: Not everyone spends a lot of time on the sites. Most of us check the sites a couple of times a day. Why punish everyone? It **should be**/ **seems likely** that people who waste
(6)
time **should**/ **will** find other ways to waste time if they can't get on social networking sites.
(7)

Erin W.: I like this idea. It's frustrating when my team members don't complete their work because they have spent too much time online. This change **would**/ **is going to** prevent
(8)
them from spending half the workday online. And my team's productivity **intends to**/ **could**
(9)
increase.

Tomas K.: I use a social networking site to update my clients on the latest design trends. Some of my clients contact me during the day on this site. If I couldn't use the site at work, I **should**/ **might** lose some of my clients. I **intend**/ **am not likely** to protest this policy if it goes
(10)   (11)
through.

Kevin L.: Friday's a bad day for this meeting. A lot of people **don't plan**/ **are not likely** to
(12)
attend because they telecommute that day. You should change the day.

B *Pair Work*   With a partner, create a role play between two managers of small businesses who have differing views on the use of social networking at work. Answer these questions in your role plays: What are you considering doing? How might the policies affect employees? How will employees react? How do you plan to address employees' reactions? Use modals and phrases that show certainty, prediction, and future action.

Student A   You are seriously considering banning the use of social networking sites through the company's computers and implementing strict rules about not accessing them on cell phones during work hours. You strongly believe that these sites cause employees to waste time, do poor quality work, and be irresponsible.

Student B   You do not believe that social networking sites should be banned at work because you believe that this will create a lot of anger and resentment from employees. You want to work with employees to create a set of policies that everyone can agree with.

A   *I'm seriously considering banning the use of social networking sites at my workplace because I think they're a major distraction for my employees.*

B   *I feel differently. I agree that there might be a need to have policies regarding their use, but I'm not sure that banning is the right solution. There may be other solutions. You're going to get a lot of criticism, you know.*

A   *I know I am. I'm planning to hold several meetings about it....*

Exercise 2.2 ◄)) Future Possibilities

Listen to two college students, Lisa and Ben, talk about social networking sites. Write *T* if the statement has a meaning similar to the one you hear. Write *F* if the statement has a different meaning. Correct the false statements so that they are true.

  is considering blocking

__*F*__ 1. Their college ~~has recently blocked~~ Internet access to social networking sites in some areas on campus.

_____ 2. Ben thinks blocking access might help students study more.

_____ 3. Lisa is going to demonstrate against it if the school blocks access.

_____ 4. Ben will demonstrate against it if the school blocks access.

_____ 5. One popular social networking site is about to charge people to use their site.

_____ 6. Lisa thinks a lot of people might delete their account if the popular social networking site charges people.

_____ 7. Ben thinks that people will pay to use the popular site.

_____ 8. Lisa might use a social networking site if she has to pay.

3 | Common Words and Phrases in Persuasive Writing 🌐

▶ Vocabulary Presentation

> In Unit 19, you learned common vocabulary used in persuasive writing to discuss opposing views. Now you will learn how to use other common vocabulary for persuasive and other kinds of academic writing.
>
> *According to the **proponents** of technology, easy access to information is one way that people benefit from new technology.*
>
> *Some educators **claim** that the networking phenomenon can be positive.*

3.1 Common Vocabulary in Persuasive Writing

a. These nouns are common in persuasive writing: When referring to people, you can use: *advocates, opponents, proponents, supporters* When referring to ideas, you can use: *argument, belief, claim, conclusion, evidence, fact, information, problem(s)*	***Opponents** of social networking sites argue that these communities deter face-to-face interactions.* *The main **argument** used by **proponents** of social networking websites is that they allow contact with people from all over the world.* *Some critics see students' dependence on SNSs as a **problem**, but there is little **evidence** of this.*
b. These verbs are common in persuasive writing: *acknowledge, admit, advocate, argue, believe, claim, control, estimate, oppose, project, refute, support*	*Some people **believe** that children should not be allowed to text in class.* *A number of parents **support** banning text messaging from schools.*
c. These adjectives are common in persuasive writing: *better, illogical, important, incomplete, little, true, unproved, valid*	*It is **important** to be familiar with the latest technology.* *It is **true** that some people spend too much time in front of the computer.* *The arguments supported by these researchers are **illogical**.*

d. These expressions are common in persuasive writing:
 	
  be in favor of (something)
  be against (something)
	*Many instructors **are in favor of** receiving homework online.*
	
	*Many teachers **are against** the use of social media in schools.*

▶ Vocabulary Application

Exercise 3.1 Vocabulary in Persuasive Writing

Read the sentences about cyberbullying. Use each word once.

argue	~~claim~~	in favor of	opponents	proponents

1. Cyberbullying occurs when people, often teenagers, are teased or humiliated by others on the Internet. Many parents and psychologists _claim_ that it can cause permanent emotional damage to children and teenagers.

2. Some people _____ that cyberbullying should be categorized as a criminal offense.

3. _____ of the idea that cyberbullying be classified as a criminal offense are _____ the approach because they believe it will decrease the amount of cyberbullying among teenagers.

4. _____ of making cyberbullying a criminal offense do not believe that criminalizing cyberbullying would be effective.

acknowledge	evidence	against	a valid point

5. While some people _____ that cyberbullying needs to be criminalized, they worry that the law will be ineffective because it is difficult to track the perpetrators.

6. The difficulty of tracking perpetrators is _____ , but the point may not be convincing in the near future since tracking devices are rapidly improving.

7. Some people who are _____ the criminalization of cyberbullying say that creating laws making it a crime violates free speech.

8. Some researchers have found that there is _____ that educational programs in early grades are effective in reducing the incidence of bullying.

Exercise 3.2 More Vocabulary in Persuasive Writing

Pair Work Work with a partner and choose one of the topics below. Discuss different views on the topic. Use the vocabulary for persuasive writing in your discussion.

- Should children under 12 be allowed to use social networking sites?
- Should parents have access to their children's and teenagers' social networking accounts?
- Should people be "friends" with their coworkers and managers on social networking sites?

I believe that children under 12 should be allowed to use social networking sites. I acknowledge that children can get into trouble, but if they use the sites responsibly, they can learn a lot about socializing and computer skills. . . .

4 | Avoid Common Mistakes ⚠️

1. **Don't confuse the noun and verb form of *claim*.**
    claim
    The ~~claiming~~ that social networking is dangerous is illogical.

2. **Don't confuse the noun and verb form of *argue*.**
    argument
    The main ~~arguing~~ against using social networking sites to communicate with people is that it is superficial.

3. **Remember to use *according to*, not *according for* or *according with*.**
    to
    According ~~for~~ a recent study, young people are losing interest in social networking.
    to
    According ~~with~~ Smith, social networking is useful as an educational tool.

Editing Task

Find and correct six more mistakes in the body paragraph from an essay on social networking.

Social Networking Sites

arguments
One of the main ~~arguing~~ against social networking sites is that people sometimes reveal information on them that often should be kept private. Recently another development has provided more support for this arguing: College admissions committees are now using social networking sites as part of the application process. According for a survey by Kaplan Test

5 Prep (2010), over 80 percent of college admissions officers use social networking sites to communicate with students. The claiming that many colleges make is that they use these sites to attract new students or to stay in contact with former students. However, some colleges admit that they are also using social networking as part of the admissions process. The main arguing for using social media is that it helps colleges evaluate candidates at a time

10 when these colleges are experiencing large numbers of applicants. According with many admissions officers, colleges need all the information they can get on applicants in order to make decisions because the admissions process has become very competitive. One college interviewer in a recent survey reported that if she has to choose between two students who are equally qualified in terms of grades and test scores, she looks at their online profiles to

15 make the final decision. In addition, applicants also use social networking sites against each other. According for another admissions officer, his office often receives anonymous messages

with links to sites that have negative information on or pictures of other applicants. Many colleges and universities do not have official policies yet on whether to use social media as part of the application process. Until these policies become clearer, prospective college

20 students should keep their social networking pages private or remove anything that might make them look less attractive to admissions committees.

5 | The Writing Process ✒

In this section, you will write a persuasive essay, which will include citations from research that you will conduct on your topic. Before you start writing, you will learn about writing strong arguments to support your point of view.

About Writing Strong Arguments

To present a strong argument, writers need to clearly identify and define their point of view and find ways to make those arguments appear convincing. The following are three methods that writers can use to make their writing more convincing:

1. **Include facts, statistics, observations, and trends based on research to support your claims.** Supporting your arguments with facts and statistical data will make your arguments stronger. Even more important is to include the sources of your information. By providing the sources, you are showing your audience that you have done your research, and you are inviting them to verify the information for themselves.

2. **Include the opinions of authorities or experts respected by your audience.** An argument will always seem stronger if you are able to provide quotations from well-known experts who hold the same position as yourself. If the experts you cite are not well known to your audience, you can convince your audience that they are authorities.

3. **Make logical connections between the information you present and any predictions or recommendations that you make.** Facts and opinions are not arguments. It is up to you to make logical connections between facts for your audience. You have to help your readers see that there may be a causal connection between facts and that therefore the course of action that you are arguing for should be taken.

Exercise

For each item, choose the type of argument strategy that is being used by the writer. Write the letter on the line.

a. Logical connection   b. Opinion of experts   c. Facts, statistics, trends

_____ 1. One study on cyberbullying has shown that the issue is widespread, with 20 percent of students reporting that they had been bullied ("Cyberbullying Research," n.d.).

_____ 2. If schools become involved, it will reduce opportunities for cyberbullying attacks.

_____ 3. According to Christina Brown and Michelle Demaray (n.d.), the authors of "School-Based Cyberbullying Interventions," school authorities must be able to identify cyberbullying, understand how it affects students, and do everything possible to create a safe learning environment.

Pre-writing Tasks

Choose a Topic

A Choose one of the topics listed below. You will write a persuasive essay in which you take a position on your topic and back it up with researched facts and opinions.

- Can educational programs prevent cyberbullying?
- Should classrooms have closed-circuit cameras to monitor teachers and students?
- A topic of your own approved by your teacher

B *Pair Work* Share your topic with a partner. Brainstorm a list of ideas to include. Suggest the sorts of facts and opinions that will be needed to support your arguments and some possible source material to go to for research.

Organize Your Ideas

A Research your topic in the library or online. Remember to find information from sources that oppose your point of view as well as those that support it. Draw the charts below on a separate sheet of paper. Write the sources and the information that you retrieved from them.

Sources	Information That Supports Your Point of View

Sources	Information That Opposes Your Point of View

B *Pair Work* Discuss the information and the logical connections you make with a partner. See if your partner finds your logic to be persuasive.

Writing Task

Write a persuasive essay. Follow the steps below.

1. Write an introductory paragraph that contains a hook, explains the issue, and provides a thesis statement.

2. Write body paragraphs that contain topic sentences that state your main ideas, present opposing viewpoints, and provide a refutation of those views.

3. Make sure your body paragraphs contain facts, statistics, and logical connections that are supported by your research.

4. Write a concluding paragraph that summarizes the main points of your essay and contains a recommendation for future action.

5. Include the following in your essay:

   • expressions that refer to future actions;

   • argumentation vocabulary;

   • at least three academic words from the essay in this unit: *access, area, aspect, beneficial, colleague, communicate, contact, contrast, create, culture, establish, estimate, focus, grade, indicate, interact, interaction, interactive, issue, lecture, link, maintain, monitor, network, networking, percent, phenomenon, policy, positive, potentially, promote, qualitatively, revolutionize, site, status, survey, visually.*

6. Create a reference list of sources at the end of your essay.

7. After you write your essay, review it and make sure you avoided the mistakes in the Avoid Common Mistakes chart on page 294.

Peer Review

A Exchange your essay with a partner. Answer the following questions as you read your partner's essay, and then share your responses.

1. Is there a thesis statement? Is the point of view clear?

2. Has the writer included any opposing views and refuted them? What are they?

3. What methods does the writer use to support his or her arguments? Does the writer use argumentation vocabulary? Underline any you find.

4. Has the writer referred to future actions or events? Circle any verbs that refer to the future.

5. Does the concluding paragraph summarize the main points and make a recommendation or prediction?

6. Does the writer include a reference list of all the sources cited in the essay?

7. Is anything confusing? Write a question mark (?) next to it.

8. Provide one compliment (something you found interesting or unusual).

B Use your partner's comments to help you revise your essay. Use the Writer's Checklist on page A2 to review your essay for organization, grammar, and vocabulary.

References

Unit 1

Grubb, A. (2011). Peak oil primer. *Energy Bulletin*. Retrieved from
http://www.energybulletin.net/primer.php

United Nations Environment Programme. (2011). *Forest facts*. Retrieved from
http://www.unep.org/wed/forestfacts/

Unit 2

Perner, L. (2008). Consumer behavior. *USC Marshall*. Retrieved from
http://www.consumerpsychologist.com/intro_Consumer_Behavior.html

United States Environmental Protection Agency. (2011, November).
Paper recycling facts and figures. Retrieved from US EPA website
http://www.epa.gov/osw/conserve/materials/paper/faqs.htm

Unit 3

Burstein, D. (2012). A minute with . . . David Jones. *Huffington Post Business*.
Retrieved from http://www.huffingtonpost.com/david-d-burstein/a-minute-withdavid
-jones_b_1288931.html

Patagonia. (2011). *Company info: Corporate responsibility*. Retrieved from
http://www.patagonia.com/us/patagonia.go?assetid=37492

Waite, L. (2007). What makes a good corporate citizen? A discussion and case study.
EzineArticles.com. Retrieved from http://ezinearticles.com/?What-Makes-a-Good
-Corporate-Citizen?-A-Discussion-and-Case-Study&id=700539

Unit 4

BP energy outlook 2030. (2011). *BP*. Retrieved from http://www.bp.com/liveassets/bp
_internet/globalbp/globalbp_uk_english/reports_and_publications/statistical_energy
_review_2011/STAGING/local_assets/pdf/2030_energy_outlook_booklet.pdf

Brown, L. R. (2009). *Plan B 4.0: Mobilizing to save civilization*. New York, NY: W. W. Norton &
Company.

Energy today and tomorrow. (2008). *ACCENT*. Retrieved from
http://www.atmosphere.mpg.de/enid/Nr2JuneO5_Context_4pu.html

Evans, S. (2007). The benefits of wind power. *Green Living Ideas*. Retrieved from
http://www.greenlivingideas.com/topics/alternative-energy/wind-energy/the-benefits-of
-wind-power

Our dependence on oil. (2010). *Environmental Defense Fund*. Retrieved from
http://apps.edf.org/page.cfm?tagID=58983

Sweet, P. (2007). Insiders see solar energy industry as ready for takeoff. *Las Vegas Sun*. Retrieved from http://www.lasvegassun.com/news/2007/aug/19/insiders-see-solar-energy-industry-as-ready-for-ta/

The true costs of petroleum: The community map. (2003). *Ecology Center*. Retrieved from http://ecologycenter.org/erc/petroleum/community.html

Unit 5

Kochan, M. (2006). Birth order and adult sibling relationships. *Revolution Health Group*. Retrieved from www.revolutionhealth.com/healthy-living/relationships/friends-family/parents-siblings/birth-order

Petersen, A. (2010). A dose of sibling rivalry. *The Wall Street Journal*. Retrieved from http://online.wsj.com/article/SB10001424052748704388504575419444247971432.html

Unit 6

Bureau of Labor Statistics. (2011, June). *American time use survey summary*. Retrieved from BLS website http://www.bls.gov/news.release/atus.nr0.htm

Robinson, L. N. (2011). Gender inequality. *InsideCounsel*, 22(238), 12. Retrieved from http://www.ccwomenofcolor.org/press/Gender_Inequality_10-11.pdf

Sasso, A. T., Richards, M. R., Chou, C., & Gerber, S. E. (2011). The $16,819 pay gap for newly trained physicians: The unexplained trend of men earning more than women. *Health Affairs*. Retrieved from http://content.healthaffairs.org/content/30/2/193.short

Unit 7

Clutter, A., & Nieto, R. (n.d.). *Understanding the Hispanic culture*. Retrieved from Ohio State University website http://ohioline.osu.edu/hyg-fact/5000/5237.html

Dr. Spock: Cultural differences in parenting. (n.d.). *Parents: Healthy Kids, Happy Families*. Retrieved from http://www.parents.com/parenting/better-parenting/teaching-tolerance/cultural-differences-parenting/

Unit 8

Galanti, G. (2000). An introduction to cultural differences. *The Western Journal of Medicine, 172*(5), 335–336.

Unit 9

Davis, S., Jenkins, G., & Hunt, R. (2003). *The pact: Three young men make a promise and fulfill a dream*. New York, NY: Riverhead Books.

Rodriguez, G. (2010). The American dream: Is it slipping away? *Los Angeles Times*. Retrieved from http://articles.latimes.com/2010/sep/27/opinion/la-oe-rodriguez-dream-20100927

Unit 10

Diner, H. (2008). Immigration and U.S. history. *America.gov*. Retrieved from http://www.america.gov/st/peopleplace-english/2008/February/20080307112004ebyessedo0.1716272.html

Economic impact of immigration in the twentieth century. (2011). *DISCovering Collection*. Gale. Retrieved from Portland Community College website https://library.pcc.edu

Migration – types of migration, theories on migration, migration and the family, migration and the global economy. (n.d.). The Marriage and Family Encyclopedia. JRank. Retrieved from http://family.jrank.org/pages/1173/Migration.html

Unit 12

Great Performances online: Howard Gardner's Multiple Intelligences. (n.d.) Used by permission of *WNET New York Public Media*. Retrieved from PBS online http://www.pbs.org/wnet/gperf/education/ed_mi_overview.html

Holland, J. L. (1997). *Making vocational choices: A theory of vocational personalities and work environments* (3rd ed.). Odessa, FL: Psychological Assessment Resources.

Unit 13

Barnard, N. D. (2011). Weird science: Should you say no to GM foods? *Vegetarian Times*, (384) 26.

Byrne, P. (2010). *Labeling of genetically engineered foods*. Retrieved from Colorado State University Extension website http://www.ext.colostate.edu/pubs/foodnut/09371.html

The Center for Food Safety. (n.d.). *Genetically engineered crops*. Retrieved from The Center for Food Safety website http://www.centerforfoodsafety.org/campaign/genetically-engineered-food/crops/

DeNoon, D. J. (2010). Genetically engineered salmon: FAQ. *MedicineNet*. Retrieved from http://www.medicinenet.com/script/main/art.asp?articlekey=120016

GM crops: Costs and benefits. (n.d.). Retrieved from University of Michigan website http://sitemaker.umich.edu/sec006group5/gm_food

Harder, B. (2008). Thinking Harder: Will we all soon eat lab-grown meat? *U.S. News & World Report*. Retrieved from http://www.usnews.com/science/blogs/thinking-harder/2008/04/24/will-we-all-soon-eat-lab-grown-meat

Katel, P. (2010). Food safety. *CQ Researcher* (20), 1037–1060. Retrieved from http://0-library.cqpress.com.library.pcc.edu/cqresearcher/

Kintisch, E. (2001). Why label food? Sticker shock. *The New Republic*. Retrieved from The Alliance for Better Foods website http://www.betterfoods.org/News/Archives/01_22_01.htm

Trivieri, L. (2011). The truth behind the definition of organic foods and farming. *Integrative Health Review*. Retrieved from http://www.integrativehealthreview.com/eating-nutrition/the-benefits-of-organic-foods/

Unit 14

American Academy of Child & Adolescent Psychiatry. (2011). *Obesity in children and teens.* Retrieved from http://www.aacap.org/cs/root/facts_for_families/obesity_in_children _and_teens

Bellows, L., & Roach, J. (2011). *Childhood overweight.* Retrieved from Colorado State University Extension website http://www.ext.colostate.edu/pubs/foodnut/09317.html

Bill Clinton on childhood obesity. (2010). *The Daily Beast.* Retrieved from http://www.thedailybeast.com/newsweek/videos/2010/03/17/bill-clinton-on-childhood -obesity.html

Carey, B. (2011). Parents urged again to limit TV for youngest. *The New York Times.* Retrieved from http://www.nytimes.com/2011/10/19/health/19babies.html?_r=1

Centers for Disease Control and Prevention. (2011, October). *Tips for parents – Ideas to help children maintain a healthy weight.* Retrieved from http://www.cdc.gov/healthyweight/children/index.html

A Change of Pace Foundation. (n.d.). *Childhood obesity.* Retrieved from http://www.changeofpace.org/childhoodobesity.html

Dietary guidelines for Americans, 2005. (2005). Retrieved from U.S. Department of Health and Human Services and U.S. Department of Agriculture website http://www.health.gov/dietaryguidelines/dga2005/document/html/executivesummary.htm

Puhl, R. (2011). Childhood obesity and stigma. *Obesity Action Coalition.* Retrieved from http://www.obesityaction.org/magazine/oacnews7/childhoodobesity.php

Virginia Foundation for Healthy Youth. (2010, April). *Virginia childhood obesity survey.* Retrieved from http://www.healthyyouthva.org/survey.asp

Unit 15

Fox, S. (2011). Health topics. *Pew Research Center's Internet & American Life Project.* Retrieved from http://pewinternet.org/reports/2011/HealthTopics.aspx

Torrey, T. (2009). Are you a cyberchondriac? Do you self-diagnose yourself using the Internet? *About.com.* Retrieved from http://patients.about.com/od/researchandresources/a/ cyberselfdiag.htm

Unit 16

Wong, J. (2010). 'Lack of time' biggest excuse for unhealthy eating. *AFN Thought for Food.* Retrieved from http://www.ausfoodnews.com.au/2010/03/04/lack-of-time-biggest -excuse-for-unhealthy-eating.html

Unit 17

Campana, J. (2012). Identity theft and fraud complaints up 19% in 2011. *Examiner.com.* Retrieved from http://www.examiner.com/identity-theft-in-national/identity-theft-and -fraud-complaints-up-19-2011-review

Collins, B. (2008). Privacy and security issues in social networking. *Fast Company.* Retrieved from http://www.fastcompany.com/articles/2008/10/social-networking-security.html

Eger, J. M. (2010). Growing concerns over Internet privacy. *San Diego State University News Center.* Retrieved from http://newscenter.sdsu.edu/sdsu_newscenter/news.aspx?s=72621

Unit 18

American Academy of Child & Adolescent Psychiatry. (2006). *Children and video games: Playing with violence*. Retrieved from http://www.aacap.org/cs/root/facts_for_families/children_and_video_games_playing_with_violence

Brocato, E. D., Gentile, D. A., Laczniak, R. N., Maier, J. A., & Ji-Song, M. (2010). Television commercial violence: Potential effects on children. *The Journal of Advertising*. Retrieved from Access My Library website http://www.accessmylibrary.com/article-1G1-248188461/television-commercial-violence-potential.html

Federal Communications Commission. (2007). *In the matter of violent television programming and its impact on children* (MB Docket No. 04-261). Washington, DC: Author.

Fredrickson, C. (2007). Why government should not police TV violence and indecency. *Buffalo News*. Retrieved from The Christian Science Monitor website http://www.csmonitor.com/2007/0906/p09s01-coop.html

Unit 19

Carr, N. (2008). Is Google making us stupid? *The Atlantic*. Retrieved from http://www.theatlantic.com/magazine/archive/2008/07/is-google-making-us-stupid/6868/

Tapscott, D. (2009). *Grown up digital: How the net generation is changing your world* (pp. 97–112). New York, NY: McGraw-Hill.

Unit 20

Brown, C. F., & Demaray, M. K. (n.d.). School-based cyberbullying interventions. *Education.com*. Retrieved from http://www.education.com/reference/article/school-based-cyberbullying-interventions/?page=3

Cyberbullying research. (n.d.). *Cyberbullying Research Center*. Retrieved from http://www.cyberbullying.us/research.php

Grabmeier, J. (n.d.). Study finds link between Facebook use, lower grades in college. *Ohio State University*. Retrieved from http://researchnews.osu.edu/archive/facebookusers.htm

Hamilton, A. (2009). What Facebook users share: Lower grades. *Time*. Retrieved from http://www.time.com/time/business/article/0,8599,1891111,00.html

Kaplan test prep's 2010 survey of college admissions officers. (2010). *Kaplan Test Prep*. Retrieved from http://press.kaptest.com/research-and-surveys/kaplan-test-preps-2010-survey-of-college-admissions-officers

Smith, A., Rainie, L., & Zickuhr, K. (2011). College students and technology. *Pew Research Center's Internet & American Life Project*. Retrieved from http://pewinternet.org/reports/2011/college-students-and-technology

Sources

The following sources were consulted during the development of *Grammar and Beyond Student's Book 4.*

Unit 1

Animals: Nat Geo wild: Bald eagle. (n.d.). *National Geographic*. Retrieved from http://animals.nationalgeographic.com/animals/birds/bald-eagle/

Blue Planet Network. (2010). *The facts about the global drinking water crisis*. Retrieved from http://blueplanetnetwork.org/water/facts

Department of Energy and Environmental Protection. (2010, October). *Bald eagle*. Retrieved from DEEP website http://www.ct.gov/dep/cwp/view.asp?q=325972

Hopkins, S. (2010). Geothermal energy in Iceland. *Green Chip Stocks*. Retrieved from http://www.greenchipstocks.com/articles/geothermal-energy-in-iceland/740

The Ministry for the Environment. (2002). *Welfare for the future: Iceland's national strategy for sustainable development 2002–2020*. Retrieved from http://eng.umhverfisraduneyti.is/media/PDF_skrar/Sjalfbar__roun_enska.pdf

Rosenthal, D. (2011). Iceland has the world's cleanest electricity. *Time*. Retrieved from http://www.time.com/time/magazine/article/0,9171,2042236,00.html

Sahagun, L. (2011). Wind power turbines in Altamont Pass threaten protected birds. *Los Angeles Times*. Retrieved from http://articles.latimes.com/2011/jun/06/local/la-me-adv -wind-eagles-20110606

Unit 2

Aitchison, S. (2012). Advertising Authority. *Klipsun magazine*. Retrieved from http://www.klipsunmagazine.com/?p=3779

Department of Energy & Environmental Protection. (2011). *Fun tidbits about recycling, energy and climate change*. Retrieved from http://www.ct.gov/dep/cwp/view .asp?a=2714&q=440320&depNav_GID=1645

Green living: Recycle glass. (n.d.). *National Geographic*. Retrieved from http://greenliving.nationalgeographic.com/recycle-glass/

Lavack, A. M. (2002). Advertising of unhealthy products. *Gale Encyclopedia of Public Health*. Retrieved from http://www.ask.com/health/galecontent/advertising-of-unhealthy -products

Neer, K. (n.d.). How product placement works. *HowStuffWorks*. http://money.howstuffworks.com/product-placement3.htm

Sauer, A. (2011). Announcing the Brandcameo Product Placement Award winners. *Brandchannel*. Retrieved from http://www.brandchannel.com/home/ post/2011/02/22/2010-Brandcameo-Product-Placement-Awards.aspx

Story, M., & French, S. (2004). Food advertising and marketing directed at children and adolescents in the US. *International Journal of Behavioral Nutrition and Physical Activity*. Retrieved from http://www.ijbnpa.org/content/1/1/3

Unit 3

Ferrell, O. C., Fraedrich, J., & Ferrell, L. (2002). *Business ethics: Ethical decision making and cases*. Boston: Houghton Mifflin Company.

Unit 4

Cru, M. (2010). Paris metro body heat to warm up building. *Reuters*. Retrieved from http://www.reuters.com/article/2010/09/06/us-heat-metro-paris-idUSTRE68522420100906

Denmark. (2010). *ThinkGlobalGreen.org*. Retrieved from http://thinkglobalgreen.org/denmark.html

Facts about wind power. (2010). *VERA*. Retrieved from http://www.northeastwind.com/resources/facts-about-wind-power

Harrell, E. (2010). The 50 best inventions of 2010. *Time*. Retrieved from http://www.time.com/time/specials/packages/article/0,28804,2029497_2030623_2029815,00.html

Lazari, S. (2006). Energy tax policy: History and current issues. *CRS report for Congress*. Retrieved from http://fpc.state.gov/documents/organization/70315.pdf

Ozcanli, O. C. (2010). Turning body heat into electricity. *Forbes*. Retrieved from http://www.forbes.com/2010/06/07/nanotech-body-heat-technology-breakthroughs-devices.html

Paulsen, M. (2011). Wind power prices drop to coal power levels: Bloomberg. *The Hook*. Retrieved from http://thetyee.ca/Blogs/TheHook/Environment/2011/02/14/Wind-power-prices-drop-to-coal-power-levels/

Piccinotti, A. (n.d.). The oil fuel issue. *Regia Marina Italiana*. Retrieved from http://www.regiamarina.net/detail_text.asp?nid=125&lid=1

Sekiguchi, T., & Roosevelt, M. (2002). The winds of change. *Time*. Retrieved from http://www.time.com/time/magazine/article/0,9171,1003118,00.html

Unit 5

DiProperzio. (2010). Understanding the power of birth order. *TODAY Parenting*. Retrieved from http://today.msnbc.msn.com/id/39459807/ns/today-parenting_and_family/t/understanding-power-birth-order/

Rawlings, S. W. (n.d.). Population profile of the United States. *United States Census Bureau*. Retrieved from http://www.census.gov/population/www/pop-profile/hhfam.html

Rosenberg, M. (2011). China's one child policy. *About.com*. Retrieved from http://geography.about.com/od/populationgeography/a/onechild.htm

Serena Williams vs Venus Williams. (n.d.). *Diffen.com*. Retrieved from http://www.diffen.com/difference/Serena_Williams_vs_Venus_Williams

Women's grand slam title winners. (2012). *ESPN.com*. Retrieved from http://espn.go.com/sports/tennis/history/_/type/women

Yarrow, A. L. (2009). History of U.S. children's policy, 1900–present. *First focus: Making children and families the priority*. Retrieved from http://www.pcya.org/SiteCollectionDocuments/History%20of%20US%20Children%27s%20Policy%20%28Yarrow%29.pdf

Unit 6

10 key areas of Title IX: Athletics. (n.d.). *TitleIX.info*. Retrieved from http://www.titleix.info/10 -Key-Areas-of-Title-IX/Athletics.aspx

Chen, P. (2010). Do women make better doctors? *The New York Times*. Retrieved from http://www.nytimes.com/2010/05/06/health/06chen.html

Francis, D. R. (n.d.). Why do women outnumber men in college? *The National Bureau of Economic Research*. Retrieved from http://www.nber.org/digest/jan07/w12139.html

Garber, G. (2001). Landmark law faces new challenges even now. *ESPN.com*. Retrieved from http://espn.go.com/gen/womenandsports/020619title9.html

Goldin, C. (2006). Women's educational attainment and early choices. *Harvard University Department of Economics*. Retrieved from http://www.economics.harvard.edu/faculty/ goldin/files/QuietRevolution.pdf

Goudreau, J. (2010). Most popular college majors for women. *Forbes*. Retrieved from http://www.forbes.com/2010/08/10/most-popular-college-degrees-for-women-forbes -woman-leadership-education-business.html

Jones, A. (2012). Five male centered professions that women are moving into. *Elephant*. Retrieved from http://www.elephantjournal.com/2012/03/five-male-centered-professions -that-women-are-moving-into--anthony-jones/

Leaving men behind: Women go to college in ever-greater numbers. (2007). *Education-Portal.com*. Retrieved from http://education-portal.com/articles/ Leaving_Men_Behind_Women_Go_to_College_in_Ever-Greater_Numbers.html

Ludden, J. (2011). Ask for a raise? Most women hesitate. Retrieved from http://www.npr.org/2011/02/14/133599768/ask-for-a-raise-most-women-hesitate

Mather, M., & Adams, D. (2007). The crossover in female-male college enrollment rates. *Population Reference Bureau*. Retrieved from http://www.prb.org/Articles/2007/CrossoverinFemaleMaleCollegeEnrollmentRates.aspx

Needleman, S. E. (2010). Is workplace advancement gender neutral? *WSJ Blogs: The Juggle*. Retrieved from http://blogs.wsj.com/juggle/2010/02/01/is-workplace-advancement -gender-neutral-men-and-women-disagree/

Professional women: Vital statistics. (2010). *DPE Research Department*. Retrieved from http://www.pay-equity.org/PDFs/ProfWomen.pdf

Williams, A. (2010). The new math on campus. *The New York Times*. Retrieved from http://www.nytimes.com/2010/02/07/fashion/07campus.html?pagewanted=all

Unit 7

Advertising quotes. (n.d.). *Altius Directory*. Retrieved from http://www.altiusdirectory.com/Business/advertising-quotes.php

International community resources: Cultural differences. (n.d.). Retrieved from Iowa State University Center for Excellence in Learning and Teaching website http://www.celt.iastate.edu/international/CulturalDifferences3.html

Unit 8

Counting the hours. (2008). *OECD Observer*. Retrieved from
http://www.oecdobserver.org/news/fullstory.php/aid/2480/Counting_the_hours.html

Cross cultural differences that affect web design. (2010). *Cenango*. Retrieved from
http://www.cenango.com/blog/2010/08/cross-cultural-differences-that-affect-web-design/

Kwintessential. (n.d.). *International etiquette guide*. Retrieved from
www.kwintessential.co.uk/resources/country-profiles.html

Würtz, E. (2005). A cross-cultural analysis of websites from high-context cultures and
low-context cultures. *Journal of Computer-Mediated Communication*, 11(1), article 13.
Retrieved from http://jcmc.indiana.edu/vol11/issue1/wuertz.html

Unit 11

Types of colleges: The basics. (n.d.). *The College Board*. Retrieved from
https://bigfuture.collegeboard.org/find-colleges/college-101/types-of-colleges-the-basics

Types of interviews. (n.d.). *About.com: Job searching*. Retrieved from
http://jobsearch.about.com/od/interviewsnetworking/a/interviewtypes.htm

Unit 12

Careers for ISTJ personality types. (2011). *BSM Consulting, Inc*. Retrieved from
http://www.personalitypage.com/html/ISTJ_car.html

Holland personality types. (2008). *North Carolina Career Resource Network*. Retrieved from
http://www.soicc.state.nc.us/soicc/planning/jh-types.htm

Jones, L. K. (n.d.). Holland's theory of career choice and you. *The Career Key*. Retrieved from
http://www.careerkey.org/asp/your_personality/hollands_theory_of_career_choice.html

United States Courts. (n.d.). *Glossary of legal terms*. Retrieved from
http://www.uscourts.gov/common/glossary.aspx

Unit 13

GMOs gain ground for the tenth consecutive year. (2006). *GMO Compass*. Retrieved from
http://www.gmo-compass.org/eng/agri_biotechnology/gmo_planting/194.docu.html

Madrigal, A. (2008). Scientists flesh out plans to grow (and sell) test-tube meat. *Wired.com*.
Retrieved from http://www.wired.com/science/discoveries/news/2008/04/invitro_meat

Schneider, A. (2009). Scientists create lab-grown pork. *The KT Radio Network*. Retrieved from
http://www.ktradionetwork.com/health/scientists-create-lab-grown-pork/

Smith, P. (2011). The environmental benefits of test-tube meat. *GOOD Worldwide, LLC*.
Retrieved from http://www.good.is/post/the-environmental-benefits-of-test-tube-meat/

Unit 14

Centers for Disease Control and Prevention. (2010, January). *Obesity & genetics*. Retrieved
from http://www.cdc.gov/Features/Obesity/

Centers for Disease Control and Prevention. (2011, January). *Genomics and health*.
Retrieved from http://www.cdc.gov/genomics/resources/diseases/obesity/obesedit.htm

Unit 16

U.S. Department of Health & Human Services. (2011). *Get enough sleep*. Retrieved from healthfinder.gov http://healthfinder.gov/prevention/ViewTopicFull.aspx?topicID=68

Unit 18

Anderson, C. A. (2003). Violent video games: Myths, facts, and unanswered questions. *American Psychological Association*. Retrieved from http://www.apa.org/science/about/psa/2003/10/anderson.aspx

Beresin, E. V. (2011). The impact of media violence on children and adolescents: Opportunities for clinical interventions. *American Academy of Child and Adolescent Psychiatry*. Retrieved from http://www.aacap.org/cs/root/developmentor/the_impact_of_media_violence_on_children_and_adolescents_opportunities_for_clinical_interventions

Unit 20

Cohen, J. (2011). Report: Facebook profiles are now part of 80% colleges' admissions outreach. *All Facebook*. Retrieved from http://www.allfacebook.com/report-facebook-profiles-are-now-part-of-80-colleges-admissions-decisions-2011-02

Driscoll, E. (2011). Attention college applicants: Admissions can see your Facebook page. *Fox Business*. Retrieved from http://www.foxbusiness.com/personal-finance/2011/03/23/attention-college-applicants-admissions-facebook-page/

Hechinger, J. (2008). College applicants, beware: Your Facebook page is showing. *The Wall Street Journal*. Retrieved from http://online.wsj.com/article/SB122170459104151023.html

Appendices

1. Parts of an Essay

INTRODUCTORY PARAGRAPH

Elements of Academic Writing

Writing in an academic style is necessary to succeed in school and in many jobs. **Nevertheless, this type of writing can seem overwhelming to students, who are used to a more informal style of writing, such as texting.** Understanding the key elements of academic writing can make it easier to manage. **Effective academic writing requires strong academic vocabulary, reliable sources, and clear organization.**

← **Hook** – draws reader in

← **Thesis Statement** – gives main idea

BODY PARAGRAPH 1

Using the right vocabulary is essential. Writers should use precise and formal vocabulary to explain their ideas. For example, in conversation someone might say, "Sometimes kids have too much stuff to do, and they can't study." In academic writing, this might be expressed as, "Sometimes students have too many commitments, so it can be difficult for them to study." One resource that can help students build their academic vocabulary is the Academic Word List **(Coxhead, 2000)**, which identifies vocabulary that is commonly found in all disciplines. Some of these words include *achieve*, *potential*, and *similar*.

← **Topic Sentence**

Supporting Details

← **Citation** – shows the source of the information

BODY PARAGRAPH 2

Another important skill is researching and citing sources. Academic writers should use reliable sources in their research and avoid sources that are biased. Writers must also avoid plagiarism by including the sources of all outside information. In academic writing, not providing a source of information is like cheating and can lead to serious consequences.

← **Topic Sentence**

Supporting Details

BODY PARAGRAPH 3

It is also necessary to organize ideas appropriately. Typically, essays contain an introductory paragraph, body paragraphs with supporting details, and a concluding paragraph that summarizes or restates the main points. In addition, different writing assignments, such as research reports and persuasive arguments, can have different patterns of organization. Good writers choose patterns that are appropriate for their purpose in writing.

← **Topic Sentence**

Supporting Details

CONCLUDING PARAGRAPH

In sum, academic essays have precise and formal vocabulary, information that is cited, and a clear organizational pattern. When writers understand the elements of academic writing, they become more effective writers. Mastering this skill can benefit students in college and, later, professionally.

REFERENCES

References

Coxhead, A. (2000). "A new academic word list." *TESOL Quarterly* **34**(2): 213–238.

2. Writer's Checklist

		Yes	No
Audience	1. Is it clear who my audience is?		
	2. Is there anything I could do to make it clearer who my audience is?		
Purpose	1. Does my writing show that I understood the writing assignment?		
	2. Is the genre (cause and effect, problem–solution) clear?		
Length	Have I stayed within the minimum/maximum length?		
Organization	1. Did I follow my outline or other organizational structure I created for the writing assignment?		
	2. For paragraph writing assignments:		
	a. Does each paragraph have a topic sentence and address one main idea?		
	b. Do I support my topic sentence with clear examples, facts, and explanations?		
	3. For essay writing assignments:		
	a. Does the introductory paragraph introduce the topic?		
	b. Is there a hook that works well?		
	c. Do I have a clear thesis statement?		
	d. Does the essay address the topic and the thesis statement?		
	e. Do I have an effective conclusion?		
	4. Have I effectively used the writing point from this unit?		
Grammar	1. Do all my sentences have subjects and verbs?		
	2. Do all the subjects and verbs agree in number?		
	3. Are the forms of verbs correct?		
Vocabulary	1. Have I used the correct forms of words (e.g., the noun form or the adjective form)?		
	2. Have I avoided informal vocabulary or slang?		
	3. Are my vocabulary choices specific and clear?		
	4. Have I used connectors, such as demonstratives (*this*, *that*, etc.), transition words and phrases (*Therefore*, *However*, *In addition*, etc.), and pronouns (*it*, *they*, etc.), to connect ideas?		
Sources	1. Have I cited information that is from outside sources?		
	2. Is it clear to my reader what the source for each idea is?		
Your Questions	1.		
	2.		

3. About Plagiarism
Definition of Plagiarism

Plagiarism is considered a form of stealing in which a writer uses another writer's ideas and/or words improperly. As a writer, you plagiarize when you:

1. copy exact words from a source without noting the name of the source and using quotation marks.
2. paraphrase in a way that is too similar to the writer's original wording, i.e., when you replace only a few words in a sentence with synonyms.
3. state specific information, for example, unique ideas, results of a study or statistics, without identifying its source.

Reasons to Avoid Plagiarism

Plagiarism is a serious offense because it is considered to be both dishonest and unethical. Educational institutions have strict policies concerning plagiarism. Students who plagiarize could risk a failing grade or even being expelled. Therefore, it is essential for you to find out all you can about your school's policies on plagiarism and learn strategies to avoid plagiarizing.

There are other important reasons to avoid plagiarism. Writers typically feel a sense of ownership about their writing, especially when they have spent a lot of time and effort to do research and to create original and effective material. Citing a writer's ideas and original text is a way to respect the person's contributions. While many people talk about plagiarism as an issue of ownership, in the end, it may be more useful to think of it as "intellectual honesty."

Another reason involves your effectiveness as a writer. Taking language without paraphrasing it or ideas without citing them may create a false sense of your understanding of the information. In other words, when you cut and paste information from someone's work into your essay, you may not really understand the information, and you may use it improperly. Also, if questioned about the material, you may not be able to respond effectively.

Finally, when a writer uses language or ideas from another source without identifying that source, it makes it difficult for the reader to find out more information about what you have written and about the topic. The citations connect readers to credible sources of information.

How to Avoid Plagiarism

Whenever you use a writer's original words or ideas in your essay, you must credit the source in the text and in a reference list that follows your essay. In order to avoid plagiarism:

1. Use quotation marks around exact words from a source and cite the source in the text using APA or MLA style. This book uses APA style in citing in-text sources, e.g., (Brooks, 2010, p. 3).
2. Paraphrase (restate in your own words) the sentences that you want to include and cite the source in the text. See Unit 4 p. 60 for a list of paraphrasing strategies.
3. Cite the source of a unique idea or specific information, such as a statistic.
4. Include a reference list at the end of your essay that has an entry for each citation in your essay.

How to Identify Plagiarism

Original Source	Excerpts From Students' Writing	Is This Plagiarism?
Primary and secondary characteristics of culture (Purnell & Paulanka, 2005, pp. 2–3) Major influences that shape people's worldview and the extent to which people identify with their cultural group of origin are called the primary and secondary characteristics of culture. The primary characteristics are nationality, race, color, gender, age, and religious affiliation. For example, two people have the same gender, age, nationality, and race, but if one is a devout Roman Catholic and the other is an Orthodox Jew, they may vary significantly in their health-care beliefs and practices. The secondary characteristics include educational status, socioeconomic status, occupation, military experience, political beliefs, urban versus rural residence, enclave identity, marital status, parental status, physical characteristics, sexual orientation, gender issues, reason for migration (sojourner, immigrant, or undocumented status), and amount of time away from the country of origin. Immigration status also influences a person's worldview. For example, people who voluntarily immigrate generally acculturate and more easily assimilate. Sojourners who immigrate with the intention of remaining in their new homeland for only a short time or refugees who think they may return to their home country may not have the need to acculturate or assimilate. Additionally, undocumented individuals (illegal immigrants) may have a different worldview from those who have arrived legally with work visas or as "legal immigrants."	Major influences that shape people's worldview and the extent to which people identify with their cultural group of origin are called the primary and secondary characteristics of culture.	**Yes.** This is copied directly from the source without quotation marks or a citation.
	"The primary characteristics [of culture] are nationality, race, color, gender, age, and religious affiliation" (Purnell & Paulanka, 2005, p. 2).	**No.** It includes quotation marks around exact text from the original source and a citation.
	For example, even with other characteristics being very similar, "a devout Roman Catholic and . . . an Orthodox Jew . . . may vary significantly in their health-care beliefs and practices."	**Yes.** Even though the statement is in quotation marks, the original source is not cited.
	Some secondary characteristics of culture include military service and political beliefs (Purnell & Paulanka, 2005).	**No.** It includes general ideas from the original source and a citation.
	Neither sojourners nor refugees may feel the need to acculturate or assimilate because they both believe that they may return to their home country (Purnell & Paulanka, 2005, p. 3).	**Yes.** Even though there is a citation, the words are still too close to the original. Acceptable: Sojourners and refugees may resist acculturation and assimilation because they see the move as only temporary. (Purnell & Paulanka, 2005, p. 3).

Final Points About Plagiarism

1. One good strategy to avoid plagiarizing is to take notes about your source rather than copying and pasting from the original to your own document. Then use your notes to write the important ideas from the source, as you understand them, without looking at the original source until you have finished.

2. Always remember to make a list of the sources. Follow the style (APA, MLA) that is preferred by your school, and make sure that you include information such as the author, year of publication, title, page or paragraph number in which you found the information, publisher and website for each source. Cut and paste urls from the websites into a document to help you keep track of them. This will also make it easier to create citations in your text and build your reference list.

3. Put quotation marks and mark the page number for *any* text that you have taken directly from a source, even if it is in your notes.

4. Just using good paraphrasing does not eliminate the risk of plagiarism because you need to include the source of ideas in the form of a citation, in addition to the paraphrase.

5. Plagiarism can be confusing for student writers because different readers, such as their instructors, may feel differently about how close is *too close,* in terms of either the source material's language or the original writer's ideas. It is always a good idea to check with your instructor for specific guidelines on plagiarism.

Academic Word List (AWL) Words and Definitions

The meanings of the words are those used in this book. ([U1] = Unit 1)

Academic Word	Definition
academic (adj) [U14] [U19]	relating to schools, especially colleges and universities
access (n) [U18] [U19] [U20]	the opportunity or ability to use something
accessible (adj) [U1] [U19]	possible to reach, approach, enter, or use
achieve (v) [U9]	do or obtain something that you wanted after planning and working to make it happen
acknowledge (v) [U15]	accept the truth or recognize the existence of something
adult (adj) [U14]	typical of, suitable for, or happening to adults
adult (n) [U6] [U7] [U9] [U14] [U15]	a person who has grown to his or her full size and strength; not a child
adulthood (n) [U5] [U7]	the part of someone's life when they are an adult
affect (v) [U2]	have an influence on someone or something
aid (v) [U7]	help or support
alternative (n) [U4] [U13]	something that is different, especially from what is usual; a choice
amendment (n) [U18]	a change or addition to a document
analyst (n) [U4]	someone who studies or examines something in detail, such as finances, computer systems, or the economy
apparent (adj) [U7]	able to be seen or understood
approach (n) [U16]	a way of dealing with something
approach (v) [U15]	meet or communicate directly with someone
appropriate (adj) [U8] [U12]	right for a particular situation
approximately (adv) [U6] [U10] [U14]	almost exactly
area (n) [U3] [U7] [U14] [U17] [U20]	a particular part of a country, city, town, etc.; a particular part of a place or anything that takes space; a subject or activity, or a part of it
aspect (n) [U2] [U6] [U8] [U20]	a particular feature or way of thinking about something
assessment (n) [U12]	a judgment or measure of the quality or importance of something
assume (v) [U8]	accept something as true without question or proof
assumed (adj) [U5]	accepting something as true without question or proof
assure (v) [U9]	promise or tell something to someone confidently or firmly, or cause someone to feel certain by removing doubt
attached (adj) [U2]	feeling close to emotionally
author (n) [U5] [U17]	a writer of a book, article, etc.; a person whose main job is writing books
available (adj) [U15]	ready to use or obtain
aware (adj) [U2] [U3] [U8] [U11] [U17]	knowing that something exists; having knowledge or experience of a particular thing
beneficial (adj) [U20]	tending to help; having a good effect

Academic Word	Definition
benefit (n) [U3] [U5] [U13] [U15] [U17] [U19]	a helpful or good effect; a service provided by an employer
benefit (v) [U15] [U19]	be helped by something or help someone
category (n) [U11] [U12]	a group of people or things of a similar type
challenge (n) [U10] [U16]	something needing great mental or physical effort in order to be done successfully
challenge (v) [U15]	test someone's ability or determination
challenging (adj) [U8] [U13] [U15] [U16]	offering a challenge
cite (v) [U4] [U13] [U16]	mention something as an example or proof of something else
code (n) [U11]	a system for representing information with signs or symbols that are not ordinary language, or the signs or symbols themselves
colleague (n) [U9] [U20]	one member of a group of people who work together
commission (n) [U18]	a group of people or an organization with the authority to gather information, establish regulations, or perform other special duties
commit (v) [U16]	promise to give yourself, your money, your time, etc., to support something
committed (adj) [U14] [U16] [U18]	loyal and willing to give your time and energy to support something
communicate (v) [U20]	give messages or information to others through speech, writing, body movements, or signals
communication (n) [U15] [U19]	the exchange of messages or information; a message, or the process by which a message or information is sent
community (n) [U3] [U14]	all the people who live in a particular area, or a group of people who are considered as a unit because of their shared interests or background
compatible (adj) [U12]	able to exist or work well with something or someone else
complex (adj) [U14]	having many, but connected, parts making it difficult to understand
component (n) [U7]	one of the parts of a system, process, or machine
computer (n) [U11] [U18]	an electronic device that can store, organize, and change large amounts of information quickly
conclude (v) [U13] [U15] [U17]	cause something to end; end; judge or decide something after some consideration
conclusive (adj) [U13]	ending any doubt or uncertainty about a situation
conduct (v) [U3] [U8] [U11]	organize and direct a particular activity
confirmation (n) [U15]	a statement of proof that something is true
consequence (n) [U1] [U4] [U14] [U16] [U17]	a result of an action or situation, especially (in the plural) a bad result
consequently (adv) [U8]	as a result; therefore
consistently (adv) [U18]	in a way that is always similar
consultation (n) [U15]	a meeting with a doctor about an illness or its treatment

Academic Word	Definition
consume (v) [U1] [U13] [U16]	use something such as a product, time, energy, or fuel; eat or drink
consumer (n) [U2] [U13]	a person who buys goods or services for their own use
consumption (n) [U1] [U13]	an amount of something that is used, or the process of using something, especially so that there is less of it
contact (n) [U20]	a person you know who may help you by sharing knowledge or information or introducing you to other people
contemporary (adj) [U9]	existing or happening now
contextualize (v) [U15]	consider something in its context
contrary (adj) [U16]	opposite
contrast (n) [U7] [U8] [U11] [U20]	an easily noticed or understood difference between two or more things
contribute (v) [U10] [U14] [U16]	be one of the reasons why something happens
controversial (adj) [U18]	causing or likely to cause disagreement
controversy (n) [U18]	a disagreement, often a public one, that involves different ideas or opinions about something
conventional (adj) [U11] [U12]	following the usual practices of the past
convert (v) [U4]	change the character, appearance, or operation of something
convince (v) [U2]	cause someone to believe something or do something
cooperation (n) [U15]	the condition of working together with someone
cooperative (adj) [U6]	showing a willingness to act or work together for a shared purpose
core (adj) [U3]	central; basic
corporate (adj) [U3]	relating to a large company
corporation (n) [U6]	a large company
create (v) [U1] [U4] [U6] [U9] [U12] [U15] [U16] [U20]	cause something to exist, or make something new or imaginative
creative (adj) [U5] [U12]	producing or using original and unusual ideas
cultural (adj) [U2] [U3] [U6] [U7] [U8]	relating to the way of life of a country or a group of people
culture (n) [U2] [U3] [U6] [U7] [U8] [U20]	the way of life of a particular people, especially shown in their ordinary behavior and habits, their attitudes toward each other, and their moral and religious beliefs
data (n) [U17]	information collected for use
debate (v) [U18]	seriously discuss or argue the different opinions people have on a particular subject
decade (n) [U4] [U6] [U9] [U16]	a period of ten years

Academic Word	Definition
define (v) [U7] [U12]	describe the meaning of something, especially a word, or to explain something more clearly so that it can be understood
definition (n) [U7] [U11] [U12]	a statement that explains the meaning of a word or phrase
design (v) [U12] [U19]	make or draw plans for something
despite (prep) [U4] [U6] [U11] [U17]	used to say that something happened or is true, although something else makes this seem not probable
discriminate (v) [U14]	treat people differently, in an unfair way
display (v) [U8]	let something become known by what you say or do, or how you look
distinct (adj) [U10]	clearly separate and different
diverse (adj) [U7] [U12]	varied or different
document (n) [U3]	a paper or set of papers with written or printed information
dominant (adj) [U6]	more important, strong, or noticeable
dramatically (adv) [U4] [U9] [U14]	suddenly or noticeably
economic (adj) [U10]	related to trade, industry, and money
economical (adj) [U2]	the careful use and management of money or of time, energy, words, etc.
economy (n) [U10]	the system of trade and industry by which the wealth of a country is made and used
element (n) [U7]	one of the parts of something that makes it work, or a quality that makes someone or something effective
eliminate (v) [U11] [U17]	remove or take away from something
energy (n) [U4]	the power to do work and activity
enhanced (adj) [U13]	improve the quality, amount, or strength of something
enormous (adj) [U12]	extremely large or great
ensure (v) [U11] [U14]	make or be certain about something
environment (n) [U1] [U2] [U3] [U4] [U5] [U6] [U12] [U13]	the air, water, and land in or on which people, animals, and plants live; the conditions that you live or work in and the way that they influence how you feel or how effectively you can work
environmental (adj) [U4]	relating to the environment
environmentalist (n) [U1]	a person who has a specially strong interest in or knowledge of the natural environment, and who wants to preserve it and prevent damage to it
establish (v) [U20]	start something that will last for a long time, or create or set something in a particular way
estimate (n) [U1] [U20]	a judgment or calculation of approximately how large or how great something is
estimate (v) [U20]	to guess the cost, size, value, etc. of something
ethic (n) [U9]	system of accepted beliefs that control behavior, especially such a system based on morals

Academic Word	Definition
ethical (adj) [U3]	good, correct
evaluate (v) [U11] [U15]	judge or calculate the quality, importance, amount, or value of something
exhibit (v) [U5] [U18]	show something, especially a quality, by your behavior
expert (n) [U2] [U4] [U5] [U17]	a person with a high level of knowledge or skill about a particular subject
expose (v) [U18]	create a situation or a condition that makes someone likely to be harmed
exposure (n) [U18]	a situation or condition that makes someone likely to be harmed, especially because the person has not been protected from something dangerous
facilitate (v) [U19]	make something possible or easier
factor (n) [U2] [U9] [U14] [U16]	a fact or situation that influences a result
federal (adj) [U18]	of or connected with the central government of some countries
final (adj) [U2]	last
finally (adv) [U2] [U11] [U12]	at the end, or after some delay
finance (n) [U3]	the management of money, or the money belonging to a person, group, or organization
financial (adj) [U6] [U7] [U17]	relating to money
flexible (adj) [U6] [U8]	able to change or be changed easily according to the situation
focus (v) [U3] [U20]	direct attention toward someone or something
format (n) [U11]	the way in which something is shown or arranged
gender (n) [U6] [U9]	the male or female sex
generate (v) [U14] [U16]	produce
generation (n) [U1] [U9]	all the people within a society or family of about the same age
global (adj) [U8]	relating to the whole world
goal (n) [U3] [U7] [U8] [U11] [U16]	an aim or purpose, something you want to achieve
grade (n) [U20]	the measure of the quality of a student's schoolwork
guideline (n) [U8] [U17]	a piece of information that suggests how something should be done
identification (n) [U13]	the ability to name or recognize someone or something
identify (v) [U12] [U15]	recognize or be able to name someone or something; prove who or what someone or something is
image (n) [U2] [U3] [U19]	an idea, especially a mental picture, of what something or someone is; a picture, such as one seen in a mirror, through a camera, in a photo, on TV, or on a computer
immigrant (n) [U10]	a person who has come into a foreign country in order to live there
immigration (n) [U10]	the process by which people come into a foreign country to live there, or the number of people coming in

Academic Word	Definition
impact (n) [U1] [U2] [U3] [U4] [U14]	the strong effect or influence that something has on a situation or person
impact (v) [U2]	have a strong effect or influence on a situation or person
implement (v) [U3] [U15]	put a plan or system into operation
inappropriate (adj) [U8]	unsuitable, especially for the particular time, place, or situation
inconclusive (adj) [U13]	not leading to a definite result or decision; uncertain
incorporate (v) [U3]	include something within something else
indicate (v) [U5] [U14] [U18] [U20]	show or signal a direction or warning; make something clear
individual (n) [U1] [U5] [U8] [U9] [U16]	a person, especially when considered separately and not as part of a group
initial (adj) [U11]	of or at the beginning; first
insight (n) [U12]	a clear, deep understanding of a complicated problem or situation, or the ability to have such an understanding
insightful (adj) [U5]	having a clear and deep understanding of a complicated problem or situation
instance (n) [U3]	a particular situation, event, or fact
intelligent (adj) [U5]	able to learn and understand things easily
intensive (adj) [U13]	needing or using great energy or effort
interact (v) [U8] [U11] [U20]	communicate with or react to each other
interaction (n) [U6] [U8] [U12] [U19] [U20]	communicating with or reacting to other people
interactive (adj) [U20]	involving a computer user in an exchange of information while a website or program is open
interpret (v) [U8]	describe the meaning of something; examine in order to explain
investigative (adj) [U12]	intended to examine something carefully, especially to discover the truth about it
investor (n) [U3]	a person or group of people that puts its money into a business or other organization in order to make a profit
involve (v) [U11] [U12] [U14] [U15]	include someone or something in an activity
involved (adj) [U8]	interested in or taking part in an activity or event
issue (n) [U7] [U13] [U14] [U15] [U17] [U18] [U20]	a subject or problem that people are thinking and talking about
item (n) [U1] [U2] [U16]	a particular thing considered as one among others of its type
job (n) [U6] [U9] [U11] [U12]	the regular work that a person does to earn money; a piece of work someone does that is of good, bad, or adequate quality
label (n) [U13]	a piece of paper or other material that gives information about the object it is attached to
label (v) [U13]	attach information about an object to that object

Academic Word	Definition
labor (n) [U3]	practical work, especially work that involves physical effort
lecture (n) [U20]	a formal, prepared talk given to a group of people, especially students
legal (adj) [U6]	connected with or allowed by the law
link (n) [U20]	a connection
location (n) [U11]	a place or position
maintain (v) [U2] [U5] [U16] [U20]	make a situation or activity continue in the same way
major (adj) [U6] [U12] [U14] [U18]	more important, bigger, or more serious than others of the same type
majority (n) [U6] [U13]	more than half the total number or amount; the larger part of something
media (n) [U14] [U17] [U18]	newspapers, magazines, television, and radio considered as a group
medical (adj) [U9] [U15] [U17]	of or relating to medicine, or the treatment of disease or injury
method (n) [U11]	a way of doing something
minority (n) [U3] [U9]	a part of a group that is less than half of the whole group; a group of people who share some characteristic by birth that makes their group smaller than some other groups in a society and may cause others to treat them unfairly
modify (v) [U13]	change something in order to improve it
monitor (v) [U18] [U20]	watch and check something carefully over a period of time
negative (adj) [U2] [U4] [U18]	having a bad effect; unfavorable
network (n) [U2] [U17] [U18] [U20]	a group of computers that are connected and can share information; a group of people who share ideas; a company that provides programs to a group of television or radio stations, or both the group and the company
networking (n) [U17] [U19] [U20]	the process of meeting and talking to a lot of people, especially to get information that can help you
neutral (adj) [U8]	not expressing an opinion or taking actions that support either side in a disagreement or war
norm (n) [U8]	an accepted standard or a way of being or doing things
normal (adj) [U14]	ordinary or usual; as would be expected
normally (adv) [U11]	usually or regularly
obvious (adj) [U18]	easily seen, recognized, or understood
obviously (adv) [U19]	certainly, without a doubt
occur (v) [U15]	happen
option (n) [U16]	a choice
oriented (adj) [U12]	directed toward, interested in, or aimed at something
outcome (n) [U8]	the result or effect of an action, situation, or event
parallel (n) [U18]	a similarity between two things

Academic Word	Definition
participant (n) [U8]	a person who becomes involved in an activity
passive (adj) [U5]	not reacting to what happens, or not acting or taking part
percent (adv) [U4] [U14] [U15] [U20]	for or out of every 100
percentage (n) [U17]	an amount of something, often expressed as a number out of 100
perception (n) [U8]	an awareness of things through the physical senses
period (n) [U10]	a particular time during a life or history
persist (v) [U14]	continue to exist past the usual time, or continue to do something in a determined way even when facing difficulties or opposition
phenomenon (n) [U15] [U20]	anything that is or can be experienced or felt, especially something that is noticed because it is unusual or new
physical (adj) [U2] [U11] [U14] [U15]	relating to the body; existing and able to be seen or touched
physically (adv) [U2]	in a way that is related to your body or appearance
policy (n) [U3] [U14] [U20]	a set of ideas or a plan of what to do in particular situations that has been agreed on by a government or group of people
portion (n) [U14]	serving of food
positive (adj) [U3] [U20]	having a good effect; favorable
potential (n) [U11]	an ability that has not yet developed
potential (adj) [U8] [U13] [U17]	possible but not yet achieved
potentially (adv) [U4] [U20]	possibly
previous (adj) [U9]	happening or existing before the one mentioned
principle (n) [U7]	a rule or belief which influences your behavior and is based on what you think is right
process (n) [U2] [U4] [U11] [U12] [U15] [U17]	a series of actions or events performed to make something or achieve a particular result, or a series of changes that happens naturally
process (v) [U15]	deal with something in a known way or according to a particular set of actions
professional (adj) [U11] [U12]	done as a job, or relating to a skilled type of work
professional (n) [U8]	a person who has a job that needs skill, education, or training
promote (v) [U20]	encourage or support something
psychological (adj) [U2]	having an effect on or involving the mind
psychology (n) [U12]	the scientific study of how the mind works and how it influences behavior
purchase (n) [U2] [U17]	something you buy or the act of buying something
purchase (v) [U2]	buy something
pursuit (n) [U3]	the act of following or searching for someone or something

Academic Word	Definition
qualitatively (adv) [U20]	in a way that relates to the quality of an experience or situation
range (n) [U12] [U19]	the level to which something is limited, or the area within which something operates
range (v) [U14]	be limited to a particular length, amount, or area
regulate (v) [U18]	control an activity or process by rules or a system
regulation (n) [U18]	rules or systems used by a person or organization to control an activity or process, or the control of an activity or process
reinforce (v) [U6]	provide proof or support for an idea or opinion
release (v) [U1]	drop, or stop carrying, holding, or containing something
rely (v) [U9]	need or trust someone or something
require (v) [U8] [U11] [U12] [U13]	need something, or make something necessary
research (n) [U4] [U5] [U13] [U15] [U18] [U19]	a detailed study of a subject or an object in order to discover information or achieve a new understanding of it
research (v) [U15]	study a subject in order to discover information
researcher (n) [U12] [U13]	a person who studies something to learn detailed information about it
resource (n) [U1] [U4]	a natural substance such as water and wood which is valuable in supporting life; something that can be used to help you
respond (v) [U11] [U19]	say or do something as a reaction to something that has been said or done
response (n) [U14] [U19]	something said or done as a reaction to something; an answer or reaction
restrict (v) [U3]	limit someone's actions or movement, or to limit the amount, size, etc., of something
restriction (n) [U18]	something that limits someone's actions or movement, or limits the amount, size, etc., of something
reveal (v) [U13] [U17]	make known something surprising or secret
revolutionize (v) [U20]	produce a very great or complete change in something
rigidly (adv) [U11]	in a way that does not permit change
role (n) [U3] [U5] [U6] [U7] [U15]	the duty or use that someone or something usually has or is expected to have
schedule (n) [U8] [U16]	a list of planned activities or things to be done at or during a particular time
schedule (v) [U8]	plan something for a particular time
sector (n) [U13]	an area of activity with its own character that a society, business, etc., is divided into
secure (adj) [U9] [U17]	free from risk and the threat of change for the worse
security (n) [U9] [U17]	freedom from risk and the threat of change for the worse
sequential (adj) [U11]	following a particular order

Academic Word	Definition
series (n) [U16]	several things or events of the same type that come one after the other
shift (n) [U13] [U15]	a change in position or direction
significant (adj) [U2] [U6] [U13]	important, large, or great, especially in leading to a different result or to an important change
significantly (adv) [U8]	in a way that is easy to see or by a large amount
simulate (v) [U11]	create conditions or processes similar to something that exists
site (n) [U12] [U17] [U20]	a website
sole (adj) [U7]	being the only one
source (n) [U13] [U15] [U16] [U19]	the cause, origin, or beginning of something; someone or something from which you obtain information
statistics (n) [U13]	a collection of numerical facts or measurements
status (n) [U20]	a state or condition at a particular time
strategy (n) [U16]	a plan for achieving something or reaching a goal
stress (n) [U14] [U16]	a feeling of worry and fear caused by a difficult situation
stressful (adj) [U12] [U16]	making you feel worried and nervous
structure (n) [U11] [U12]	the arrangement or organization of parts in a system
structure (v) [U11] [U12]	arrange or organize something
style (n) [U7]	a way of doing something that is typical to a person, group, place, or time
subordinate (adj) [U6]	having a lower or less important position
substitute (n) [U4]	the use of someone or something instead of another person or thing
survey (n) [U15] [U20]	a set of questions to find out people's habits or beliefs about something
survive (v) [U9]	continue to live, especially after a dangerous situation
target (v) [U2]	intend to achieve an effect or purpose, or to direct toward a particular person or group
task (n) [U11] [U12] [U16]	a piece of work to be done, especially something difficult or unpleasant
team (n) [U11]	a group of people who work together, either in a sport or in order to achieve something
technical (adj) [U12]	involving or needing special skills or knowledge
technique (n) [U2]	a specific way of doing a skillful activity
technological (adj) [U13]	relating to or involving technology
technology (n) [U19]	the method for using scientific discoveries for practical purposes, or a particular method by which science is used for practical purposes
tension (n) [U16]	anxiety and worry
theory (n) [U12]	something suggested as a reasonable explanation for facts, a condition, or an event
topic (n) [U11] [U15]	a subject that is written about, discussed, or studied
tradition (n) [U8]	a custom or way of behaving that has continued for a long time in a group of people or a society

Academic Word	Definition
traditionally (adv) [U7]	according to tradition
trend (n) [U14]	the direction of changes or developments
unaware (adj) [U2]	not knowing that something exists, or not having knowledge or experience of something
unethical (adj) [U8]	not morally acceptable
unique (adj) [U5]	different from everyone and everything
unstructured (adj) [U11]	not arranged or organized in a systematic way
variation (n) [U5]	a change in quality, amount, or level
vary (v) [U8] [U10]	change or cause to be different
version (n) [U9]	a form of something that differs slightly from other forms of the same thing
via (prep) [U19]	by way of
virtual (adj) [U17] [U19]	happening on or with a computer without going anywhere or talking face-to-face with anyone; almost, but not exactly or in every way
visually (adv) [U20]	in a way that involves seeing or appearance
volume (n) [U19]	the number or amount of something having a lot of units or parts

Glossary of Grammar and Writing Terms

active sentence a sentence that focuses on the doer and the action.
People spoke English at the meeting.

adjective a word that describes or modifies a noun.
Large ecological footprints cause problems.

adjective clause *see* **relative clause**

adverb a word that describes or modifies a verb, another adverb, or an adjective. Adverbs often end in *-ly*.
*Consumers need to shop **wisely***.

adverb clause a clause that shows how ideas are connected. Adverb clauses begin with subordinators such as *because, since, although,* and *even though*.
*Some consumers purchase products they do not need **because they are on sale***.

adverb clause of concession a clause that is used to contrast two things or ideas and particularly to indicate that the idea in the main clause is surprising. Adverb clauses of concession are introduced by the subordinators *although, even though, though,* and *while*.
***Even though face-to-face communication is preferred**, sometimes business has to be conducted virtually*.

adverb clause of contrast a clause that is used to contrast two things or ideas. Adverb clauses of contrast are introduced by the subordinators *while* and *whereas*.
*The official language of Brazil is Portuguese, **while in Colombia, it is Spanish***.

adverb clause of purpose a clause that answers the question *why*. Adverb clauses of purpose are most often introduced by the subordinator *so that,* or just *so*.
*He cut down on fatty food **so (that) he could lose weight***.

adverb of degree an adverb that makes other adverbs or adjectives stronger or weaker.
*Solar energy is **very** clean*.

adverb of manner an adverb that describes how an action happens.
*People can get into debt **easily***.

adverb of time an adverb that describes when something happens.
*Firstborns are generally smarter than siblings who are born **later***.

agent the noun or pronoun performing the action of the sentence.
*An **interviewer** screens candidates*.

appositive a noun phrase that either defines, restates, or gives important additional information about the noun phrase it follows.
*John Holland, **a leading researcher in vocational psychology**, developed a theory about career choices*.

article the words *a/an* and *the*. An article introduces or identifies a noun.
***A** new family moved in across **the** street from my house*.

auxiliary verb (also called **helping verb**) a verb that is used before a main verb in a sentence. *Do, have, be,* and *will* can act as auxiliary verbs.

*Natural resources **are** becoming scarce.*

*The Earth **does** not have time to renew the resources.*

base form of the verb the form of a verb without any endings (*-s* or *-ed*) or *to*.

come   go   take

citation a statement of the source of information cited, or used, in an essay. It includes who wrote the original material and/or what publication the original material came from.

*" 'Car culture,' both in the cities and suburbs, causes the smog that helps make many California cities unhealthful" **("The True Costs of Petroleum: The Community Map," 2003)**.*

citing (in essay writing) stating who wrote the original material and/or what publication the original material came from.

*Producing 20 percent of its energy from wind power, Denmark is the world leader in wind energy production **(Evans, 2007)**.*

clause a group of words that has a subject and a verb. There are two types of clauses: **independent clauses** and **dependent clauses**. A sentence can have more than one clause.

  INDEPENDENT CLAUSE   DEPENDENT CLAUSE
Future generations will suffer** if **pollution is not reduced.

cohesive device a device that a writer uses to connect back to previously stated ideas or information. Cohesive devices include pronouns, demonstratives, repetitions of words and phrases, different word forms, synonyms, and signal words and transition words.

*Visual learners are defined as people who learn through seeing. **For this reason, these** learners need to see the teacher's facial expressions to fully understand the content of a lesson.* (transition expression, demonstrative)

comma splice two independent clauses combined with a comma. To correct a comma splice, you can use a period between the two independent clauses.

Humans cause many environmental problems, it is our responsibility to resolve them. (comma splice)

Humans cause many environmental problems. It is our responsibility to resolve them. (correction)

comparative the form of an adjective or adverb that shows how two things or ideas are different.

*Immigrants in the United States often have **larger** families than Americans.* (adjective)

*Some people talk **more quickly** than others.* (adverb)

complex noun phrase a noun phrase that includes modifiers, such as adjectives, prepositional phrases, and relative clauses.

         ADJECTIVE   NOUN   RELATIVE CLAUSE
*Sometimes **professional women who start their own businesses** have trouble getting loans.*

complex sentence a sentence with an independent clause and a dependent clause introduced by a subordinator.

  INDEPENDENT CLAUSE   DEPENDENT CLAUSE
Bikeshares are becoming popular** because **they are a great way to reduce pollution.

compound sentence a sentence with at least two independent clauses that are connected by a coordinating conjunction (*and, but, or, so, yet*). Use a comma before the coordinating conjunction.

There are efforts to clean up the oceans, but the health of our oceans remains critical.

concluding paragraph the last paragraph in an essay in which the writer tries to make an impact. The writer may link back to ideas in previous paragraphs, ask a thought-provoking question, discuss potential consequences, or include a relevant quote.

conditional a sentence that describes a possible situation and the result of that situation. It can be a real or unreal condition/result about the present, past, or future. The possible situation, or the condition, is in the *if* clause.

If companies recycle, employees generally recycle, too. (present real conditional)

If I had read the privacy policy carefully, I would have avoided the problem. (past unreal conditional)

coordinating conjunction a word such as *and, but, so, or,* and *yet* that connects single words, phrases, or clauses.

Some gases trap heat in the air, **so** *the Earth gets warmer.*

count noun refers to a person, place, or thing you can count. Count nouns have a plural form and take plural verbs.

Large **families** *are enjoyable.*

definite article the word *the*. Use *the* with a noun when both the reader and the writer share common knowledge or information about the noun, when the noun is unique, or when the noun was introduced earlier.

In American families, it is common for **the** *wife and* **the** *husband to share household duties.*

The *president spoke about mobility in U.S. society.*

Each person in a family has a moral responsibility to aid other members of **the** *family.*

demonstrative the words *this, that, these, those*. Demonstratives are used to show physical distance from the speaker, to show distance in time, or to connect ideas that are close to each other in a text.

Chapter 2 is about immigration. In **this** *chapter, the author describes immigration in the mid-1800s.*

Immigrants came from all over Europe. Most of **these** *immigrants became farmers.*

dependent clause a clause that cannot stand alone. A dependent clause is not a complete sentence, but it still has a subject and verb. Some kinds of dependent clauses are adverb clauses, relative clauses, and time clauses.

Although people try to save energy*, global use of it increases every year.*

determiner a word that comes before a noun to limit its meaning in some way. Some common determiners are *some, a little, a lot, a few, this, that, these, those, his, a/an, the, much,* and *many*.

This *unit is about immigration. Let's look at* **the** *first page.*

A *young Latina woman is* **the** *new student in* **my** *class.*

Few *women are CEOs.*

direct object the person or thing that receives the action of the verb.

An interviewer screened the **candidates***.*

direct speech (also called **quoted speech**) repetition of a person's exact words. A direct speech statement consists of a reporting clause and the exact words of a person inside quotation marks.

The manager said, "Workers need to use creativity*."*

-ed phrase a phrase that begins with a past participle that acts as an adjective and modifies a noun.

Women **elected to Congress** *are in the minority.*

element a part of a sentence that works as a grammatical unit, such as a subject, a verb, an object, an adjective, an adverb, or a prepositional phrase.

SUBJECT   VERB PREPOSITIONAL PHRASE

The topic of greenhouse gases is often in the news.

formal a style of writing or speech used when it is not appropriate to show familiarity, such as in business interactions, a job interview, speaking to a stranger, or speaking to a person who you respect. Academic writing is a kind of formal writing.

Good evening. I'd like to speak with Ms. Smith. Is she available?

Swanson (2010) has argued that labeling may be a short-term solution to the problem of GM foods.

fragment an incomplete sentence in which the subject or verb is missing. Avoid fragments by making sure all sentences have a subject and a verb.

In the future, will probably be much warmer on Earth. (fragment, missing subject)

frequency adverb an adverb that describes how often an action happens.

*Ozone and other greenhouse gases are **often** debated in the news.*

future a number of verb forms that describe a time that has not yet happened. The future is expressed in English by *will*, *be going to*, modals, and a variety of words and phrases.

*The Internet **will continue to** allow for a greater exchange of ideas.*

*Some colleges **are going to** ban access to social networking sites on campus.*

*The use of social networking sites by recruiters for jobs **could increase** in the next few years.*

*The company **is about to** introduce a new app.*

future real conditional a sentence that describes a possible situation or condition in the future and its likely result. The verb in the *if* clause is in the simple present, and the verb in the main clause is *be going to* or a modal such as *will* or *might*.

If I get a raise, we will be able to buy a new car.

future unreal conditional a sentence that describes an imaginary situation in the future and gives the result as if it were true. The verb in the *if* clause is in the past, and the verb in the main clause includes one of these modals: *would*, *could*, *might*.

If we were socially responsible, we would attract more customers.

gerund the *-ing* form of a verb that is used as a noun. It can act as a subject or object.

***Reducing** our ecological footprints is crucial.*

habitual past a verb form that describes repeated past actions, habits, and conditions using *used to* or *would*.

*I **used to** study on the bus to school every day.*

*While I was living in my country, I **would** go for long walks.*

helping verb *see* **auxiliary verb**.

hook a part of an essay that tries to interest readers and motivate them to keep reading the essay. Hooks may be a surprising fact, a thought-provoking question, or a quotation. The hook is usually the first or second sentence in the introductory paragraph.

identifying relative clause a relative clause that modifies a noun and gives necessary information about the noun. Without that information, the sentence would be incomplete. Do not use commas with identifying relative clauses.

*The study examines characteristics **that are common in firstborn children**.*

if clause the condition clause in a conditional. It describes the possible situation, which can be either real or unreal.

If a company does not make a profit, it will go bankrupt.

imperative a type of clause that tells people to do something. It may give instructions, directions to a place, or advice. The verb is in the base form.

Listen to the conversation.

Don't open your books.

indefinite article *a/an* is the indefinite article. Use *a/an* with a singular count noun when the noun is not specifically identified or when it is first mentioned and new to the reader. Use *a* with consonant sounds. Use *an* with vowel sounds.

There is a new student in my class.

The class read an article about cultural values.

indefinite pronoun a pronoun used when the noun is unknown or not important. There is an indefinite pronoun for people, for places, and for things. Some examples are *somebody, anyone, nobody, one, somewhere, anywhere, nothing, everything*, etc. Use singular verb forms when the indefinite pronoun is the subject of the sentence.

Nobody in her family had ever attended college before.

First, one needs to acknowledge that a problem exists.

independent clause (also called **main clause**) a clause that can be used alone as a complete sentence.

Although people try to save energy, global demand for energy increases every year.

indirect object the person or thing that receives the direct object.

Many merchants offer consumers green products.

indirect speech (also called **reported speech**) tells what someone says in another person's words. An indirect speech statement consists of a reporting verb (*see* **reporting verb**) such as *say* in the main clause, followed by a *that* clause. The word *that* is optional and is often omitted in speaking.

The expert said (that) junk food was unhealthy.

informal a style of speaking and writing used to communicate with friends, family, or children.

Hey, there. Nice to see you again.

infinitive *to* + the base form of a verb.

It is difficult to find time to exercise every day.

infinitive of purpose an infinitive that answers the question *why*. Infinitives of purpose can be introduced by *in order to* and *so as to*. If the meaning is clear, it is not necessary to use *in order*.

Doctors place brochures in their waiting rooms (in order) to provide patients with valuable information.

Doctors should discuss treatment options with patients so as to address any concerns.

-ing participle phrase a phrase that begins with the *-ing* form of a verb. It can act as an adjective and modify a noun or it can express cause and effect.

The number of women starting their own businesses is increasing. (adjective modifying a noun)

Using wind energy, we can lower the cost of electricity. (cause)

Some countries give tax credits for wind energy, lowering costs for consumers. (effect)

it construction a construction such as *it* + *be* + adjective + *that* clause, *it* + *be* + adjective + infinitive, *it* + *appears/seems* + *that* clause, *it* + *appears/seems* + adjective + *that* clause. These constructions are commonly used in academic writing to make the text more impersonal and objective.

It is true that people who exercise usually have more energy.

It is important to find an exercise that is enjoyable.

It seems that people who eat healthier are frequently in a good mood.

main clause *see* **independent clause**.

main verb a verb that functions alone in a clause and can have an auxiliary verb.

Solar energy *is* very clean.

The government is *investing* large sums of money in alternative energy projects.

modal a verb such as *can, may, should,* and *will.* It goes before the main verb to show such things as ability, permission, possibility, advice, obligation, necessity, or lack of necessity.

We *might* buy a hybrid car.

The gifts *should* not be expensive.

modal-like expression a verb such as *have to, be going to,* and *be supposed to* that acts like a modal but changes its form of the verb.

The country *had to* change its policies.

She *was supposed to* major in education, but she decided to change her major to economics.

modifier a word or a phrase that is added to another phrase to change or describe it. Adjectives, prepositional phrases, and adverbs are examples of modifiers.

Receptions *for weddings* involve *delicious* foods. (prepositional phrase, adjective)

They *commonly* involve music. (adverb)

noncount noun ideas and things that you cannot count. Noncount nouns do not have a plural form and so use a singular verb.

My cousin borrowed some *money* from me.

nonidentifying relative clause a relative clause that provides additional information about a noun. The sentence would be complete without the information in the relative clause. Use commas with a nonidentifying relative clause.

National Institute of Mental Health, *which is a government agency,* conducts research on the effects of violence on children.

noun a word for a person, place, or thing.

Some *consumers* buy "green" *products*.

noun clause a clause that acts as a noun and that can be the subject or object in a sentence. Noun clauses often start with *that*. They can also start with *wh-* words and *if/whether.*

Experts suggest *that the consumption of fast food has increased.*

Readers have to decide *which experts they trust.*

Students who use online sources should check *whether the sources are reliable or inaccurate.*

noun clause with *wh-* words a clause that starts with a *wh-* word (*who, what, where, when, why,* and *how*). These noun clauses function as nouns and can act as subjects, objects, or objects of prepositions. They use statement word order.

Students have to learn *how they can evaluate sources.*

Experts disagree on *what the benefits of Internet use are for students.*

noun phrase a phrase that includes a noun and modifiers.

DETERMINER ADJECTIVE NOUN   PREPOSITIONAL PHRASE

***The** extremely **sensitive issue of gender inequality** has been discussed for many decades.*

object a noun or pronoun that receives the action and usually follows the verb.

*Many researchers study **families**. They analyze **them**.*

object relative clause a relative clause in which the relative pronoun is the object of the verb in the relative clause.

*There are several strategies **that parents can use to help their only children**.*

parallel structure a list in which each item follows the same grammatical pattern.

              ADJECTIVE   ADJECTIVE   ADJECTIVE

*Boys are encouraged to be **aggressive, outgoing,** and **strong**.*

paraphrase to state the information in a different way from the original without changing its meaning.

"Denmark leads the world in wind energy, generating 20 percent of its energy from wind power" (Evans, 2007, para. 3).

Paraphrase: ***Denmark is the world leader in wind energy. Twenty percent of its energy comes from wind power. (Evans, 2007)***

passive a sentence that focuses on the action or on the person or thing that receives the action. The object is in the subject position. The verb form in the passive is a form of *be* + past participle.

The results of the survey were presented by the committee at the meeting.

past modal modals such as *had to/did not have to, should have/should not have, could have/could not have,* and *might have*. Speakers use these modals to give their perspective on past events.

*They **had to** find a way to pay for their education.* (past necessity)

*He **could have** found out about the job opening at the career center.* (possible action in the past)

past participle a verb form that can be regular (base form + *-ed*) or irregular. It is used to form perfect forms of the verb and the passive. It can also be an adjective.

*Researchers have **examined** the situation carefully.*

*Auditions are **known** to be effective interview tools.*

*The **increased** cost of housing has affected many students.*

past perfect a verb form that describes the first of two completed events in the past. It can also describe an action or situation that goes back to an earlier time in a narrative or description. In narrative and academic writing, it is used to give background reasons and explanations for later past events. Its form is *had* + past participle.

*By midnight, he **had finished** most of his work, so he decided to go to bed.*

*Nesreen was nervous on her first day of work. She**'d** never **had** a job before.*

*For years, many people **had considered** the American dream to be achievable. Then the economy changed.*

past perfect progressive a verb form that emphasizes an ongoing past action leading up to a point in the past or a past action that had been occurring when another action took place. Its form is *had* + *been* + verb + *-ing*.

*He**'d been talking** about applying to medical school for a long time. Finally, last January, he applied.*

*They**'d been working** for about an hour when the bell rang.*

past unreal conditional a sentence that describes a hypothetical situation – an untrue situation in the past. Past unreal conditionals describe something that was possible but did not happen. The verb in the *if* clause is in the past perfect. The verb in the main clause uses the modal *would have*, *could have*, or *might have* and the past participle form of the verb.

If the author had discussed education in his article, the text would have been stronger.

phrase a group of words about an idea that is not a complete sentence. It does not have a main verb.

about the environment

in the future

preposition a word such as *to, at, for, with, of, in, on,* or *above* that goes before a noun or pronoun to show location, time, or direction.

*Stores put snack foods **on** low shelves so that children can see and ask **for** them.*

prepositional phrase a phrase with a preposition and an object, which is usually a noun or pronoun. It can be part of a noun phrase or a verb phrase. Some reduced relative clauses are also prepositional phrases.

*The debate **on immigration** has heated up recently.*

*Immigration has increased **over the past 20 years**.*

present perfect a verb form that describes a past event that is still important in the present. This event may be completed, or it may continue into the future. The form is *have/has +* past participle.

*Some researchers **have demonstrated** that genetically modified food may cause damage to humans.*

*The consumption of GM foods **has increased** significantly in the last 10 years.*

present perfect progressive a verb form that describes an action that started in the past and emphasizes that the action continues to the present and may continue into the future. The form is *have/has + been +* verb *+ -ing*.

*Researchers **have been studying** the impact of GM foods on our health.*

present real conditional a sentence that describes a possible situation or condition in the present and its likely result now. The verbs in the *if* clause and the main clause are in the simple present.

If companies donate to charity programs, they set good examples for other companies.

present unreal conditional a sentence that describes an imaginary situation in the present and gives the result. The verb in the *if* clause is in the past, and the verb in the main clause includes one of these modals: *would, could, might*.

If employees became involved in the community, they would feel good about themselves.

quantifier a word that indicates the amount or degree of something. Some examples of quantifiers are *all, almost all, most, several, some, few, both,* and *no*.

Most toys are gender-specific.

relative clause (also called **adjective clause**) modifies or describes a noun and follows the noun that it modifies. It begins with a relative pronoun such as *who, whom, which, that,* or *whose*.

*Children **who have siblings** are often very close to their parents.*

reporting verb a verb that writers use to report ideas or findings from a source. Reporting verbs are followed by *that* clauses or noun phrases. Common reporting verbs include *say, show, explain, mention, report,* and *state*.

*The authors of the study **conclude** that childhood obesity can be very harmful.*

run-on sentence two independent clauses that are not separated by a period, semicolon, or coordinating conjunction. To correct a run-on sentence, use a comma and a coordinating conjunction to connect the two independent clauses.

Gases trap heat in the air the Earth gets warmer. (run-on sentence)

Gases trap heat in the air, so the Earth gets warmer. (correction)

sentence a complete thought or idea that has a subject and a main verb. In writing, it begins with a capital letter and has a punctuation mark (. ? !) at the end.

The Earth is becoming warmer.

signal words words that help the reader know that the writer has finished writing about one step in the process and started writing about another. Signal words include words and phrases such as *first*, *the first thing to do*, *second*, *next*, *after that*, and *finally*.

simple sentence a sentence with only one clause, which is called an independent clause or a main clause. Like all sentences, it has a subject and a verb.

Small changes can make a difference.

subject the person, place, or thing that performs the action of a verb.

People should buy less.

subject relative clause a clause in which the relative pronoun is the subject of the verb in the relative clause.

Researchers who study families have different views.

subordinator (also called **subordinating conjunction**) a word that shows the relationship between the two ideas. It introduces an adverb clause. Some common subordinators are *before*, *after*, *while*, *because*, *since*, *if*, *although*, *whether*, *whereas*, and *as if*.

Some consumers buy products because they want to be like their friends.

superlative the form of an adjective or adverb that compares one thing or idea to others in a group.

Latinos are currently one of the largest ethnic groups in the United States. (adjective)

Americans are among the groups who say things the most directly. (adverb)

supporting detail a detail or example that explains or supports the main idea of the paragraph.

***that* clause** a clause that acts as a noun and that can be the subject or object in a sentence.

The expert recommended that people read food labels carefully.

thesis statement a sentence that states the main idea of an essay and gives a preview of what the writer is going to say about the topic. It is often the last sentence in the introductory paragraph.

time clause a clause that shows the order of events and begins with a subordinator such as *after*, *as*, *before*, and *while*.

After I finished high school, I had to find a job.

time signal a word or phrase that makes the sequence of events or ideas easier to follow. They are important in narrative writing. Common time signals are *after*, *over (the course of)*, *by*, *for; already*, *always*, *ever*, *just*, *lately*, *never; every day*, *once*, *once again*, *twice; later*, *earlier*.

Over the next 10 years, immigration is likely to decrease.

We've always lived in this neighborhood.

Years later, I returned to Boston to go to medical school.

topic sentence a sentence that introduces the main idea of a body paragraph in an essay. It often appears at the beginning of a body paragraph.

transition word or phrase a word or phrase that connects two independent clauses to make the relationship between two ideas very clear. Transition words and phrases signal a number of different relationships, such as cause and effect, concession, contrast, and steps of a solution. Use a comma after a transition word or phrase.

Environmental values might affect some purchases; **consequently,** *merchants offer green products.*

U.S. executives prefer time limits for meetings. **In contrast,** *Greeks see them as less necessary.*

First, *it is important for people to find an activity that is enjoyable.* **Next,** *they need to commit to doing it.*

verb a word that describes an action or a state.

People **use** *a lot of resources in developed countries. Many of them* **know** *that they should reduce their ecological footprints.*

verb phrase a phrase that includes a main verb, any modals or auxiliary verbs, and elements such as adverbs, direct objects, and prepositional phrases.

VERB   PREPOSITIONAL PHRASE
Solar energy **will grow in importance**.

Index

a/an, 104, 105
  a few, 88
  a great deal of, 88
    Academic Writing Tip, 95
  a great many, 88
  a little, 88
  a lot in common, 108
  a lot of, Academic Writing Tip, 95
  a number of, 195, 198
abbreviations, 104, 179
Academic Writing, elements of, A1
according to, 268, 294
acronyms, 104, 179
active vs. passive, 57, 60, 160
adjectives
  be, 83
  cause, 12
  comparatives, 98–100
  demonstratives, 148–149, 153
  difference, 74
  factor, 12
  graphics, 212
  it constructions, 237, 238
  noun phrases, 82
  parallel structure, 91
  persuasive writing, 292
  position, 82
  reason, 12
  show effect, 26
  show result, 26
  superlatives, 98–100, 104
adverbs/adverb clauses and phrases
  be, 153, 224
  commas, 117, 123
  comparatives, 98–100
  -ing forms, 224
  logical connectors, 279
  modals, 208
  of concession, 116, 117, 123
  of contrast, 116–117

of purpose, 220, 221
of time, 131, 137–138, 151, 153
passive, 168, 208
past perfect, 131, 224
past progressive, 224
present perfect, 191, 224
present progressive, 224
quantifiers, 88
reduced, 224
show cause, reason, or purpose, 20
simple past, 224
simple present, 224
superlatives, 98–100
usage, 116–117
used to avoid overgeneralizations, Academic Writing Tip, 273
affect, 29
after, 8, 130, 137, 138, 151, 224
agent, passive, 160, 161
all, 88
almost all, 88
already, 191
although, 8, 117
American Psychological Association (APA), A3, A5
  Academic Writing Tip, 216
and, 6, 14
animate nouns, 181
another vs. *the other,* 123
anticipate, 289
appear, 236, 237, 268
appositives
  be, 178
  commas, 179
  dashes, 179
  graphics, 179
  indicating credentials, 265
  noun phrases, 178
  placement, 179

punctuation, 179
relative pronouns, 178
usage, 179
argue, 294
articles
  definite, 104–105
  indefinite, 104, 105
  omission of, 104–105, 109
as, 137, 138, 208, 213
  as . . . as, 70
  as a consequence, 24
  as a result (of), 5, 21, 24
  as if, 8
  as many . . . as, 70
  as much . . . as, 70
  as soon as, 138
audience (being addressed in writing), 154–155
auxiliary verbs (*see also* modals and modal-like expressions), 5, 99, 276
base form of verb, 37, 40, 45
based on, 168
be
  + adjective, 83
  adverb clauses, 224
  adverbs of time, 153
  appositives, 178
  auxiliary verbs, 5, 99
  be going to, 134, 288
  definitions, 174, 175
  + infinitive, 241
  modals, 213
  nouns that show cause, 11, 12
  passive, 161, 213
  relative clauses, 82
  relative pronouns, 82
  stative verb, 131, 134
because (of), 8, 14, 20, 21, 29
  Academic Writing Tip, 17
before, 8, 130, 137, 138, 224
begin, 241

best, 109

both, 88

brainstorm, 214

but, 6, 120, 123, 134

by, 55, 151
   by the time, 130

can / cannot / can't, (*see also could*), 5, 37

categories, 169

cause, 11, 12, 14, 29, 57

cause and effect
   relationships / writing, 4, 8, 11, 15, 23, 26, 30, 36, 40, 41, 46, 53, 57

citations, 60, 179, A1

citing sources, Academic Writing Tip, 216

claim, 294

classification
   essay, 169
   words and phrases, 164–165
   writing, 164, 183

classifying ideas or things, 169

clauses (*see also* adverbs; *if* clauses; noun clauses)
   dependent, 8, 20, 137
   independent, 4, 5, 6, 8, 20, 23
   main, 4, 36, 37, 142
   parallel structure, 85, 91
   relative, 66–68, 75, 82, 175, 178, 181, 264–265, 270

cohesive devices, 183

commas
   adverb clauses of concession, 117, 123
   adverb clauses of contrast, 117, 123
   appositives, 179
   compound sentences, 6
   coordinating conjunctions, 6
   dependent clauses, 8
   if clauses, 36, 37, 40, 251
   -ing participle phrases, 52
   nonidentifying relative clauses, 264, 265

only if, 43

splice, 6

transition words, 5, 23, 107, 120, 123, 241

comparatives
   adjectives, 98–100
   adverbs, 98–100
   explicit usage, 100
   implicit usage, 100
   quantifiers, 88

compare and contrast items in a series, 85

comparison and contrast
   essay / writing, 66, 67, 70, 73, 83, 88, 98, 104, 107, 110, 116, 120, 124

complex nouns, 82–83

complex sentences, 8

compound sentences, 4, 6

conclusions, 124–125

conditionals, real / unreal (*see* real conditionals; unreal conditionals)

conjunctions
   coordinating, 6
   subordinating, 138

consequently, 5, 24

consider, 289

considerably, 88

contrast and concession, 120–121

contribute to, 57, 59

conversely, 120

coordinating conjunctions, 6

could / could not / couldn't (*see also can*), 37, 40, 133, 237, 252, 289

could (not) have, 134, 251, 252

count nouns, 70, 88, 105, 198

coz, 14

cuz, 14

dashes, appositives, 179

definite articles
   omission of, 109
   usage, 104, 105
   vs. indefinite articles, 104–105

   with superlative, 104

definitions
   be, 174, 175
   formation, 174, 175
   gender-specific singular pronouns, 175
   identifying relative clause, 175
   passive, 174, 175, 181
   plural nouns, 181
   prepositional phrases, 175
   singular nouns, 181
   usage, 175, 176

demonstratives
   Academic Writing Tip, 157
   adjectives, 148–149, 153
   cohesive devices, 183
   it constructions, 148
   pronouns, 148
   usage, 148–149

dependent clauses, 8, 20, 137

describing information in charts, 211–212

describing the steps of a solution, 245

despite, 121

details, supporting, 92, A1

differ, 73

difference, 73, 74

do, auxiliary verb, 5, 99

due to, 21

-ed phrases, 82

effect, 26, 29

e-mail messages, Academic Writing Tip, 127

emphasizing ideas, 143

emphasizing the significance of a problem, 199

emphatic condition, 43

-er
   adjectives, 99, 100
   adverbs, 99, 100
   comparisons, 109

error log, Academic Writing Tip, 247

-est
  adjectives, 99, 100
  adverbs, 99, 100
evaluating proposed solutions, 231
even
  even if, 43
  even though, 117
ever, 191
every time, 138
exclusive condition, 43
expressions, persuasive writing, 292
factor, 12
few, 88
fewer, 88
first, 241
for
  for example, 230
  + noun phrases, 236
fragments (sentence), 5, 8, 14, 68
  Academic Writing Tip, 17
from, 151
furthermore, 5
future actions, expressing, 288–289
future real conditionals (*see* real conditionals)
future unreal conditionals (*see* unreal conditionals)
gender-specific singular pronouns, definitions, 175
general nouns, 175
generalizations, 105
gerunds, 4, 55
graphics (charts, figures, graphs, tables)
  adjectives, 212
  appositives, 179
  as . . . , 213
  nouns, 211
  passive, 211
  verbs, 212

had
  auxiliary verb, 140
  had to / did not have to, 133
  vs. *having* (adverb clauses), 224
have
  auxiliary verb, 5, 99
  having, vs. *had* (adverb clauses), 224
  stative verb, 134
hedging, 268
his / her vs. *their,* definitions, 175
hook, 15, 30, 124, 271, A1
hope to, 289
how, 276
however, 5, 120
hypothetical situations, 251
identifying object relative clauses (*see also* relative clauses), 67
identifying relative clauses (*see also* relative clauses), 66–68, 82, 175
identifying subject relative clauses (*see also* relative clauses), 67, 75
if
  cause and effect relationships, 8
  if . . . not, 43
  negative subject, 43
  noun clauses, 276
  vs. *whether,* 276, 282
if clauses
  comma, 36, 37, 40, 251
  emphatic condition, 43, 45
  real conditionals, 36–37
  subject and verb agreement, 45
  unreal conditionals, 40, 251
impossible to, 244
in, 55
  in contrast, 73, 120, 121, 123
  in fact, Academic Writing Tip, 261
  in most cases, 268
  in my opinion, 255
  in order (not) to, 221, 222
  in spite of, 121

inanimate nouns, 75
indefinite articles
  usage, 104, 105
  vs. definite articles, 104–105
independent clauses, 4, 5, 6, 8, 20, 23
infinitives
  be, 241
  of purpose, 220, 221
  with passive, 162
-ing forms / participle phrases
  adverb phrases, 224
  comma, 52
  express future action, 289
  formation, 52
  noun phrases, 121
  relative clauses, 82
  show cause, 54–55
  show effect, 52–53
  show reason, 54–55
  usage, 52–53
  vs. gerunds, 55
instead (of), 120, 121
intend to, 289
Internet searches, improving, Academic Writing Tip, 79
introductory paragraph to a persuasive essay, 271
involved in, 168
irregular plurals, Academic Writing Tip, 170
is about to, 289
is due to, 289
it constructions
  adjectives, 237, 238
  demonstratives, 148
  formation, 236–237
  modals, 237
  noun phrases, 236
  overgeneralizations, 268
  passive, 237
  present perfect, 237
  reporting verbs, 237
  usage, 236–238
it is important to, 244

know
   if/whether noun clauses, 276
   stative verb, 131

lead to, 57

less
   + adjective/adverb, 99
   quantifier, 88

like, before a clause, 108

likely, 268

likewise, 107

little, 88

logical connectors, 279

look likely to, 289

lots of, Academic Writing Tip, 95

main clause of a sentence, 4, 36,
   37, 142

mainly, 268

many, 88
   Academic Writing Tip, 95

may, 37, 237, 289

means, definitions, 174, 175

might, 37, 40, 237, 252, 289

might have, 134, 251, 252

modals and modal-like
   expressions (*see also* auxiliary
   verbs)
   adverb clauses, 208
   be, 213
   examples, 133–134
   expressing certainty, 288–289
   future real conditionals, 37
   future unreal conditionals, 40
   it constructions, 237
   making predictions, 288–289
   passive, 161, 168, 208, 213
   past, 133–134
   past unreal conditionals,
     252, 257
   present an opposing view, 279
   present unreal conditionals, 40
   real conditionals, 45
   simple sentences, 5
   unreal conditionals, 45
   usage, 133–134

wh- noun clauses, 276

Modern Language Association
   (MLA), A3, A5
   Academic Writing Tip, 216

modifiers, 82, 83

more, 88, 99, 109

most, 88, 109

much, 88

narrative writing, 131, 137,
   142, 151

narrowing down a topic, 214

negative conditions, 43

never, 191

nevertheless, 120, 121

next, 241

no vs. *none,* 88

noncount nouns, 70, 88, 105, 198

none vs. *no,* 88

nonetheless, 120, 121

nonidentifying relative clauses
   (*see also* relative clauses), 178,
   264–265, 270

not as . . . as, 70, 99

noun clauses/phrases
   adjectives, 82
   appositives, 178
   complex, 82–83
   if/whether, 276
   -ing forms, 121
   it constructions, 236
   of, 194–195
   parallel structure, 85, 91
   prepositional phrases, 82
   reporting verbs, 205, 213
   similar, 107
   that clauses, 195–196
   types of, 4
   wh- words, 276

nouns
   animate, 181
   count, 70, 88, 105, 198
   general, 175
   graphics, 211
   inanimate, 75
   noncount, 70, 88, 105, 198

persuasive writing, 292
   plural, 105, 170, 181
   proper, 265
   quantifiers, 88
   shell, 194
   show cause, 11, 12
   show effect, 26
   show result, 26
   singular, 105, 181
   specific, 104, 105

object pronouns, 88, 99

object relative clauses (*see*
   identifying object relative
   clauses; relative clauses)

of, with noun phrases, 194–195

on the contrary, 120, 123

on the other hand, 120, 121, 123

once, 138

one thing in common, 108

only if, 43

opposing views
   common phrases, 279
   presenting and refuting, 283

or, 6
   or not, 282

otherwise, 45

over, 151, 153

overgeneralizations
   examples, 268
   it constructions, 268
   limiting, 268
   quantifiers, 88
   replaced by adverbs, Academic
     Writing Tip, 273
   words that limit, 268

parallel structure, 85, 91

paraphrasing, 60–61, 110, 258

parentheses, appositives, 179

participles, past, 140, 251, 257

passive
   adverbs, 168, 208
   agent, 160, 161
   be, 161, 213
   common verbs, 162, 163
   definitions, 174, 175, 181

formation, 160, 161
graphics, 211
infinitives, 162
it constructions, 237
modals, 161, 168, 208, 213
prepositions, 162
receiver, 160
usage, 160–162
vs. active, 57, 60, 160

past participles, 140, 251, 257

past perfect
adverb phrases, 224
adverbs of time, 131
formation, 140
narrative writing, 131
time clauses, 130
usage, 130–131, 138
vs. past perfect progressive, 131
vs. simple past, 140

past perfect progressive
usage, 130, 131
vs. past perfect, 131
vs. past progressive, 140

past progressive
adverb phrases, 224
vs. past perfect progressive, 140

past unreal conditionals, 251–252, 257

past vs. present in narratives, Academic Writing Tip, 144

periods, 5, 6

personal vs. general examples, Academic Writing Tip, 113

persuasive essay/writing, 268, 271, 276, 283, 292, 295

phrases
introducing problems, 227
introducing solutions, 227

plagiarism, 60, A3–A5
Academic Writing Tip, 62

plan to, 289

plural nouns
articles, 105
definitions, 181

irregular, Academic Writing Tip, 170

points of an essay, main, 46–47

possessive pronouns, 88

possibility in the future, expressing, 289

prepositional phrases
definitions, 175
noun phrases, 82
time signals, 151

prepositions
expressions with *cause, result, effect,* 29
show cause, reason, or purpose, 20–21
show contrast and concession, 121
with passive, 162

present (*see also* simple present)
summary–response writing, 254
vs. past in narratives, Academic Writing Tip, 144

present perfect
adverb phrases, 191, 224
it constructions, 237
summary–response writing, 254
time signals, 151
usage, 138, 190, 191
vs. present perfect progressive, 190, 192
vs. simple past, 191

present perfect progressive
time expressions, 192
usage, 191–192
vs. present perfect, 190, 192

present progressive, 224

present real conditionals (*see* real conditionals)

present unreal conditionals (*see* unreal conditionals)

presenting and refuting opposing views, 283

prioritize ideas, 214

problem–solution essay/writing, 190, 194, 220, 227, 231, 236, 238, 242, 245

produce, 57

pronouns
cohesive devices, 183
demonstrative, 148
object, 88, 99
possessive, 88
relative, 67, 75, 82, 178, 181, 264, 265, 270

proper nouns, 265

punctuation (*see* commas; dashes; parentheses; periods; semicolons)

purpose
adverb clauses, 220, 221
infinitives, 220, 221
writing, 155

quantifiers
Academic Writing Tip, 95
adverbs, 88
comparatives, 88
difference, 74
examples, 88
nouns, 88
of, 88
overgeneralizations, 88

questions, thought-provoking, Academic Writing Tip, 186

quotation/quote, 30, 125
Academic Writing Tip, 62
scare, Academic Writing Tip, 285

quotation marks, Academic Writing Tip, 79

real conditionals
future, 36, 37
if clauses, 36–37
modals, 37, 45
present, 36–37

reason, nouns that show cause, 12

receiver, passive, 160

references, Academic Writing Tip, 62

refutation
  persuasive writing, 283
  phrases that introduce, 280

relative clauses
  be, 82
  identifying, 66–68, 82, 175
  -ing phrases, 82
  modifiers, 82
  nonidentifying, 178, 264–265, 270
  object, 67
  pronouns, 181
  restrictive, 66
  subject, 67, 75

relative pronouns
  appositives, 178
  be, 82
  nonidentifying relative clauses, 178, 264–265, 270
  object relative clause, 67
  omission of, 67, 82, 265
  subject relative clause, 67, 75
  usage, 181
  use vs. omission, 67, 75

reporting verbs
  examples, 204–206
  it constructions, 237
  noun phrases, 205, 213
  source of information, 110
  that clauses, 205, 213
  usage, 205–206

restrictive relative clauses, 66

result, 26, 29
  result from, 57, 59
  result in, 57, 59

result in *if* clauses, 37

run-on sentences, 6

scare quotes, Academic Writing Tip, 285

see, 276

seem, 131, 236, 237, 268, 270, 289

semicolons, 5, 23, 120

sentences
  complex, 8
  compound, 4, 6
  run-on, 6

simple, 4–5
  topic, 76, 92, A1
  variety, 142

series of items, 85

several, 88

shell nouns, 194

should, 37, 289

should (not) have, 134

signal words/phrases, 183, 245

significantly, 88

similar, 107

similarities, 107

similarly, 107

simple past
  adverb phrases, 224
  completed action, 130
  summary–response writing, 254
  vs. past perfect, 140
  vs. present perfect, 191

simple present (*see also* present)
  adverb phrases, 224
  formation, 4–5
  in narratives, Academic Writing Tip, 144
  usage, 4, 5

simple sentences, 4–5

since, 8, 20, 138, 151, 192

singular nouns, 105, 181

slightly, 88

so, 6, 20
  so as (not) to, 221, 222
  so that, 20, 221

solutions
  describing the steps of, 245
  evaluating proposed, 231

some, 88, 105

something in common, 108

specific nouns, 104, 105

splice, comma, 6

statement, thesis (*see* thesis statement)

stative verbs, 131, 134, 191

subject of sentence, 4

subject relative clauses (*see* identifying subject relative clauses; relative clauses)

subordinating conjunctions, 138

subordinators, 8, 20–21, 116, 117, 137–138

substantially, 88

such, 88

summarizing, 110

summary–response writing
  common phrases, 254–255
  guidelines, 258–259
  present, 254
  present perfect, 254
  simple past, 254

superlatives, 98–100, 104

supporting details, 92, A1

synonyms, 60, 181, 183

tend, 268

than, 99, 100
  vs. *then,* 244

that
  demonstratives, 148–149, 153
  identifying relative clauses, 66, 67, 68
  nonidentifying relative clauses, 265, 270
  quantifiers, 88
  reporting verbs, 205

that clauses
  appear, 236
  noun phrases, 195–196
  reporting verbs, 205, 213
  seem, 236

the, 88, 104, 105, 109
  the fact that, 198
  the least + adjective/adverb, 99
  the most + adjective/adverb, 99
  the other vs. *another,* 123
  the problem of, 230
  the same as, 75, 109

their vs. *his/her,* definitions, 175

then, 36, 241
  vs. *than,* 244
thereby, 53
therefore, 24
Thesaurus, Academic Writing Tip, 233
these, 88, 149, 153
thesis statement
  definition, 15
  general, 15
  introductory paragraph, 169, 271, A1
  specific, 16
  topic sentence, 76
this, 88, 148, 149, 153
  this is the first time, 151
those, 88, 149, 153
though, 117
through, 151
thus, 24, 53
time clauses/expressions (*see* adverbs)
time signals, 151–152, 153
to, 151
topic sentences, 76, 92, A1
transition phrases/words
  commas, 5, 23, 107, 120, 123, 241
  complex sentences, 8
  differences in meanings, 120–121
  examples, 5, 120–121, 241
  indicating steps of a solution, 241
  problem–solving writing, 242

punctuation, 5
semicolon, 23, 120
show cause, reason, or effect, 23–24
simple sentences, 5
to indicate steps of a solution, 241
to signal contrast and concession, 120
with *similarly* and *likewise,* 107
transitional expressions, 183
typically, 268
unless, 43, 45
unlike, 73
unreal conditionals
  future, 40
  if clauses, 40, 251
  modals, 40, 45, 252, 257
  past, 251–252, 257
  present, 40–41
until, 138
used to, 134
vague references, Academic Writing Tip, 157
verb phrases
  parallel structure, 85, 91
  replaced by complex noun phrases, 83
verbs (*see also* the names of tenses)
  auxiliary, 5, 99, 276
  graphics, 212
  persuasive writing, 292
  reporting, 110, 204–206, 213, 237
  show cause and effect, 57

stative, 131, 134, 191
was
  vs. *were,* 40
  was supposed to, 134
were vs. *was,* 40
wh- noun clauses, 276
what, 276
when, 37, 130, 138, 224, 276
when clauses, 130, 140
whenever, 37
where, 276
whereas, 8, 116
whether
  noun clauses, 276
  subordinator, 8
  vs. *if,* 276, 282
which, 66, 67, 264
while, 8, 116, 130, 137, 138, 177, 224
who/whom, 66, 67, 68, 75, 181, 264, 276
whose, 66, 67, 264
why, 20, 221, 276
will, 5, 37, 288
wonder, 276
would, 40, 134, 252, 289
would have, 251, 252
Writer's Checklist, A2
writing strong arguments, 295
yes/no choice, 276
yet, 6, 191
you vs. *individuals, one, people,* Academic Writing Tip, 48

Art Credits